D1590734

IDEOLOGIES OF IDENTITY IN ADOLESCENT FICTION

CHILDREN'S LITERATURE AND CULTURE
VOLUME 8
GARLAND REFERENCE LIBRARY OF SOCIAL SCIENCE
VOLUME 1094

CHILDREN'S LITERATURE AND CULTURE

JACK ZIPES, *Series Editor*

Ideologies of Identity in Adolescent Fiction
The Dialogic Construction of Subjectivity

Robyn McCallum

Garland Publishing, Inc.
a member of the Taylor & Francis Group
New York and London
1999

Library of Congress Cataloging-in-Publication Data

Ideologies of identity in adolescent fiction : The Dialogic Construction of Subjectivity / by Robyn McCallum.
    p.   cm. — (Children's literature and culture ; v. 8. Garland reference library of social science ; v. 1094)
    Includes bibliographical references (p. 267) and index.
    ISBN 0-8153-2290-9 (alk. paper)
    1. Children's literature.   I. Title.   II. Garland reference library of social science ; v. 1094.   III. Garland reference library of social science. Children's literature and culture ; v. 8.
Z7164.S42L55   1995
866'.9.3—dc20   93–37236
                                       CIP

PN
3443
.m38
1999

Printed on acid-free, 250-year-life paper
Manufactured in the United States of America

CONTENTS

GENERAL EDITOR'S FOREWORD

Dedicated to furthering original research in children's literature and culture, the Children's Literature and Culture series includes monographs on individual authors and illustrators, historical examinations of different periods, literary analyses of genres, and comparative studies on literature and the mass media. The series is international in scope and is intended to encourage innovative research in children's literature with a focus on interdisciplinary methodology.

Children's literature and culture are understood in the broadest sense of the term *children* to encompass the period of childhood up through late adolescence. Owing to the fact that the notion of childhood has changed so much since the origination of children's literature, this Garland series is particularly concerned with transformations in children's culture and how they have affected the representation and socialization of children. While the emphasis of the series is on children's literature, all types of studies that deal with children's radio, film, television, and art are included in an endeavor to grasp the aesthetics and values of children's culture. Not only have there been momentous changes in children's culture in the last fifty years, but there have been radical shifts in the scholarship that deals with these changes. In this regard, the goal of the Children's Literature and Culture series is to enhance research in this field and, at the same time, point to new directions that bring together the best scholarly work throughout the world.

Jack Zipes

Acknowledgments

I owe thanks to John Stephens, for his expert advice, critical insights and readiness always to find the time to read and discuss my work; to Rod McGillis, Peter Hunt and Peter Hollindale, who made invaluable comments on an earlier version of this work; to Laurie Upfold, who assisted in proofreading the manuscript; to Greg Upfold, who has been a very patient, understanding and supportive friend; and to my parents, Mary and Robert McCallum, for their continued support and encouragement.

IDEOLOGIES OF IDENTITY IN ADOLESCENT FICTION

I INTRODUCTION

The ideological frames within which identities are formed are inextricably bound up with ideas about subjectivity—that sense of a personal identity an individual has of her/his self as distinct from other selves, as occupying a position within society and in relation to other selves, and as being capable of deliberate thought and action. Concepts of personal identity and selfhood are formed in dialogue with society, with language, and with other people, and while this dialogue is ongoing, modern adolescence—that transition stage between childhood and adulthood—is usually thought of as a period during which notions of selfhood undergo rapid and radical transformation. It should come as no surprise, then, that ideas about and representations of subjectivity pervade and underpin adolescent fiction. Conceptions of subjectivity are intrinsic to narratives of personal growth or maturation, to stories about relationships between the self and others, and to explorations of relationships between individuals and the world, society or the past—that is, subjectivity is intrinsic to the major concerns of adolescent fiction. There are two important corollaries to this observation. First, the formation of subjectivity is dialogical, as has been argued by many theorists in the areas of linguistics, philosophy and psychology (such as Bakhtin, Lacan, Vygotsky and Vološinov). There are some significant differences between the positions of these theorists, but a common formulation is that an individual's consciousness and sense of identity is formed in dialogue with others and with the discourses constituting the society and culture s/he inhabits (*see also* Smith, 1988 and Levine, 1992). Second, the formation of subjectivity is thus always shaped by social ideologies. My purpose in this book is to examine the representation of dialogic conceptions of subjectivity in adolescent and children's fiction using a Bakhtinian approach to subjectivity, language and narrative.[1]

Mainstream children's and adolescent fiction has been dominated by premodern conceptions of the individual, the self and the child associated with liberal humanism and romanticism. This orientation, combined with moral assumptions about writing for and about children, perhaps accounts for the reluctance in children's and adolescent fiction to embrace anti-humanist ideologies. Although the humanist subject has been systematically put into question by structuralist, poststructuralist and Marxist literary and critical discourses, the question in adolescent and children's fiction is not whether the subject exists, but what kind of subject it is and what are the conditions of its coming into being. This question lies at the heart of fiction for young people and it is also fundamental to this study. I am centrally concerned with the images of selfhood that these fictions offer their readers, especially the interactions between selfhood, social and cultural forces, ideologies and other selves.

SUBJECTIVITY, HUMANISM AND CHILDREN'S LITERATURE

It is not within the scope of this book to include a thorough discussion of the theoretical issues surrounding subjectivity—suffice it to say that they are complex and impinge on a range of disciplines, especially philosophy, linguistics, education and sociology. I will touch these issues and areas where they are relevant to my specific concerns with the dialogic representation of subjectivity in children's and adolescent fiction, though for the most part, I am using a Bakhtinian approach to subjectivity, language and narrative.

Key terms in theories of subjectivity are **individual**, **subject** and **agent**, but because there is a tendency to conflate these terms it is essential to indicate how they are to be used. In *Discerning the Subject* (1988) Smith makes the following distinctions. The subject is to be understood as a conglomeration of provisional subject positions "into which a person is called momentarily by the discourses and world s/he inhabits" (p. xxxv). A person is not, however, "simply determined or dominated by the ideological pressures of any overarching discourse or ideology, but is also the agent of a certain discernment" (p. xxxiv). Agency, then, refers to "the place from which resistance to the ideological is produced and played out" (p. xxxv). Thus, subjectivity is an individual's sense of a personal identity as a subject—in the sense of being subject to some measure of external coercion—and as an agent—that is, being capable of conscious and deliberate thought and action. And this identity is formed in dialogue with the social discourses, practices and ideologies constituting the culture which an individual inhabits.

Many critical discussions of subjectivity throughout this century have shown that modern ideas of the self and the individual are relatively recent cultural constructs (Vološinov, 1986, 1987; Smith, 1988; Levine, 1992; Booth, 1993), as are concepts of childhood and adolescence (Aries, 1962;

Spacks, 1981; Kessen, 1983; Wartofsky, 1983; Neubauer, 1991). The meanings that are conventionally attached to terms such as self, individual, or child emerged from the political, economic, cultural and moral programs of liberal humanism and romanticism in the eighteenth and nineteenth centuries (Wartofsky, 1983; Howe, 1992); the modern concept of adolescence is an even more recent cultural invention (Spacks, 1981; Russell, 1988; Neubauer, 1991).

Humanist ideologies appeal to notions of a common core of humanity, or essential humanness (Soper, 1986, p. 12) and insist on the inherent value of individual human beings and the centrality of human experience (Bullock, 1985, p. 155). Underpinning these ideologies are assumptions about the uniqueness of the individual and the idea of selfhood as essential. Thus, poststructuralist theorists such as Althusser, Derrida and Foucault have dismantled humanist ideologies on the basis that they are logocentric. In other words, humanism is a system of thought which relies on an extra-systemic validating presence or center which underwrites and fixes linguistic meaning, but is itself beyond scrutiny or challenge (*see* Derrida, 1978 and Hawthorn, 1992, p. 94). As poststructuralist theorists have argued, the posited presence that underwrites humanist ideologies is the concept of an essential and universal individual human subject—the point being that this concept is a cultural construct rather than a universal. However, many writers have noted that the idea of an individualized unique and essential self has been systematically undermined virtually since its invention (Howe, 1992; Booth, 1993), particularly within modernist writing (Hutcheon, 1989, p. 108; Gloege, 1992, p. 59). The poststructuralist deconstruction of the humanist self can be understood as an explication of what has always been implicit in the humanist tradition. In admitting the fictionality of the humanist self, contemporary humanists, such as Bullock (1985), Lodge (1990), Howe (1992) and Booth (1993) have stressed the political, social and ethical contexts within which this fiction has been posited and which poststructuralist critiques often ignore. For example, it has premised the social and political agendas of social philosophers like Locke and J. S. Mill, and the American and United Nations Declarations of Human Rights. Thus, the humanist invention of the individual self has also been instrumental in the sociopolitical and ethical constructions of childhood, which for example were an aspect of the child labor reforms of the nineteenth century (Kessen, 1979, p. 266). As Wartofsky (1983) has argued, the cultural construction of the self and of the child "is not simply a matter of reflection in thought, but also of the whole range of practices, interactions and institutions that comprise the social and historical life-world" (1983, p. 190)—of which literature for children and adolescents is an integral part.

A central problem for any theory of subjectivity is how to conceive of the relationship between an individual and society without structuring this relation as an opposition in which one term is privileged over the other. In other words, we need to avoid both essentialist conceptions of the human subject, which ground subjectivity in either consciousness, agency or essential selfhood—as humanism tends to do—and mechanistic social theories of subjectivity, which conceive of the subject as "determined by the social object"—as structuralism and poststructuralism have tended to do (Giddens, 1979, p. 120). As Giddens has argued, the first "takes subjectivity for granted, as an inherent characteristic of human beings," and hence assumes "that the subjective is not open to any kind of social analysis," and the second "reduces subjectivity to the determined outcome of social forces" (1979, p. 120). Smith (1988) has also shown that the interrogation of the humanist subject central to Marxist, structuralist and poststructuralist approaches also discounts a theory of agency. Instead, these approaches tend to represent the subject as disempowered by the sociolinguistic structures within which it is passively constructed and to ignore the status of a person as both subject (and hence situated in relation to social practices and discourses) and agent (and hence capable of conscious action and resistance to the social and the ideological). However, it has been claimed by many theorists that Bakhtin's concept of dialogism overcomes the opposition between individuals and societies, and between humanism, structuralism, Marxism and poststructuralism (Holquist, 1981 and 1983b; Polan, 1983; A. White, 1984; Lodge, 1990, p. 21).[2]

The cultural construction of the child was coincident with and contingent upon the construction of the humanist self, and there has been a historical complicity between children's literature and liberal humanism which Rose (1984, p. 8) sees as based on Rousseau's and Locke's philosophical conceptions of childhood and of the role of education. As was suggested earlier, mainstream children's and adolescent fiction has been dominated by liberal humanist conceptions of the individual, the self and the child. However, as Bullock's history of the humanist tradition (1985) has demonstrated, humanism is not a homogeneous ideology (*see also* Soper, 1986). In many of the novels discussed in this book, premodernist concepts of the subject, that is, as essential and unique, are questioned, but almost always within the context of a dominant humanist ethic. Thus, the ideological scope of modern forms of humanism emerges through the varied thematic concerns of the novels—with the relations between the self and others, the individual and society, and with the influences of language and social and cultural practices on the formation of consciousness and a sense of personal identity.

Many of the novels examined also implicitly inscribe reading positions which interrogate the universalist and essentialist implications of humanism.

Representations of subjectivity in fiction are always based on ideological assumptions about relations between individuals, and between individuals, societies and the world. The preoccupation with personal maturation in adolescent fiction is commonly articulated in conjunction with a perceived need for children to overcome solipsism and develop intersubjective concepts of personal identity within this world and in relation to others. Solipsism is the inability to distinguish between one's own self and the otherness of the world and of other people. It takes two main forms: a person may be unable to perceive an other as another self, and hence denies that other a subject position independent of his/her self—the solipsistic child's attachment to the primary caregiver, for example; or a person may be unable to perceive her/his own selfhood as independent of the world, and to construct a sense of her/his self as an agent. In the first instance, it is a viewpoint which denies an other agency; in the second, it is the inability of a person to construct a sense of self as agent. There has been a common tendency in contemporary adolescent fiction to represent the move out of solipsism as one which conceives of the selfhood of an individual as essential, presocial and prelinguistic. However, this move is also represented as one which situates that individual within dominant social and ideological paradigms, a prestructured social order within which s/he is ultimately represented as disempowered and passive. Underlying these representations is an opposition between the individual and society, which also logocentrically opposes subjectivity and agency. Adolescent fiction, and many of the discussions which surround it, typically assume and valorize humanistic concepts of individual agency, that is the capacity to act independently of social restraint. However, the image of empowered individuals capable of acting independently in the world and of making choices about their lives offers young readers a worldview which for many is simply idealistic and unattainable. The question, then, is how to strike a balance between these two ideologies of identity.

Most of the texts discussed in this book are adolescent novels, though a few are children's novels, such as *Antar and the Eagles* (Mayne, 1989), *Finders, Losers* (Mark, 1990) and *Charlotte Sometimes* (Farmer, 1969/ 1992).[3] The criterion for selecting novels to discuss is twofold, and it is largely determined by my interests in the work of Bakhtin, Vološinov and Lacan on the novel and subjectivity and in adolescent fiction. While Bakhtinian and Lacanian theories are relevant to a wide range of fiction, they have a particular pertinence to adolescent fiction. The main focus is on novels which represent subjectivity as being dialogically constructed through inter-relationships with others, through language, and/or in a relation to social and cultural forces and ideologies. My second interest is in novels which use overtly "dialogical" narrative strategies to structure the narrative and to represent subjectivity and intersubjectivity.[4] The corpus of texts examined evinces a range of genres and narrative techniques, but special reference is made to polyphonic, multistranded, intertextual and mixed genre narrative forms and historical genres. Most of the novels I am concerned with are complex and sophisticated in their narrative techniques and thematic concerns, and many of them express or reflect highly complex philosophical and psychological ideas. A typical criticism of some of these novels is that they are "too difficult" for children or adolescents, and not really "children's books"—for example *Red Shift* (Garner, 1973)—and this is a comment that might be leveled at many of the texts that I discuss. The charge of difficulty is often accompanied by calls for "relevance" and equal access to education. The problem is that this concern is often taken to mean that "all books should be relevant and accessible to all children." Thus, the idea that a book is too difficult for some children comes to mean that it is too difficult for all children, and is more indicative of the assumptions of its adult readers about children and about complex ideas. As Hunt (1991) has observed, "it may be correct to assume that child-readers will not bring to the text a complete or sophisticated system of codes, but is this any reason to deny them access to texts with a potential of rich codes?" (p. 101). Furthermore, many of the novels I discuss do set out to teach readers the kinds of interpretative strategies needed to deal with more complex forms of writing—for example *Finders, Losers* (Mark, 1990) or *Backtrack* (Hunt, 1986).

The texts examined are implicated in a range of complex and subtle issues which narratively work upon readers, but which I would not expect the intended readers to be able to articulate at the level of implication. Discussion will center on the representations of subjectivity and the potential significances that texts may offer, rather than the meanings that an intended (actual) audience may or may not directly perceive or comprehend, though these representations will of course impact on readers' interpretations and reading strategies. This interest has two main focuses: the conceptions of subjectivity that are either implicit in or explicitly constructed by texts; and the positioning of implied readers (as distinct from actual readers) as subjects within texts. First, insofar as childhood and adolescence are typically seen as transitional stages leading (ideally) from a solipsistic childhood to an intersubjective adulthood, narrative representations of maturation are inscribed with ideological assumptions about the nature and possibilities of subjectivity. Thus, even children's or adolescent novels which are not overtly about subjectivity but which are about personal, social or intellectual growth, maturation, and understanding, entail more or less implicit concepts of selfhood, identity and agency. Second, the genre of children's and adolescent fiction is a particular kind of discursive practice which is culturally situated and which constructs an implied audience position inscribed with the values and assumptions of the culture in which it is produced and received. Implicit here is a distinction between an actual reader and an implied reader. An implied reader designates a subject position inscribed in and by the discourse of a text as a specific conceptual and ideological position (*see* Stephens, 1992a, pp. 54–59). Implied reader positions may influence the positions that actual readers adopt in relation to a text and the kinds of meanings that readers infer, but they do not determine either of these aspects. Insofar as childhood, adolescence and adulthood are culturally constructed categories, the relations between which are primarily determined by processes of education, enculturation and maturation, then the implicit audience positions inscribed in literature for children and adolescents will be informed by wider cultural assumptions about what constitutes these cultural categories and the processes involved in moving between them.

BAKHTINIAN CONCEPTS

Bakhtin and Vološinov occupy a central place in my theoretical approach, and to a lesser extent, I also use theoretical approaches adapted from the work of Lacan, Vygotsky and Althusser, as well as concepts derived from more recent narrative theory and critical approaches to subjectivity. One advantage of using a Bakhtinian approach to the study of the representation of subjectivity in narrative is that many of Bakhtin's and Vološinov's ideas about subjectivity are formulated in the context of their study of language and narrative. My intention, however, is not to impose these theories on texts, but rather to examine conceptions of subjectivity implicit in texts in the light of the insights offered by the theories.

Over the last ten to fifteen years, the rediscovered work of Bakhtin and Vološinov has had a profound influence on theories of subjectivity, language, culture and narrative, but so far has had a limited impact on the criticism of children's literature. A notable exception to this is the work of Maria Nikolajeva (1988; 1989; 1996). Nikolajeva first introduced Bakhtin's concept of the chronotope to the study of children's literature in her study of fantasy, *The Magic Code* (1988), and her recent book, *Children's Literature Comes of Age* (1996), has extended the application of Bakhtinian ideas, such as polyphony and the chronotope, to children's literature.[5]

Bakhtin was a major proponent of the dialogic construction of subjectivity and of the novel as a dialogic form, and his theories of subjectivity, language and narrative have a significant contribution to make to the study of narrative technique and the representation of subjectivity in children's and adolescent fiction. Adolescent fiction has in common with Bakhtinian writings a predominant concern with the relations between the self and others, and the influence of society, culture and language on cognition and maturation. Bakhtin's theoretical writings are a peculiar mix of humanist ideologies and methodologies which prefigure the strategies of structuralism, Marxism and poststructuralism (Ivanov, 1975; A. White, 1984). Likewise, despite the central humanist assumptions of most adolescent fictions, many novels do also borrow extensively from various kinds of postmodernist cultural texts and forms. Bakhtin's concept of dialogism thus provides ways of theorizing the interaction between various textually constructed ideological positions. His theories of narrative, in particular his formulation of concepts like polyphony, intertextuality and parody, combined with concepts derived from more recent narrative theory, provide ways of analyzing narrative strategies and techniques that have gained popularity in contemporary children's and adolescent fiction, such as the use of multiple narrative strands and narrational voices, and the mixing of literary and nonliterary genres and discourse styles. Finally, Bakhtin's and Vološinov's theorizing of the link between language and cognition, and of the dialogic orientation of discourse toward other discourses and toward an addressee (listener or interlocutor) has important implications for a theory of reading. This supplements other approaches to reading and provides a more sophisticated theory of reading than simplistic reader response theories which have tended to dominate the criticism of children's literature.

Bakhtinian theory utilizes a specific discourse, and as this discourse is central to my argument, I will outline six key concepts which I see as having important implications for the production and representation of subjectivity in narrative and for the production of implied readers as subjects in texts. These are heteroglossia, polyphony, dialogism, monologism, intertextuality and addressivity. Bakhtin's approaches to subjectivity and narrative are based on a theory of language, and each of these concepts can be used to discuss language, subjectivity and narrative. Although each concept has a specific field of reference, their semantic fields intersect and many terms are often used interchangeably—for example, "heteroglottic," "dialogic" and "polyphonic" are often used to refer to the same textual phenomena. For the convenience of readers, these and other technical terms are gathered into a glossary placed at the end of the book.[6]

Heteroglossia literally means "many languages." The term refers to the "internal stratification of any single national language into social dialects, characteristic group behavior, professional jargons, generic languages, languages of generations and age groups, tendentious languages, languages of the authorities, of various circles and of passing fashions, languages that serve the specific socio-political purposes of the day" (Bakhtin, 1981, pp. 262–263). These "languages" are also referred to as "socially typifying languages" (Bakhtin, 1981, p. 290) and "speech genres" (Bakhtin, 1986), and Allon White (1984, p. 124) has also introduced the linguistic concepts of "register" and "sociolect" to describe Bakhtin's conception of the heteroglottic structure of language. Generally, I refer to these languages as "discursive genres" so as to avoid confusion with either a language or narrative genre, and so as to include both spoken and written forms of language variation. Discursive genres are relatively stable types of utterance that correspond to specific social conditions (Bakhtin, 1986, p. 60), such as the discourses of law, religion, finance and so on. These genres have a socio-ideological basis. They represent "specific points of view on the world" and are "forms for conceptualizing the world in words" (Bakhtin, 1981, pp. 291–292) which coexist, intersect and often conflict. Thus, any one language comprises multiple coexisting and competing social discourses and ideologies which "encounter and co-exist in the consciousness of real people" (Bakhtin, 1981, p. 292). Any one speaker will typically speak and write using a range of identifiable discursive genres. As many commentators have remarked, Bakhtin's implicit politicizing of language and relativizing of meaning in his notion of heteroglossia prefigures both sociolinguistics and deconstruction, but moves beyond the limitations of both of these approaches (*see* A. White, 1984; Crowley, 1989; Lodge, 1990, p. 21;).

Bakhtin's conception of language—and society—as heteroglottic has two main implications for theories of subjectivity and adolescent narrative fiction. First, for Bakhtin and Vološinov, thought is virtually impossible outside language, and the formation of consciousness and subjectivity is thus inextricable from the acquisition of language. The link between consciousness, subjectivity and language suggests an analogy between the heteroglottic structuring of language and the formation of subjectivity. For Bakhtin, an individual's subjectivity is formed through the selective appropriation and assimilation of the discourses of others, and these discourses position a speaker within a heteroglossia and equip speakers with socio-ideological viewpoints. Subjectivity is the product of an intense struggle for hegemony among various ideological discourses and voices (Bakhtin, 1981, p. 346). Thus, he claims that "for any individual consciousness living in it, language is not an abstract system of normative forms, but rather a concrete heteroglot conception of the world" (1981, p. 293). As will be discussed in Chapter 4, the representation of characters who are culturally and linguistically alienated can foreground the construction of subjectivity and consciousness within society and language.

Second, Bakhtin sees the novel as a heteroglottic genre, in that it draws upon and represents the extra-literary strata of a national language. For him, novelistic discourse is always represented discourse. Novels typically appropriate and represent "a multiplicity of social voices" and socio-ideological discourses from within a heteroglossia (1981, p. 263) and they deploy a range of narrational strategies, voices and discursive styles. For these reasons, he defines the novel as an inherently **polyphonic**—or "many voiced"—narrative form. The term **polyphony**, as he uses it, acquires a specific meaning, referring to the construction of dialogical interrelationships between speakers and voices represented in narrative. Novelistic discourse is also always voiced; that is, it is discourse spoken by a speaking person—a character or a narrator—and Bakhtin's emphasis on "the speaking person in the novel" allocates narrator and character discourse a central place in his theory of the novel. He conceives of speaking persons in novels as **ideologues** and their discourse as **ideologemic**; that is, they are subjects occupying specific social and discursive positions in relation to each other and to the represented world, and they represent particular socially and ideologically situated ways of viewing the world (1981, pp. 332–333). Chapter 2 examines the use of overtly polyphonic narrative forms, such a multistranded and multivoiced narration, to explore and represent forms of intersubjectivity, and social and cultural interactions. Chapters 7 and 8 focus on texts which are overtly heteroglottic; that is, they foreground the diverse range of nonliterary discourses which structure them, and in doing so represent the subject as textually constructed.

The concept of **dialogism** is central to Bakhtinian theory, though it is probably the most difficult to define. Interpretative problems stem mainly from the range of functions that it has in Bakhtin's work and in secondary material. It is used to describe language, narrative and subjectivity. A general sense of its meaning is that of "dialogue": a verbal interchange between individuals where there is an exchange of words, ideas and viewpoints, as opposed to monologue, wherein only one person speaks. **Dialogic** thus describes a particular kind of relation between two positions—between the self and others, between the subject and language or society, between two ideologies or discourses, two textual voices, and so on. In this sense, dialogism is an analytic strategy which enables the conceptualization of a relation which is neither oppositional (i.e. differences between the two positions are not irreconcilable), nor dialectical (in the sense that it does not entail a synthesis of the two positions), nor monological (neither position is dominant).

There are two main ways that Bakhtin uses the concept of dialogism. It can refer to particular kinds of "dialogic" discourses as opposed to "monologic" discourses, and it is used as a descriptive metalinguistic concept that refers to the "dialogic orientation" of all discourse (Hirschkop, 1985a, pp. 674–675). As many commentators on Bakhtin's work have pointed out, these two formulations seem to imply contradictory notions of dialogism and of language. If, as Bakhtin suggests, all language is heteroglottic and all discourse has a dialogic orientation, then what constitutes monologism, and how do monologic discourses emerge?[7]

Monologism and dialogism can be understood as centripetal and centrifugal forces within language. Monologism is associated with "historical processes of linguistic unification" (Bakhtin, 1981, p. 270) and sociopolitical and cultural centralization (p. 271), and dialogism is associated with conflictual forces within language and culture, linguistic diversification, and decentralization (p. 272). Monologic forces "guarantee a certain maximum of mutual understanding and a real although still relative unity" (p. 270), but insofar as these forces can only "operate within the midst of heteroglossia" (p. 271), dialogism is a condition of monologism. For example, monologic forces are expressed in the idea of a "unitary language" or "a system of linguistic norms" which is manifest as an official dominant language and ideology. However, "a unitary language is not something given but is always in essence posited—and at every moment of its linguistic life it is opposed to the realities of heteroglossia" (p. 270). In other words, monologic discourses are essentially logocentric, first because they are posited on the idea of a central still point at which linguistic meaning can be fixed, and second because they are always oriented toward the repression of the inherent heteroglossia of language and hence the repression of difference. Thus, as Hirschkop (1985a, p. 674) has argued, monologism can only operate in the context of dialogism and is to be understood as a form of dialogism.

The concepts of monologism and dialogism have a range of implications for theories of subjectivity and the novel. The two approaches to the subject discussed by Giddens (1979) that I outlined earlier both represent monologic theories of subjectivity in that both logocentrically privilege either the individual or society.[8] Ideally, Bakhtin's concept of dialogism implies a dialogue between individuals and society. Totalizing theories of narrative can also express the monologic forces of language. An approach which assumes a unitary structure, language or significance within a narrative will privilege some aspects and marginalize others in order to arrive at a single unified meaning. Further implications of dialogism and monologism for narrative will be discussed shortly.

The second way that the concept of dialogism is used is as a metalinguistic concept that refers to the **dialogic orientation** of discourse (Bakhtin, 1981, p. 275). According to Bakhtin, any word, text or utterance is oriented toward other preceding or subsequent words, texts or utterances and toward an other and that other's anticipated answering word (p. 280). The terms **intertextuality** and **addressivity**[9] have been used to refer to these two orientations which combine to construct discursive and interpersonal contexts in which meanings are shaped and modified.

The dialogic orientation of discourse has implications for the role of language in the formation of subjectivity, and for the textual production of meanings and readers. The **intertextuality** of discourse entails that "no living word relates to its object in a *singular* way: between the word and its object, between the word and the speaking subject, there exists an elastic environment of other alien words about the same object, the same theme" (Bakhtin, 1981, p. 276). The theory of intertextuality entails that meaning lies in the space between the focused text and its intertexts and is the product of their interrelations. There are parallels between Bakhtin's ideas, linguistic sign theory and deconstruction, namely that there is a gap between the word (sign) and its object (referent) and between a speaker and his/her discourse, which is mediated by other words. The implication that any word or utterance is always a quotation prefigures Derrida's idea of language as a "play of signifying references" (1976, p. 7).

The **addressivity** of discourse entails that "every word is directed toward an *answer* and cannot escape the profound influence of the answering word that it anticipates" (Bakhtin, 1981, p. 280). This highlights the role of language in relations between the self and other selves: "language, for the individual consciousness lies on the borderline between oneself and the other. The word in language is half someone else's" (p. 293). Although addressivity, as it is formulated by Bakhtin, is a dialogic orientation, an implication of the relation between dialogism and monologism discussed earlier is that addressivity can also have a monologic orientation—or, to put this another way, monologism is a lack of addressivity. In this sense, it is a stance toward an other and her/his discourse that either ignores her/his response or denies her/him a subject position from which to respond. As Bakhtin has suggested, "monologism, at its extreme, denies the existence outside itself of another consciousness with equal rights and equal responsibilities, another *I* with equal rights *(thou)*" (1984a, p. 292). Whereas dialogism is associated with the formation of intersubjectivity, monologism refers to a form of solipsism which fails to recognize or effaces the subjectivity of the other. Conversely, addressivity can also describe the strategies of response toward the discourse of a text or speaker utilized by an addressee or reader.

The dialogic orientation of discourse implies that reading is an interactive process: meanings are the product of intertextual and intersubjective relations generated by a text. I use the term "intertextuality" in its widest sense, to refer to the range of cultural and literary discourses, genres, pretexts and generic precursors, as well as specific texts referred to or quoted within a focused text. Intertextuality is an implicitly polyphonic narrative strategy because it enables the representation of multiple simultaneous intersecting voices and discourses within a text. The interrelations between these voices and discourses can express forms of intersubjectivity. The intertextual construction of a narrator or character discourse can also foreground the linguistic and textual status of the narratorial subject.

Many commentators have noted connections between Bakhtin's concept of addressivity and reception theory, in particular Iser's concept of the implied reader (1974; 1978; *see also* Bernstein, 1983; A. White, 1984, pp. 128–129; Booth, 1985; Allen, 1987; Shepherd, 1989). Addressivity entails that the discourse of a speaker is inscribed with both an anticipated response and an idea of the other to whom an utterance is addressed. This formulation implies a distinction between the actual response of an addressee and the anticipated response of that addressee, and between the actual addressee and the speaker's conception of that addressee. Both the anticipated response and the speaker's conception of the other are inscribed in the discourse of a speaker or text, and are thus comparable with Iser's notion of an implied reader to whom a text is addressed. The implied reader is "a textual structure anticipating the presence of a recipient" (Iser, 1978, p. 34).

The approaches of Bakhtin and Iser are similar insofar as both see texts as constructing and inscribing an interpretative position. However, the concept of an implied reader informing Bakhtin's work differs from that of Iser in ways which highlight problems with Iser's theory, particularly as it has been used in the criticism of children's literature—for example, Chambers (1985) or Thomson (1987). The main difference between Bakhtin and Iser is how they conceive of the relation between text, reader and implied reader. For Iser the implied reader is a textual role or position that mediates the text and reader. It "incorporates both the prestructuring of the potential meaning by the text and the reader's actualisation of this potential through the reading process" (1974, p. xii). Thus, although Iser describes reading and interpretation as active processes, the relation between text, implied reader and reader that he describes entails that a reader must align with the implied reader position in order to arrive at a successful reading—that is, one which "actualizes" the meaning of a text. Thus, he seems to assume a single reading position and a single unified textual meaning—an approach which by implication privileges monological textual strategies and assumes a limited range of reading positions and strategies. For Bakhtin an implicit addressee (reader) is to be understood as an interlocutive position contingent upon the enunciative position of the speaker (or narrator). Thus, the relations between a text, its inscribed readers and actual readers hinge on a dialogue and disparity between subjects occupying different discursive positions, rather than on a relation of alignment. Bakhtin's approach is thus inclusive of two specific aspects of reading and narration that Iser's approach would exclude. These are a reader who refuses the subject position constructed by a text, but who in choosing to read against a text arrives at an equally valid reading, and texts which construct multiple implicit reading positions and thereby deny readers a stable interpretative position. In other words, Bakhtin's concept of addressivity entails a range of strategies for reading and response, and his conception of the novel as a dialogical and heteroglottic genre which typically incorporates a diversity of discourses and voices implies that texts can potentially construct a range of implied reader subject positions in dialogic relation to these discourses and voices.

Finally, Iser and Bakhtin also differ in the degrees of passivity and activity they attribute to readers. As Shepherd (1989) and Stephens (1992a, pp. 55–56) have both argued, Iser's concept of the implied reader entails that by identifying with implied readers, readers occupy passive and disempowered positions and that "a reader's subjectivity is effaced as part of the reading process" (Stephens, 1992a, p. 4). It is this implication that Chambers (1985) has taken to its extreme when he claims that "a requirement of fulfilled readership is a willingness to give oneself up to the book" (p. 37). The idea that the "best" readings are produced through strategies of identification places limitations on both reading strategies and narrative techniques. As Hunt (1988b) has argued, the processes whereby texts construct meaning and readers comprehend texts are complex and the latter involve a range of learned rules, codes and strategies. Bakhtin's approach envisages a much broader range of narrative techniques, reading positions and interpretative strategies than that of Iser. For Bakhtin, the addressivity of a text is to be understood as a cognitive, ideological and social stance toward an other—analogous to the self's relation to another—which assumes degrees of both activity and passivity in the production of meanings. Bakhtin's approach is not opposed to that of Iser, but rather includes Iser's implied reader within a wider conception of reading strategies and strategies for addressing and constructing implicit readers as active and passive subjects.

As I suggested earlier, Bakhtin sees the novel as an inherently dialogic genre in that it typically utilizes a range of narrative techniques and types of discourse representation and incorporates a range of social and ideological discourses. However, his association of the novel with heteroglossia and dialogism implies a misleading opposition between dialogic discourses—such as the novel—and other monologic discourses—such as the epic and the lyric (*see* his "Epic and Novel," 1981). Clearly, some narrative fiction, in particular a substantial proportion of children's fiction, attempts to construct and impose a unified (monologic) worldview upon readers, and in doing so represses the dialogic potential of the novel genre. It is, however, open to debate as to whether any fiction can be wholly successful in achieving this aim; even the most didactic narratives will disclose contradictions and fissures in meaning and open themselves to divergent and recalcitrant readings. Conversely, as I argue in Chapter 2, the dialogic effects of polyphonic, intertextual and heteroglottic strategies for constructing narrative and representing subjectivity can be subverted through the presence of underlying monologic ideologies and monologic forms of closure. An implication of this is that particular narrative forms or techniques are neither inherently dialogic nor inherently monologic. Rather, like language, the novel genre is structured by an interaction between monologic and dialogic forces. In general, monologism is associated with the hegemony of authorial control and the limitation of narrational techniques, discursive styles and ideological viewpoints represented in novels (*see* Hunt, 1988a). These are strategies which situate implied readers in restricted and passive subject positions (*see* Stephens, 1991; 1992a). Dialogism is associated with the relinquishing of authorial control, and with narrative techniques which disguise or efface an author's presence so as to construct more active and analytic strategies for reading. These comments might be extended to interpretative practices in general, my own in particular. In producing readings of novels, there is always a risk of imposing a single unified meaning on a text, and in doing so ignoring the range of other possible readings that a text might open up and that might be produced through another reader's engagement with that text. The interpretations of texts offered in the chapters that follow are interpretations which I prefer, for a range of ideological, intellectual, personal and at times probably quite idiosyncratic reasons, but they are always provisional interpretations and hence open to further dialogue.

Most of the novels I examine and discuss use a range of dialogical narrative structures and discursive techniques which represent subjectivity as dialogically constructed and which construct implied readers who are actively involved in the production of meanings. Some of these novels, mainly those discussed in Chapters 3 and 4, are not overtly dialogical in their narrative techniques; rather, the focus in these chapters is on the dialogic representation of subjectivity and the use dialogic narrative structures, such as the motif of the double, or *doppelgänger,* and stories of cultural, social or psychological alienation and displacement, to explore the nature of the subject and the social and linguistic influences on its formation. Most of the texts examined in Chapters 2 and 5 to 8 are more overtly dialogical in their narrative techniques and discursive strategies. They use multiple narrators or character focalizers and multistranded narration, or overtly intertextual and heteroglottic forms of discourse to foreground the polyphonic and dialogic structuring of the narrative discourse.

Chapter 2 outlines dialogic narrative strategies for representing intersubjectivity, in particular intertextuality, polyphony, and multivoiced and multistranded narration. Here I argue that the representation of characters as subjects is contingent upon their construction within a narrative as focalizing agents and that the representation of intersubjectivity in narrative depends on the inclusion of two or more character focalizers. These strategies are also instrumental in the construction of implied readers in active subject positions. This chapter also looks at strategies for repressing dialogism and thus disabling intersubjectivity.

Chapters 3 and 4 outline the major theoretical issues surrounding subjectivity. Chapter 3 examines Bakhtin's and Lacan's approaches to the relationship between the self and the other and the representation of interpersonal relations in narrative. In adolescent novels humanist assumptions about subjectivity, meaning and history are called into question through dialogic narrative structures and techniques. Often this results in a more or less overt affirmation of humanist ideas and principles; nevertheless, notions of an essential selfhood are destabilized by an emphasis on interpersonal relationships, intersubjectivity, fragmentation and alienation, or on the social and linguistic influences affecting the formation of subjectivity. The discussion focuses on the use of the *quest* motif, wherein the formation of subjectivity is represented as a "quest for the self," and the double, or *doppelgänger.* This motif is used to express the idea that a sense of personal identity is shaped by a relation to an other and to represent a dialogue between different conceptions of the subject, namely the ideas of an essential subject, a subject constructed through interpersonal relations and/or social processes, and a split or fragmented subject. The idea, most frequently identified with

Lacan, that the subject is inherently split, and that subjectivity is hence always experienced as a form of alienation, is reflected in the use of the double and in stories of cultural and psychological alienation. Chapter 4 examines theoretical perspectives on the influences of language, society and culture on the formation of subjectivity and their implications for representations of cultural displacement, alienation and transgression in narrative. Narratives about cultural, social, temporal or psychological displacement express analogies between personal and cultural forms of solipsism, that is, between personal and cultural perceptions and constructions of otherness. These narratives also reflect ideas about how language, society, individuals and ideologies of identity interact, and hence, explore the construction of subjectivity in relation to specific social, cultural and linguistic codes and practices. They thereby raise questions about the limitations that cultural conventions can place on experience, agency and subjectivity.

Chapter 5 examines the incorporation of modernist thematic concerns and narrative techniques into adolescent fictions and the implications these have for humanist assumptions about the possibility of subjectivity and intersubjectivity. The chapter focuses on the representation of positive and negative variants of modern humanism in two polyphonic multitemporal novels, *Unleaving* (Walsh, 1976) and *Red Shift* (Garner, 1973). These novels explore modernist themes and philosophical ideas that are not often dealt with in children's fiction, and they use complex and diverse narrative and intertextual strategies to represent interrelations between subjectivity and personal and mythic time.

Chapter 6 is also concerned with the representation of subjectivity in polyphonic multitemporal narratives, but its focus is now on representations in novels which include a historical dimension. It argues that historical narratives have a primary function in the inscription of universalizing notions of historical process, human experience and subjectivity. Interpretations and representations of the past are frequently based on concerns in the present, and multitemporal narratives, that is, novels which incorporate multiple narrative strands located in multiple time contexts, foreground how interrelationships between a (conceived of) past and a present are used to forge meaning(s). The chapter examines how dialogic relationships between versions of the past and the present can be constructed by depicting characters as focalizing agents in both the past and the present, through the use of intertextual strategies and through the construction of alternative and subversive historical narratives.

Chapters 7 and 8 focus on different aspects of the textual and discursive construction of subjectivity in texts which are overtly heteroglottic.

Chapter 7 examines the use of extra-literary genres and discourses, in particular diary and epistolary genres, to represent the subject as constructed in and through discursive and textual codes and structures. These strategies represent the socio-ideological contexts in which subjects are positioned and through which subjectivity itself is figured as an intersection of heteroglottic discourses and textual codes, and they can also be instrumental in the construction of active implied reader positions.

Chapter 8 examines the relations between the past and its textual representation in history writing and in fictions which incorporate historiographic generic conventions. It argues that textual and discursive forms can impose a constraint on the representation of subjectivity and on the apprehension of the subjectivity of an other. The narrative strategies of historiographic metafictions foreground problems associated with the inscription of subjectivity in history which conventional forms of historical writing usually mask. In doing so, they represent the past as a fragmented heteroglottic text and draw attention to the process through which the past is interpreted and represented.

ENDNOTES

1. The authorship of works by Mikhail Bakhtin, Valentin Vološinov and Pavel Medvedev has been in dispute since 1973, when Ivanov claimed that Bakhtin wrote many texts published under the names of Vološinov and Medvedev (Ivanov, 1975). As Bakhtin neither denied nor confirmed Ivanov's claims, the question of authorship has remained unresolved. Arguments in support of Ivanov are presented by Holquist (1983b), Clark and Holquist (1984) and Todorov (1984), and refutations of Ivanov's claims are presented by Titunik (1984). Terms like "Bakhtinian" and "the Bakhtin circle" refer collectively to the work of this group of writers, of whom it seems clear Bakhtin was the intellectual leader, though wherever I refer to particular texts I use the authorial name under which they were originally published.

2. This claim has also been questioned by a range of commentators on Bakhtin's work. See for example, Hirschkop (1985a, 1986b, 1989) Stam (1988) and the exchanges between Young (1985–1986) and White (1987–1988), and Hirschkop (1985a) and Morson (1985).

3. There is not space here to examine issues such as what constitutes the category "adolescent fiction," and whether it does or should exist. For my purposes, an "adolescent" novel is one that has been classified and marketed for high school-aged people (ages 12–17). The "children's" novels that I will be discussing are aimed at a primary school-age audience (ages 8–11).

4. These "dialogic" narrative strategies will be outlined and discussed in Chapter 2. The term "intersubjectivity" suggests that subjectivity is not specific to the individual, but exists within interrelationships with others. This idea, and narrative strategies used to articulate it, will be discussed in Chapters 2 and 3.

5. Stephens (1992a) has used Bakhtin's idea of carnival to discuss transgression in children's literature; and Hunt (1991) has referred to Bakhtin's conception of the novel as a polyphonic form in his discussion of open and closed texts (p. 81). Bakhtin's notion of carnival is developed in *Rabelais and his World* (1984b), but will not be dealt with here. Polyphony and the chronotope are discussed in Chapters 2 and 6.

6. Publication dates for the work of Bakhtin and Vološinov refer to English

translations. Full publication details are given in the References section.

7. This question has been formulated in various ways by Holquist (1983b), Todorov (1984, pp. 63–64), Hirschkop (1985a), Morson (1985), Pechey (1989) and Lodge (1990, p. 90). My own understanding of the ambiguity that the question pinpoints is mainly dependent on Hirschkop's explications (1985a; 1986b; 1989).

8. These two approaches are versions of what Vološinov has termed "individualistic subjectivism" and "abstract objectivism" (1986, p. 48).

9. The term "addressivity" has mainly been used by Holquist (1983b, pp. 311–312; 1990, p. 48) to describe these ideas and the philosophical idea of "answerability" developed in Bakhtin's early essays of the 1920s (in *Art and Answerability*, 1990). My use of the concept of "addressivity" is more concrete than Holquist's in that I am interested in the implications that it has for the representation of intersubjective relations and the textual construction of implied reader subject positions in narrative.

Representing Intersubjectivity

Polyphonic Narrative Techniques

The fundamental condition, that which makes a novel a novel, that which is responsible for stylistic uniqueness, is the speaking person and his dis- *course. The speaking person in the novel is always, to one degree or another, an* ideologue, *and his words are always* ideologemes. *A particular language in a novel is always a particular way of viewing the world, one that strives for a social significance.*

Bakhtin, *The Dialogic Imagination*

This chapter focuses on narrative strategies for representing intersubjectivity and polyphony, with particular reference to focalization, intertextuality, and multivoiced and multistranded narrative. These strategies have important implications for the representation of selfhood as being formed in dialogue with others and with the physical, social and cultural world and for the positioning of implied readers in active subject positions. My approach extends the Bakhtinian concept of polyphony by linking it with two related clusters of concepts deployed by other narrative theorists. These concepts are, on the one hand, narrative voice, point of view, focalization, and speech representation, and on the other, narrative time, order and structure.[1]

Although Bakhtin claimed that the novel as a genre is an inherently "polyphonic" form (that is, it is by definition "many-voiced"), my analysis in this chapter is confined to novels which use multivoiced and/or multistranded narrative and are thus overtly polyphonic.[2] These terms refer to two kinds of narrative technique which have recently gained popular status in adolescent fiction. Multivoiced narratives use two or more character focalizers or narrators from whose perceptual and attitudinal viewpoints events are narrated. Multistranded narratives comprise two or more interwoven or interconnected narrative strands through which events (or different versions of events) are narrated. These strands may be differentiated by shifts in narrative point of view (who speaks or focalizes) and/or by shifts in the spatial or temporal relationships (or what Bakhtin terms "chronotopic" relationships). This chapter will focus on a selection of multivoiced and multistranded novels in which narrative strands are situated in the same time and place, but narrated from different narratorial or character points of view—*Goldengrove* (Walsh, 1972/1985), *The Chocolate War* (Cormier, 1974/1988), *Slake's Limbo* (Holman, 1974/1986), *Salt River Times* (Mayne, 1980), *The Lake at the End of the World* (Macdonald, 1988/1990) and *Finders, Losers* (Mark, 1990).[3] All of these novels are also overtly concerned with interrelations between the self and others, and between the self and the physical and social world. The chapter will focus on the use of polyphonic narrative strategies to structure and shape these themes.

Maria Nikolajeva has outlined the concept of polyphony in *Children's Literature Comes of Age* (1996), where she uses Bakhtin's schema for the historical development of literature (*see* "Epic and Novel" in *The Dialogic Imagination,* 1981) to chart the stages of development in children's literature. According to Nikolajeva, this development proceeds from adaptations of existing adult literature and folklore through to "polyphonic" children's novels of the seventies, eighties and nineties (pp. 95–99). Most of the novels which I discuss in this chapter as examples of explicit polyphony also fall into Nikolajeva's fourth category ("polyphonic, or multivoiced, children's literature"). However, my approach differs from that of Nikolajeva insofar as I don't see polyphonic narrative as a particularly recent phenomena, but rather as an inherent feature of narrative fiction. Certainly, multiple narrators and/or character focalizers and modernist and postmodernist narrative strategies have become popular with contemporary writers for children, and recent fiction may hence appear more explicitly polyphonic than earlier fiction, but the examples of early ("didactic" and "epic" as opposed to "polyphonic") children's literature that Nikolajeva cites are more "polyphonic" than her analysis would suggest. For example, Nikolajeva cites *Treasure Island* (Stevenson, 1883) as an example of "didactic" (and therefore presumably nonpolyphonic) fiction in that is it narrated retrospectively "from the viewpoint of a clever adult." As John Stephens and I have argued in *Retelling Stories* (1998), along with other critics such as Nodelman (1983) and Gannon (1985), a central ambivalence is created in the novel through its implicit doublevoicedness: it is narrated retrospectively by an older wiser Jim Hawkins, but from the viewpoint of a younger more impressionable and naive Jim, and despite the dominance of the narrator's voice, young Jim's voice and viewpoints constantly surface and engage dialogically with the position implied by that narrative voice.[4] A difference between my approach and that of Nikolajeva, then, is that rather than seeing some children's fictions as polyphonic and others as not polyphonic, I would follow Bakhtin's argument that the novel as a genre is inherently polyphonic and that fiction for children, by virtue of the fact that its evolution was simultaneous with the adult novel, is also inherently polyphonic. Insofar as polyphony may be a more or less overt aspect of the structure and narrative technique of a novel, I would also distinguish between implicit and explicit forms of polyphony. In this way, I would refer to texts which Nikolajeva designates "polyphonic" as "explicitly polyphonic;" and I would refer to many of the earlier texts which she excludes from the category "polyphonic," such as *Treasure Island,* as "implicitly polyphonic." This is not simply a quibble over definitions, but rather a recognition that Bakhtin's notion of polyphony is relevant to a wide range of literature.

There are three main implications of polyphony that interest me here. These are: (1) the effects of narrative strategies for the construction of characters and narrators as subjects and for the representation of intersubjectivity; (2) the positioning of implied readers as active subjects within a narrative discourse; and (3) the implications for intersubjectivity of the relationships between monologic and dialogic tensions in polyphonic narrative. The representation of characters as subjects is dependent on their construction within a narrative as focalizing agents. Intersubjectivity (i.e. the idea that subjectivity exists within interrelationships with others and with the world) depends on the dialogic orientation of focalizing and narratorial positions. Although the narrative techniques that I discuss in this chapter are potentially dialogic, this potential can be contained and suppressed through monologic narrative strategies, in particular monologic forms of narrative closure and the inscription of logocentric or hegemonic metanarratives. Insofar as the representation of intersubjectivity is contingent upon the dialogic structuring of a narrative discourse, strategies which repress dialogism also place a limitation on the possibility of representing positive (nonsolipsistic) interrelations with others. Furthermore, these strategies also limit the range of implicit reading positions and strategies constructed in texts and deny readers active subject positions. The next section will examine more closely Bakhtin's concept of polyphony and its implications for the representation of subjectivity in multistranded and multivoiced adolescent novels.

HETEROGLOSSIA, POLYPHONY AND THE NOVEL

Bakhtin's theory of the novel centers on its representation of language and of the speaking person. For Bakhtin, the novel is an inherently heteroglottic and intertextual genre which appropriates and represents various primary speech genres as well as other socially stratified languages, both literary and extraliterary, from within a heteroglossia (1981, pp. 301–330; 1986, pp. 65–67). It characteristically deploys a range of narrational strategies, voices and discursive styles and is thus defined by a diversity of social speech types and a diversity of individual voices. There are four primary compositional forms for appropriating and representing heteroglossia in the novel (1981, p. 301–320). These are:

1.   The parodic representation, stylization and playing with other discursive styles—literary, generic, professional, class-and-interest groups, and everyday, or "common" speech (p. 311)
2.   The language used by narrators or authorial figures (p. 312)
3.   The language used by characters: direct and indirect forms of character speech and thought (p. 315)
4.   Incorporated extra-literary genres—such as confession, diary, biography, letters, songs, poems (p. 320)

These forms for representing heteroglossia in the novel "permit languages to be used in ways that are indirect, conditional and distanced" (p. 323) that is to be the object of representation. In this chapter I will mainly be looking at the interrelations between the second and third of these forms for representing heteroglossia—narrator and character discourse—but will also examine the use of literary intertexts in *Goldengrove*.[5] Bakhtin's emphasis on "the speaking person in the novel" allocates narrator and character discourse a central place in his theory of the novel, and for my purposes, the interrelations between these two forms have important implications for the representation of intersubjectivity.

The idea that the novel is a "dialogized system" of the images of "languages," styles and consciousnesses is central to Bakhtinian theory (Jefferson, 1989, p. 173). As Jefferson has argued, this is not, however, simply a question of placing language at the center of a critical approach, but rather a conception of novels as constituted by the represented discourse of speaking persons. Conversely, Bakhtin's emphasis on "the speaking person" does not reduce his theory of the novel to a theory of character. For Bakhtin "the formal elements of fiction," such as plot or character, are devices for incorporating and organizing speech variety in the novel. Thus characters "are not primarily bodies or minds to be depicted . . . they are just speakers providing vehicles for different types of discourse" (Jefferson, 1989, p. 173). Similarly, the novelistic plot is subordinated to the task of coordinating and organizing social languages and ideologies (Bakhtin, 1981, p. 365).

In "Discourse and the Novel" (1981), Bakhtin claims "the fundamental condition, that which makes a novel a novel, that which is responsible for its stylistic uniqueness, is the *speaking person and his discourse*" (p. 332). There are three aspects to this conception of the novel. First, a speaker and his/her discourse is the "object of *verbal* artistic representation." The discourse of a speaker "is not merely transmitted or reproduced" within a novel; rather, "it is, precisely, *artistically represented . . . by means of* (authorial) *discourse*" (p. 332). Hence, novelistic discourse always incorporates at least two voices or discursive positions: the (represented or reported) discourse of a speaker, and the (representing or reporting) narratorial context. The novel is thereby characterized by a range and variety of narrative techniques for representing speech—including direct and indirect forms of discourse representation, as well as focalization strategies (*see* McHale, 1978; Pateman, 1989). Furthermore, it also means that novelistic discourse is always internally dialogized or double-voiced (Bakhtin, 1981, p. 315; pp. 324–325). The novel is thus an inherently polyphonic (or many-voiced) form. Since the speech of a character or narrator is the appropriated speech of another in another's language, this discourse is then verbally and semantically autonomous. Thus, while it may serve to express refracted authorial intentions (p. 324), and hence constitute a second language for the author, there is always a potential dialogue embedded within the speech of characters and narrators in relation to an authorial context or position. This dialogue can thus represent intersubjective relations between speaking positions and voices.

Second, "the distinctive qualities of a character's discourse always strive for a certain social significance, a social breadth; such discourses are always potential languages" and therefore "may also be a factor stratifying language, introducing heteroglossia into it" (p. 333). No one voice can ever be effectively cleansed of other voices constituting it, so the novel, as comprising the represented discourse of others, is a radically intertextual form, characterized by its capacity to incorporate and represent other socially stratified languages from within a heteroglossia. The language of a speaker thus functions as representing discourse, as well as represented discourse.

Third, Bakhtin describes the speaking person in the novel as "always, to some degree or another, an *ideologue*," and his words as *"ideologemes"* (p. 333). A comparable contemporary linguistic concept might be that of "idiolect"—"an individual's personal variety of a particular language system" (*Macquarie Dictionary,* 1981). The language of any one speaker is situated within a particular (shared) social, ideological and discursive context, but their "idiolect" is characterized by particular linguistic usages, peculiar to that speaker (Bernard and Delbridge, 1980, pp. 184, 288). This double function of the discourse of a speaker is implicit in Bakhtin's concept of character as an ideologue. A speaking person in a novel brings "with them their own unique ideological discourse, their own language" or "ideologeme" (pp. 332–333). This language "is always a particular way of viewing the world," but it is also "one that strives for a social significance" and is thus socially and ideologically situated (p. 333). A speaker, according to Bakhtin, is to be conceived of as occupying a particular ideological position, or "language world view," which "functions as one ideology among other possible ideologies" (p. 334). This position is "always open to contest" (p. 334) and it is ideologically demarcated from the representing (authorial or narratorial) discourse. Implicit here is the notion that a speaker in a novel occupies a discrete subject position not dominated by the authorial or narratorial voice or position. Characters and narrators alike are constructed in and through language. They are constituted by a particular intersection of social and ideological discourses and they occupy discrete subject positions which are discursively and ideologically situated within a represented social world in dialogue with each other. By making the "speaking person" a condition of the novel, Bakhtin defines the novel as an inherently dialogic, or "polyphonic" form, which is characterized by: (1) the variety and range of narrative strategies used to represent the discourse (speech, thoughts and "language world views") of others; (2) its capacity to appropriate and represent a multiplicity of social and ideological discourses and viewpoints; and (3) its capacity to represent characters and narrators as speakers and as subjects.[6]

In Bakhtin's writing and in the secondary literature about Bakhtin, the term "polyphony" has often been used interchangeably with dialogism and heteroglossia to refer to particular types of novels as well as to the novel genre in general. Bakhtin had developed the concept of polyphony in his early work on Dostoevsky (1984a; first published in Russian in 1929), but in his later work he clearly came to see polyphony as characteristic of novelistic discourse in general (*see* "Discourse and the Novel" in *The Dialogic Imagination,* 1981). The lack of precision in many contemporary usages of the term as simply meaning "many-voiced" does, however, reduce its analytic force as a concept for describing particular kinds of interrelations between voices and subjects in narrative. Polyphony does literally mean "many-voiced," but it acquires more specific meanings as it is used by Bakhtin, as it does in musicology, from which it is derived. In music, "polyphonic" is used to refer to a musical composition, such as a fugue or a canon, which consists of two or more voices, or parts, which are counterpointed against each other. Although each voice is a repetition or variation on the same subject or theme and the relations between voices are harmonic, no one voice dominates the composition. It is the modulations and variations within voices and the intervals and relationships between voices that are of musical importance. Thus the fugal form is conceived of as a system of interrelationships between distinct voices, rather than a harmonious blend of indistinct voices. Similarly, in *Problems of Dostoevsky's Poetics* (1984a) Bakhtin uses the term "polyphonic" to describe not just the "plurality of voices" in Dostoevsky's novels but, more specifically, the particular ways in which these "voices" are represented within narrative, and the peculiar interrelationships among them. In the following description, Bakhtin stresses the independence of and interrelations between voices in Dostoevsky's novels:

> *A plurality of independent and unmerged voices and consciousnesses, a genuine polyphony of fully valid voices is in fact the chief characteristic of Dostoevsky's novels.* What unfolds in his works is not a multitude of characters and fates in a single objective world, illuminated by a single authorial consciousness; rather a *plurality of consciousnesses, with equal rights and each with its own world,* combine but are not merged in the unity of the event. Dostoevsky's major heroes are, by the very nature of his creative design, *not only objects of authorial discourse but also subjects of their own directly signifying discourse.* (pp. 6–7)

From this description, we can extrapolate two primary features of polyphonic narrative. The first feature refers us to the question of how polyphony is represented. Characters and narrators are conceived of as "unmerged voices and consciousnesses," that is, as speaking subjects situated in particular discursive positions in relation to, but independent of, the (reporting) authorial context. As such, they are "subjects of their own directly signifying discourse" and they occupy subject positions not dominated by an authorial or narratorial voice or position. The second feature refers to how polyphony is organized. These voices are independent of each other, but they also have shape and meaning in dialogue with each other. As in a fugue, it is the interrelations between voices, the differences and patternings rather than relations of identity or of hierarchy, that are of interest. Thus, polyphony also enables the conception of intersubjective relations in narrative, that is, the idea that a speaker occupies a discrete subject position in a text in a dialogic relation to others and to the textual world.

A categoric use of the term "polyphony" to distinguish between polyphonic and nonpolyphonic forms of narrative would seem fairly limited. Most narrative fiction is polyphonic in the sense that it consists of more than one voice, even first person narration.[7] My understanding of the concept of polyphony is that it relates to the interrelationships between representing and represented voices in narrative fiction, and that it is these interrelationships which are of importance, not simply the existence of multiple voices. In this sense, polyphony is not so much either a generalized category of discourse (narrative fiction) nor a specific category of the novel (the polyphonic novel), as it is a dialogic orientation within narrative fictions. Insofar as some novels, such as *Salt River Times* (Mayne, 1980) and *Finders, Losers* (Mark, 1990), use multiple narrative voices as a structuring principle, whereas others, such as *Goldengrove* (Walsh, 1972/1985), *Arilla Sun Down* (Hamilton, 1976/1977) or *Eva* (Dickinson, 1988) incorporate multivoicedness as an aspect of the discourse, we can distinguish between more or less explicit and implicit forms of polyphony. All novels are polyphonic in that they are constructed out of represented and representing discourses, but as the gap between these discourses widens, polyphony becomes more explicit.

There are three main strategies for representing and organizing polyphony, which have become increasingly more common in contemporary adolescent fiction. These are the use of multiple character focalizers or narrators, implicit and explicit forms of intertextuality, and the use of multistranded narrative. These strategies are not exclusive, and are in fact often combined in various ways, and they all tend to foreground polyphony. In *Goldengrove* (1972/1985) Walsh uses three character focalizers and extensive intertextual references; *The Chocolate War* (Cormier, 1974/1988) has thirteen character focalizers. *Slake's Limbo* (Holman, 1974/1986), *Salt River Times* (Mayne, 1980), *The Lake at the End of the World* (Macdonald, 1988/1990) and *Finders, Losers* (Mark, 1990) all combine multiple character focalizers and/or narrators with multistranded narrative. In the next section, Bakhtin's concept of polyphony is linked with the more recent concept of focalization. Focalization and the interrelations between narrative and character discourse are particularly important for the representation of intersubjectivity and for the positioning of characters and implied readers as subjects and as agents in texts.

FOCALIZATION AND SUBJECTIVITY IN MULTIVOICED AND MULTISTRANDED NARRATIVE

The narrative technique of focalization is probably the most characteristic strategy for representing polyphony. It facilitates the construction of speakers in independent subject positions and the representation of a plurality of voices and consciousnesses. It is thus crucial for the representation of agency and intersubjectivity. Focalization is an indirect mode of narration occurring in first and third person narrative whereby events are narrated from the perceptual point of view of a character situated within the text as if seen through the eyes of that character (Stephens, 1992a, p. 27). In third person narrative, it is an intrinsically double-voiced mode which combines the narrative position and voice of a third person narrator with the perceptual viewpoint, and often the discourse and conceptual point of view, of a character. In first person narration, double-voicing is usually more implicit and produced through unreliable narration and temporal shifts. There are two main effects of focalization which concern me here. First, focalization is instrumental in constructing a character as an ideologue. By situating narrative point of view within the perceptual and conceptual purview of a particular character, that character is constructed as a specific ideological and discursive position, that is, as a "language worldview." Characters are thus represented as occupying subject positions in relation to contextual discourses and voices. Second, although the effect of extensive focalization from the viewpoint of one character in third person narrative can be very similar to that of first person narration, double-voicing is more explicit. Third person character focalized narration combines two narrative positions and discourses, and shifts between a third person narrator and a character focalizer are important for the construction and representation of intersubjectivity, because such shifts correlate with a character's changing subject position from focalized subject to focalizing subject.

In third person narration, there are three main strategies for indicating character focalization: verbs denoting the perceptual viewpoint of a character, for example, "saw" or "looked"; shifts between (narrated) direct speech and (character focalized) indirect speech and thought; and the use of indirect discourse more appropriate to a particular character than the narrator. The following passage from *Finders, Losers* (Mark, 1990) demonstrate some of these strategies.

> When Dad got the job of artist-in-residence at Shapton College, the first thing that Philip had said was, "In *residence*? Does that mean you'll be living there?"
>
> "Not all the time," Dad said. "I'll be home in the holidays and some weekends. It's only for a year." Evidently a year did not seem very long to Dad. To Philip it seemed like forever.
>
> "Actually, it's only eleven months," Dad said, "from September to July." Eleven months did not sound much better. It was not as if he were used to his father being away from home, even during the day. Dad was a potter and worked in an outhouse at the end of the garden . . . (p. 9)

That this is predominantly indirect narration from Philip's point of view is sig-naled by the frequent omission of nominal qualifiers (such as "Philip's" or "his") in "when Dad," "Dad said" and "Dad was." However, subtle shifts in narrative point of view occur throughout the passage through shifts between direct and indirect narration. In the reported (direct) dialogue between Philip and his father, their voices and that of the narrator are fairly clearly differen-tiated, though the speech tags—"Dad said"—imply a blurring of the narrator's and Philip's point of view. It then shifts to indirect character thought ("To Philip it seemed like forever") to free direct character thought ("Eleven months did not sound much better") then back to third person narration ("It was not as if he were used to his father") and finally back to indirect character focalized narration ("Dad was"). These instances of indirect narration are strictly speak-ing narrated material, but in using language appropriate to Philip's viewpoint, they combine character discourse with that of the narrator. The positions de-noted by these two discourses are, however, quite closely aligned. The voice and position of the narrator is for the most part effaced, and the double-voicedness of the narrative discourse remains fairly implicit. As I will show later in this chapter, the polyphonic effects of Mark's narrative strategies are more apparent when we consider the interrelations between various narrative strands, each of which is focalized by a different character.

The extent to which character focalized narration is more or less ex-plicitly double-voiced is dependent upon the interrelations between charac-ter discourse and narrator discourse. This can be seen in the range of focal-ization strategies used by Mayne in *Salt River Times* (1980). A passage from this novel shows the way in which character focalized narrative can be more overtly double-voiced through the construction of divergent narrator and character discourses:

> The next day after that, Thursday, Sophia had got tired of her, be-cause really Gwenda treated every friend in the way she treated her mother. No one liked her for four days in a row.
>
> On Thursday she had fallen out with Sophia so she went along by the river alone. It was not a dirty river, she thought. Of course there was mud in it. You get mud if you mix water and earth. You get wa-ter and earth if you mix rivers with land. And the other way about.
>
> In fact the river was cleaner than coffee. Or Gwenda was think-ing that before she looked. She had thought how clean it was when she went down the gravel road to the water. . . .
>
> . . . Now she thought she would look at the river and find it was clean and make her mother agree. She knew she must be right, be-

cause she had thought of it so clearly.

The river hadn't been thinking clearly. It was the colour of coffee. (my ellipsis, pp. 11–12)

The shifts between third person narration and character focalized narration are foregrounded by phrases which repeat the same information, but from a different narrative point of view, as in "Sophia had got tired of her" and "she had fallen out with Sophia." The combination of indirect discourse as a means of representing character discourse ("In fact the river was cleaner than coffee") and free indirect discourse ("You get mud if you mix water and earth") with quite a lot of third person narration ("or Gwenda was thinking that before she looked") sets the conceptual viewpoint of the character against the perceptual viewpoint of the narrator. By foregrounding the disparity between character thought and the object of perception, the discourse constructs Gwenda as a specific language worldview which is distinct from that of the narrator, thereby representing Gwenda as both focalizing and focalized subject. The frequent shifting between character and narrator discourse culminates in an ironic alignment of narrator and character point of view: "The river hadn't been thinking clearly. It was the colour of coffee." The overall effect of double-voiced narration here is to force a collusion between the attitudinal viewpoints of implied readers and the narrator in a way which views character focalized narration ironically.

In first person (narrator focalized) narrative, polyphony is often much more implicit than it is in third person character focalized narration, because the gap between represented and representing discourse is frequently less perceptible. Double-voicing can emerge, however, when the narrator is unreliable: when the viewpoints of other characters indicate that the narrator's view of the world is limited or based on misapprehension; or when that viewpoint conflicts with consensus views of reality. In the first instance, the viewpoints of other characters constitute other voices in the narrative which have as much (or more) validity as that of the narrator. In the second, multivoicedness arises out the process of reading and understanding—readers in effect supply those other voices which make the text interpretable. Double-voicing can also emerge when the narration is retrospective or when it shifts between the narrator's present and his/her past. In this way, the narrator's present voice is representing discourse and retrospective narration is represented discourse. This distinction is quite clear-cut in first person narratives like Stevenson's *Treasure Island* or Dickins's *Great Expectations,* where events are clearly narrated at a much later time in the voice of an older narrator, but from the viewpoint of the narrator's young self.

In first person narratives, such as *Arilla Sun Down* (Hamilton, 1976/ 1977), which move back and forth in time, the relationship between representing and represented discourse also shifts. This novel is narrated in the present tense by twelve-year-old Arilla, and it uses various strategies which dialogize the narrator's discourse—or make it double-voiced. That Arilla's view of the world is limited is frequently highlighted through the reported dialogue of other characters, though the limitations of other character's viewpoints is also often indicated by snatches of free indirect thought (stream of consciousness) and remembered dialogue. For example, Arilla's observations about the girls she invites to her party evince an ambiguous mixture of naivety and insight: "Girls older than me can change like that, from something worse than ordinary into these creatures out of mysteries, and right before my eyes. I don't know what causes them to change. It hasn't rained in a week, and I know for sure not one of them's done any outside reading since the last book report" (1977, pp. 47–48). Shifts in narrative voice and point of view in those sections of the narrative which are narrated from the viewpoint of a much younger Arilla also dialogize the discourse, as in the opening of the novel, for example:

> Late in the big night and snow has no end. Taking me a long kind of time going to the hill. Would be afraid if not for the moon and knowing Sun-Stone Father is sledding. Way off, hear him go, "Whoopeeeee!" Real thin sound, go, "Whoop-eeeee!"
> If Mother could see me, she would say, *What you doing up? Get back under the covers. Catching your death.* But Mama sleeping on. I can slip on out to the moondust snow. She not seeing everything I do, like she say. (p. 1)

The discourse of the novel in general is marked by the use of the present tense and frequent omission of finite verbs, strategies which, in part, represent dialect speech. However, nonstandard grammatical formations and short abrupt syntax are more conspicuous in those sections of narrative which take place in Arilla's early childhood, such as this passage, where these strategies also represent the conceptual viewpoint of a small child. The narrative voice slips, however, with the inclusion of indirect and direct dialogue. Arilla's reporting of her father's "Whoop-eeeee!" remains in the voice of her younger self ("Way off, hear him go") whereas her indirect reporting of her mother's speech ("If Mother could see me, she would say") slips into an older voice.

In an episode about halfway through the novel, Arilla's writing of a story about James False Face draws attention to the extent to which language is double-voiced. The story that Arilla tells about her friend is quite different than that which emerges through the novel, and Arilla's story is interrupted by her own commentary on what she is writing, in comments such as "Don't think," "That's a lie" and "Don't tell anything about your feelings" (pp. 135, 136). The episode highlights the way in which narrative can be used to fabricate and to conceal rather than reveal, but also the extent to which the act of narration enacts a split between represented and representing discourse and hence between a narrating and a narrated self. Read back onto the rest of Arilla's narrative, the episode self-reflexively draws attention to those gaps in her discourse, where her language simultaneously obscures and discloses significance, and where it implicitly blends and clashes with the language of other characters whose voices she also records.

As Stephens (1992a) has shown, focalization in narrative is crucial for the positioning of implied readers. Through mediating the textual world and implied readers, focalization strategies construct an implicit position from which to "see" and interpret this world. This position is usually aligned either with the language worldview of the focalizing character/narrator or that of the (third person) narrator—depending on how explicitly double-voiced the narrative is. Stephens has also observed that it is unusual to find narratives written for children which are extensively focalized by more than a narrator plus one main character, and that this restriction of narrative points of view frequently has the effect of restricting the possible subject positions available to implied readers (1992a, p. 27). In many children's novels, character focalized point of view and narratorial point of view tend to be either implicitly aligned so that the attitudes of character, narrator and implied reader coincide, or in an unequal relation with the narrator occupying the privileged position. Both of these strategies tend to have the monologic effect of repressing or marginalizing the discourse of characters and of implied readers, and hence of denying both characters and readers agency. The positions denoted by character focalized discourse are constructed as subordinate to that of the dominant narratorial discourse, and implied reader positions are thereby constructed as passive and disempowered. In this way, while focalization is a primary way of incorporating and representing intersubjectivity and polyphony, it is not in itself an inherently dialogical narrative technique.

Many of the novels with which I am concerned in this chapter incorporate two or more character focalizers and are thematically preoccupied with the relations between the self, others and the world. Character focalization is a key strategy for representing these interrelations. Novels such as *Goldengrove* (Walsh, 1972/1985), *The Chocolate War* (Cormier, 1974/1988), *Slake's Limbo* (Holman, 1974/1986), *Salt River Times* (Mayne, 1980) and *Finders, Losers* (Mark, 1990) incorporate multiple character focalizers who are located in the same narrative space and time. These novels vary in the complexity of narrative techniques used to structure and represent character's voices and viewpoints. *Goldengrove* exemplifies a narrative technique which is quite unusual in children's fiction in that it interweaves the viewpoints of three focalizing characters within third person narration. Cormier's use of thirteen character focalizers in *The Chocolate War* is probably the most complex use of this narrative technique in children's fiction to date, though the range of ideological positions represented through these characters is limited and character ideologemes collude to construct a hegemonic metanarrative. The construction of multiple separate, but interconnecting, story strands in *Salt River Times* or *Finders, Losers* is a more common strategy for incorporating the viewpoints of more than two focalizing characters.

The use of multiple focalizers has three main effects. First, it enables the representation of a plurality of narrative voices, social and cultural discourses, and the construction of a range of perceptual, attitudinal and ideological viewpoints associated with the subject positions occupied by characters—hence it is also an important way of incorporating and representing heteroglossia. Second, it enables the construction of characters within multiple focalizing and focalized positions, and is thereby a crucial strategy for representing and examining forms of intersubjectivity. Third, the incorporation of multiple focalizers can efface, and thereby destabilize, a reader's sense of an implicit single authoritative narratorial position. In this way, narrative strategies using polyfocalization are instrumental in the positioning of implied readers. However, the presence of two or more speakers or focalizers, or the construction of two or more narrative strands, does not automatically ensure the dialogic character of the narrative discourse. What determines this is the "dialogic angle" at which narrative voices, viewpoints, subject positions, "styles and dialects are juxtaposed or counterposed in the work" (Bakhtin, 1984a, p. 182). As I suggested earlier, Bakhtin's notion of polyphony is similar to that of a polyphonic fugue. It refers to the interrelationships between voices, the differences and patternings among voices, rather than simply the number of voices. Dialogic relationships between narrative voices, "languages," social dialects and so on, are possible insofar as these "languages" are "perceived not as the impersonal word of language but as a sign of someone else's semantic position," that is, an "ideologeme" or "language world view" (Bakhtin, 1984a, p. 184). In narrative, it is through the interrelations between the represented direct and indirect discourse of narrators and characters that speakers are represented as subjects not dominated by a hegemonic authorial discourse. However, as my discussion of texts will show, the dialogic potential of multivoiced and multistranded narrative is frequently contained through implicit authorial control manifest in the narrative, and thematic and intertextual structures used to organize and structure the various narrative strands or voices. These strategies also deny characters agency and disable intersubjectivity. The following section will examine the use of multivoiced narrative and intertextuality in *Goldengrove*.

POLYPHONIC DISCOURSE: MULTIVOICED NARRATIVE, INTERTEXTUALITY AND INTERSUBJECTIVITY IN JILL PATON WALSH'S *GOLDENGROVE*

The title of *Goldengrove* (Walsh, 1972/1985) is a quotation from the first lines of Gerard Manley Hopkins's poem "Spring and Fall"—"Margaret are you grieving, / Over Goldengrove unleaving?" (1953, p50). Although the poem is only really alluded to indirectly in the text itself, it forms a context for the novel's thematic concerns with time, personal maturation and the self. The poem, read in the context of the novel, discloses a common view of the transition from childhood to adulthood which implies that the processes through which an individual negotiates this transition necessarily entail a loss of childhood and of self. These thematic concerns are explored in Walsh's novel through polyphonic narrative strategies which, by constructing a dialogue between the language worldviews or ideologemes associated with particular characters, suggest that the transition from solipsism to intersubjectivity is coincident with the development of interpersonal relations and can only ever be partially achieved.

Goldengrove is a multivoiced, though not overtly multistranded, novel. It is narrated in the third person and it incorporates the voices and viewpoints of three character focalizers (Madge, Paul and Gran). Events in the novel take place during a summer vacation spent by Madge and Paul at their grandmother's house at St. Ives, on the Cornish coast. Paul and Madge are supposedly cousins, though they discover toward the end of the novel that they are in fact brother and sister. The novel centers upon the implications that this discovery has for Madge, for whom it is made too late (1985, pp. 123–124). She feels unwanted by her father (p. 109) and that she has missed out on having a brother when she needed him (p. 123). As Townsend has suggested, the connection between the novel and Hopkins's poem is thematic (1979, p. 160). Walsh's novel makes overt what is implicit in Hopkins's poem, that is, that the experience of grief for the passing of time or for another is also to some extent grief for oneself and one's own loss of self. Furthermore, to the extent that these sentiments are associated with and implicitly voiced by Madge, Hopkins's poem also functions as an ideologeme, that is, "a particular language and way of viewing the world" (Bakhtin, 1981, p. 333), which is constructed through narrative discourse focalized by Madge, and which is indicative of a larger ideologeme which underlies the broader thematic concerns of the novel. This is not to say that Hopkins's poem dominates the novel's significances. Rather, the poem and the novel take on particular nuances of meaning read in conjunction with each other, and significances arise within the intertextual space between the two texts.[8]

Madge, Paul and Gran are all represented as focalizers, and their voices and viewpoints are juxtaposed and interwoven throughout the novel. They are each comprehensible as a particular way of looking at and talking about the fictional world; that is, in Bakhtin's terms they are identifiable as "ideologues" or "semantic positions" (1984a, p. 184). This can be seen in the opening of the novel (pp. 7–8), where the train journey to Goldengrove is narrated first from the viewpoint of Paul and then from that of Madge. There is a contrast in the narrative techniques used to represent the perceptions and thoughts of the two characters, as well as in the selectivity of their viewpoints (Paul anticipates seeing the sea, while Madge anticipates seeing the lighthouse) and the kinds of language they both use to describe and represent what they see.

Frequent shifts in point of view also construct a multiplicity of possible perceptual and interpretative positions, thereby dialogizing the discourse. Shifts in point of view in the following passage show this.

> No mackerel for breakfast today, for the fishing fleet, says Gran, stayed safely tucked up in the harbour last night, and Paul who slept through every sound of it, and slept through Gran walking with a lamp in her hand, trembling at the thought of death in the watery darkness, clearly thinks that the storm cannot have been excuse enough to miss the sweet firm pink and grey flesh flaking off the web of thin translucent bones on his morning plate. Amy has provided kippers instead, and I like kippers quite a lot, thinks Paul, but they're not the same because we eat them at home, and mackerel only here. . . . He grins to himself.
>
> "Nice kipper, dearie?" says Gran.
>
> "Fine, thanks, Gran," and, "Do hurry up, Madge. We'll be late down to the beach," says Paul. (my ellipsis, p. 19)

The passage incorporates and interweaves the voices of Gran, Paul and, implicitly, that of Madge, using indirect modes of discourse representation.

The shifts between Paul's and Gran's points of view are ostensibly marked by "says Gran," "Gran . . . at the thought," "Paul . . . clearly thinks." However, the qualifier in "Paul . . . clearly thinks," implies the point of view of a third person—the narrator, Gran or Madge? The sentence structure whereby Gran's "thought of death" is grammatically embedded within the clause referring to Paul's thoughts and the delay between the subject (Paul) and the verb (thinks) also implies the existence of multiple simultaneously perceiving and thinking subjects. It is not clear whether Madge is present at the beginning of this passage—in the immediately preceding passage she is upstairs looking out of the window—but she is obviously present by the end of the passage when Paul speaks to her. So either she has already entered but remained silent, or enters at some point during the passage. However, Madge's voice is identifiable as a particular ideologeme. In general, the discourse of narrative focalized by Madge tends to be emotive, elevated and often self-consciously literary. Her voice—and possible entry into the room—in this passage is indicated by odd shifts in register and discursive style characteristic of her particular idiolect. There is a clash of register in "Amy has provided kippers instead, and I like kippers quite a lot" (which is clearly marked as the free indirect thought of Paul) and "sweet firm pink and grey flesh flaking off the web of thin translucent bones" (the tone and language of which is more characteristic of Madge than of Paul or Gran). Likewise, the emotive language used to represent Gran's thoughts, "trembling at the thought of death in the watery darkness," would seem to be more likely that of Madge than Gran. In this way, while she remains silent throughout the passage, Madge's voice is inscribed within, though it is not inextricable from what is ostensibly the narrator's discourse. Her presence as a silent focalizing character has the effect of dialogizing (or making double-voiced) the narrative discourse and of inscribing Madge as a particular subject position within the discourse. This literal interweaving of the thoughts and speech of characters implies that the represented fictional world is multilayered, heteroglottic and intersubjectively constructed.

Ostensibly, the use of multiple character focalizers allows readers access to a range of different characters' thoughts, perceptions and interpretative positions, and frequent shifting of point of view denies readers a stable position from which to identify fully with any one character. Instead, implied readers are situated in a range of possible subject positions. However, although Paul and Gran do focalize a significant amount of the narrative, Madge is the primary focalizer and the implied reader point of view is mostly aligned with her. Thematically she is the most central character, and the external textual world (the sea and the lighthouse in particular) is primarily represented from her point of view. Walsh's use of indirect modes of discourse representation to incorporate Madge's voice, as in the passage quoted above, does at times implicitly align Madge's point of view with that of the narrator, and in doing so often disguises and implicitly privileges Madge's viewpoint. But this alignment does not destroy the novel's polyphonic interrelationship of voices and viewpoints, because while Madge's voice and viewpoint is predominant, it does not dominate the discourse. The narrative always offers another way of looking at the world and at characters. Furthermore, Madge is also frequently the object of irony—a strategy which in turn withdraws privilege from her point of view.

A primary way in which character focalized discourse is dialogized through irony is by the incorporation of other literary intertexts. During the course of the novel, Madge befriends Ralph Ashton, a blind professor of literature, to whom she reads from texts such as William Empson's *Seven Types of Ambiguity,* Jane Austen's *Northanger Abbey* and Milton's *Paradise Lost,* and quotations from these texts are often inserted in the narrative. While readers who recognize the quotations may read the novel differently as a result of the other meanings they potentially bring to it, literary intertexts do not, on the whole, function as "keys" to meaning(s). Instead, they usually serve to imply an ironic viewpoint on the characters, thereby constructing implied reader positions which are not aligned with character point of view. In the case of Madge, these strategies establish her naivety and unreliability as a narrative voice. Irony is an implicitly double-voiced narrative strategy because it depends upon a reader's recognition of two implicit meanings and hence enables the representation of two simultaneous voices and viewpoints. Thus, irony is achieved in the novel through the incorporation of quotes which mean one way when read in the context of the novels themes, but which mean quite differently as characters use these quotes to interpret the world around them. For example, there are thematic connections between the passages about John Donne's "A Valediction: of Weeping" that Madge reads from Empson's *Seven Types of Ambiguity* (quoted on pp. 40–41 of *Goldengrove*) and recurring motifs in the novel, such as the sea and a sense of grief. There are also structural connections: Empson's comments focus on the structure of Donne's poem and its ambiguity, and hence might offer a way of reading Walsh's novel as a text in which "the same idea is being repeated" (p. 40) and which might be read "forwards and backwards" (p. 41). Ironic effects are produced, however, through a clash between the content of what Madge reads and how she reads and interprets it. For example, on page 40, she reads of a "change in tone" in a voice which is "flat and expressionless"—the irony suggests her alienation from what she reads. On the following page, there is an apparent merging of the quoted text—*"What it may doe too soon," since the middle line may as usual go forwards or backwards, . . ."*—and the reporting context—"It doesn't go anywhere. I suppose it's because his face has no direction"—as Madge's thoughts are interwoven with the passage she reads. However, the connection between the quoted text and the reporting discourse is only by way of the signifier "go," denoting "direction"—Empson is talking about the structure of Donne's poem, whereas Madge is thinking about Ralph's smile. At this level we don't need to know the text that Madge is reading from, just that she is misappropriating it as a way of reading the world—though readers who are able to analyze the connections between the texts are perhaps more empowered than Madge, who clearly feels alienated by the cultural knowledge represented by the text that she reads from.[9]

Madge's readings of Empson and Milton's *Paradise Lost* (on pages 76–78) are clearly tangential readings; they are not misreadings or incorrect readings, but in using them literally as a way of reading the world, she does reveal her naivety and youth. For example, when she reads the passage from *Paradise Lost,* in which blindness is used metaphorically, her understanding of its significance is literal and shaped by the situational context in which it is read, that is, as it relates to Ralph's (literal) blindness and her pity for him. In contrast, Paul's comprehension of the same passage is even more limited; his interpretation is based on the sound of the words, rather than their "sense" or meaning, and what that sound reminds him of—"a magnificence in which he cannot find the sense" (p. 76).

These intertwinings of character, narrative and intertextual voices function in the construction of characters as ideologues, that is, as socially and personally situated ways of seeing and encoding the world. Gaps between intertexts and the reporting context often foreground the extent to which characters' interpretations of each other are limited, if not misguided. Madge and Ralph both use borrowed literary intertexts to interpret and represent each other, and by drawing attention to the limitations of their viewpoints the discourse reinforces the larger thematic concerns of the text with selfhood and intersubjectivity. Charlotte Bronte's *Jane Eyre* and Jane Austen's *Northanger Abbey*, are two intertexts through which they construct themselves and each other. While reading from *Northanger Abbey* Madge imagines herself as Jane and Ralph as Mr. Rochester (p. 49)—two characters from *Jane Eyre.* In the same episode Ralph calls Madge "Catherine" (p. 48), presumably confusing her with Catherine in *Northanger Abbey.* He thus confuses the fictional character with the actual person, and from Madge's point of view, he associates her with the wrong character—though ironically, he is quite right in that Madge, like Catherine, interprets her relationship with Ralph using the conventions of romance fiction. Ironically though, Madge's representation of Ralph as a character out of a romance novel is also accurate in that the blind, embittered and tormented figure of Rochester is also an aspect of the image which Ralph projects of himself. Both characters misread the world because they are each unable to perceive the viewpoint of the other and, hence, the intersubjective relation between self and other.

BLINDNESS WITHOUT INSIGHT, POLYPHONY WITHOUT DIALOGUE: RESTRAINTS ON INTERSUBJECTIVITY IN POLYPHONIC NARRATIVE

Novels such as *Goldengrove* (Walsh, 1972/1985) and *The Chocolate War* (Cormier, 1974/1988) use polyphonic narrative strategies to represent and explore intersubjectivity. However, both novels are fairly negative about the possibility of attaining intersubjective relations with an other. For both Walsh and Cormier, there are restraints on intersubjectivity and the movement out of solipsism is only ever partial. In *Goldengrove,* these restraints are explored metaphorically through the use of perceptual motifs—in particular, blindness and visual perception. In *The Chocolate War,* restraints emerge in part out of Cormier's political agenda, but also as a consequence of the way in which narrative strategies are used. Thematically, Cormier's novel is structured around an opposition between individuals and societies which sees intersubjective relationships as limited, if not impossible, and a primary function of multivoiced narration in the novel is the articulation of this theme. While the novel incorporates an astonishing number of focalizing characters for a children's novel, there is on the one hand a sameness in the world views that these characters represent and on the other hand an inability on the part of characters to engage and enter into dialogue with each other. Thus, the dialogic potential of polyphonic discourse is restricted.

Perceptual motifs, such as blindness and myopia, are often used in fiction as metaphors which articulate characters' worldviews and their perceived place in the world. Such motifs can also have a self-reflexive quality: they can implicitly draw attention to how narrative strategies like focalization and point of view work in narrative to represent characters' perceptual (and conceptual) views of others and the world. Ralph's blindness in *Goldengrove* (Walsh, 1972/1985), functions in various ways. Significantly, and perhaps ironically, he does not focalize in the narrative at all. We never see events from his point of view, and we only have access to his character through narratorial descriptions, Madge's naive and romantic representations and interpretations of him and through his own dialogue, which is often ironically undercut. For example, his self-conscious use of heightened and emotive language is often ironic, as in his repetition of "how much of what I am is blindness and how much is me." Ralph's blindness is conceptual as well as physical, and it is analogous with his solipsistic inability to perceive Madge as another self with her own needs. Instead, he wants her merely for her eyes and her voice (p. 113). His solipsistic effacement of her, however, reflects Madge's view of him as well as her own image of herself. She, in a sense, cannot see beyond his blindness and also perceives him only in relation to her self, seeing herself as the center and as the cause of his happiness. However, she also interprets this relation as one which effaces her. She describes herself as a mirror which "just reflect[s]" what is going on around her: "And all sorts of things happen in a mirror when there are people moving around it, but when it's alone it's empty, glassy and still." (p. 85). Her image of herself is analogous to Ralph's representation of her as a voice: that is, she is merely a vehicle for the other. She recognizes the necessity of a relation to an other in order to construct an idea of selfhood, but sees, or desires, this relation as involving the self-effacing integration of self and other, rather than as maintaining the distinction between self and other as discrete entities. This is clear in her idea of a future with Ralph as his scribe/housekeeper (p. 111)—an ironic reference to the fate of Milton's daughters, perhaps.

Madge's inability to maintain a distinction between self and other and to construct a sense of self as intersubjective is also implicit in her representations of the physical world, wherein there is an assumed correspondence between the perceiving subject and the object of perception, as in the following passage—this follows Ralph's request of Madge to describe what the waves look like.

> Madge watches first. The waves rise and run towards her in glassy straight ridges, and break, spilling froth and diamond-bright flying droplets, and spending and exhausting themselves in creamy foam; then they fall back, sleeking and glossing the yellow slope of the sand . . . "Well," she says, "the waves rise up along the edge of the sea, and run forwards, and break all frothy on the sloping sand. They make it wet and smooth." (pp. 91–92)

The heightened and emotive language of the first description of the waves, as they are focalized by Madge, contrasts with the objectivity and banality of Madge's description as it is narrated as direct speech. This disparity between represented speech and represented indirect thought implies the phenomenality, or thingness, of both the referent (the waves) and the subjective experience of the referent anterior to its encoding in language. Madge recognizes that signs do not refer unequivocally to things—that is, that words are not exchangeable for waves (p. 92)—but from her point of view, meanings are inscribed not through language, but in a reality which impacts upon a passively perceiving subject. This dialogic play with perception, language and the representation of reality is further elaborated in Ralph's description of the view from the top of the cliff, as he remembers it in his "mind's eye," from which he omits the lighthouse. The omission is significant from Madge's viewpoint, not just because of the meanings she has attributed to the lighthouse, but also because, for her, these meanings are inscribed within it and impinge upon her own experience of subjectivity. Thus, the point at which the actuality of things and of being is most emphatically asserted (because she can see it) is the point at which that actuality is destabilized, because it potentially does not exist for someone else—and, by implication, potentially the subject does not exist outside of a relation with an other.

As has been argued by many commentators, *The Chocolate War* (Cormier, 1974/1988) is a political allegory in which the school structure is analogous with larger social structures (for example, *see* Macleod, 1994). It is ostensibly a school story which centers on an annual sale of chocolates to raise money for Trinity, a Catholic private boys' school, but it is also an allegory about the operation of power within institutions. Students are manipulated by the Vigils, a secret organization, and by Brother Leon, the deputy principle. When Jerry Renault refuses to sell chocolates, against the wishes of the Vigils, he is systematically victimized, and at the close of the novel, physically and psychologically beaten. However, the novel does not offer any simple unequivocal readings, partly because of the way in which Cormier's ending repudiates the "long American tradition of the triumphant lonely hero tale" (Macleod, 1994, p. 191), and partly because of the narrative strategies that Cormier uses.

The tradition of the dissenting lone hero is evoked by a key intertext for the novel, a line from T.S. Eliot's "The Love Song of J. Alfred Prufrock", "Do I dare / Disturb the universe?" (1954), which is written on a poster inside of Jerry's locker. And the register used to narrate Jerry's stand against selling chocolates has epic connotations. However, toward the end of the novel, after Jerry has been beaten and is waiting for an ambulance to take him to the hospital, he realizes the cost and inevitable impossibility of "disturbing the universe" and attempts to communicate this to Goober: "They tell you to do your own thing but they don't mean it. They don't want you to do your thing, not unless it happens to be their thing, too. It's a laugh,

Goober, a fake. Don't disturb the universe, Goober, no matter what the posters say" (1988, p. 186). In this way, Jerry's defeat and capitulation offer a vision of society in which individuals are fundamentally powerless in relation to institutions and corruption is systemic. At this level the novel offers its readers two main positions: we can agree with the implied worldview and concede that the nonconforming individual will always get beaten into line by the system; or we can refuse this worldview and affirm that hope for the human species lies simply in the recognition of corruption and the possibility of refusing to toe the line. The novel offers support for both readings: the first is supported by Archie's speculation on "What a great year it was going to be" (p. 188), which implies that nothing has changed; the second is given support by characters who begin to question the system (such as Carter and Cochran) and by Brother Leon's lesson about power early in the novel (Chapter 6). A central message emerges from this lesson that the operation of power depends upon the cooperation and acquiescence of individuals, and this tenet is repeated in Jerry's later realization that he "had allowed Archie to do this to him" (p. 182). As Macleod has suggested, Cormier has "evoked a political world in which evil is . . . a collaborative act between individuals and political systems that begins when the individual gives over to the system the moral responsibility that is part of being human" (1994, p. 196).

A third reading position is offered through analysis of the narrative strategies that Cormier uses to construct these two worldviews. The novel is a multivoiced narrative comprising thirteen character focalizers, and characters tend to fall roughly into two main groups in terms of the worldviews they represent: a dominant worldview represented mainly by Archie (Obie, Janza and six minor focalizing characters: Sulkey, Casper, Consatro, Caroni, Chartier and Randell also represent this worldview); and an oppositional worldview represented by Jerry. A third group of characters emerges by the end of the novel; these are characters who at various points begin to question the dominant view represented by Archie and are positioned in the middle of these two main groups (Goober, Carter and Cochran). Between them, Archie and Jerry focalize approximately half of the novel, and this suggests an oppositional structuring of Cormier's argument, if it were not for the movement of characters between the worldviews that they represent. While the presence of thirteen focalizing characters implies that this might be a radically polyphonic novel, point of view in the novel is actually quite limited. Only the school boys focalize—the teachers and parents do not—and despite the rough divisions between groups of characters, there is a sameness about the ways that different characters view the world—the way that they all perceive women, for example. Cumulatively, the viewpoints of all these characters combine to imply a pervasive spiritual and emotional poverty within characters and in their relations with each other. Furthermore, despite their sameness, all of these characters are ultimately unable to engage in dialogue with each other. Jerry is (physically) unable to communicate his revelation to Goober at the close of the novel; Goober locks himself in his room, unable to communicate with Jerry; Carter's disgust and sense of guilt remains unvoiced (p. 174–175); and so on. A third oppositional reading position emerges out of this recognition of the limitations that Cormier's strategies pose, and it involves reading against the text. Two premises which ground Cormier's novel are that social institutions exist independent of individuals (and individuals and society are hence fundamentally opposed) and that individual human beings are essentially monadic—that is, existing singly in isolation from each other. Cormier shapes and limits narrative point of view so as to articulate this argument. It follows, then, that intersubjectivity is an impossibility in the world of the novel because individuals are fundamentally solipsistic beings. An oppositional reading thus recognizes the ideological implications of Cormier's narrative techniques and refuses the ideological premises of the novel.

Polyphonic narrative techniques are used in *Goldengrove* (Walsh, 1972/1985) to construct ideologemic discourses associated with the viewpoints and subject positions of characters which are intertwined and placed in dialogue with each other. In contrast, Cormier is using polyphony in *The Chocolate War* (1974/1988) to construct a novel in which there is essentially no dialogue—in the Bahktinian sense. The dialogicality of this novel comes instead from the range of reading positions which readers may take up and the extent to which it requires that readers engage dialogically with the worldviews it articulates. In Walsh's novel, although the discourses and voices of characters are distinct from each other, they are to some extent subservient to a dominant thematic concern with the relation between self and other and the transition from childhood to adulthood. A primary function, then, of multivoiced narrative in *Goldengrove* is to represent concepts of selfhood as intersubjective and formed in dialogue with the discourses and viewpoints of others, though the novel suggests that intersubjectivity is only ever partial. In Cormier's novel, however, these same strategies serve a quite different thematic function. The discourses and voices of characters also collude and are subservient to a dominant metanarratival ideology, but it is one which denies even the possibility of intersubjectivity. The extent to which multivoiced narrative can be made subservient to, and thereby subsumed by, a larger metanarrative forms part of the focus of the next sections, where I will be looking at novels which use overtly multistranded narrative, as well as multiple character focalizers, to explore similar concerns with intersubjectivity.

POLYPHONIC VOICING AND INTERSUBJECTIVITY IN OVERTLY MULTISTRANDED NARRATIVES

Slake's Limbo (Holman, 1974/1986), *Salt River Times* (Mayne, 1980) and *Finders, Losers* (Mark, 1990) have in common a thematic concern with the relations between a sense of physical, cultural and social place and the formation of concepts of selfhood. These themes are explored in each novel through multivoiced and multistranded narrative. *Slake's Limbo* has two interlaced, but initially unconnected, narrative strands which intersect toward the close of the novel: the story of Slake, a teenage boy who lives for four months in the New York subways; and the story of Willis Joe, a train driver who rescues Slake when he walks onto the railway tracks in front of the train that Willis Joe is driving. Both strands are narrated by a third person narrator who frequently comments on events and characters, but access to character thought is limited to the two primary characters and is conveyed via narrated indirect thought and focalization. The narrative structures of *Finders, Losers* and *Salt River Times* are more complex. Both novels comprise a number of apparently separate "story" strands, each of which is focalized by a different character. These story strands are represented successively, almost as separate stories. (Both novels are, in fact, marketed as "collections" of short stories.) However, the narrative strands in both novels are spatially, temporally and thematically interconnected, and readers are able to infer from these interconnections a central "story": the mystery of the boat in *Salt River Times* and the interconnectedness of events in one day in *Finders, Losers*. Both novels thereby overtly position implied readers in active subject positions. The address to a narratee in the preface to *Finders, Losers* quite explicitly suggests that story and meaning are constructed by readers rather than artifacts of the text.[10]

While the "story" connections between the two narrative strands in *Slake's Limbo* do not emerge until the close of the novel, spatial and temporal links between Slake's and Willis Joe's narratives are made clear by the use of temporal markers. Thematic connections between the two narratives are less explicit, however, and emerge out of the way in which the two narratives are structured in parallel with each other. Slake's narrative is shaped by a trajectory which proceeds from a state of extreme solipsism to a state of emerging intersubjectivity; his literal descent into the subway at the opening of the novel and anticipated ascent up to the rooftops at its close metaphorically charts this trajectory. In contrast, Willis Joe's narrative proceeds in the opposite direction: he progresses from an outward-looking aspiring young man with an ambition to become a sheephand in Australia to a solipsistic train driver who perceives his passengers as sheep to be rounded up. Like Slake, however, he does emerge out of this solipsism when he realizes toward the close of the novel that each "sheep" is in fact "a single person like him" (1986, p. 87). Willis Joe's realization echoes Slake's much more gradual awareness of other people which can be seen emerging in the questions he asks himself about them—as in "What happened to them? . . . Where did they go?" (p. 61)—and in the connections he begins to feel with them (pp. 61, 68).

The narrator's comments also stress physical and causal connections between Slake and the world around him, which he is not aware of, and these also have a crucial role in elaborating thematic concerns in the novel. For example, on page 17 the narrative digresses to give an account of how Slake's hideout came to be there; the hideout is a cave within the wall of a subway tunnel which was created as a result of mistakes made by workmen building the Commodore Hotel next door some fifty years earlier. The narrator stresses the implications that these earlier events have for Slake in a discourse which features relations of causality: "it is only one of the many unknown facts that operated to affect or not affect him, it is fairly safe to say that the simple practical results—the existence of the room and his presence in it—were all that really mattered" (p. 17). In this way, narrator commentary stresses the interconnectedness of events and of Slake's narrative with other narratives happening around him, despite his limited awareness of those narratives. These ideas also work metaphorically in the elaboration of the novel's central theme: the need for characters to develop an intersubjective awareness of other people around them and interconnect with them.

The sections of the novel which focus on Willis Joe are headed "On Another Track," alluding to the narrative structure of the novel—these sections represent another narrative "track" or path. They also allude to the function of train travel in the novel as a metaphor for life. Repeated references to the masses of commuters who travel on the trains, Slake's wonderings about the people he meets and sees (p. 61), and his use of the subway system to explore and define the parameters of his world, all combine to suggest the feeling that traveling on trains can give of progressing through one's life along with other people but ultimately alone. For example, a group of commuters will travel on the same train, but each has his/her own "track" of life, purpose or direction. In this way, the setting of the novel implies a vision of a world populated by people who are all very much like

Slake and Willis Joe, each locked into their own world and each with limited abilities to relate to and connect with others.

Slake's glasses also have a central metaphoric role in the novel. Just as Ralph's blindness is symbolic of his limited insight in *Goldengrove* (Walsh, 1972/1985), Slake's myopia and fragmented vision is symbolic of his alienation. His inability to see the world more than ten feet in front of him (Holman, 1986, p. 8) is thematically linked with his solipsism and his limited perception of other people. At the opening of the novel his glasses have been "abandoned" (p. 8), but while living in the subway he finds a pair of broken glasses. He puts them on, and looking at himself in a mirror "which he had put together on the floor from bits of broken mirrors" he sees himself as "fragmented" (p. 54). The fragmentation is in a sense doubled because of the mirror and because the lenses of the glasses are smashed. It is also tempting to read this episode in terms of Lacan's mirror phase: in recognizing its image in the mirror, the child experiences itself as a site of fragmentation (Grosz, 1990, p. 39). The mirror phrase signals the moment that the child recognizes the distinctions between self, other and world, and hence the initial stage of the transition out of solipsism.[11] Slake removes the broken lenses, sorts through his collection of odd lenses, and finding two which seem to help him to see better, fits them into the broken frames. One lens fits quite well, but the other, which is "tinted a light pink" is too big so he "fixed its position firmly with a piece of wire that bisected his vision" (Holman, 1986, p. 54). While he now sees the world brighter and sharper—and the metaphoric implication is that he is now able to engage more with the world—his vision is now fragmented and split and, to spell out Holman's joke, he is now seeing through at least one rose-coloured glass. At the end of the novel, Slake is given a new pair of glasses, and now sees things from a different "angle": "not peering at the pavement, but straight out and across and even up? Because it was amazing what the new glasses did to the world." (p. 92). Whereas Slake's experience of himself and the world seen through his first pair of glasses would seem to parallel Lacan's vision of the subject as fragmented and grounded in a sense of loss, his second pair of glasses offers a vision of a subjectivity which, on the one hand, approaches a sense of completion or greater coherence with the world, and on the other, is still in a process of becoming—the novel ends as follows: "Slake did not know exactly where he was going, but the general direction was up." (p. 93).

In *Finders, Losers* (Mark, 1990) there are six "stories" (or six narrative segments of one story) each taking place on the same day, in the same place, on and around a university campus. Each is narrated by a nonintrusive third person narrator and focalized by a different character—Philip, Hiroko, David, Sallie, Mary and Derek. The title alludes to the children's playground rhyme, "finders keepers, losers weepers," but it also summarizes and inverts the narrative movement of each narrative from lack to plenitude. Each "story" hinges on a character's search for something, though what is found is not always exactly what was being sought, and each characters' search is explicable as a quest for a sense of selfhood and for intersubjectivity. This is most obvious in the first and last narrative, in that Philip and Derek are both looking for friends, and they both inadvertently find and lose things which link them with other characters and with each other. Philip finds Sallie's note and Peter's map, and Derek loses his dog and finds Peter's gun. Hiroko's need to conquer, and hence lose, her fear of heights is inextricable from her need to construct a more positive sense of herself; she also finds Mary's glasses. Sallie finds a letter from a mysterious stranger whom she spends the morning waiting for, and in doing so is able to construct for herself an other self, separate and secret from her domineering sister. David helps his brother Peter look for his guns, but his actions are motivated by the need to make his parents recognize the serious implications of Peter's extreme solipsism. Mary loses (and finds) her glasses and her key, and her glasses, like Slake's, work as a metaphor for the interrelations between the self and the world. This narrative movement, between things lost and found, gives each "story" a sense of narrative and thematic closure. Temporally, however, the six stories are interlaced, so that there is often a disparity between story order and text order. For example, Hiroko finds and returns Mary's glasses before she loses them, and the story of Sally and Joe is only retrospectively put together in chronological order by readers.

The narrative techniques of *Salt River Times* (Mayne, 1980) are more complex and varied: there is a nonintrusive third person narrator, seven main character focalizers (Mel, Gwenda, Joe, Sophia, Elissa, Dee and Kate) and one secondary first person narrator (Morgan), who partially narrates two chapters.[12] (Chapter 19 in particular combines the points of view of at least four characters, Morgan, Joe, Dee and Kate, and some chapters comprise almost entirely of character dialogue.)[13] There is one central "story" strand which runs through and connects most of the twenty-one individual "stories" or chapters. This is the mystery of the boat which had belonged to old Mr. Young (Joe's grandfather) and sank in a flood many years before. The various narrative strands are also connected, again at the level of "story," through the interrelations between characters, events such as the flood and the burning of old Mr. Young's house (this is narrated twice in two separate chapters from the point of view of

Jack and that of the narrator), and things such as the dragon head from the boat which is found by Gwenda.

Each of these three novels is thematically concerned with perception and interpretation and with relations between self and place, self and other. In *Slake's Limbo,* thematic concerns emerge from the parallels between the narrative strands and from repeated motifs which gain metaphoric significance—in particular, Slake's glasses and references to visual perception. In *Finders, Losers* and *Salt River Times,* focalization strategies are used to explore the relations between perceiving characters and the textual world and, hence, to disclose the particular ideologeme of each character. The use of multiple focalizers in these novels highlights a particular problem. One effect of polyphony is that characters are successively represented as focalizers and as focalized. To the extent that the representation of a character's subjectivity is contingent upon the construction of that character as a focalizer, the shift from focalizer to focalized can entail a loss of subjectivity. Characters such as Hiroko in *Finders, Losers* and Joe in *Salt River Times* become "alien," and are thus denied subjectivity, when they are focalized by other characters and thereby inscribed as objects within the discourse of others. While *Slake's Limbo* is not heavily focalized, references to how Willis Joe in particular perceives other people—that is, as "sheep"—also highlight this problem.

Finders, Losers as a whole can be seen as an elaborate exercise in narrative and ideological point of view. Each of the six main characters is represented as a focalizing and focalized subject. Some characters, such as Peter, Sally and Joe, do not focalize at all and are thereby denied subject positions. Peter's way of reconstructing the world, wherein he sees all non-Anglo-Celtic students as "foreigners," is clearly pejorated in the novel through the collusion of other focalizing characters' attitudes. This collusion subordinates the ideologemes of each character to the larger ideologies driving the metanarrative.

A common concern with forms of physical, social and cultural displacement, alienation, and the formation of concepts of selfhood provides a thematic link between the various narrative strands. Each of the narrative strands is located in the same place, on the same day, though the ways in which the setting is represented from each character's point of view varies. The campus setting represents a social microcosm. As a whole, it is represented selectively and partially, and characters' points of view are dependent upon the positions they occupy in relation to place. These positions are defined socially as well as spatially, and the relationship of each character to the textual world can be conceived of as varying forms of physical and social displacement as seen in Table 1–1:

Table 1–1. Socio-spatial Placement of Characters in *Finders, Losers* (Mark, 1990)

Character	Physical position	Temporal position	Legal Status	Transgressive Function
Philip	outsider	temporary	legitimate	trespasses; eavesdropper
Hiroko	insider	temporary	legitimate	trespasses within campus
David	insider	permanent	legitimate	
Sallie	insider	permanent	legitimate	trespasses outside
Mary	insider	temporary	legitimate	
Derek	outsider	temporary	legitimate	trespasser and lawbreaker

A number of patterns emerge from this which link various characters and which construct the campus setting as a microcosm or specific social world. Philip and Derek are both outsiders to the university. Philip is a legitimate visitor, who spends much of his time eavesdropping and spying, and who trespasses in a minor way on the garden beds. Derek not only trespasses on the campus grounds but also walks his dog there against regulations. Mary and Hiroko are both temporarily living on campus, and Hiroko inadvertently eavesdrops and trespasses within the college, on the roofs of the buildings. David and Sallie are both permanently living on campus. Socially, all of the children only marginally belong on the campus. All except Derek are there because of their parents, and their parents represent a crosssection of campus residents. Sallie's father is a porter, David's father is the gardener, Hiroko's mother is a student and Philip's father is a resident potter. Only Mary's father is an academic, and her family is only living there temporarily. This marginal status is emphasized in each of the narratives, through the common motifs of trespassing, isolation and displacement. Derek trespasses onto the campus, while Sallie trespasses outside of it and Hiroko trespasses within it. David and Philip are the only characters who don't overtly trespass. Loneliness is also a common thread in the narratives of Philip, Derek and Sallie, and all characters are represented as socially isolated. The opening of Sallie's narrative sets up a series of oppositions between the village and the city, as in "village, church tower, farmland and woods, college" as opposed to "city, housing estates and factories, cathedral spire." A traditional "town/gown" opposition also underlies Derek's narrative (Mark, 1990, p. 163). He lives in the village and goes to the cathedral school in the city, while the children who live on campus go to the village school. There is an implication that Derek's trespass is social as well as physical.

The openings of Derek's and Philip's narratives both give an account of each characters' entry into the grounds of the college through the gates of Shapton Court, and each character perceives and represents the setting according to different socially determined ideologemes. Both are visitors to the university, though Derek's perception himself as a trespasser—and as a lawbreaker (p. 175)—influences the way in which the setting is represented from his point of view: the gates are "built to keep people out," the campus is seen as "a place apart," "on the edge of the village" (p. 163). Both boys see the signs on the gate, but they each read different signs, as well as focusing on different aspects of the signs' meanings. The sign which Philip reads says: "Shapton College. Faculties of Science and Technology and Design" (p. 12). The sign which Derek reads says: "Shapton College. This is Private Land. No Right of Way. The Exercising of Dogs on these Premises is Strictly Forbidden" (pp. 163–164). When Philip asks his father what the sign means, he is concerned with the denotative aspect of the words he reads—what the words refer to. His interest in words and their meanings recurs through his narrative (for example, see the conversation between Philip and his father about the term "campus" on pages 9–10). Derek is more concerned with the intentional aspect of the signs, that is, what they do and what implications they have for his own actions. Three of the signs which Derek reads are prohibitory in tone as well as in meaning. For Derek, they demarcate boundaries and proscribe actions, and they are also thereby attributed with attitudinal as well as intentional meanings. They are seen as "unfriendly," and their role in prohibiting certain actions and movements effects the way in which Derek perceives himself.

This concern with relations between self and place recurs throughout the novel, especially in the varying names that different characters have for places and things. The physical setting is represented in ways which correspond with the way that characters perceive themselves and the positions they occupy. David's narrative centers on an underlying opposition between him and his brother, Peter, which is displaced onto the physical setting: for David, the campus is like "the Garden of Eden," whereas Peter sees it as "an enormous battlefield" (p. 71). For Hiroko, the Cedrus Libani has a special significance, but ironically, the same tree has a special, but different, significance for Sally and Joe, who get the name of the tree wrong twice, and for Peter, who calls it "the Gallows Tree." Similarly, there is a small corner of woodland on the campus, which is termed "Elephant wood" by David, "Cathedral wood" by Derek and "Death wood" by Peter. While for each character the significance of the wood is similar—it is their own special and private place set apart from the rest of the campus—each character sees and encodes this same place differently, according to his own experiences and social values.

These differences in the ways that characters see and encode the campus setting, as well as particular places and things, highlight the different social and personal ideologemes by which characters are positioned in the world. The viewpoints of each character are semantically distinct—they each have a particular way of looking at the world and locating themselves in it—but they are not autonomous. Each character's worldview engages dialogically with other characters' worldviews. The novel, in this sense, is truly polyphonic. However, the thematic repeated patterns and motifs, especially isolation and loneliness, which link the narratives, suggest that each of these children are in the process of developing more positive ways of relating to each other and to place. A larger ideologically driven metanarrative which links the various strands, then, is one which sees the move out of solipsism as essential and values intersubjective relationships.

In *Salt River Times* (1980), Mayne also uses multiple focalizing characters to incorporate social and cultural diversity, and to explore the relations between the construction of subjectivity and the social and cultural positioning of characters. This is also inextricable from the physical and historical positions within which characters are situated, and a concern with how characters represent and interpret the relations between self and the world is a primary interconnecting theme. There is a range in both the strategies used by characters to interpret and represent the world and others, and in the extent to which characters are able to conceive of their selves, others and the world as distinct, though interconnected, entities. Narrative which is focalized by Gwenda and Morgan, for example, represents degrees of solipsism: Morgan is unable to make the distinction between the phenomenality of the world and his own imaginative representations of it; and Gwenda is unable to make the distinction between the otherness of objective reality and of other selves. Narratives involving characters such as Mel, Jack and Mary are concerned with the kinds of narrative strategies used to interpret and represent events in the present, and in the case of Mel, in particular, to represent and mediate the past and the present. The story of the boat is mostly revealed in narrative focalized by Mel (Chapters 1, 9 and 17), and in the process of inferring this story, he is involved in constructing a sense of the past as a coherent and chronological narrative sequence. Concepts of subjectivity are dependent upon a sense of the past, and the various narrative strands work to construct different concepts of the past as a social, cultural and physical phenomena. Kate's collections of "bits of people" are one way of representing the world, the past and people as physical objects. Narrative focalized from Joe's point of view is concerned with the more distant past, before the town and city were there. The physical displacement of the birds—"The birds had remembered the land as it was, and had come back to it and found there was nothing left. There was nowhere for them, nowhere to settle, nowhere to take fish and frogs" (p. 21)—reiterates the sense of displacement that Joe experiences—"Joe thought that he had woken into nowhere and nothing, or perhaps was still asleep in nowhere and nothing" (p. 19)—and is analogous to the sense of cultural displacement that both Joe and Elissa experience.

Polyphonic narrative techniques are used in *Slake's Limbo* (Holman, 1974/1986), *Salt River Times* (Mayne, 1980) and *Finders, Losers* (Mark, 1990) to construct distinct ideologemic character discourses, to represent social and cultural diversity and to explore characters' constructions of selves, others and the world. In all of these novels, as well as in *Goldengrove* (Walsh, 1972/1985) and *The Chocolate War* (Cormier, 1974/1988), characters are located within a single cultural or social context, and ideologemic dialogue occurs through the range of contrasting positions that characters occupy, thereby stressing cultural heterogeneity within a specific social context. The next section will examine the use of double-stranded narrative and dual narration to represent an ideologemic dialogue between radically different cultural and social discourses and positions.

IDEOLOGEMIC DIALOGUE, INTERSUBJECTIVITY AND MONOLOGIC CLOSURE IN *THE LAKE AT THE END OF THE WORLD*

The Lake at the End of the World (Mcdonald, 1988/1990) uses polyphonic narration to construct a dialogue between two different cultural ideologemes and to explore the possibilities of intersubjectivity for characters located in radically different cultural and social contexts. Like *Goldengrove* (Walsh, 1972/1985), *The Chocolate War* (Cormier, 1974/1988), *Slake's Limbo* (Holman, 1974/1986), *Salt River Times* (Mayne, 1980) and *Finders, Losers* (Mark, 1990), this is a multivoiced novel in which the narrative strands are situated in the same spatial and temporal context. However, in Macdonald's novel events are represented from the points of view of two first person narrators. As with *Slake's Limbo*, the novel is structured as two parallel narrative strands which are interlaced together in alternating chapters or segments of narrative. Each narrator shares an approximately equal proportion of the narrative.[14] The interlacing of parallel narrative strands structures the novel as a "dialogue" between different cultural and ideological positions. Whereas the three novels by Walsh, Mark and Mayne in various ways either refuse or problematize story and thematic closure, the combination of dual narration and what is essentially a binary "plot dependent" narrative structure (Bakhtin, 1984a, p. 252) in Macdonald's novel entails the resolution of the narrative through monologic closure.

Since *The Pigman* (Zindel, 1969), interlaced binary narrative has become a common technique for structuring multivoiced narrative in adolescent fiction. Parallel narrative strands are narrated either by two narrators (e.g., *Thicker than Water* (Farmer, 1989) or *The Hillingdon Fox* (Mark, 1991)), or in the third person from the viewpoint of two character focalizers (e.g., *Going Up* (Hunt, 1989), *What Are Ya?* (Pausacker, 1987), *Winter Quarters* (Mayne, 1982), *Come Lucky April* (Ure, 1992), or *A Bone from a Dry Sea* (Dickinson, 1992)).[15] These strategies can overtly structure a novel as a dialogue between two social, cultural, gendered or historical positions. However, interlaced dual narration has tended to settle into its own formulaic conventions and, as my discussion of *The Lake at the End of the World* will indicate, it can be a particularly problematic form. The tendency to structure narrative points of view oppositionally often entails that one dominant narratorial position is privileged and dialogue is thus subsumed by monologue. This seems to be more common in first person narration, such as Macdonald's novel, than in third person character focalized narration, where the more frequent use of indirect modes of discourse representation and shifts in point of view tends toward the generation of a plurality of textual positions and voices (as in *Come Lucky April*, for example). Dual narration would thus seem to constitute a variant of the "narrator plus one main character focalizer" pattern which Stephens has remarked on (Stephens, 1992a, p. 27).[16]

The Lake at the End of the World (Macdonald, 1988/1990) is a postecological disaster novel set in the year 2025 and the two narrators, Hector and Diana, are members of two very different kinds of societies. Hector has lived all his life in an underground bunker in a repressive and totalitarian society, and he finds his way through the underground tunnels to the outside world, where he meets Diana, who has lived above the ground all her life knowing only her parents in a family-oriented subsistence community. The underground community was originally established to survive a nuclear war and has been isolated for over fifty years, and Hector has only ever lived underground. Parallel narration by Hector and by Diana thus juxtaposes two radically different social and ideological positions and viewpoints. After leaving the underground, Hector lives with Diana's family, and the two narratives reflect Diana's and Hector's gradual negotiation of the other's point of view. When Hector returns with Diana to the underground to obtain medicine for Beth, Diana's mother, Hector sees his old life differently. After a flood in the tunnels and the death of the Counselor (the leader of the community), the people living underground follow Hector and Diana out of the tunnels to the outside world, where they will live with Diana and her family and form a new community.

Louise Lawrence's *Children of the Dust* (1985) is perhaps a pretext for Macdonald's image of two opposing postdisaster societies. [17] In both novels, traditional humanist values associated with the outside society are privileged. The underground and outside societies denote two cultural positions of which Hector and Diana are representative. Ostensibly, the double narrative structure offers the possibility of a dialogue between these two cultural positions and for both characters to attain intersubjectivity via their relationship with each other. However, these two positions are structured as binary oppositions and the close of the story, in which the underground community joins the outside, has thematic implications which create problems for the possibility of cultural or intersubjective dialogue. The ideologies of the underground society are clearly pejorated, thereby privileging the cultural and ideological assumptions implicit in the outside community. Insofar as intersubjectivity is made possible through cultural and social dialogue, narrative and thematic closure also places in question the possibility of attaining intersubjectivity.

The use of two narrators explores aspects of intersubjectivity within a cultural context, in particular the idea of individual and cultural solipsism. The narrative techniques foreground the limitations of any one perceptual and interpretative viewpoint, in a similar way to the use of multiple focalizers in the novels I have been discussing. There is a lot of repetition in the two narrative strands, as the same episodes are often narrated twice (that is, from each narrators' point of view), and these repetitions foreground the extent to which Hector's and Diana's interpretations and misinterpretations of each other and of each other's community are grounded in, and thereby limited by, their own cultural assumptions and experiences. The physical differences between their worlds and societies are emphasized in the opening pages: the brightness of the outside world, the loudness of Diana's voice and her physical strength (from Hector's viewpoint); and Hector's paleness and red eyes, his apparent physical weakness and the quietness of his voice (from Diana's point of view). These physical oppositions between the two characters emerge as characters shift from focalizing to focalized positions in the narrative and they underline their perceptual, conceptual and cultural differences. Both characters initially see the world of the other as strange, alien and primitive, and both progressively move toward a less culturally and individually solipsistic position. However, as I have suggested, this movement is inhibited by the oppositional structure of the narrative. While Diana's narrative point of view is clearly limited, the ideological assumptions implicit in the cultural position that she occupies are privileged.

Thematically, the novel hinges upon an ideological opposition between two variants of humanism. The outside world is informed by a liberal humanist ideology which takes for granted such values as the "naturalness" of the nuclear family, individual freedom and choice (p. 111) and the inherent value (and power) of the natural world. The lives of Diana, Beth and Evan are oriented toward a subsistence level of existence, the natural setting is represented in almost idyllic terms, and the stories of the power of the lake ally the natural world with conventional humanist values of freedom against capitalist self-interest. The ideology of the underground society is grounded in the homocentric extreme of humanist thought, which in its aim to "continue human endeavor beyond global destruction" (p. 152) results in an intellectual elitism which is ultimately allied with capitalism (p. 137) and fascism in the figure of the Counselor (the "visionary" (p. 85) or "mad" (p. 153) leader of the underground community). Furthermore, this opposition is constructed so as to "naturalize" and thereby privilege the liberal humanist values of the outside world. This is set up quite early in the novel, where the opposition between the underground and the outside is constructed in metaphoric terms, which oppose light and dark, freedom and repression (Diana's ability to fly and the brilliance of the blue of her wings as opposed to Hector's constructed, dark and colorless world).

A primary intertext for Hector's journey from the underground world to the outside world is Plato's cave simile, and this is instrumental in representing Hector's physical transition as an analogy for a process of intellectual growth and ideological empowerment. Plato's cave simile represents the stages in "the ascent of the mind from illusion to pure philosophy" (Plato, 1974, p. 316) and can be summarized as follows. In an underground cavelike chamber are people who have been prisoners there since they were children. They are able to see only shadows (or illusions) reflected upon a wall, and in the absence of evidence to the contrary, assume that the shadows they see are the real thing. If a prisoner were released, taken outside and made to look at the sun, "his eyes would be so dazzled by the glare of it that he wouldn't be able to see a single one of the things he was now told were real." However, once s/he grew accustomed to the light of the sun, s/he would be able to perceive and recognize the shadows on the wall for what they are (illusions) (1974, pp. 316–325). When Hector first emerges from the underground, he is initially unable to see at all:

> They told me there was nothing left outside. They said the world was
> empty, finished.

The first time I go outside I believe them. I can see nothing. They for-
got to tell me that the light outside is so brilliant it is blinding. (p. 1)

As with Ralph in *Goldengrove*, Hector's blindness is both physical and metaphoric. When he returns to the underground after living on the outside for
sometime, he goes back to the library, where he sees the books he read as a
child "with altered eyes," and recognizes the way in which these books constructed a "carefully filtered" view of the world, so that he would know of
no other (pp. 157–159). In this way, Hector is able, through the knowledge
and cultural experiences that he has gained in the outside world, to recognize the limitations of the cultural assumptions of the underground community and to interrogate the ideologies which inform these assumptions. In
other words, "Hector has been empowered to reread the texts of his society in such a way as to see their ideological assumptions" (Stephens, 1992a,
p. 50).

However, while the subject position from which Hector rereads his
own culture is a more empowered one than that which he had previously
occupied, it is one which is informed by ideological assumptions which are
associated with the outside society, and there is no analogous interrogation of the ideologies of this society. Although Diana is represented as also
moving toward intersubjectivity, she is not ideologically empowered by this
process to reflect on the assumptions of her own society, and readers are
not offered a position from which to do so either. In this way, the ideological dialogue implied by the narrative structure is closed off because it
only operates in one direction. This is reinforced by strong story and thematic closure in the novel, wherein the ideologies of the outside world are
"naturalized." The final emergence of the "cave people" from the underground—an aspect of story closure—is described in terms which are ideologically laden:

> It's as if they are now fully aware they are released from the hypnotic
> influence of the Counsellor. Someone else laughs, and gradually the
> sense of liberation spreads, until everyone is laughing and calling
> 'Happy New Year!' and whistling and cheering into the night. They
> are free. It's their new world—or their old world. (p. 183)

Diana is narrating this passage, and the repetition of terms denoting freedom, recuperation and a new beginning inscribes the close of the story with
the liberal humanist ideologies of her own cultural position. In this way, by
the end of the novel both Hector and Diana interpret the narrative of the

underground community from the same cultural viewpoint, and the cultural dialogue between these two characters is thereby monologically resolved. The cultural differences between the two communities are repressed in favor of a vision of a homogeneous social whole, and the narrative is thus also thematically closed. Insofar as intersubjectivity is made possible via the dialogic structuring of the positions and viewpoints of the central characters, monologic thematic closure places the possibility of intersubjectivity in question. An implication of the ending of the novel is that intersubjectivity is only, if at all, possible within certain culturally proscribed boundaries.

Like *The Chocolate War* (Cormier, 1974/1988), *The Lake at the End of the World* foregrounds a crucial problem with multivoiced narration, which is that the ideologemic discourses associated with characters can be made subservient to the metanarrative of a novel. Here the potential of polyphonic narrative techniques to represent dialogic forms of intersubjectivity and to construct a dialogue between different ideological positions is contained through the incorporation of monologic closural strategies. Macdonald's novel is more closed than *The Chocolate War* precisely because the ideologies that are privileged reflect dominant social ideologies. The temptation to "read against" the close of Cormier's novel arises in part because the worldview that it reflects conflicts so radically with worldviews usually offered in children's novels.

Ure's *Come Lucky April* (1992) and Hunt's *A Step off the Path* (1985) are two double-stranded novels, both of which provide an interesting comparison to *The Lake at the End of the World*. Like Macdonald, Ure uses a double-stranded narration to construct a dialogue between the cultural ideologemes of two postdisaster societies. However, although these two societies are represented oppositionally, Ure's use of character focalized third person narration prevents the privileging of one narrative viewpoint over the other, and ironically foregrounds the limitations of both. Hunt also uses doublestranded narration to construct a dialogue between two cultural and social positions. *A Step off the Path* is a double-stranded metafictive novel in which a story told by a character (Jo) in one narrative strand is a version of events occurring in the other strand. The story concerns a group of knights (descendants of their Arthurian namesakes) who exist on the margins of mainstream society and culture. Although the knights have been displaced by the dominant culture, their own culture and traditions have been appropriated and reconstructed by that culture in the form of popular medieval romance fictions. And the story that Jo tells is constructed out of these popular fictions. Thus, the novel hinges on the discrepancy between the knights (as they are represented in the primary narrative) and their "fictional" counterparts (as they are represented in Jo's narrative). The point is that by appropriating the stories and culture of one social group and rewriting it as "romance" (and hence "fiction" or "myth"), the dominant culture effectively writes this group out of "history" and out of the present. Whereas in *The Lake at the End of the World* the ideologies of the mainstream culture dominate and subsume those of the other culture, Hunt inverts and subverts this relationship by allowing the ideologies of the other culture to metafictionally interrogate and dismantle those of the dominant culture.

The inclination toward monologic closure is also resisted in *Goldengrove* (Walsh, 1972/1985), *Salt River Times* (Mayne, 1980) and *Finders, Losers* (Mark, 1990) in ways which contrast with *The Lake at the End of the World* (Macdonald, 1988/1990). In *Goldengrove*, the possibility of a dialogue between story and thematic closure is asserted through the presence of a double ending:

> At the turn of the path they stop, and look out for a moment over the beach and harbour and town, over the serenely restless sea, tossing and dreaming eternally in the great bight of the bay.
>
> "I don't see what you meant just now, when you said it was too late, Madge, honest I don't," says Paul.
>
> "Lucky you, Paul!" She turns her back on the wide view and walks slowly on. Behind her in the early lilac dusk the yellow light of Godrevy winks on. "Ralph said some things couldn't be mended, some things were too late to put right. And I just thought that sounded sick and wicked, I didn't understand what he meant at all. But now I see." (1985, p. 124)

Descriptive terms such as "serenely" and "eternally" ostensibly imply a recuperative and closed ending for the novel. However, they also parodically reiterate an earlier description of this view seen by Madge during the picnic episode: "The wide sea filling and frilling the great bight of the bay, and the fishing fleet scattered over the dreaming water . . ." (p. 54). Furthermore, the register of the language and the visual image it conveys is a parodic quotation of cliched filmic endings and undermines the sense of closure it offers. The short exchange between Madge and Paul which follows constitutes a second, more negative, ending which makes overt the impossibility of full intersubjectivity. For Madge, the move out of solipsism entails loss and grief, because of the loss of aspects of the self that it necessitates, and because relationships with an other can only ever be partial. Madge's action in turning "her back on the wide view" implies a refusal of the cliched romance ending, and, also, a recognition of its impossibility.

Mayne and Mark both use polyphonic narration to represent the heteroglottic multicultural structure of the textual world, a feature which can potentially create tension between narrative and ideological closure. The possibilities of story and thematic closure are flaunted in both novels, though Mark's novel is the more closed of the two. While it is asserted on the cover of *Finders, Losers* (Mark, 1990) that the "stories" can be read "in any order," the effect is cumulative and the final story, narrated from Derek's point of view, does provide the narrative information to close the sequence at the level of story and theme. Each of the narrative strands is incomplete, though they are temporally and thematically interconnected so as to retrospectively complete each other, but the point of closure lies outside of the narrative and is aligned with the implied reading positions. As I have suggested, however, the text implies thematic closure through the connections between various character ideologemes. The ending of Derek's narrative in which the three boys, Derek, Philip and David, "find" each other, constructs intersubjectivity as an element of thematic closure and ascribes it with social value.

Story closure in *Salt River Times* (Mayne, 1980) is fairly strong: the discovery of the boat and its contents in Chapter 20 resolves the central mystery. However, Mayne's novel overtly plays with notions of closure in the addition of an extra chapter which is not overtly connected to this central story strand and which leaves the question of intersubjectivity unresolved. The three characters in this chapter reflect the disablement and impossibility of intersubjectivity. Sophia's desire for interpersonal relationships makes her the victim of Gwenda's solipsism, and Kate's desire to collect "bits of people" reflects a solipsistic inability to perceive the selfhood of an other. Finally, despite the different viewpoints on intersubjectivity expressed in *Salt River Times* (Mayne, 1980) and *Finders, Losers* (Mark, 1990), the narrative techniques of both novels represent cultural difference as a plurality of coexisting and conflictual possibilities, contrasting with *The Lake at the End of the World* (Macdonald, 1988/1990) and *The Chocolate War* (Cormier, 1974/1988), wherein cultural differences are represented as mutually exclusive.

Conclusion

Multivoiced and multistranded narrative techniques are especially important strategies for representing polyphony and intersubjectivity. Bakhtin came to see polyphony as a characteristic of narrative fiction in general, but in this chapter I have focused primarily on novels which are explicitly polyphonic, that is, novels which incorporate polyphony as a structural element through the use of multivoiced and multistranded narrative. Polyphony in its broadest sense refers to the interrelations between representing and represented voices and discourses, and these interrelations have enormous implications for the representation of intersubjectivity. These implications can be summarized as follows: the construction of characters and narrators as subjects is dependent on their representation as focalizing agents and on their occupying subject positions within a narrative. Such characters and narrators function as particular socially and subjectively situated ways of seeing and encoding the world. The use of multiple focalizers (or narrators) is one way of representing a plurality of voices, consciousnesses and discourses within narrative, of structuring a narrative as a dialogue between different cultural and ideological positions, and of representing forms of intersubjectivity.

A primary effect of using multiple character focalizers or narrators is that characters are successively represented as focalizing and as focalized and, as they shift from one position to the other, they are denied subjectivity by the focalizing position of the other. This draws attention to perceptual and cultural differences between the ways that characters conceive of the world, and it has a range of implications for the possibilities of attaining intersubjectivity and for its representation in narrative. *Goldengrove* (Walsh, 1972/1985), *Salt River Times* (Mayne, 1980), *The Lake at the End of the World* (Macdonald, 1988/1990) and *The Chocolate War* (Cormier, 1974/1988) are all, for different reasons, fairly negative about the possibility of intersubjectivity. In Macdonald's novel, this negativity arises from the narrative structures through which intersubjectivity is represented and thereby disabled. In Cormier's, it arises from his vision of the interrelations between individuals and society; for Cormier, individuals are always radically alienated from others and from the world around them. In Mayne's and Walsh's novels, intersubjectivity is put into question through thematic concerns with modernist concepts of self and with problems arising from the need to negotiate within interpersonal relationships. In these latter two novels, there is a recognition that intersubjectivity depends upon an individual's ability to move out of solipsism, and that this transition is often only ever partial.

In most of the novels discussed in this chapter characters are located in a single social or physical setting within which dialogue occurs between a range of represented ideological positions. Although the discourses and voices of characters in each of these novels are distinct from each other, they are all to some extent subservient to dominant thematic concerns. Though the ideologemes represented in these novels do not "add up" in any simple way to an ideological whole, they do combine to construct a coherent polyphony of discourses which are ideologically situated within the metanarrative of each novel. An implication of this is the possibility that by making ideologemic discourses subservient to the metanarrative, the dialogic potential of polyphonic narrative strategies may thus be repressed, as my discussions of *The Lake at the End of the World* and *The Chocolate War* have demonstrated.

This chapter has focused on the implications of overtly polyphonic narrative techniques for representing intersubjectivity, such as multivoiced and multistranded narrative. I have restricted my discussion here to novels in which narrative strands and voices are situated in the same time and place, but are differentiated by narratorial or character viewpoints. In Chapters 5, 6, 7, and 8, I will turn my attention to explicitly polyphonic narratives, in which voices and narrative strands are differentiated by shifts in temporal and spatial relationships, as well as narrating and focalizing positions. In Chapters 3 and 4, I will examine Bakhtinian and Lacanian concepts of subjectivity and the dialogic construction and representation of subjectivity in fiction. Most of the novels discussed in these two chapters are not as overtly dialogic or polyphonic in their narrative techniques as those so far discussed. Instead, these novels are implicitly polyphonic, and my interest is in the use of dialogic motifs to explore the construction of subjectivity.

ENDNOTES

1. Secondary literature which has sought to combine the approaches of narrative theory and Bakhtinian theory include Jefferson (1980), Shukman (1980), Thibault (1984), Malcuzinski (1984) and Phelan (1989).

2. In Chapters 3 and 4, I will discuss some less overtly polyphonic novels—that is, novels, such as *Eva* (Dickinson, 1988) and *The Blue Chameleon* (Scholes, 1989), in which polyphony is an aspect of the discursive and thematic structure.

3. Chapters 5 and 6 will examine the narrative techniques of multistranded novels in which narrative strands are differentiated by chronotopic (time-space) relationships, as well as narrative voice and point of view.

4. Nikolajeva's first stage in the development of children's literature, adaptations of existing adult literature and folktale, is also problematic in that adaptations, retellings and reversions are always dialogically situated, in relation to their pre-texts and in relation to the culture which produces them (*see* Stephens and McCallum, 1998).

5. Bakhtin's fourth category of discourse representation, incorporated extraliterary genres, will be discussed in Chapters 7 and 8.

6. The ideologeme has also been used by Jameson (1981) and Kristeva (1980) in different ways. Jameson has defined the term in a fairly limited way, so that its meaning is closer to that of "sociolect"; that is, it is "the smallest intelligible unit of the essentially antagonistic collective discourses of social classes" (Jameson, 1981, p. 76). Kristeva (1980, p. 36–37) has extended its meaning to refer to the radical intertextuality of texts; the ideologeme of a text is thus the intersection of discourses and intertexts within and around that text.

7. *See* discussions of first person narratives in this chapter and in Chapters 3 and 7.

8. The relation between Hopkins's poem and Walsh's novel highlights a curious intertextual phenomena, wherein the focused text may potentially influence and change the way in which the intertext is read. I can no longer remember how I first read Hopkins's poem, and so am not entirely sure of the extent to which my reading of "Spring and Fall" has influenced my reading of *Goldengrove*, or whether my reading of *Goldengrove* has colored my reading of "Spring and Fall." Certainly, the poem does not provide any magical key to the novel, nor does the novel provide a key to the poem, but the common concerns in each engage dialogically to produce a reading which lies somewhere in the intersections between the poem and the novel.

9. I am grateful to Rod McGillis, whose comments on an earlier version of this discussion of intertextuality in *Goldengrove* drew my attention to the complexity of the interrelations between the text and its intertexts in these passages and alerted me to the range of possible ways that the passages might be read.

10. The concluding paragraph of the preface reads: "By the time you have read all six, [stories] you will know exactly what happened on that day, and why, but you'll be the only one who does" (Mark, 1990, p. 6).

11. Lacanian theories of language and subjectivity are discussed more fully in Chapter 3.

12. Morgan is clearly the narrator of Chapter 4, but Chapter 19 shifts frequently between character focalized third person narration, indirect and free direct discourse. This shifting, as well as the fragmentation which characterizes narrative focalized by Morgan, emphasizes Morgan's utterly solipsistic state, as reflected in his inability to differentiate between the self and rest of the world.

13. Stephens (1993) has outlined the distribution of chapters among focalizers as follows:

primary narrator (7, 11 12, 18, 20, 21)
Mel (1, 5, 9, 17)
Joe (3)
Sophia (6, 15)
Elissa (8)
Dee (13, 15)
Kate (16)
Morgan (4, 19)

14. This interlacing of narrative strands also occurs briefly in *Goldengrove*, where the narrative is at some points structured as discrete interlaced strands—in particular, in the opening (pp. 7–10), and later when Paul goes to the lighthouse, while Madge remains with Ralph (pp. 83–92)—though, for the most part, this multistranding remains implicit within the discourse of the novel.

15. *A Bone from a Dry Sea* (Dickinson, 1992) and *The Hillingdon Fox* (Mark, 1991) use double-stranded narration to construct a dialogue between different cultural and historical positions, and these two novels will be examined in Chapters 6 and 7. Variations on double-stranded narrative occur in Mayne's *Drift* (1985), Garner's *Red Shift* (1973) and Hunt's *A Step off the Path* (1985). In *Drift* the story is told first from one character's viewpoint, and then retold from the other character's viewpoint; *A Step off the Path* is a double-stranded novel but uses multiple character focalizers in each strand; and *Red Shift*, which I will discuss in Chapter 5, has three interlaced narrative strands located in different times. The combination of interlaced binary narrative with typographical experimentation and overt genre mixing has also become widespread in recent popular children's fiction, for example *Came Back to Show You I could Fly* (Klein, 1989), *Dodger* (Gleeson, 1990), *Dear Nobody* (Doherty, 1991),

The Hillingdon Fox (Mark, 1991) and *Going Up* (Hunt, 1989). These forms will be examined in Chapter 7.

16. Jan Mark's *The Hillingdon Fox* (1991) is a notable exception to this pattern.

17. This theme seems to have become quite common in futuristic postdisaster fictions, and there are any number of literary and popular culture pre-texts for it: *Dr. Who* ("Genesis of the Daleks" or "The Face of Evil" for example). Rod McGillis has also suggested William Morris's *The Well at the World's End* and George Macdonald's *Day Boy and Night Girl* and certain *Star Trek* episodes as pre-texts.

3   Dialogism and Subjectivity

Doubles and the Quest for Self

To be *means* to communicate . . . *To be means to be for another, and through the other, for oneself. A person has no internal sovereign territory, he is wholly and always on the boundary; looking inside himself, he looks* into the eyes of another *or* with the eyes of another.

Bakhtin, *Problems of Dostoevsky's Poetics*

In their preoccupation with personal growth, maturation and the development of concepts of selfhood, adolescent novels frequently reflect complex psychological ideas about the formation of subjectivity. As I suggested in Chapter 1, liberal humanist and romantic concepts of subjectivity usually underpin narratives of maturation. The infiltration of modernist and structuralist conceptions of the subject into children's literature has been limited and tends to occur within the dominant liberal humanist ethic. This ethic privileges concepts such as the uniqueness of the individual and the essentiality of the self, as opposed to concepts of the self as fragmented or plural, or of subjectivity as being formed through language and in dialogue with social ideologies and practices. In many of the novels with which I am concerned in this book, different representations of the subject—as essential and unique, internally fragmented or socially constructed—are juxtaposed and represented in dialogue with each other. In doing so, these novels implicitly problematize humanist and romantic conceptions of subjectivity by constructing positions from which essentialist assumptions can be interrogated. However, these strategies do not automatically subvert the dominant conceptions of the subject. In fact, they often implicitly reassert humanist paradigms.[1]

Representations of subjectivity in fiction are always grounded by ideological assumptions about relations among individuals, and between individuals, societies and the world. This chapter focuses on the exploration of subjectivity within intensely interpersonal and introspective contexts, with special reference to the notion of essential selfhood. Chapter 4 will deal at greater length with the sociocultural influences on subjectivity, with particular attention to alienation and transgression. For purposes of discussion, I am separating concepts that are not strictly separable, of course, but I am examining them as significant structures within narratives. The books discussed in the two chapters all use the *quest* as a primary narrative structure to depict the formation of subjectivity. Central characters are represented as internally fragmented and/or solipsistic, and their stories articulate a quest for a sense of identity which is stable, coherent, unique and whole. In novels such as *Charlotte Sometimes* (Farmer, 1969/1992), *A Game of Dark* (Mayne, 1971), *Stranger with my Face* (Duncan, 1981/1995), *Jacob have I Loved* (Paterson, 1981/1983), *Eva* (Dickinson, 1988) and *Speaking to Miranda* (Macdonald, 1990) this quest is situated within a narrative context which represents subjectivity as fragmented, partial and subject to social discourses and practices. The commonplace notion of "finding one's self" underlying the idea of the formation of subjectivity as a quest for a stable identity has clear ideological and teleological implications which are interrogated and subverted through their dialogic representation in these novels. The disparity between the object of the quest and its representation within the narrative discourse implies a dialogue between the idea of the selfhood of an individual as constructed within a series of provisional subject positions via specific social and discursive practices, and the self as a unique and essential entity which exists prior to and in opposition to society. The idea of a unique, singular and essential self is an assumption which underlies a person's own sense of, or more specifically desire for, a single and stable personal identity within, and in relation, to the world and to others. In *Eva* and *Speaking to Miranda,* this assumption is represented as a necessary fiction, the desire against which an experience of fragmentation is measured. In *Charlotte Sometimes* and *Stranger with my Face,* there is a more positive evaluation of essentialist concepts of self, in that there is a recognition of the necessity and value of such concepts, in the context of severe loss and fragmentation of self within time, space and social institutions.

The versions of the quest narrative with which I am concerned in these chapters exhibit three main narrative strategies. First, the double, or *doppelgänger*, is used to represent intersubjective relationships between self and other as an internalized dialogue and the internal fragmentation of the subject—the split subject. Second, characters are seen to experience temporal, cultural or psychological displacement or marginalization. To the extent that notions of selfhood are dependent upon and constructed within specific social, linguistic and historical contexts, characters who are displaced out of their familiar surroundings are apt to be depicted as undergoing some form of identity transformation or crisis. Displacement can effect a fragmentation of the subject and social or cultural alienation. It can be used to foreground the social construction of subjectivity, as it does in *Antar and the Eagles* (Mayne, 1989), but also to assert an essentiality of self, as it does quite explicitly in *The Blue Chameleon* (Scholes, 1989) and more implicitly in *Charlotte Sometimes* (Farmer, 1969/1992). The motif of displacement runs through most of the novels discussed here and takes a number of forms: temporal displacement, as in timeshift narratives such as *Charlotte Sometimes;* spatial and social displacement, as in *The Blue Chameleon* (Scholes, 1989), *Antar and the Eagles* (Mayne, 1989), *Stranger with my Face* (Duncan, 1981/ 1995) and *Eva* (Dickinson, 1988); and/or psychological or emotional displacement, as in *A Game of Dark* (Mayne, 1971) and *Stranger with my Face* (Duncan, 1985/1991). Representations of subjectivity in narrative are necessarily tied up with character function and setting and with the discursive strategies used to construct these components. Further, notions of subjectivity are always grounded in ideological assumptions about the relations between individuals and societies. The positioning of characters on the margins of, or in a transgressive relation to, a represented society or culture provides a way of exploring the interplay between subjectivity and agency, and of interrogating the dominant cultural and social paradigms for the construction of subjects. These implications will be taken up more fully in Chapter 4. The third narrative strategy to which I will be referring is intertextuality. This term covers the range of literary and cultural texts, discourses and genres used to construct fictions, but my focus here is on its use to represent subjectivity as constructed within language, that is, as the intersection of a variety of social and cultural discourses and texts. This is foregrounded in *Speaking to Miranda,* where the subjectivity of characters is represented as a bricolage of appropriated texts and discourses. Chapter 4 will examine at greater length the construction of subjectivity within language and social codes in *The Blue Chameleon* and *Antar and the Eagles.*

Some of the novels discussed in this chapter and in Chapter 4 also use overtly polyphonic and dialogic narrative techniques, such as multistranded narration and multiple character focalizers. Most are not, however, predominantly dialogical in their narrative technique, and my interest here is more in the dialogic representation of subjectivity. The remainder of this chapter will focus on the representation of interpersonal relations in narrative, in particular the relation between self and other, and the representation of concepts of essential selfhood. Each of the novels discussed explores the idea that a sense of personal identity is shaped by an other and represents a dialogue between images of the self as essential and as multiple and internally fragmented. These conceptualizations of the subject are also central to the theoretical approaches of Bakhtin and Lacan. The following section will examine Bakhtinian and Lacanian accounts of subjectivity and their implications for the analysis of representations of interpersonal relations in adolescent fiction.

SELF AND OTHER

It is frequently claimed that the Bakhtinian concept of dialogism overcomes the opposition between individual and society by recognizing that individual subjectivity is intersubjective; that is, it is formed in a dialogic relation with an other and with social discourses and practices. Bakhtin's ideas about subjectivity were developed in the context of a theory of narrative and may perhaps appear more directly relevant to the analysis of narrative than those of Lacan. There are, however, some important points of convergence between Bakhtinian and Lacanian theories of subjectivity,[2] and Lacan's recognition of the interplay between subject formation and language also has implications for the narrative representation of subjectivity. Both theorists were concerned with the dialogical relationship between self and other and with the construction of the subject through the other and through language. Both were also preoccupied with the image of the mirror and the gaze to describe the interrelationship between self and other (Stam, 1989, pp. 2–4). Furthermore, for Bakhtin and Lacan, the idea of the subject as a unitary entity which is the source and agent of action or meaning, central to a humanist theory of subjectivity, is an essentializing fiction which ignores the construction of that subject in relation to an other and within social and ideological discourses, and it represents, in Bakhtinian terms, a desire for the monological effacement of the other.

There are, however, some crucial differences between Bakhtin and Lacan. An obvious difference is that Bakhtin's work discounts Freudian theories of the unconscious, upon which Lacan's work is premised. As Emerson has argued, Bakhtin's model of the formation of consciousness and subjectivity through language and social interrelations has "no room for—and perhaps no conceptual possibility of—an independent unconscious" (1983, p. 250). Accordingly, for Bakhtin, the Freudian unconscious is a myth which evades history and social process (1983, p. 251).[3] Both Lacan and Bakhtin see subjectivity as dependent on the recognition of the position of the other and of the distance between self and other. For Lacan, this distance is the site of an ontological split in the subject and of an irremedial loss and alienation: the subject is defined by lack and imperfection (Stam, 1989, p. 5). Bakhtin takes a more positive view of the relationship between self and other, emphasizing the role of the other in completing the self. Individual consciousness is impossible outside of a relation with an other:

> I am conscious of myself and become myself only while revealing myself for another, through another, and with the help of another. The most important acts constituting self-consciousness are determined by a relationship toward another consciousness, (towards a *thou*). Separation, dissociation, and enclosure within the self as the main reason for the loss of one's self. Not that which takes place within, but that which takes place on the *boundary* between one's own and someone else's consciousness, on the *threshold*. (Bakhtin, 1984a, p. 287)

For Bahktin, loss is located outside of, or, in the absence of, the relation between self and other, rather than because of it. The "other" constitutes a position of outsidedness needed to complete the self.

In an early essay written in the 1920s, "Author and Hero in Aesthetic Activity" (in *Art and Answerability*, 1990), Bakhtin had conceived of the relation between an author and a character as analogous to that between the other and the self in the sense that the author (or other) constitutes an exotopic position in the relation to a character (or self) from which the character (or self) is perceived and represented as whole and complete. His approach is predicated on the recognition that the relation between self and other is "determined by the fact that one does not see oneself as one is seen by others" (Jefferson, 1989, p. 153). This relation is described in physical perceptual terms, and Bahktin's description might be paraphrased as follows: When I contemplate an other human being who is situated outside of me, our concrete, actually experienced horizons do not coincide. Regardless of our positions and proximity, I shall always see and know something that s/he, from her/his place outside me, cannot see: parts of her/his body that are inaccessible to her/his own gaze (her/his head, her/his face and its expression), the world behind her/his back, and a whole series of objects and relations, which are accessible to me but not to her/him (pp. 22–23). Bakhtin continues: "It is possible, upon assuming an appropriate position, to reduce this difference of horizons to a minimum, but in order to annihilate this difference completely, it would be necessary to merge into one, to become one and the same person" (p. 23). In other words, the categories of self and other depend upon the situatedness of persons and their outsidedness in relationships with each other. The distance between persons is irreducible to the extent that it grounds the relation between self and other, and hence the constitution of subjectivity. Since we can never see ourselves directly, we construct a sense of ourselves by appropriating the position of the other, outside of the self. It is in this sense that the other is necessary for the completion of the self and that the position of the other is analogous to that of the author, in that the other "authors" the subject.

There are, however, some problems with Bakhtin's formulation in his early work. As Jefferson (1989) has shown, the relation between self and other as it is conceived of in "Author and Hero in Aesthetic Activity" has a "non-dialectic basis," and the subject (or character) is constructed in a position of passivity (1989, p. 156). Bakhtin conceives of the relationship between a character and author as a love relation in which "the author-lover is the active partner and the beloved-hero his passive counterpart" (Jefferson, 1989, p. 155). Although Bakhtin describes the role of the author as "a nonauthoritative and unfounded other" (1990, p. 33), the relation between author and character can function as a power relationship in which the position of the author (other) is dominant. With the concept of dialogism which he developed in his later work, Bakhtin introduced a linguistic dimension into his formulation of the relation between self and other. The subject is constituted within and by the language of the other. Thus, the relation between self and other is always mediated by language which lies beyond the subject and to which the subject has limited access and control. Jefferson has argued that Bakhtin's concept of dialogism is, then, an implicit acknowledgment that the scenario he described in "Author and Hero in Aesthetic Activity" has its darker side, and that author (other) and hero (self) are linked as much by conflict as by love (Jefferson, 1989, p. 163). Bakhtin's analogy between the relation between self and other, and characters and authors, has implications for how we interpret narrative representations of these relations, such as those in *Speaking to Miranda* (Macdonald, 1990), for example. Furthermore, to the extent that the author is conceived of by Bakhtin as a function of narrative (a position of outsidedness in relation to character), it has implications for how the relations between the subject and larger social processes which "author" the subject are conceptualized.

Lacan's approach stresses a "darker side" of the relation between self and other which, for Lacan, implies a fundamental split in the subject. The subject first senses and identifies itself in the image of the other and the construction of self occurs via an imaginary identification of the subject with that image (Wilden, 1975, p. 100). "The subject, to be a subject at all, internalizes otherness as its condition of possibility," and subjectivity is thus grounded in internal fragmentation and alienation (Grosz, 1990, p. 43). As

Emerson has suggested, the gap between self and other, between inner and outer, is for both Bakhtin and Lacan a cause of pain, but whereas for Bakhtin "it is the pain of inarticulateness," for Lacan "it is the pain of desire" (Emerson, 1983, p. 256). Whereas Bakhtin represents conflict and crisis for the subject as external and social, Lacan sees conflict as internal, and thus grounds subjectivity in an internal alienation.

Bakhtin and Lacan both use the image of the mirror and the gaze to describe the interrelationship between self and other.[4] Lacan's theory of the mirror phase is crucial to his conception of the inherently divided, split subject (1977a, pp. 1–7). The mirror phase refers to the point at which a child (age six to eighteen months) recognizes as such, and takes delight in, his/her own image in a mirror (pp. 1–2). The specular image which the child apprehends "is given to him only as *Gestalt*," that is, "in an exteriority," which fixes and inverts the image of the subject "in contrast with the turbulent movements that the subject feels are animating him" (p. 2). Bakhtin's comments about the contemplation of one's own image are similar. When we look in a mirror, we still do not see ourselves directly. Rather, "we see a *reflection* of our exterior, but not *ourselves* in terms of our exterior," and this reflection of an "exterior does not encompass all of me [because] I am in front of the mirror and not in it" (1990, p. 32). As both writers observe, there is a gap between the subject as perceived and the subject as perceiver. For Lacan, the mirror phase marks the point at which the subject is internally split, "divided between itself and its mirror reflection" (Grosz, 1990, p. 15). The child perceives its image in the mirror as stable, fixed and whole, as "a unified totality," but it "experiences itself in a schism, as a site of fragmentation" (p. 39).

Lacan and Bakhtin both see the process through which the specular image is perceived and recognized as representing the process whereby subjectivity is constructed via an internalized other. According to Bakhtin, "since we lack any approach to ourselves from outside . . . we project ourselves into a peculiarly indeterminate possible other" from whose position we "give form to ourselves" (1990, p. 32). In this way, "our own relationship to our exterior . . . pertains only to its possible effect on others" and "we evaluate our exterior not for ourselves, but *for* others *through* others" (p. 32). For Bahktin, the event of self-contemplation cannot express a "unitary and unique soul," because it always implies a second participant, "a fictitious other, a nonauthoritative and unfounded author" (pp. 32–33). For Lacan, however, it is the otherness of the specular image that is stressed. The mirror phase is to be understood as an "identification" and as formative of the function of the "I" (1977a, pp. 5–7). The subject, "I," is constructed via an imaginary identification with the other—that is, the specular image (p. 2). But, in identifying with its mirror image, the subject's relation to that image is alienated: "the image both is and is not an image of itself"; it is also always an image of another (Grosz, 1990, p. 40). Again, Lacan's emphasis is on the fragmentation and alienation of the subject.

Lacan's account of the mirror phase has two main implications. First, the child's recognition that it is not complete in itself marks the initial stages of the transition out of solipsism. It signals the moment of the child's recognition of the distinction between the self and the other, and between the self and the world, and the child's first attempts to construct an identity independent of the other and to locate a position in the world (Grosz, 1990, p. 34–35). In this sense, Bakhtinian and Lacanian positions are roughly analogous. Second, the mirror phase marks the child's first recognition of lack or absence, and it represents the child's first concerted attempts to fill this lack by identifying with its own specular image. It is at this point that Bakhtin and Lacan would seem to part company. Although for both the idea of the unified subject is an essentializing fiction, they give this fiction a slightly different emphasis. For Bakhtin, the lack of the unified singular subject and the construction of subjectivity through relationships with others is to be viewed positively; a person experiences subjectivity as social, multiple, discontinuous and as always in a state of becoming. The stress in Lacan's account on fragmentation and division grounds a person's experience of subjectivity in loss, lack and absence, and as always oriented by an unrealizable desire for completion or presence.

Bakhtinian and Lacanian accounts of the relation between self and other have implications for the analysis of the representations of these relations in adolescent fiction. Both Bakhtin and Lacan see the formation of subjectivity as an aspect in the developmental process of the child, and both are interested in the transition from solipsism to intersubjectivity. These concerns provide a clear parallel with that central preoccupation of adolescent fiction, personal maturation. The theoretical approaches of Bakhtin and Lacan are also of particular relevance to the dialogic representation of subjectivity in narrative. They provide ways of analyzing the use of narrative strategies and motifs in adolescent fiction, such as the double and the *quest*—strategies which are often used to explore the idea that a sense of personal identity is shaped by an other and that subjectivity is the site of multiplicity and fragmentation. The idea that the unified subject is an essentializing, but unrealizable, fiction is central to Lacan and Bakhtin's accounts. But this fiction also underlies the use of the *quest* motif for the representation of subject formation as a quest for a stable and coherent sense of identity in many adolescent novels. Each of the novels examined in the next section combine the quest and the double to represent a dialogue between images of the self as essential, and as fragmented and provisional.

The Double and the Dialogic Representation of Subjectivity

The double, or *doppelgänger,* is frequently used in narrative to explore the idea that personal identity is shaped by a dialogic relation with an other and that subjectivity is multiple and fragmented. In *Charlotte Sometimes* (Farmer, 1969/1992), *A Game of Dark* (Mayne, 1971), *Stranger with my Face* (Duncan, 1981/1995), *Jacob Have I Loved* (Paterson, 1981/1983), *Eva* (Dickinson, 1988), *The Blue Chameleon* (Scholes, 1989) and *Speaking to Miranda* (Macdonald, 1990) each main character has a double or counterpart, internal or external to that character, which is crucial for the construction and representation of that character's subjectivity. In *Stranger with my Face* and *Jacob Have I Loved,* the double is the narrating characters' actual twin in relation to whom the narrator defines herself and who, to some extent, displaces the narrator. In *Charlotte Sometimes* and *Eva,* the double is an actual other with whom the main character has changed places, and whose body, time and place this character occupies. In *Speaking to Miranda* and *A Game of Dark,* the double is an internalized or imagined other.

A primary effect of the double is to destabilize notions of the subject as unified, or coherent, or as existing outside of a relation to an other. It does this by representing an internal fragmentation and alienation of the subject and/or an internalization of the intersubjective relation between self and other. To the extent that the concept of the split subject is contingent with the relation between self and other, the distinctions between these two functions blur. The double is frequently both an other and another aspect of the self, an internalized other. In *Jacob Have I Loved* (Paterson, 1981/1983), for example, Louise (the narrator) depicts herself as growing up in the shadow of her twin (Caroline). Caroline becomes an internalized other for Louise—another self in relation to whom her own sense of selfhood is defined. In *Stranger with my Face* (Duncan, 1981/1995), a novel about identical twins separated as babies, Laurie (the narrator) describes Lia (her twin) as her other self: "myself, yet not myself. The other half of me" (p. 82). Studies of the double (Crook, 1981; Hallam, 1981; Jackson, 1981; Dolar, 1991) have focused on its use in fantasy fiction, particularly gothic and romantic fiction, and have been influenced by Rank's *The Double* (1971) and Freud's account of the *doppelgänger* in "The Uncanny" (1919/1959, pp. 368–407)—in particular his descriptions of Hoffmann's "The Sand-man." In both Freud's account and in gothic novels, such as Mary Shelley's *Fran-*

kenstein or Stevenson's *Dr. Jekyll and Mr Hyde,* the double is a mirror inversion of the subject which is located externally—as in *Frankenstein* and "The Sandman"—or internally—as in *Dr. Jekyll and Mr Hyde.* The relationship between a character and its double is usually oppositional and typically has a moral function (*see* Freud, 1919/1959, pp. 387–89 and 402). As I have argued elsewhere, Freud's ideas are useful in analyzing the function of the double in novels in fantasy genres, where the double is frequently a symbolic manifestation of a character's alterego and often represents that character's other "evil" self (*see* McCallum, 1996a). In gothic novels closure is usually achieved through the death of both the double and the hostcharacter. Hence, the relation between character and double is structured monologically: there is no possibility of either dialogue or dialectic synthesis between the character and its double.

This schema for the double occurs in *Stranger with my Face* (Duncan, 1981/1995). The narrator, Laurie, gradually becomes aware that she has a double, a mystical presence, Lia, who is her identical twin sister. Their mother was a Navajo, and they have both inherited the Navajo ability to astral travel—though at the opening of the novel, Laurie is unaware of her inheritance and has not yet learned this skill. Lia has been institutionalized after causing the death of her fostersister, and now astral travels to the island where Laurie lives. The double motif is in a sense twofold: Lia and Laurie are doubles for each other; and the astral travel motif which enacts a split between mind and body, also has a doubling effect. Lia is clearly represented as the "evil" twin—her inherent "evil" quality is sensed by Helen (p. 62) and by Laurie's adopted mother (p. 71)—and as Laurie's other "evil" self— they are "two sides of a coin . . . the dark and the light side" (p. 177). However, unlike the gothic pre-texts, while Laurie is clearly changed by the events which occur, Lia's death does not entail her own.

Nevertheless, a pervading sense of loss permeates the narrative. Initially, when Laurie first finds out that Lia is her sister, she experiences feelings of loss (p. 77). Her search for Lia is also a quest for her own identity—that is, it is a search for a sense of selfcompletion, her "other half" (p. 82), as well as for her real family and past. Laurie also experiences a sense of detachment from her self, identifying with Lia's position. For example, on page 65, while kissing Gordon she feels her mind "detaching itself" and, finding herself "standing back, looking at this boy and girl kissing," she realizes that this must be how Lia feels: "She stands apart and watches" (p. 65). The episode is echoed later in the novel, when Laurie finds herself trapped outside of her own body while astral traveling. In her absence, Lia has taken her place and now occupies her body. It becomes clear that Lia's actions are motivated by this desire to take Laurie's place. She causes accidents to happen to people, such as Helen and Jeff, whom Laurie is close to and can talk to about Lia, and as Laurie becomes more obsessed with Lia, she also becomes more introverted and withdrawn from her friends and family. Her involvement with Lia thus entails a progressive alienation from the people around her. The episode in which Laurie is trapped outside of her body is used by Duncan to raise questions about the nature of selfhood. While watching Lia in her place, Laurie asks, "if *she* was Laurie Stratton—then, who was I?" (p. 227). However, Megan recognizes that Laurie is now Lia which implies, on the one hand, an essentialist concept of selfhood, but on the other, that identity is shaped and defined through the ways in which others perceive Lia/Laurie. Despite the satisfying resolution—in which Laurie regains possession of her body—and the characterization of Lia as unequivocally "evil," a sense of loss and isolation prevails, which both problematizes notions of selfhood and blurs distinctions between "good" and "evil." Lia's presence remains as a trace in Laurie's house after her body has been pronounced dead and cremated, and it is clear that the experience has changed Laurie, leaving her isolated and alone: "Of the three people I could talk to, two are gone and the third is very young" (p. 3).

In many contemporary adolescent fictions the double is represented as an aspect of the developmental process, and is better understood in the context of Lacanian and Bakhtinian theories of subjectivity. States of fragmentation and/or multiplicity experienced by characters as a consequence of the double motif are conceptualized as conditions of the possibility of subjectivity, rather than as aberrations. The relation between character and double in *A Game of Dark* (Mayne, 1971) and *Speaking to Miranda* (Macdonald, 1990) is oppositional insofar as it articulates a split between the subject and the agent, and the relation between the two worlds represented in *A Game of Dark* is, to some extent, allegorical, although the moral implications of this allegorical structure are suppressed. In *Jacob Have I Loved* (Paterson, 1981/1983), Louise perceives and represents Caroline as her opposite, but it becomes clear that Louise's narration is unreliable as a result of her extreme solipsism. Often the double is perceived by a character as a threat to their sense of selfhood, as it is in *Stranger with my Face*. However, in novels such as *Speaking to Miranda* (Macdonald, 1990), *Eva* (Dickinson, 1988) and *Charlotte Sometimes* (Farmer, 1969/1992), the relation between a character and her/his double is not directly oppositional, nor is it structured morally as it is in Duncan's novel. Instead, the double in these novels is represented as an aspect of the developmental process. That is, the double represents another possible position that the character might occupy, an internalized aspect of otherness, and/or is indicative of the internal division of the subject.

In *Speaking to Miranda* (Macdonald, 1990), *A Game of Dark* (Mayne, 1971) and *Jacob Have I Loved* (Paterson, 1981/1983) the relation between characters and their doubles provides a way of exploring agency, that is, a person's sense of themselves as capable of conscious action or meaning. In Macdonald's and Mayne's novels' the relation between character and double articulates a split between the subject and the agent. In Paterson's realist novel, this split is related to how the narrator Louise perceives herself, that is, as displaced and disempowered by her twin, Caroline.

In *Speaking to Miranda* and *A Game of Dark,* the double is an internalized or imagined other and the subjectivity of characters is thereby represented as internally fragmented. Agency is located with the double, or internalized, imagined other; hence characters are subject to or, at least, perceive themselves as subject to their double. The relation between characters and their doubles is thus grounded in a relationship of power, and in both novels this manifests itself in a concern with the possibilities of constructing a sense of oneself as subject and as agent independent of social forces and practices. In *A Game of Dark,* this is expressed in the construction of two narrative strands: a primary narrative which represents the "real" world occupied by Donald Jackson; and a secondary narrative which represents a fantasy medieval world entered, or constructed, by Donald, where he takes on the role of Jackson and kills the worm which threatens the medieval town. The fantasy world functions primarily as a place in which Donald is able to achieve a position of intersubjectivity and agency which he is denied in the real world. As I have suggested, the relation between the two worlds is to some extent allegorical, but there is not a one-to-one correspondence between events and things in the real and fantasy worlds.

In *Speaking to Miranda,* Miranda is the name of an imaginary other with whom the narrator, Ruby, speaks throughout the novel; but as Ruby discovers, Miranda is in fact her own name, and Ruby the name of her half sister who died the night she herself was conceived.[5] This confusion of names is based in an act of denial: Ruby/Miranda's mother, Emma/Magda, renamed Miranda "Ruby" in an attempt to pretend that Ruby's death had never happened. The relation between Ruby and Miranda articulates a split between Ruby/Miranda's sense of herself as subject and as agent. Ruby perceives Miranda as responsible for decisions and actions (p. 30), thereby locating agency with Miranda. Their relation is also represented as that between a narrator or character and an author, as in the following passage:

I heard mocking laughter and was aware of a deep antagonism. *What are you? Nothing. The sum total of you is what I've made of you. You are nothing—and will be nothing—without me. You'll always do what I want. I have created you, moulded you, and I can destroy you at any time.* [Italics indicate Miranda's speech] (p. 26)

The representation of Miranda and Ruby as author and character compares with Bakhtin's analogy between the relations between self and other, and character and author. For Bakhtin, the author corresponds to an other, from whose position a character (self) can be perceived and represented as complete. Miranda takes on the role of an authoritative and antagonistic author, however, and this draws attention to one of the more problematic aspects of Bakhtin's approach: that the relation between author and character is a power relationship in which the author/other is dominant. Furthermore, insofar as Ruby also attributes agency to Miranda, there is a correlation here of the other, authorship and agency, which puts in question the possibility of constructing a subjectivity outside of the constraints put in place by the other. The connection between agency and the other also suggests the possibility that a search for selfhood merely represents the desire for the other—which in Lacanian terms represents an unrealizable desire for completion or presence.

Jacob Have I Loved (Paterson, 1981/1983) is a realist novel in which the double is an actual other, Louise's fraternal twin, Caroline, whom Louise perceives as being the favored twin. The novel is narrated by Louise, an unreliable and fallible narrator, and her depiction of Caroline and their relationship is determined by her own self-image. Descriptions of Caroline and Louise foreground their differences:

> There is a rare snapshot of the two of us sitting on the front stoop the summer we were a year and a half old. Caroline is tiny and exquisite, her blonde curls framing a face that is glowing with laughter, her arms outstretched to whoever is taking the picture. I am hunched there like a fat dark shadow, my eyes cut sideways toward Caroline, thumb in mouth, the pudgy hand covering most of my face. (1983, pp. 16–17)

Louise clearly perceives herself as Caroline's opposite—unloved, unattractive and untalented. Descriptions of their physical appearance constantly contrast Louise's darkness with Caroline's fairness, Louise's glumness and Carline's easygoing likeable temperament. The twins' aging grandmother often also doubles for Louise by voicing her secret fears and desires—for example, Louise's attraction to the captain—and articulating Louise's own sense of self in relation to Caroline. This culminates with the grandmother's quotation of the biblical passage which gives the novel its title: "Jacob have I loved, but Esau have I hated" (p. 156)—Louise perceives Caroline as the loved twin. Louise reads the rest of the passage (from Romans 9) which continues: "Therefore hath he mercy on whom he will have mercy, and whom he will he hardeneth"; and Louise concludes: "God had chosen to hate me. And if my heart was hard, that was his doing" (p. 159). The passage from Romans is often quoted in arguments about free will versus predestination, and it highlights a key theme running through Paterson's novel: that it is imperative that Louise acquire a sense of her own agency and not see her own actions and personality as being shaped by external forces. The novel does not enter into the predestination debate, but it does suggest that a belief in free will is more empowering than a belief in providence. Louise's conclusion—that "God had chosen to hate me"—locates agency outside of the self, and so implies a conception of herself as disempowered. It thus corresponds with the second form of solipsism outlined in Chapter 1, that is, the inability to perceive one's own selfhood as independent of the world and to construct a sense of one's self as an agent. As long as Louise perceives herself as the hated twin (rather than the twin who has chosen to be hated, regardless of whether or not she is less favored) and hence constructed by the attitudes and viewpoints of others, she is unable to make what she perceives as independent choices and act in the world. Instead, she perceives the world and others as acting upon her.

Louise's solipsism also informs her representation of Caroline and herself. In this sense, it conforms to the first form of solipsism outlined in Chapter 1: the inability to perceive an other as another self, and hence the denial of a subject position for that other independent of one's self. Louise's reaction to Call and Caroline's marriage is partly attributable to this viewpoint. Throughout her narrative, she represents Call in very objectified (and disparaging) terms. She is unable to see either Call or Caroline as other selves with their own viewpoints on the world—this is clear, for example, on page 150, in Louise's reaction to Caroline's expressed desire to leave the island. Louise's oppositional representation of herself and Caroline is also an aspect of her solipsism. Insofar as she is unable to perceive herself and Caroline as independent of each other, Caroline's achievements define her lack of achievement. The novel is not simply about sibling rivalry. It is as much about Louise's need to perceive her own difference from others in a positive light as difference, rather than deficit. When Caroline leaves the island in the latter part of the novel, Louise seems to lose agency altogether: she leaves school and works with her father on the fishing boat and withdraws from society and her family. It is only when she realizes that she needs other people that she also realizes that she too is needed and that others do in fact understand and empathize with her (p. 191). It is at this point, too, that she realizes that there are other things she wants to do with her life and that she must (and can) leave the island in order to construct a sense of her own self—as both agent and subject.

The Double as Supplement

As I suggested earlier, the double in *Charlotte Sometimes* (Farmer, 1969/ 1992) and *Eva* (Dickinson, 1988) is an actual other with whom the main character has changed places, and whose body, time and place this character occupies. The interrelation between the character and its double in these two novels can be understood in the context of the Derridean concept of the *supplement* (Derrida, 1976). The supplement has two significations. On the one hand, it "adds itself, it is a surplus, a plenitude enriching another plenitude, the *fullest measure* of presence" (p. 144). In this sense, the supplement corresponds to Bakhtin's notion of the other as completing the self and to the Lacanian desire for presence. On the other hand, the supplement substitutes, that is "it adds only to replace" and "as substitute, it is not simply added to the positivity of a presence . . . its place is assigned in the structure by the mark of an emptiness" (pp. 144–145). In this sense, the supplement corresponds to Lacan's conception of the subject as constructed through identification with the other and the internalizing of otherness. The other is a sign which stands in for the self and thus inscribes selfhood as an absence. The double fulfils both of these functions in *Eva* and *Charlotte Sometimes*. It represents a position of outsidedness necessary to complete the self and to construct the self as presence; and it is a substitute or proxy, which also constructs selfhood as a form of absence, and thus threatens to take the place of and efface the self.

Charlotte Sometimes is a time-shift narrative which takes place in a girls' boarding school in two different times, 1918 and 1958. Charlotte wakes up on her first morning at the school to find that she has slipped forty years into the past and changed places with Clare. Other characters automatically assume that she is Clare and only Emily, Clare's sister, eventually recognizes that she is not. For a while Charlotte and Clare change places each day, but when Clare's and Emily's move away from the school is delayed a day, Charlotte remains stranded in Clare's time.

The novel is narrated entirely from Charlotte's point of view. Clare is absent from the narrative as either a represented character or as a focalizer. Clare does, however, have a textual presence, in that the messages she writes to Charlotte in their diaries are represented in the novel. Clare is also made present in two other main ways. Her story is inscribed as a "trace" within Charlotte's narrative and can be inferred by readers. Charlotte's awareness of her also represents her as an absent presence. This awareness is mainly constructed out of the knowledge which Charlotte gains of Clare through the ways in which others, who think that she is Clare, behave toward her, and through her perception of the expectations that others have of her, as Clare. In this way, her idea of what Clare is like comprises a particular conglomeration of behavior codes and character traits corresponding with the position that she occupies. Much of Charlotte's behavior in the past is determined by her awareness of and inferencing about how Clare might have behaved. Clare is thus present as a specific subject position: a particular way of perceiving and behaving in the world.

A central concern in the novel is with the extent to which a sense of personal identity is dependent upon a relationship with an other and that other's recognition of the subject. Underlying this concern are questions about the constructedness of the subject on the one hand and the essentiality of the self on the other. This complex is articulated in the following passage:

> And, she thought uncomfortably, what would happen if people did not recognize you? Would you know who you were yourself? If tomorrow they started to call her Vanessa or Janet or Elizabeth, would she know how to be, how to feel like, Charlotte? Were you some particular person only because people recognized you as that? (1992, pp. 73–74).

Charlotte's ruminations implicitly raise existential questions such as: If my sense of myself (as particular, unique and distinct from any other self) is dependent upon an other's recognition of me as such, and I am consistently mistaken for someone else, how can I be sure that I am who I think I am? Duncan's *Stranger with my Face* (1981/1985) also obliquely postulates such questions, but Farmer's treatment of them is more sophisticated. For Charlotte, the constant changing between being Clare and being Charlotte means that she finds it hard to remember whether she is "Charlotte, or Clare, or someone different again" (p. 37). When she becomes stranded in 1918, the distinction between being Clare and being Charlotte becomes, for Charlotte, more blurred. As she feels impelled to behave in ways that she thinks Clare would have behaved, she begins to lose a sense of herself as Charlotte and to think of herself as Clare. That she is not always sure who she is destabilizes the notion of the self as essential and unique, and implies that an individual's own sense of selfhood is constructed within particular contexts. On the other hand, the fact that Charlotte in Clare's time and place is indeed someone else, as both Emily in Clare's time and Elizabeth in Charlotte's time, recognize, implies an essentialist view of subjectivity, which locates selfhood with the conscious mind of an individual. And Charlotte's return to her own time and to being herself ostensibly affirms such essentialist notions of self.

The relation between Clare and Charlotte is supplementary. On the one hand, Clare adds to or completes Charlotte's sense of herself. Charlotte's sense of selfhood is inextricable from her idea of Clare, and of both being Clare and not being Clare. It becomes imperative that she ascertain the differences between herself and Clare, both in 1918 and in her own time: "her need was to define herself, Charlotte, as much as Clare" (1992, p. 184). She becomes herself through Emily's and her own perception of her difference from Clare. Concepts of selfhood are thus contingent upon our own perceptions of our similarities and differences from others as well as other people's perceptions of us. It is as crucial for Emily that Clare return, as it is for Charlotte that they change places again, because for Emily, Charlotte represents not only the loss of Clare, but also a loss of herself, or at least those aspects of self which emerge in Clare's presence.

On the other hand, Clare and Charlotte function as the replacements or substitutes of each other. This is not just because each is in the other's place in time. Farmer inverts the supplementary relation so that it is the proxy (Charlotte) who feels (or fears) that she is effaced and displaced by the subject position of the other (Clare). Underlying this is a fear of being absorbed by the other and of a loss of self. The prospect of remaining in Clare's time is one which for Charlotte represents an irreconcilable loss of self, because it means being constructed (by others and by the society in which she has been placed) and constrained within the subject position of an other. This is also represented metaphorically in her dream of changing places with Agnes. The use of the dream and the motif of sleep, through which the exchange between Clare and Charlotte takes place, locates the point at which a stable sense of identity is undermined within the unconscious. This further undermines the concept of essential selfhood.

The *quest* motif, which I outlined in the opening of this chapter, is inscribed in *Charlotte Sometimes* at the level of story in Charlotte's need to return to her own time and to being herself. It is also present as a theme in her quest for a sense of identity as distinct from Clare. The resolution of this quest is ambivalent. Charlotte's final return to her own time and to being Charlotte works in part to affirm a sense of the self as stable and singular, but Clare's death both confirms and denies that singularity. Her sense of herself is still inextricable from Clare. Clare is her absent double, who she both is and is not. Charlotte's grief for Clare represents a grief for both the other (an other whom she knew only as an absence) and for the self: that is, for the unavoidable loss of self entailed in the loss of the other. The climactic scene near the close of the novel when Charlotte recovers Clare's diary from 1918 hidden inside one of the bedhead posts underscores the doubleness of this sense of loss. Charlotte opens the diary, expecting a final message from Clare, and finds instead only a message from herself, left there in 1918 the night before Clare and Emily were to leave the school. The shock of this discovery for Charlotte and for readers lies in the text's deferral of closure. Charlotte's expectation of a final message represents a desire for a sense of completion for her own narrative and that of Clare—"it would have seemed conclusive, appropriate, even a little comforting" (p. 195). The message is in fact one from her past self addressed to an other (Clare), but read by her present self. Her anticipated apprehension of the other (like that of readers) is thus mediated by and inscribed within her own address to that other. The episode emphasizes Clare's incompletion as a subject, and hence as an other self, and it reinforces her status in the text as a "trace," or a lack of presence. But in doing so, it stresses that Charlotte's status as a subject is also provisional, by juxtaposing two representations of the subject (past and present) and by implying that a sense of self (as complete, whole, or singular) is contingent upon a sense of the other's completion. Charlotte's desire for a message from Clare is, then, a desire for confirmation of the other's selfhood, and hence for confirmation of her own selfhood.

Eva (Dickinson, 1988) is a fantastic futuristic narrative about the transplanting of a young woman's (Eva's) neurones into the body of a chimpanzee (Kelly). As in *Charlotte Sometimes,* the main character, Eva, literally takes the place of another character, Kelly. The implication underlying *Charlotte Sometimes* that concepts of stable identity are undone at the level of the unconscious is explicit in *Eva.* The relation between Eva and Kelly is made more complex than that between Charlotte and Clare by the fact that Kelly's unconscious is present as a kind of race memory, coexisting with Eva's own human unconscious mind. Further, in *Eva* there is a correlation between the construction of subjectivity and the body—the absent human body as well as the present chimpanzee body. Whereas in *Charlotte Sometimes* there is a fairly conventionalized split between the mind and the body, Eva/Kelly effectively has the mind of a human being, the body of a chimpanzee and an unconscious corresponding to both, the coexistence of which puts into question conventional mind/body binarisms as well as notions of the subject as either essential or as simply constructed. The concept of the supplement is again useful for describing the ambivalence of the relation between Kelly and Eva. To the extent that Kelly's body and unconscious mind are both present, and Eva is a mind without a body, so to speak, Eva and Kelly add to or complete each other. However, the process of neurone transfer involves the effacement of Kelly's consciousness. Furthermore, in order to deal with her new state of being and to become a person, Eva must repress or displace her own (human) unconscious associated with her old body and allow Kelly's unconscious or instinctive emotions expression. The characterization of Eva/Kelly represents the subject as internally fractured and the construction of subjectivity as an interplay between a range of conscious, unconscious, instinctive and social forces. Thus, the novel is centered around a dialogue between essentialist and constructivist conceptions of subjectivity.

Essentialist notions of selfhood are implicit in *Eva* in three main ways, and they are linked with consciousness, the unconscious and the body. First, the idea of "neurone memory" (p. 22), that is, the unique genetic pattern or arrangement which constitutes an individual and which defines Eva as human and as the particular individual that is "Eva," implies an essential and unique element associated with her humanness and her human capacity for conscious thought, action and the ability to manipulate linguistic signs. In this sense, Eva exists as a conscious mind and as a past human self which is present in her conscious memories of her past. Second, Eva/Kelly comprises both a present chimpanzee body and an absent past human body, which is present as an aspect of her human memory. This copresence is described in the following passage:

> The ghost of a human arm still trying to work, to reach and touch at the mind's command. You couldn't see it but it was there, moving slightly out of synch as the chimp arm moved, with the elbow wrong and the invisible fingertips wavering among the chimp knuckles. When she closed her eyes she saw in her mind the pale slim fingers, helpless, trapped in this strange hairy place, lost. (pp. 35–36)

Eva is thus present not just as consciousness, but also through her memories of her past body, or what Lacan has termed "an autonomous body schema" which is inscribed at the level of the (human) unconscious (Grosz,

1990, p. 44). Eva's past body corresponds to "the space occupied by the imaginary body" which has been displaced by the "real" anatomy of the chimpanzee body (Grosz, 1990, p. 44). Third, Kelly also exists as a kind of archetypal or race memory, as the following passage suggests:

> Kelly was dead, gone, would never come back, but something was still there. Not a particular chimp with particular memories . . . but a chimp still, with older, deeper memories. (p. 39)

Both the past Eva and past Kelly denote aspects of self located more or less at the level of the unconscious. They are the trace of that which has been displaced by the other: the human body and the chimpanzee mind. This fracturing of the subject represents subjectivity as the site of loss and absence. Eva realizes that in order to function as a person she needs to become "whole," and to allow the two aspects of self, Kelly and Eva, to become one. Thus, the *quest* for self motif is inscribed in the narrative as a Lacanian desire for presence and completion.

The coexistence of both Eva's neurone memory and Kelly's primal memory deconstructs the rationalist opposition between the mind and the body upon which a conventional humanist privileging of the unique self is grounded, and of which Eva's desire for wholeness and for singularity is in part an expression. However, her project of attaining wholeness involves both a repression of her past self (the longing for her old body) and an acceptance of those aspects of her unconscious which are Kelly: "The only way to become whole was to pull the wall down, to let the other side back in . . . A new pattern, not Eva, not Kelly—both but one" (p. 39). Being "one" thus involves being both Eva and Kelly. In other words, subjectivity is constructed out of a heterogeneity of past and present voices and bodies, images and conceptions of selfhood.

The status of Eva's notions of both her chimp and human selves is made problematic by her human knowledge, human self-consciousness and her access to language. This can be seen in her analysis of the dream about trees, which recurs as chapter epigraphs and which is represented as a primal memory of Kelly's. It is not possible that it is Kelly's actual memory—that is, one based on experience—as she had no experience of trees or of forests (p. 26). As Kelly's mind has been "emptied out," this memory is associated metonymically with the body. Eva's human experiences and interpretative skills also mean that the dream changes through her own awareness of herself as a human mind: "she had thought about the dream, knowing everything the human Eva knew, so now as she reached and clambered and rested she carried the human knowledge with her" (p. 32). Moreover, the structure of the dream itself is changed through her ability to use the logical structures of language to represent it as a narrative and interpret it (pp. 32–33). Eva makes a distinction, though, between these later dreams and the first (unrepeatable) dream, "Kelly's dream" (p. 32), which constitutes an originary, prelinguistic moment transcendent of human language associated with Kelly and the body.

Eva's narrative represents the psychological and social development of a child and an individual's quest for a stable sense of identity. The novel is narrated in the third person. Focalization techniques align reader point of view with that of Eva, so that, through strategies of defamiliarization, the narrative discourse replicates the processes of recognition and misrecognition that this development involves. The novel opens with Eva in a hospital, waking from a coma. Her mother is represented from Eva's visual point of view:

> Dim white blur. A misty hovering shape, pale at the center, dark at the edges.
>
> "Darling?"
>
> With a flood of relief Eva dragged herself out of the nightmare. Mum's voice. The mist unblurred a little, and the shape was Mum's face. (p. 7)

The discourse represents the external world as it impacts upon Eva's consciousness. The image which she sees gradually comes into focus and makes sense through the association of visual shape and sound.

The opening chapters detail the social development of an individual, a process which involves Eva's recognition of others (her parents) and of the image of the other she sees in the mirror as an image of herself. The stages whereby she perceives and recognizes this image as an image of herself are explicable in the context of Lacan's account of the mirror phase. The following passages detail this:

> For an instant all she seemed to see was nightmare. Mess. A giant spider-web, broken and tangled on the pillows with the furry black body of the spider dead in the middle of it. And then the mess made sense.
>
> She closed her right eye and watched the brown left eye in the mirror close as she did so. The web—it wasn't broken—was tubes and sensor-wires connecting the machines around the bed to the pink-and-black thing in the centre. (pp. 18–19)

> The face in the mirror, surrounded by its tangle of tubes and
> cables, was still that of a stranger. Large pale ears stuck out either
> side through strong black hair; in the middle was the pinky-brown
> hummock of the face-parts, with the huge lips, the nothing nose and
> the forward-facing nostrils; the brown eyes were bright with thought.
> (p. 25)

Eva is initially unable to discriminate between the different components of
the image. Rather, she sees the figure and the background as a whole. The
emotive terms in which the image is described—"nightmare," "broken,"
"tangled," "dead"—and its alien otherness emphasizes her horror and in-
comprehension. Her recognition of the image as that of herself is represented
as a form of play, whereby she watches the image replicate her actions in a
manner which echoes Lacan's description of a child's playful response to its
visual image (Lacan, 1977a, pp. 1–2). The use of the definite article and of
objective and attitudinally neutral terms—"large," "huge," "face-parts,"
"hummock," "forward-facing"—in the second passage constructs the visual
image of the self as an objectified other. The image is seen as a bundle of
visual components—ears, hair, face-parts, lips—rather than as something
which represents a whole or which is meaningful. The relation between the
perceiver and the perceived is one of complete exteriority, analogous to
Bakhtin's stress on the radical outsidedness which characterizes the relation
between self and other. The image of the self is perceived from the position
of an other and it is understood as the image of an other.

In Lacan's account of the mirror phase, the child identifies with its
mirror image which it perceives as a stable and fixed whole, but it experiences itself as fragmented, partial and changeable. This is heightened in Eva's
recognition of herself and the specular image as "Eva" and as "Kelly." For
Eva, the relation between the self as perceiving subject and the self as object of perception is always ambivalent, and there is a split between chimp
and human selves, language and codes of behavior. Selfhood is for Eva a form
of otherness; her subjectivity is grounded in the internalizing of the dialogue
between self and other. Her perception of herself as chimp (not human) is
dependent upon her perceived differences from others, as in her observation
of the "oddness of people not having hair on their bodies" (p. 37), for example. At the same time, her recognition of herself as human (not chimp) is
grounded upon her perception of her own difference, or otherness (as chimp),
from her human self, as in "when she closed her eyes she saw in her mind
the pale slim fingers, helpless, trapped in this strange hairy place, lost" (p.
36). As the narrative progresses, her gradual entry into chimp society, her

abandonment of human society and her final discarding of the keyboard which she uses to communicate with humans (and hence her discarding of human language) shows her becoming more chimp than human. She remains different from the other chimps, but the approximation of wholeness that she achieves means the rejection of aspects of her humanness and of her human self. She is thus symbolically trapped in the mirror phase, in that she comes to identify with the specular image and to reject or repress the fragmentation of self she experiences as a subject within human society.

In both *Eva* and *Charlotte Sometimes*, the double is used to represent subjectivity as inherently split and to represent an internalized relation between self and other. The meanings and values attributed to this fragmentation and to the position of the other in the two novels correspond with the varying emphases placed on the intersubjective construction of subjectivity by Lacan and by Bakhtin. The representation of subjectivity in *Eva* closely parallels Lacan's account of the split subject, emphasizing Eva's radical sense of fragmentation and alienation. Although her human and chimp selves are not actively hostile (as they are for other chimp/human characters in the novel, Caesar/Stefan and Angel/Sasha), Eva's experience of subjectivity as either chimp or human is grounded in loss and a sense of displacement by the other. Eva is able to attain an approximate sense of wholeness only through repressing and rejecting one aspect of self (her humanness). The relation between self and other in *Charlotte Sometimes* is expressed in terms closer to a Bakhtinian account. For Charlotte, the construction of a sense of selfhood is contingent upon the other, and loss of the other entails an unavoidable loss of self. Thus, the novel expresses a more positive view of the necessity and value of intersubjective relationships. Both novels close with a powerful sense of loss and grief. In *Charlotte Sometimes*, this is represented in personal terms: Charlotte's grief for Clare and for her own personal loss is modernist in tone. The loss which informs the close of *Eva* is expressed more in cultural and social terms, focusing attention on the cultural implications of antihumanist discourses. These aspects of *Eva* will be taken up again in Chapter 4.

The following section on *Speaking to Miranda* anticipates some key ideas about the dialogic construction of the subject through language, which provide the focus of Chapter 4. One reason for examining this novel here, though, is that, like *Charlotte Sometimes* and *Eva,* it constructs a dialogue between essentialist and constructivist notions of selfhood. It does this by combining the motif of the double with two other narrative strategies: the quest for a sense of identity is represented parallel with a quest for the subjectivity of an other; and intertextual strategies are used to represent subjectivity as the intersection of a range of appropriated cultural discourses and texts.

The position of the other in *Speaking to Miranda* (Macdonald, 1990) is occupied by two characters: Miranda, Ruby's internalized double whom I discussed earlier; and Emma/Magda, Ruby's dead mother who deliberately effaced and concealed her past and origins. Ruby's quest for the identity of her mother entails a parallel reconstruction of her own identity. This reconstruction is articulated primarily through her appropriation of the image and the identity which her mother, Magda, had constructed for herself (that of Emma Blake) and her replication of her mother's actions. An underlying concern in the novel is with the interrelation between the possibility of inferring a subjectivity for an other, namely Emma/Magda, and of achieving a sense of oneself as subject and agent. Implicit here is a concern with the relation between notions of individual freedom and agency and the constraints put in place by social, cultural and linguistic structures within and through which subjectivity is made possible.

As in *Charlotte Sometimes* (Farmer, 1969/1992) and *Eva* (Dickinson, 1988), the relation between self and other in *Speaking to Miranda* is structured so as to represent a dialogic interplay between different concepts of subjectivity, that is, between the idea of essential selfhood and the idea of the subject as constructed within a series of provisional subject positions. The following passage, with which the novel closes, is part of a conversation between Ruby, the narrator, and Rob, her adoptive father. It crucially juxtaposes different representations of Emma/Magda as subject.

> Then he [Rob] goes on, lightly, "And, anyway, you know that I've never found another Emma.'
>
> I nod. It's what he believes. But a small voice from a corner of my head wonders if it's merely a romantic dream of his, an ideal love for ever lost to him. If she hadn't died, how long would they have stayed together? But then perhaps Emma/Magda was extraordinary. She's left a strong image with everyone who knew her, but the images are all in different shades, flickering, changing, and I wonder if I'll ever be able to distil the essential Magda.
>
> Before, at times like this, I might have asked Miranda about it. But I'm on my own now. (pp. 184–185)

The desire to "distil the essential Magda" and Ruby/Miranda's image of herself as alone assumes a concept of the selfhood of the other, and of one's self, as unique and essential. However, the description of Emma/Magda as a series of fragmentary images "flickering" and "changing" represents her on the one hand as fundamentally inaccessible and unknowable, as the transcendent signified which consistently resists the structures used to represent it, and on the other hand, as constructed within a range of contingent positions subject to the perceiving consciousness of others. These different conceptions of the subjectivity of the other define the parameters within which notions of selfhood are explored in the novel.

Both Rob and Ruby represent Emma/Magda as a projection of their own selves, in effect, as an image of their own desires. As Ruby observes, for Rob, Emma represents the object of desire, an "ideal love." Ruby's quest for her mother is concomitant with her search for her own identity. By putting into question the possibility of constructing a coherent idea of and knowing an other (Emma/Magda), the narrative also puts into question the possibility of constructing a coherent and stable self. Ruby's quest takes two forms in the narrative. The terms in which she attempts to narrate and represent both her mother and herself are informed by assumptions about individual subjectivity as unique and singular. For Ruby, Emma/Magda represents the desire for that significant other which might guarantee a secure and authentic sense of selfhood. However, her knowledge of Emma/Magda is mediated by the images and representations constructed by others and by Emma herself. In this way, there is a disjunction between the story as mystery or quest (especially as the narrator's unresolved desire to "distil the essential Magda") and the realization of this quest in the narrative discourse, wherein the quest for an individual identity (for either Emma/Magda or Ruby/Miranda) as stable and singular is persistently disclosed as only a deconstructive possibility.

While Emma's name and past are revealed, there are crucial "story" gaps in the novel: the mystery of her death; the identity of Ruby/Miranda's real father; the history of the original Emma Blake; the absence of Emma/Magda's parents; and certain unexplained periods of time. The main functions of these narrative gaps are to imply the construction and circumscribing of the character of Emma/Magda within social and discursive practices and to convey the sense of a past which is not objectively knowable and is always already implicated in problems of language, point of view, representation and narration. For Ruby, and for readers, Emma/Magda is present in the text only as a series of partial and fragmentary images, representations of the other as this other is constructed within the consciousnesses, memories and desires of other characters, in particular Rob and Sonny (Emma/Magda's husband), Ruby's two "father" figures. A range of narrative techniques, in particular intertextuality, combine to represent the selfhood of the other and of the self precisely as representation.

A major intertext for the novel, for both its story and its concerns with subjectivity, is John Fowles's *The French Lieutenant's Woman* (1969/1985). Ruby acquires and wears a black cloak which is a replica of that worn by Emma/Magda and by Sarah/Anna/Meryl Streep in the film version of Fowles's novel, and Magda's disappearance replicates that of Sarah. Furthermore, the account of Magda's behavior on the night of Miranda's conception, as it is given by Sonny and his mother,—"your trashy mother" (Macdonald, 1990, p. 151) who "put on her lipstick and her big black cloak and went to town" (p. 158)—reproduces a particular social construction of the whore, an image which compares with Sarah's representation of herself as "the French Lieutenant's Whore" (Fowles, 1985, p. 152). Rob's reference to Sarah (as she is represented in the film version of the novel) as, "What's-her-name standing on the pier with the stormy sea all around and the wind whipping at her black cape?" (p. 10) ironically draws attention to the way in which Sarah (and by implication, Emma) functions as an idea, as a textual sign. Compare Fowles's description of Sarah:

> Its clothes were black. The wind moved them, but the figure stood motionless, staring, staring out to sea, more like a living memorial to the drowned, a figure from myth, than any proper fragment of the petty provincial day. (1985, p. 9)

Sarah and Emma/Magda are imaged as the mysterious enigmatic female figure, and it is the image and the idea that they both represent that is significant, not the person or the name.

In Sonny's account of his relationship with Magda, Fowles's novel is again a major intertext. The following passages demonstrate this.

> "You know how your memory can play tricks. Your present brain can change the past. When we tell our own past stories, we can never be sure how much we're deceiving ourselves." (Macdonald, 1990, p. 156)
>
> You do not even think of your own past as quite real; you dress it up, you gild it or blacken it, censor it, tinker with it . . . fictionalize it in a word, and put it away on the shelf—your book, your romanced autobiography. We are all in flight from the real reality. That is a basic definition of Homo Sapiens. (Fowles, 1985, p. 87)

Though there is a downward shift in linguistic register, Sonny's comment about the relationship between the past, memory and narrative reconstruction is an overt quotation of Fowles's narrator. The implication that the past is never objectively knowable works ironically to foreground the limitations of Sonny's own account, wherein he represents Emma/Magda primarily as mother and wife. These limitations are inferred by Ruby—who is aware of Emma/Madga's other aspirations, namely, a swimming career—and her narration draws attention to the discontinuities in Sonny's account of Madga (as in, "It doesn't add up to me, doesn't make sense the way Sonny's telling it" (p. 158)). The effect of drawing attention to these discontinuities is to negatively imply a subjectivity for Emma/Magda as agent, that is, as occupying a subject position outside the cultural assumptions and narrative structures through which Sonny represents and thereby attempts to circumscribe her.

The novel illustrates the two forms of solipsism referred to earlier in my discussion of *Jacob Have I Loved* (Paterson, 1981/1983). Both Rob and Sonny represent the other, Emma/Magda, from within a solipsistic viewpoint, in that they are both unable to conceive of her as an agent or as another self independent of themselves. In the case of Rob, this applies also to his perception of Ruby, as is made clear early in the novel through his representation of himself and Ruby as "Summerton and Daughter," to which Ruby ironically—and subversively—replies, "Why not Summerton and Summerton . . . Or even Summerton and Blake?" (p. 3). Rob's refusal to speak of Emma denies both Emma and Ruby a subject position independent of himself, as does Sonny's representation of Magda as wife and mother. Ruby's solipsism conforms with the second type, in that she is unable to perceive her own selfhood as independent of the world and is thus unable to construct a sense of herself as an agent. Instead, as suggested in my earlier discussion of the double, Ruby's experience of subjectivity is grounded in an internal split between her sense of herself as subject (Ruby) and as agent (Miranda).

The relation between Miranda and Ruby can also be understood within the context of Vygotsky's (1962) study of language acquisition and child egocentric speech and Bakhtin's concept of the formation of subjectivity as determined by the struggle for hegemony between authoritative and internally persuasive discourses (1981, p. 345). Vygotsky observed that a child's egocentric speech is extremely sensitive to social factors, and he concluded that such speech is the direct internalization of speech which is socially and environmentally oriented. It is a "transitional stage in the evolution from vocal [social] to inner speech" (p. 19), the latter being the coincidence of thought and speech which constitutes the basic structure for adult thought (pp. 47–51). Similarly, Bakhtin sees the formation of subjectivity as integral with a person's appropriation and assimilation of the discourse of others through which an "internally persuasive discourse," or inner speech, is constructed. Miranda's presence in the novel is taken for granted by Ruby—the novel opens: "Miranda was always there . . ." (p. 1)—and her accounts of her early childhood relationship with Miranda clearly construct her as a kind of imaginary friend, symptomatic of a child's egocentrism. She is described as the "trace of a voice," and the title and references to Ruby "speaking to Miranda" imply Miranda's existence as the partly internalized speech of an other. The relation between Ruby and Miranda represents an internal dialogue between self and other. Insofar as this relation is antagonistic, it represents a struggle between competing social and ideological discourses, and the representation of Miranda as an author implies a connection between the other and the social structures which author the self. Miranda is also Ruby's link with the past, her identity, and her mother, so their relation also suggests the construction of subjectivity out of a play of appropriated discourses, voices, images, memories and desires. Miranda thus allegorically denotes the position and function of the Other in the Lacanian sense; she indicates the field of the other constituted by the subject's move into language and the social, as well as the internalized other.

The relation between Ruby and Miranda has two main functions: it represents Ruby's quest for subjectivity as a process through which she appropriates and assimilates the discourses of others; and, as I argued earlier, it suggests a correlation between the other, agency and authorship. These two functions are interrelated, in that those discourses which enable the construction of a subjectivity also constitute a constraint and limitation upon it. By representing subjectivity as constructed through the discourse of others, and by associating agency and authorship with the other (Miranda), Macdonald puts into question the possibility of constructing a subjectivity outside of the constraints put in place by others. Underlying this is a concern with the concept of individual freedom which, combined with the notion of authorship—as a position which both creates and limits the subject—has strong echoes of Fowles's similar concerns expressed in *The French Lieutenant's Woman* (1985, p. 86). These ideas are primarily explored through the representation of Emma/Magda. Magda's transgression of social conventions and deliberate self-effacement can be read as an analogy for existential freedom, wherein she is cast, like Fowles's Sarah, as the "free outcast." Her actions thus imply the limitations of conventional social and narrative structures to represent the subject, and hence the limitations of textuality itself. However, the desire to prove the existence of the self as independent of the structures that limit it leads to a loss of self, because those structures also define, represent and enable the construction of a subjectivity. Emma/Magda's act of self-effacement is thereby replicated by the discourse of the text, within which she is effectively denied an active subject position. In this way, she remains a present figure of absence within the novel, mystified and obscured by the representational discourses in and through which she is simultaneously constructed and made present.

The possibility of individual freedom is further explored through Ruby/Miranda's attempts to construct an empowered subject position from which to speak and act. Her wearing of the black cloak, her obsession with its authenticity and her replication of Magda's deliberate disappearance represent an attempt to appropriate the identity of Emma/Magda, the discourse of the other, and to thereby construct a subject position independent of that constructed for her by Rob. However, the representation of the other which she appropriates is precisely that which has been constructed by Rob and Sonny, and even by Emma/Magda herself, as is apparent in the following passage:

> I cradled the baby, wrapping the edge of my cloak around him because the coldness of the night was creeping in against the dwindling fire. I thought about Rob's story of my mother cradling me beside a beach fire the first night he met her . . . I noticed Sonny and his mother looking at me from the other side of the embers. Their faces were full of meaning as if they were seeing Magda sitting with Ruby. (Macdonald, 1990, pp. 175–176)

As the retrospective reference makes clear, this scene is a repetition of an earlier description of Emma by Rob (p. 48). In describing herself as a replication of Emma as she has been represented by Rob and as she is seen by Sonny and his mother, Ruby encodes herself as an image. As a representation of Ruby/Miranda/Magda/Emma, she simultaneously occupies all, but none, of these positions. Ruby/Miranda's appropriation of the image of the other then involves an effacement and loss of self, analogous to that of Emma/Madga herself. In this way, Ruby/Miranda's attempt to construct herself as agent, independent of Rob, merely involves her in a process of replication.

There is a disjunction between the "story" and the discourse, which is instrumental in constructing a rather ambivalent and unresolved ending. Ruby/Miranda's desire for a secure and authentic sense of selfhood is inscribed in the text at the level of "story"—the mystery/quest narrative of which she is the narrator. Retrospective narration throughout the novel stresses the sense in which Ruby/Miranda's personal history is one which is derived from places she has lived, rather than from a family she belongs to. So there is a strong sense in the ending of the novel of a recuperation of the past, of family, and of self in her return to her original home, which seems to offer some degree of "story" and thematic closure. Ruby's insistence, then, toward the end of the novel, during a conversation with Rob, on her name being "Miranda" is also an insistence upon a subject position independent of Rob's representation of her. In this way, it represents a crucial move for Ruby out of her own solipsism, toward the construction of a sense of selfhood as subject and as agent. However, the discourse undercuts this by persistently disclosing that such notions of selfhood are provisional and dialogical. Ruby/Miranda's assertion of an experience of oneness—"I'm on my own now" (p. 185)—ultimately depends upon the prior existence of the other, Miranda/Ruby, and upon her unrealized (and unrealizable) desire to "distil the essential Magda" (p. 185). The discursive and intertextual structures used to represent images of selfhood foreground the status of those images as representation, and as circumscribed within social, discursive and textual practice. One implication of this is that a subjectivity for either Emma/Magda or Ruby/Miranda as agent can only be posited negatively, that is, as a subject position outside of the cultural assumptions, social and narrative structures in and through which both characters have been represented. In other words, subject positions for Emma/Magda and Ruby/Miranda as agents can only be posited by reading against the text, and by implication, by reading against the cultural assumptions in and through which it is situated. To the extent, however, that the text represents this reading position as desire, then such a reading conflates agency with the humanist subject, as that source or agent of conscious meaning or action extrinsic to cultural and discursive structures and relationships.

Thematically, *Speaking to Miranda* hinges upon a dialogic interplay between the idea of an individual as subject and as agent, that is, between the individual as being constructed within a series of provisional subject positions, and as capable of conscious or directed meaning or action outside social discourses and practices. By leaving this dialogue ostensibly unresolved, the novel articulates the complexity of ways in which individual subjectivity is formed in dialogue with the social discourses, assumptions and practices which constitute a culture. In this way, the move out of solipsism would involve a rather tenuous series of empowering and disempowering relations between individual desire and the dominant social and ideological paradigms within which a person can speak and act.

This chapter has examined the representation of interpersonal relations and conceptions of subjectivity in narrative in the light of the theoretical approaches of Bakhtin and Lacan. In both, the emphasis on the importance of relations between self and other for the formation of subjectivity and the transition from solipsism to intersubjectivity are particularly relevant to the central concerns of adolescent fiction. Further, the use of the image of the mirror and the gaze to describe the relation between self and other in physical, cognitive and psychological terms provides us with useful interpretative paradigms for understanding how these images are used as narrative devices in fiction.

The novels discussed in this chapter use two narratives motifs—the quest and the double—to explore the formation and nature of subjectivity. Each novel also engages in a dialogue about essentialist and constructivist concepts of selfhood. Ideas of selfhood as either existing independently and prior to language and society on the one hand, or as utterly determined and inscribed by social practices and discourses on the other hand, are both put into question. The concepts of selfhood represented are given a varying emphasis and valuation, but there is a common tendency to avoid monologic closure. The endings of *Charlotte Sometimes*, *Eva* and *Jacob Have I Loved* implicitly suggest a negative evaluation of the personal and cultural implications of fragmentation and alienation and the value of positive intersubjective relations, but these novels do not present these concerns unproblematically. The novels discussed illustrate three strategies for destabilizing notions of essential selfhood: an emphasis of intersubjectivity, of fragmentation and alienation, and of social and linguistic influences on the subject. Farmer's stress in *Charlotte Sometimes* on the necessity and value of intersubjective relations is closest to a Bakhtinian approach, and ultimately asserts humanist sentiments regarding the value of the individual. Dickinson's stress on fragmentation and representation of social and psychological development of the subject corresponds closely with Lacan's theoretical frame.

The discussion has touched on some issues which anticipate my concerns in Chapter 4: the themes of temporal and cultural displacement (in *Charlotte Sometimes* and *Eva*), the use of the double to explore both the relations between subjectivity and agency and those between individuals and societies, the use of intertextual strategies to represent the circumscription of the subject within larger social discourses and practices, and the relations between subjectivity and language. These issues will be examined in the light of sociocultural influences on subjectivity, with particular attention to alienation and transgression.

1. Many of the ideas in this chapter—in particular, material on the double and Bakhtinian and Lacanian theories of subjectivity—have been extended in "Other Selves: Subjectivity and the Doppelgänger in Australian Fiction" (McCallum, 1996a).

2. Ivanov (1975) describes Lacan as "a beneficiary of Bakhtin's `semiotic re-interpretation' of Freud," (p. 314), but it should be noted that, as Emerson has argued, Ivanov makes very wide claims for Bakhtin's influence (Emerson, 1983, p. 255).

3. Vološinov (1976, p. 85) reformulates the distinction between the unconscious and consciousness as a distinction between two modalities of verbal consciousness: official consciousness, which refers to that which social and ideological structures allow one to express openly; and unofficial consciousness, which deviates from socially accepted norms (Stam, 1989, p. 4), and which represents "a struggle among various motives and voices within the conscious" (Emerson, 1983, p. 251). The first is to be correlated with authoritative discourses; and the second with the development of internally persuasive discourses.

4. Pirog (1989, p. 406) has also compared Lacan's and Bakhtin's use of the mirror.

5. An earlier version of the discussion in *Speaking to Miranda* in this chapter was published in *Papers: Explorations into Children's Literature* (*see* McCallum, 1992).

4 ALIENATION AND TRANSGRESSION AS FUNCTIONS OF THE SOCIAL CONSTRUCTION OF SUBJECTIVITY

I give myself verbal shape from another's point of view, ultimately from the point of view of the community to which I belong. A word is a bridge thrown between myself and another. If one end of the bridge depends on me, then the other depends on my addressee. A word is territory shared by both addresser and addressee, by the speaker and his interlocutor.

Vološinov, Marxism and the Philosophy of Language

The focus of this chapter is on the social dimension of the concepts of solipsism and alienation and their thematic function in representing subjectivity in children's fiction. If solipsism is the inability to perceive the otherness of the world and of others, then alienation is an extreme form of solipsism. In general terms, alienation in its various aspects—powerlessness, meaninglessness, normlessness, social isolation, self-estrangement and cultural estrangement—denotes the radical, perceived or actual, separation of the self from the social world, the inverse of intersubjectivity.[1] Solipsism can also be extended to refer to what Bakhtin calls "ethical" or "cultural" solipsism, so suggesting an analogy between the solipsistic construction of subjectivity and the construction of a social or cultural identity, an identity which is unable to perceive and comprehend another culture in its otherness. In this sense, the concept of solipsism has broader implications in the dialogue between humanist and cultural relativist ideologies, a dialogue generated, at least in part, by the ideological opposition that structuralist and poststructuralist theories pose to a humanist-based view of culture and meaning. Humanism and cultural relativism face a common challenge: that is, how to conceive of the strangeness of another culture without marginalizing that culture. Both approaches are liable to fall into one of two possible misconceptions of otherness. The strangeness of an other culture or self may be understood by postulating a center of meaning common to both the perceiving and perceived culture or subject which, by enabling the other to be conceived as a reflection of one's own culture or self, hence entails an assimilation of that other to one's own culture or self. Alternatively, the other's strangeness may be conceived from the position of the alienated subject as being so utterly different that it is rendered wholly incommensurable with one's own self or culture or any other culture (Gombrich, 1987, p. 687). In other words, both approaches operate through strategies of exclusion, whereby the other is marginalized, whether it be through a logic of identity or nonidentity.

In the novels discussed in this chapter, the thematic interrelations between individual solipsism and cultural or ethical solipsism are explored through three intersecting narrative motifs: displacement, alienation and transgression. Novels such as *Charlotte Sometimes* (Farmer, 1969/1992), *A Game of Dark* (Mayne, 1971), *The Language of Goldfish* (Oneal, 1980/ 1987), *Fade* (Cormier, 1988/1990), *Eva* (Dickinson, 1988), *Antar and the Eagles* (Mayne, 1989), *The Blue Chameleon* (Scholes, 1989) and *Speaking to Miranda* (Macdonald, 1990) all depict characters whose solipsism is represented as a form of cultural, social, temporal or psychological displacement, alienation or marginalization. Characters are displaced from their families or their pasts, or from familiar social, cultural or temporal surroundings. They are thereby situated within alienated subject positions: either as the cultural other within an alien society (as in *Antar and the Eagles*, *The Blue Chameleon* or *Eva*); and/or as the socially marginal other in relation to their own society (as in *The Language of Goldfish*, *Fade*, *A Game of Dark*, *Speaking to Miranda* or *Eva*). In these last four novels, characters are alienated through their transgression of received social or cultural codes or conventions. Alienation and transgression are categories of personal experience and action, both of which are generated via the social construction of subjectivity. Both designate positions of otherness, or outsidedness, in relation to cultural or social structures from which those structures can be represented and examined. Robert Cormier's novels of the 1970s and 1980s marked the emergence of the alienated subject in American teenage fiction, a trend which has more recently begun to surface in Australia in novels by John Marsden (such as *Checkers*, 1996 or *Dear Miffy*, 1997), Sonya Hartnett (such as *Sleeping Dogs*, 1995) and Gary Crew (*Strange Objects*, 1990).

There are three main aspects of these narrative strategies that are of interest. First, to displace a character out of his/her familiar surroundings can destabilize his/her sense of identity and hence undermine essentialist notions of selfhood, though it can also affirm these concepts. Second, such displacement can offer ways to explore linguistic and sociocultural influences on cognition and the formation of subjectivity, especially where a character is depicted as learning, decoding and interpreting alien social codes and discourses. Third, representations of transgressive modes of behavior or being in fiction can construct interpretative positions from which to examine and interrogate the limitations that the dominant cultural and social discourses and practices of a given society or culture place on experience, action and subjectivity.

There has been a considerable amount of theoretical and philosophical writing about the sociocultural influences on subjectivity and its construction through language. These discussions usually hinge on the relationships between social structures and subjectivity, language and consciousness. The following section will examine some key concepts arising of out these debates and their implications for representation of subjectivity in narrative, with particular reference to the work of Bakhtin and Vološinov on the relationship between language acquisition and subject formation. The latter is particularly pertinent to my discussion of *Antar and the Eagles* (Mayne, 1989), *The Blue Chameleon* (Scholes, 1989) and *Speaking to Miranda* (Macdonald, 1990). (Some of these ideas have been touched on in Chapter 3, in my discussion of *Speaking to Miranda,* and are explicated more fully here.)

The Construction of Subjectivity in Language and Society

A common concern with the relation between language, society and the formation of subjectivity underlies the approaches of Bakhtin and Vološinov and those of structuralist and poststructuralist theorists to the problem of subjectivity. Saussure (1959), Vygotsky (1962), Bakhtin (1981) and Vološinov (1986) have all stressed the interrelationship between thought, language and society. For Saussure and Vološinov, thought is virtually impossible outside language, and individual consciousness is thus inextricably bound up with the acquisition of language (e.g., *see* Saussure, p. 65; Vološinov, pp. 11–15). Vološinov's work stresses the implications of this for the formation of subjectivity within and through language which, in Saussurian terms, is a social fact (*see* Saussure, pp. 8–9). For Vološinov, subjectivity is formed in dialogue with the discursive practices of the society which a person inhabits: "I give myself verbal shape from another's point of view, ultimately, from the point of view of the community to which I belong" (Vološinov, 1986, p. 86). As I commented in Chapter 3, neither Vološinov nor Bakhtin expound a theory of the unconscious, the existence of which would presuppose concepts of self or of subjective experience prior to their expression in language. According to Vološinov (1986), "there is no such thing as experience outside of [its] embodiment in signs" (p. 85). Subjectivity is explicable "solely in terms of the social factors that shape the concrete life of the individual in the conditions of his social environment" (pp. 25–26). This means that any expression or articulation of an experience, including "self-experience," is also social because it is articulated in a language which is always already socially and ideologically oriented (pp. 89–90). Furthermore, essentialist theories of subjectivity—or what Vološinov terms "individualist subjectivism"—which conceive of the self as radically separate from language and from social practice, are in fact also social and ideological constructs. This also implies that narrative representations of subjectivity have a social and ideological basis. These ideas are particularly pertinent to novels which assert essentialist concepts of selfhood.

In "Discourse and the Novel" (1981), Bakhtin described the formation of subjectivity as a process whereby a person selectively appropriates and assimilates the ideological discourses of others (pp. 341–342). This occurs within a heteroglottic social and linguistic context. Within any one society, various socially typifying languages coexist and intersect, representing different socio-ideological groups and interests. These languages, or speech genres, are "specific points of view on the world in words." That is, they are ideologically inscribed discursive positions which imply enunciative positions for speakers (pp. 290–291). The multiplicity of ideological discourses which constitute a society correspond to a multiplicity of subject positions occupied by social groups and persons. For Bakhtin, then, the formation of subjectivity is tied up with the appropriation of social and ideological discourses with which to speak and, hence, a subject position from which to speak.

There are similarities between Bakhtin's position and those of Althusser and Lacan. Bakhtin's conception of the sociolinguistic construction of subjectivity is comparable with Althusser's thesis that individuals are "interpellated"; that is, they are called into position as "subjects" by social discourses and ideologies (Althusser, 1971, pp. 160–165). Similarly, Lacan's thesis is that the subject is formed via entry into the symbolic order (*see* Grosz, 1990). The point at which these three part company, however, is where they locate power in the configuration of individual, subject and social practice. As Smith (1988) has shown, Althusser's view that "subjectivity is constructed through ideological intervention" conceives only of a "dominated subjectivity" which is passively constructed within the constraints of social practice (p. 17). It leaves no room for either agency or resistance, nor for a conception of a person as occupying multiple or contradictory subject positions. Stam (1989) has made a similar suggestion that Lacanian "entry into the symbolic order entails submission to a pregiven place and role" wherein discourse "speaks the subject" (p. 54). For Bakhtin

(1981), language "lies on the borderline between oneself and the other" and is always "someone else's" (p. 293), but it is not a homogeneous whole (or *langue*) which pre-exists the subject. "One's own discourse" is formed through the processes of appropriation and assimilation of the discourses of others and the construction of a subject position. Language is a heteroglottic multiplicity of discourses that exist in dialogue with the subjects that appropriate and speak them. Thus, Bakhtin's dialogic approach to subjectivity, language and society allows that individuals as subjects "simultaneously constitute and are constituted by conflictual social and cultural institutions and contexts" (Stam, 1989, p. 54). They are simultaneously constrained and empowered by language, rather than simply constructed within it.

The close interrelation between language, society and consciousness in Bakhtin's work suggests an analogy between the heteroglottic structuring of society on the one hand, in which various intersecting and often conflictual socially stratified languages coexist, and the formation of subjectivity as the product of an intense struggle for hegemony among various alien ideological discourses and voices on the other hand (1981, p. 346). He distinguishes between two forms of ideological discourse: authoritative discourse and internally persuasive discourse (pp. 341–348). Authoritative discourses, such as political, religious or moral discourses, are binding and unassimilable. They demand unconditional acknowledgment. Internally persuasive discourse is discourse which "is denied all privilege, backed up by no authority" and which "is frequently not even acknowledged by society" (p. 342). The development of an individual consciousness is determined by the struggle and dialogic interrelationships between these two categories of ideological discourse (p. 345). Initially, an individual consciousness cannot "separate itself" from the surrounding ideological discourses, but once "thought begins to work in an independent, experimenting and discriminating way" there "occurs a separation between internally persuasive discourse and authoritarian enforced discourse" (p. 345). Internally persuasive discourse is formed through the "process of distinguishing between one's own and another's discourse, between one's own and an other's thought" and is linked with the development of "one's own discourse" or inner speech, which is gradually wrought out of others' words which have been acknowledged and assimilated (p. 345).

Bakhtin's and Vološinov's ideas about the sociolinguistic construction of subjectivity are developed within the context of their concerns with the discourses of narrative fiction, and have a range of implications relevant to representations of subjectivity in adolescent fiction. First, Vološinov's work foregrounds the social and ideological basis of language and of thought and, thus, of concepts, theories and narrative representations of selfhood. This applies particularly to approaches which would attempt to essentialize the self and locate selfhood outside language and social structures. Second, Bakhtin's view of language and society as heteroglottic implies that individual subjectivity, representations of subjectivity and the novel itself are also heteroglottic. Characters, like Bakhtinian and Lacanian "subjects," are constituted by and within language, and can be understood in similar terms. That is, they are constituted by a range of intersecting social and ideological discourses and they occupy discrete subject positions which are discursively and ideologically situated within a represented social world.[2] Third, Bakhtin's ideas about language acquisition are pertinent to the analysis of novels which represent the movement out of solipsism as taking place within a context which is culturally and/or linguistically alien and which depict characters appropriating and assimilating the discourses of others—for instance, *A Game of Dark* (Mayne, 1971), *Antar and the Eagles* (Mayne, 1989) and *The Blue Chameleon* (Scholes, 1989). Finally, to the extent that narrative, society and subjectivity are each discursively structured, the represented relations between characters and social settings are also indicative of ideological assumptions about the relations between individual subjects and social and discursive practices. These relations hinge on the degree to which the subject is represented as empowered or disempowered by the social and linguistic structures through which it is constituted, and thus have implications for the possibilities of agency, resistance and transgression.

One way in which the interrelations between individuals, subjectivity, society and language are explored in narrative is through the social, temporal, cultural or psychological displacement and alienation of characters. Characters are removed from their familiar surroundings and placed in an environment which is physically, culturally or linguistically alien. This displacement can also be psychological, that is, characters, while not physically displaced, experience a state of alienation from their social surroundings. To the extent that concepts of selfhood are dependent upon and constructed in relation to social, linguistic and historical contexts, this displacement of a character can destabilize and place in question their concepts of personal identity, though it can also be used to assert the idea of an essential self which transcends social or cultural structures. The configuration of interrelations between the subject and society are important. There are two main possibilities. First, the selfhood of a character can be represented as radically separate from, or transcendent of, the social context into which or from which this character is displaced. In *Charlotte Sometimes* (Farmer, 1969/1992) and *The Blue Chameleon* (Scholes,

1989), the prior selfhood of characters is essentialized and thus represented as transcendent of the social structures through which characters are repositioned. Second, selfhood can be represented as constructed and provisional. Characters can be represented as more or less actively involved in, and thereby empowered by, the processes through which they are positioned and constructed, as in *Antar and the Eagles* (Mayne, 1989). Antar is represented as actively constructing a sense of self out of the discourses and texts of the culture into which he has been displaced. In other novels, characters are represented as more passively constructed and thus constrained within and disempowered by the social contexts in which they are positioned. In *Fade* (Cormier, 1988/1990), the experience of displacement and alienation is ultimately disempowering, while in novels such as *The Language of Goldfish* (Oneal, 1980/1987), *Eva* (Dickinson, 1988) and *Speaking to Miranda* (Macdonald, 1990) the psychological, cultural and social alienation of characters represents the relations between the subject and society as involving degrees of empowerment and disempowerment.

CULTURAL DISPLACEMENT AND ALIENATION

Two novels which use the cultural displacement of characters to explore the formation of subjectivity within an alien social and linguistic context are Mayne's *Antar and the Eagles* (1989) and Scholes's *The Blue Chameleon* (1989). In both novels the language, social codes and conventions of the societies into which characters are displaced are entirely different from their own. In *The Blue Chameleon* Beni Ish-Mahel, a member of a nomadic African clan in the Sahara, is separated from his tribe, from his twin brother Ziad and from his cultural traditions. He is sent to live with his Arabic-speaking uncle in Melbourne, from where he stows away on an Australian ship bound for Antarctica. In *Antar and the Eagles,* Antar climbs to the spire of the church on which his father is working, and is carried away by mountain eagles who want him to perform a quest for them: to regain a stolen egg which will hatch into their next Great Eagle. Though Beni in *The Blue Chameleon* is eventually able to communicate with his Australian companion Chris, he only partially assimilates the alien culture. By comparison, Antar is placed in a nest, where he is fed, cared for and resocialized according to the cultural codes of eagle society to the point that when he returns to human society he has begun thinking of himself as an "eagle." Whereas Antar is virtually resocialised and almost entirely assimilates eagle-culture, Beni retains much of his past traditions, and, in his attempts to interpret events and people, he transposes the codes and conventions of African nomadic culture onto the alien (Australian) culture.

Both Beni and Antar are physically and emotionally isolated from their own culture and alienated within the new alien culture. However, the displacement and alienation each experience functions quite differently in the two novels. Whereas Antar's subjectivity is represented as provisional, and subject to the social discourses and structures within which he is displaced and resocialised, Beni's subjectivity is represented as transcendent of the alien social context. Ultimately, Mayne uses displacement in *Antar and the Eagles* to assert a cultural relativist viewpoint, wherein cultures and the meanings generated within different cultures are radically different. In *The Blue Chameleon,* Scholes uses displacement to assert a logocentric view of culture and meaning, which posits the existence of a transcendent signified which would assimilate and obscure cultural difference.

Antar and the Eagles is an allegory of the socialization of a child within a foreign culture. The opening chapters stress Antar's father's plans for him: he is to go to school to learn "reading, writing and figuring" (p. 8), and so will enter the literate community. Schooling marks a crucial stage in a child's entry into the symbolic order; it is significant, then, that Antar is stolen by the eagles the day before he is to start school, before he has fully learned the social and discursive codes of his own culture. The novel is also a parody of socialization, and to this purpose it replays crucial events. His time in the eagle's nest replicates the past six years: the eagles initially treat him as completely dependent on them, like the young eagles with whom he shares the nest. In eagle society, Antar symbolically moves to adolescence and adulthood. He learns the language and conventions of eagle society, "grows" wings, learns to fly and literally (and metaphorically) leaves the nest. He is sent on a quest to regain the egg which will hatch into the new Great Eagle, and when he returns and loses the egg on the way, he is symbolically stripped of his feathers, alienated from eagle society and sent into the earth to retrieve the egg.[3] When he finally returns with the newly hatched Great Eagle, Antar is reassimilated as an adult. He becomes the egg mother/father to the new great eagle, settles down to the task of rearing a family and makes a new set of wings from the feathers of the old Great Eagle. The latter part of the novel is a parody of conventional gender-typed child-rearing practices in human society, with Antar involved in the "nestkeeping" (p. 189). Antar's eagle friend, Garak, teaches the young bird, while Antar sits close with his sewing, listening and learning and sometimes having "to put everything down and peck with his hand at the young bird to make it listen" (p. 191). Antar's socialization into eagle society also involves a measure of resistance in that he is not passively assimilated by this society. His use of fire and his insistence on cooking his food and not eating the kitten represent instances of resistance to the authoritative social codes of eagle society.

Whereas Antar's subjectivity is represented as almost entirely constructed within the other society, the formation of subjectivity in *The Blue Chameleon* is represented as taking place not so much within the discourses and practices of the foreign culture as on their margins. Beni's misreading of the other culture is much more extensive and sustained than that of Antar, and his enculturation into and comprehension of the alien culture is more limited. Certainly, Beni begins to move out of his solipsistic state through his relationship with Chris, an Australian scientist, but the narrative tends toward the assertion of essentialist concepts of self and meaning which would transcend social structures and cultural differences. Beni's story represents three interrelated quests: for Ziad (his twin brother, who is thought to be dead for most of novel), for a sense of his own selfhood as separate and distinct from Ziad, and for the purpose and meaning of his journey to Melbourne and to Antarctica. Ultimately, these three quests come together to construct a powerfully logocentric and teleological metanarrative: Beni's search for subjectivity and meaning is also a quest for the transcendent signified (God) which would guarantee authenticity of self and of meaning.

Underlying Beni's quest for a sense of subjectivity separate from that of Ziad is a concern with the uniqueness of the individual and the essentiality of the self. As I have argued elsewhere, the scene in which Beni sees his reflection in a mirror for the first time parallels and reverses Lacan's descriptions of the mirror phase (McCallum, 1996a). Beni's approach to the mirror phase is complicated by the fact that Ziad is his identical twin brother, and hence the image of himself in the mirror is also the image of an actual other. In an attempt to differentiate his own image from that of Ziad, and hence distinguish between self and other, he cuts his face, telling himself that "Ziad is dead. You are Beni . . . *This is your mark . . . Beni Ish-Mahel*" (p. 17). Thus, in a move which reverses Lacan's conceptualization of the mirror phase, Beni effaces rather than internalizes the other, so that the image in the mirror coincides with the self and the subject is essentialized rather than fractured. The desire for an essential and authentic self is further explicated through the repetition and shifting meaning of the phrase, "You've got to be your own black dog." The phrase signifies Beni's isolation from his family, culture and past (p. 84), his alienation from both his own culture and the other culture in which he has been placed (p. 111) and his need to be his own person separate from Ziad and to have a sense of his own place within a larger order of things (p. 127).

A crucial aspect of Beni's quest for subjectivity is his need to construct a narrative which would make sense of the events occurring around him and which involve him—namely, the purpose and meaning of his journey to Australia and to Antarctica. He does this by making causal links between apparently contiguous events and people and by using the stories and religious beliefs of his own culture to interpret events in the alien culture. Furthermore, the narrative that he thereby constructs is one in which he and Ziad have a central role. For example, in the opening of the novel, Beni is performing a ritual of hanging gifts upon a tree when he inadvertently witnesses a car accident and helps one of the victims. He later refers to the blood from the cut he makes to his chin to differentiate himself from Ziad as "the omen of blood that came from the Tree" (p. 17), thereby linking it with the blood on his clothes and hands from the accident (p. 5) and with the bloodstain on the Blue Chameleon, Ziad's talisman which he now carries with him (p. 16). He thus constructs a series of causal and semantic connections between events (the accident, and his own action of cutting his chin) and objects (the Tree, the Blue Chameleon) which are only spatially and temporally linked and, ultimately, these connections form a larger order of meaning. The discursive register of Beni's thoughts also defamiliarizes and mythicizes events and objects (as in "the omen of blood that came from the Tree," for example) and implies that Beni is interpreting events occurring in Australia (and later on the boat to Antarctica) through the interpretative schemas of his own culture, thereby assimilating the other culture to his own. The discourses of Beni's own culture function, in Bakhtinian terms, as "authoritative discourses." This process is replicated by the larger macronarrative structures of the novel, wherein the mythic narratives of Beni's culture construct a metanarrative that determines the meanings of events which have occurred in Antarctica.

Both *The Blue Chameleon* and *Antar and the Eagles* are narrated in the third person and extensively focalized by characters whose viewpoints are limited. Beni and Antar are both linguistically alienated from the cultures into which they are placed, and this draws attention to the cultural specificity of the meanings constructed through language. In both novels, characters initially misinterpret situations because of their lack of cultural and linguistic knowledge. For example, when Antar first arrives at the eagles' nest, he sees the young eagles as "a group of hobgoblins with open mouths" and assumes that he is about to be eaten (p. 48), perhaps an ironic comment on the typical assumptions of the "civilized" culture about the "barbaric" other. Similarly, Beni misinterprets aspects of Australian society through his use of inappropriate interpretative codes, such as his assumption that the men on the ship watch violent videos in order to learn from them (p. 60). However, Mayne and

Scholes differ radically in their treatment of the relations between linguistic and semiotic signs and the things in the world to which these signs refer, and this has implications for the underlying assumptions in the two novels about meaning, subjectivity and cultural difference. Whereas Mayne constantly plays on the gap between signs and things, thereby emphasizing cultural difference, Scholes closes off the gap between signs and things through the assertion of abstract meanings which transcend cultural difference.

In *Antar and the Eagles*, Antar's learning of eagle-language follows the pattern of a child's learning. He successively acquires more complex speech functions within specific social contexts. The following passage occurs not long after Antar has been placed in the nest:

> They began to squabble and peck and climb on one another to get to the warmest places. When they pecked Antar he hit back with his fists. Under the down they were rigid with bone. He did not hurt them, and they did not make a fuss. Pecking and squawking were their ways of communicating. Antar joined in the squawking too, without knowing what the sounds meant. (p. 54)

Antar acquires instrumental speech functions and behavioral codes before informational or semantic functions. That is, he uses language to achieve material needs and to establish relationships with others before being able to construct and communicate independent meanings. Through Garak, Antar begins to acquire more complex speech functions, and the interactional function of language is emphasized, as in the following passage:

> Together they walked to the next tumble of water. Together they stood by it and discussed it. Neither of them knew what the other said, but they agreed, even if they did not know what that was either. (p. 65)

It does not matter that Antar and Garak do not understand each other; the exchange is important for establishing a relationship and a context in which learning can occur. Antar begins to acquire the semantic functions of eagle speech through learning the names for things (p. 66), and idiomatic meanings, as in the Great Eagle's use of the word "eat" in phrases like "I cannot eat that" (p. 92), "I wished to eat his sense for myself" (p. 94) and "I eat your understanding" (p. 98). The text also draws attention to the distinction between linguistic competence and performance, whereby Antar is able to interpret the wing signals of other birds—"a separate language of its own" (p. 86)—but is literally unable to "speak" this "language."

Antar's acquisition of eagle-language is also represented as occurring simultaneously with his learning of eagle cultural codes and conventions and historical narratives. Meanings are always, to some extent, culturally constructed, and the learning of another language entails learning the cultural codes through which a linguistic community represents and makes sense of the world. This is foregrounded, for example, in Garak's description of the human town as a "nesting ground." Furthermore, the same signifier "nest" is used to refer to a house, a cupboard and a basket (p. 96). Garak has no names for the things which do not exist in eagle society. Similarly, the only words the eagles have for the kitten are "food" or "snack," although they do come to understand that the kitten has a different significance for Antar.

By constantly playing on the gaps between signs and things, the discourse foregrounds the cultural differences between the kinds of meanings that are constructed in the two represented cultures. Although Antar does initially misread eagle culture, he acquires and gains competence in the eagle language, social behavior and cultural history and conventions. Likewise, the eagles, in particular Garak, also learn about aspects of human society. In this way, the novel represents a fairly positive view of the possibilities of cultural exchange, without assimilating one culture to the other and without representing one society as more culturally impoverished than the other— thus avoiding the two extremes of cultural solipsism. Furthermore, Mayne's representation of Antar's maturation and formation of friendships within eagle society implies a connection between the formation of individual intersubjectivity and nonsolipsistic forms of cultural exchange and interaction. An important aspect of Antar's socialization in eagle society is his recognition and understanding of otherness as a form of difference, rather than as an opposition. At first Antar is unable to distinguish between the eagles, but he gradually learns how to perceive their differences, "mostly where their beaks joined the heads" (p. 57). This is a two-way process, and Garak also comes to recognize Antar's difference, as is implicit in Garak's reaction when he pecks Antar too hard:

> The eagle spread its wings, bowed its head, and stood before him ashamed, with eyes closed. It was meant not to hurt him. Antar knew that it had merely treated him like another eagle. Now it cowered before him as if he were the king. (p. 64)

The idea that subjectivity exists within interrelationships with others is also conveyed in Garak's comment to Antar, "I have told you so much that if you die I shall lose it all" (p. 144), and Antar's understanding that "Garak had taught him to fly, had taught him another language, and had given Antar so much of his self that Antar could not go away with it and give nothing in return" (p. 176).

Mayne's novel stresses the differences between cultures. Although Antar is able to learn about and gain some understanding of Eagle society, this is made possible only through his actual entry into this society. He assimilates much of the eagle culture, and thus becomes alienated from his own culture: "Even thoughts of that [home] became faint in his mind, because he could not remember anything about home. What was happening now was what filled his mind; and he did not know where home was" (p. 56). Though he still has alien status within eagle society, he clearly thinks of himself more as "eagle" than as "human" when he arrives in the human town and automatically gives chase to a mouse (p. 118) and straightens his feathers (p. 114). Antar's capture in the town enacts a further social displacement and he perceives human society from the position of an outsider: he was "mostly furious because these things were happening to an eagle and he was cross too because they were happening to him" (p. 124).

Whereas *Antar and the Eagles* implies a connection between concepts of cultural and individual intersubjectivity, the narrative strategies used in *The Blue Chameleon* inadvertently affirm an inverse analogy between individual and cultural solipsism. This occurs through the combination of two interrelated strategies: the use of a solipsistic character focalizer who (mis)interprets the textual world by confusing signs with things; and the construction of a metanarrative which, by assuming a logocentric relationship between signs and things, perpetuates and authorizes those misinterpretations. In this way, the problem of cultural difference is resolved through positing transcendent meanings. This, however, entails the assimilation of one culture to the other, and thereby suggests an analogy between Beni's solipsism and cultural solipsism.

Unlike Antar, Beni's acquisition of and competence in the linguistic and cultural codes of the other culture is only ever partial and fragmentary. Beni uses two interpretative strategies to make sense of the alien culture into which he has been displaced. First, he transposes the fragmentary knowledge of Australian culture that he has acquired from watching television onto the actual world. For example, his interpretation of the car accident with which the novel opens presupposes a direct correspondence between the actual physical world and the textual discourses (such as television) through which that world is represented and mediated. In other words, he confuses things and events in the world with the signs used to represent them. Although Beni's confusion of signs and things in this episode is clearly represented as a misreading, the same confusion is replicated in the second strategy that he uses to interpret events and in the narrative structures through which the novel achieves closure.

Second, he transposes the cultural codes and conventions of his own culture onto that into which he has been displaced. This strategy also assumes a direct correspondence between signs and things, but whereas this assumption leads to a misreading in relation to the discourses of the other culture, it enables him to produce a textually valid reading when he uses the discourses of his own culture which are thereby attributed with a mythic and transcendent status. This can be seen in the representation and function of the Dome in the text. The Dome is a glass snowstorm which was found with Goma, Beni and Ziad's mother, who came to the clan as a baby. The description of the Dome (pp. 37–38) is part of a textual game. For most readers, a snowstorm would be a familiar and easily recognizable object, but the discourse obscures and mystifies it through the use of the unfamiliar name ("the Dome"), capitalization and archaic syntax (as in "The Dome with the sign of red lines crossing" or the Red Cross insignia). These same strategies are used in representing the narratives and discourses of Beni's culture, whereby stories and rituals are inscribed with a mythic status, or what Scutter (1991, p. 33) has referred to as a purity or "thisness." For the clanspeople, the snowstorm is a "sign" or text, which has significance for the clan itself, though its specific meaning is ambiguous. Their attempts to make sense of it and assimilate its otherness depend on their ability to make links between it and their own culture—for example, the "roofs" of the buildings inside it are "shaped like tents" and the "snowflakes" like "manna from heaven." In this way, the snowstorm is appropriated and assimilated into their narratives according to the signifying systems of their own culture, and as a mysterious (but significant) sign, it is inscribed with abstract and transcendent meanings intrinsic to their overtly teleological narratives.

This assimilative process is analogous with Beni's interpretative approach to the Antarctic and to Australian culture. He uses objects, such as the Dome and the Blue Chameleon, as well as stories, such as the story of the clan and of Ziad and himself, to reconstruct micrographic images of a plant and to find his way around a camp in the Antarctic. Furthermore, insofar as these interpretations are textually valid, the Dome, the Blue Chameleon and the stories of his culture come to function as transcendent signifiers which imply a direct correspondence between signs and things and which attribute meaning to Beni's journey and the world that he encounters. Ultimately, this journey is part of a grand plan to revegetate the desert and save the clan. However, to the extent that meaning and truth are correlated with the discourses and interpretative practices of Beni's culture, the process whereby this grand narrative operates is culturally solipsistic. Radical differences between Australian and African nomadic cultures are resolved by an evocation of meanings which transcend those differences but which also inadvertently assimilate and efface the "otherness" of the other (Australian) culture. Beni's journey and the events in the Antarctic are explicable only within the context of his cultural and religious tradition.

Beni's initial misinterpretations of Australian society imply a cultural relativist position: the two cultures, their traditions, meanings and values, are seen as radically different and, hence, not assimilable. Mayne's position in the beginning of *Antar and the Eagles* corresponds with this viewpoint. Further, in both novels cultural differences are ameliorated through the development of intersubjectivity. The move out of solipsism for both Antar and Beni is facilitated by their relationships with others. However, the two novels differ radically in how cultural differences are understood and addressed, and in the implications that this has for an understanding of the relation between subjectivity and society. In *The Blue Chameleon,* cultural differences are resolved monologically by postulating a center of meaning (for which the Dome is metonymic) common to both cultures which transcends the differences between them and which thereby essentializes meaning and subjectivity. In *Antar and the Eagles,* intersubjectivity promotes understanding and learning, and the relation between Antar and the eagles is represented as one of cultural exchange, rather than replication or assimilation. Thus, whereas subjectivity is represented in *Antar and the Eagles* as provisional and subject to the social discourses and structures within which Antar is resocialized, subjectivity in *The Blue Chameleon* is represented as transcendent of these kinds of social and cultural influences.

In this section, I have been looking at the uses of cultural displacement to explore the formation of subjectivity within an alien social and linguistic context and analogies between forms of individual and cultural solipsism. These analogies will be examined further in historical genres in Chapters 6 and 8. The next section of this chapter examines the representation of psychological alienation.

PSYCHOLOGICAL ALIENATION AND DISPLACEMENT

The Language of Goldfish (Oneal, 1980/1987) and *Fade* (Cormier, 1988/ 1990) are two novels which depict characters whose extreme solipsism takes the form of psychological and social alienation. In *Fade*, a fantasy novel, the consequences of extreme alienation and solipsism are explored through the use of doubles and the fantastic motif of being able to make oneself invisible, or able to "fade." *The Language of Goldfish* is a realist novel about a young girl, Carrie, whose emotional and personal maturation is arrested as she approaches puberty, resulting in a progressive psychological and social alienation.

Fade is a multistranded fantasy novel with two temporal settings. The primary narrative is set in the 1930s and narrated by thirteen-year-old Paul Moreaux—it emerges that Paul's narrative is the unpublished manuscript of author Paul Roget. The latter part of the novel switches between narration by Susan, Paul Roget's niece (in the 1980s) and the second part of Roget's manuscript, which is set in the 1960s and which alternates between first person narration by Paul Moreaux (now a famous author, like Roget) and third person narration focalized by Ozzie, his nephew, who was given up for adoption at birth. The narrative structure of *The Language of Goldfish* is less complex. It is narrated in the third person and focalized by Carrie. However, the discourse slips frequently into free direct discourse, using truncated syntax and minimal verbs so as to represent Carrie's frequently chaotic thoughts and (mis)perceptions of the world around her.

Fade tells the story of how at the age of thirteen, Paul Moreaux develops an ability to "fade," or become invisible, an inherited skill which is passed on through his family from an uncle to a nephew. Paul's uncle, Adelard, arrives the summer that Paul's ability begins to manifest itself. The "fade" comes to hold metaphoric significance in the novel. Paul initially does not comprehend Adelard's ambivalence about his ability to "fade," but as he grows up he comes to understand that it is a burden, rather than a gift. It is described in terms evocative of the Lacanian notion of desire: "The experience of the fade was always disappointing, however. The fade did not provide the freedom it promised" (1990, p. 78). "Fading" places a strain on him physically and emotionally, and in enabling him to become invisible, he learns other people's secrets—secrets which he would prefer not to know. In this way, the fade motif discloses the doubleness of the world and the people around him: beneath the surface of appearances is a world which is sordid, corrupt and perverse. This knowledge becomes a burden for Paul. He inadvertently witnesses sexual acts, which he finds perverse—such as Mr. Dondier's relationship with a thirteen-year-old girl and an incestuous relationship between his friend, Emerson, and sister, Page, whom Paul secretly desires. The knowledge that he gains by fading leads him to feel increasingly separate from the world and other people (pp. 69, 78 and 79). His difference is personally debilitating because it prevents him from forming intersubjective relationships with others and leads to a solipsistic alienation in which the self is perceived as radically separate from the world.

The Language of Goldfish tells the story of thirteen-year-old Carrie, who, faced with the prospect of growing up, retreats from the world around her and from adolescence. She begins to experience strange "dizzy spells" (1987, p. 11) during which she sees a kaleidoscope of colors and hears a roaring noise, and becomes disoriented and loses track of time. During one of these episodes, she takes a drug overdose. The novel chronicles the onset and development of Carrie's psychological disorder and her recovery after leaving the hospital. However, the discourse is almost entirely focalized by Carrie, which means that interpretations of her condition are determined largely by her limited capacity to understand and articulate what is happening to her. The novel never states objectively what is wrong with her. Instead, this is to be inferred from Carrie's thoughts and memories (especially of her childhood) and from the descriptions of her drawings and of an island that she "sees" and draws. Carrie's feelings of separation from her family and school friends are marked in the opening chapters by her lack of interest in dances, clothes and boys and her mother and sister's attempts to impose these interests on her. The idea that a fear of growing up underlies Carrie's condition is also made clear in her reaction to the pervasive sexuality and violence of Beardsley's drawings (p. 44). Her sense of difference, however, becomes manifest after the experience at the hospital and with her daily visits to a psychiatrist.

An implication in both novels is that psychological alienation, wherein a character becomes extremely solipsistic, or centered in on the self, is contingent with social alienation, a separation of self from society, and with a fragmentation or dissolution of self. Both novels use metaphors to articulate these processes of social alienation and psychological fragmentation. In *Fade*, alienation and fragmentation are expressed through the motif of "the fade" itself, which leads to a separation of self from society, and through a complex use of the *doppelgänger*, or double. Paul's character is doubled through the "fade" motif. In his "faded" state he, in a sense, takes on another identity. And Paul is also doubled by Ozzie, his nephew, who functions as his *doppelgänger* in the latter part of the novel. The "fade" becomes a psychological burden for Paul because his "fade" self, the person he becomes in a fade, comes to represent an asocial and more perverse and corrupt aspect of himself. In his invisible state he is overcome by the desire to act in otherwise socially transgressive ways. He is able to stare at and touch women and he kills two other people (Rudolphe Toubert, the man partly responsible for the outbreak of fighting between police, "scabs" and strikers in which Paul's father is injured, and Ozzie, Paul's nephew). In this sense, the "fade" motif functions in a similar way to a "Jekyll and Hyde" type of *doppelgänger,* where an individual character is internally fragmented into "good" and "evil" selves. Ozzie is also characterized as fragmented, though the split between the two selves is sharper and is represented in the discourse as an internal dialogue. Ozzie's "fade" self manifests itself as an internal voice which speaks to him and, as his alienation increases, as a voice which speaks through him to other characters. Paul and Ozzie are also each other's *doppelgänger,* insofar as Ozzie is an inadequately socialized version of Paul and acts out Paul's repressed desires. Whereas Paul is able to curb the behavior of his "fade self" by refusing to fade voluntarily, Ozzie's "fade self" is allowed free reign; thus, Ozzie's extreme alienation articulates a nihilistic view of the world in which life is an amoral struggle for power. Like so many of Cormier's novels, there is a political subtext which is alluded to in a reference to Hitler in Nazi Germany and the possibility that a future "evil fader" might use the fade for "terrible purposes" (1990, p. 88). As in *The Chocolate War* (1974/1988), Cormier seems to be implying that there is an inherent propensity for "evil" within society which manifests itself through the acquiescence of individuals to authority. However, whereas the earlier novel suggests that power and the capacity for evil has its basis in social institutions, Cormier's use of the *doppelgänger* motif in *Fade* seems to imply that this propensity has its basis within the (asocial) desires of individuals and that it can only be repressed and curbed through education and socialization.

In *The Language of Goldfish,* fragmentation and alienation are expressed through Carrie's drawings and her visions of an island which is literally a small pile of rocks in the middle of a fishpond in her garden. This island comes to represent, for her, her own childhood, which she fears losing as she moves into adolescence. Metaphorically, the island also represents her personal and social alienation. The drawings have a *mise en abyme* function; that is, they are self-reflective devices which parallel her retreat into and emergence from a solipsistic and alienated state.[4] In the opening chapters, she begins a series of abstracted drawings based on "the idea of making patterns in which the real object disappeared" (1987, p. 31). The description parallels descriptions of Carrie's hallucinations, especially the episode at her parent's cocktail party where the discourse slips between descriptions of what Carrie sees and hears in her head and what is happening in the room, blurring distinctions between external objective reality and Carrie's internal imagined reality (*see* pp. 67–68). In wanting to draw the "slow descent" of a leaf (p. 19) and capture "not the leaf but the movement itself" (p. 26), she seems to express a desire to encapsulate time, to catch the moment of something. Insofar as her condition seems to be preempted by the idea, and fear, of growing up, the ideas lying behind her drawings suggest a desire to catch and hold onto the moment of childhood. The metaphoric connection between Carrie's drawings and her sense of self is made quite explicit as she watches her reflection in the goldfish pond: "She wanted it to hold still, stay that way. But even while she watched, the water rippled and her reflection broke apart and joggled in disconnected fragments on the surface" (p. 28).

In the latter part of the novel, after she comes out of the hospital, Carrie begins a new series of drawings, a series of watercolors based on the island that she sees in her head. Descriptions of the drawing process imply that the sketches are a manifestation of her imaginings and subconscious desires. The first drawing begins as an idle sketch which "seemed to be finding its direction without her" (1987, p. 116) and it is only when she shows the drawing to Saskia (her drawing teacher's daughter) that she realizes that it is in fact the island that she has drawn. Initially, she is afraid of drawing the island and draws still lifes instead in an attempt to repress the idea of the island, but she finds that "even in the course of sketching them, the apples became rocks and moss and water" (p. 119). However, even when she decides to draw the island, and begins the watercolor series, she does not immediately see the direction that the drawings are taking. It is only later, looking at twelve sketches from the series that she and her teacher choose for entry in a competition, that she sees that the pictures "formed a kind of progression" as the details in each successive picture grow clearer: "It was as if the cliffs were slowly emerging from mist, as if morning sun were burning off a haze" (pp. 151–152). In this way, the drawings metaphorically illustrate their own process of construction, in which the island becomes clearer as Carrie externalizes it. They also illustrate her recovery, which is represented as a process of externalization. In order to develop out of the alienated and solipsistic state into which she had withdrawn, she needed to recognize the existence of the island as a thing in the external world and hence realize the relationships between internal and external, and self and world.

These two novels contrast in the extent to which de-alienation is seen as a possibility. The central character of *Fade*, Paul, does not make the move out of solipsism. Instead, his progressive social alienation is represented by his literal and metaphoric "fading" away and his increasing reclusiveness. In contrast, Carrie is depicted at the end of *The Language of Goldfish* as emerging out of the extreme alienation that has arrested her development as she externalizes the image of island which has dominated her thinking about the world. The title of the novel refers to a childhood game that she had played with her sister, Moira, beside the goldfish pond (the location of

Carrie's actual island) in which they whistled to the goldfish in the "language of goldfish," a phrase which clearly suggests metaphorically a concept of childhood as a way of conceptualizing the world. The novel closes with Carrie teaching her young neighbor, Sara, "the language of goldfish," just as Moira taught it to her, and her final recognition that the island had "been there all along" (an object in the real world) and that "it was a very small island" (p. 179).

In this section I have focused on concepts of psychological and social alienation. The next section examines the possibility and forms of resistance to and transgression of the social structures and discourses which dialogically inform the formation of subjectivity.

RESISTANCE AND TRANSGRESSION

Many of the novels I have been discussing here and in Chapter 3 represent a character's developing subjectivity as resistance to and/or transgression of existing social discourses, structures and codes of behavior. These ideas are articulated through narrative strategies, such as the displacement and alienation of characters or the *doppelgänger* motif, which structure texts around a dialogue between notions of identity as being constructed within language and society on the one hand, and as situated on the margins of, or in a conflictual relation to, social and discursive practice on the other hand. Texts which situate characters on the margins of a culture or society can offer positions from which to interrogate the social and cultural boundaries which limit subjectivity, and hence question dominant social and cultural paradigms of identity formation.

The conceptualization of transgressive or resistant actions or modes of subjectivity poses a problem for theoretical and narrative representations of subjectivity. Stated simply, "transgression is the act of breaking rules" (A. White, 1982, p. 51). It involves "an inversion or subversion of some existing socially valued norm, rule, structure or contract" (p. 52). The possibility of resistance or transgression is premised on the existence of social, ideological, legal or cultural codes and conventions which constitute boundaries and constraints upon a person's actions, speech, thoughts and sense of identity. These boundaries imply that subjectivity is subjection to a particular set of constraints. Hence, agency lies in actions which counter or violate boundaries and thereby situate a person in conflict with existing social practice. However, the act of transgressing or resisting does not simply constitute agency. Such actions also position and construct a person, albeit in a conflictual relation, to the received social codes and conventions. In other words, they also imply the status of that person as a subject. The possibility of either transgression or resistance thus presumes the coexistence of two aspects of individual subjectivity: a sense of a personal identity as a subject, who is thus positioned in a relation of compliance or conflict to social and discursive practice; and a sense of identity as an agent, who thereby occupies a place or position from which resistance to or transgression of social boundaries can be produced. In Bakhtinian terms, the concepts of resistance and transgression necessitate a conception of subjectivity as dialogical: individual subjects are simultaneously constrained and empowered by the social and cultural discourses and institutions in and through which they are constituted.

Notions of transgression, resistance, subjectivity and agency are inherently bound up with how the interrelations between individuals and society are conceptualized. As I suggested in Chapter 1, an underlying problem is how to conceive of the relation between individuals and society without structuring this relation as oppositional, that is, as a relation in which one term is privileged over the other. By essentializing concepts such as the self, consciousness, or the individual, humanist approaches tend to ignore the formation of subjectivity within and through language and social interaction. On the other hand, by stressing the construction of the subject within social and linguistic practice, structuralist and poststructuralist approaches often represent the subject as disempowered by social structures, thus foreclosing the possibility of agency or resistance. Transgressive and resistant actions are dependent on two conditions: the constraining force of social institutions and discourses to be resisted; and the directedness of resistant or transgressive actions. The opposition between individuals and societies, and agency and subjectivity underlying humanist and structuralist discourses problematizes concepts of transgression and resistance by negating one or the other of these conditions of possibility.

As suggested in Chapter 3, Mayne's use of the double in *A Game of Dark* (1971) represents Donald's subjectivity as internally split between a sense of personal identity as subject and as agent. Double-stranded narration in this novel also structures the relation between subjectivity and agency dialogically and suggests a correlation between agency and the transgression of social codes. The primary narrative concerns Donald's relationship with his parents, from whom he is painfully alienated as a consequence of his inability to comprehend his father's illness and their stern religious beliefs. The secondary narrative takes place in a medieval town which is threatened by a voracious "worm" which kills the knights who challenge it. Here Donald takes on the role of Jackson and challenges and kills the worm. Parallels between the two narratives suggest interpretative possibilities: the connections between Berry, the minister in the real world with whom Donald is friends, and the lord in the fantasy world; Cecily, Donald's dead sister, and Carrica, the young woman in the fantasy world; Donald's parents' religious beliefs and the codes and conventions governing behavior in the fantasy world; and the worm and the guilt and repulsion which Donald feels toward his father. Some interpretations of the novel have suggested a closer connection between the worm and Donald's father, thus interpreting the novel as a reworking of the Oedipal narrative (Babbitt, 1971). The relationship between the two narrative strands is certainly metaphoric, but the significance of the worm for the primary narrative is more subtle than this interpretation would allow. The story of the worm in Mayne's novel is a version of "The Worm of Lambton Hall,"[5] in which the worm represents a projection of the principal character's failings. The worm embodies Donald's sense of disempowerment and alienation in the real world, the emotional barrenness of his relationships with his parents, and his ambivalent feelings toward his father, which are grounded in his own solipsism and inadequacies. Donald feels a sense of repulsion toward his father as an invalid, which is evoked in the repeated references to the stench of the sickroom and the hospital and that of the worm. He also experiences a sense of guilt related to his own inability to perceive his father as another person. The physical representation of the worm powerfully represents an outward manifestation or projection of both his father's self-preoccupation and the destructive and self-consuming nature of Donald's own emotions toward his parents.

It is clear that the secondary narrative constitutes a fantasy world which Donald constructs and withdraws into and that this world functions as a place in which he is able to achieve a position of agency and intersubjectivity through his appropriation of the role of Jackson. The double narrative structure articulates a split between the representation of character as subject and as agent, and furthermore suggests a correlation between agency and transgression, through the character of Jackson. As in "The Worm of Lambton Hall," the worm can only be destroyed by the character who is responsible for its existence, and it can only be killed through unconventional means. The feudal society which it terrorizes has constructed an array of accepted social codes for dealing with the worm and for challenging it, and when Jackson runs away from the worm he is effectively cast out from this society. He no longer has any status as a person—he is "the same as a dead man" (p. 126)—and is placed outside of the law and "out of grace" (p. 127). Jackson realizes that the accepted ritualized ways of dealing with the worm, through honor and order, are bound to fail, and that the only way that the worm can be killed is through what the society deems are dishonorable and unacceptable actions. Jackson's killing of the worm is described in negative terms:

> It was slain in unfair combat, and no glory from its death could come to him. He had accomplished no duty. He was not restored to honor. (p. 141)

His actions are described in terms which negate the conventions valued by the society—fair combat, glory, duty, honor—and his transgression of these conventions places him outside that society. But it is only through transgressing those social conventions and thus placing himself on the outside that he can defeat the worm and thereby attain agency, and life for himself and for others.

The ending of the novel is ambivalent. The two narrative strands are closely intertwined, so as to imply a series of analogies between Jackson and Donald: Jackson's social alienation from the feudal society parallels Donald's psychological alienation from the real world; Jackson's choice to leave the town once he has killed the worm parallels both Donald's choice to return to the real world and his father's death. Donald's construction of a sense of agency, as Jackson, and his realization that he does now know how to love his father (p. 142) offers the possibility that he has overcome his own solipsism and will be more able to construct for himself an active subject position in the real world to which he returns. But the means through which agency is achieved represents the move out of solipsism into intersubjectivity as inextricable from the act of transgressing the social conventions in and through which a person is situated. In other words, Donald can only attain intersubjectivity and agency through violating social conventions, and this act of violation also repositions him as subject and as agent within society.

A Game of Dark thus highlights a particular problem for the representation and interpretation of transgressive forms of action in narrative. Transgressive actions are defined as such by their being situated in a conflictual relation to existing social rules or structures. They do not automatically subvert these structures, and often, in fact, implicitly reassert the social codes which they transgress, even though the social boundaries determining these codes may be modified. The point is that the ideological value and significance of transgression can only be ascertained contextually. This is something that assertions of the inherent transgressive or subversive nature of children's literature, such as those of Lurie (1990), usually elide. Allon White (1982) makes a similar point in his discussion of the political basis of theories of transgression. He has outlined two models which have dominated theories of transgression. The first, associated with Bakhtin's work on carnival (1984b) and Kristeva (1980) emphasizes the capacity for transgression to "destabilise existing social structures" (p. 52). It is thought of as always "intrinsically radical" (p. 52), and thereby entails what White sees as a "false essentialising of transgression" (p. 60). The second model recognizes the capacity for transgressive actions to implicitly reassert the structures they subvert, but interprets this as a generalized complicity. It holds that "transgression is merely a licensed infraction of the rules which in fact consolidates and conserves the rules by periodically allowing them to be broken" (p. 60). Both approaches are nonhistorical, and, as White points out, they polarize the problem of transgression. In doing so, they pose the crucial question: "How far does carnivalesque transgression remain complicit with the rules and structures which it infringes, and how far does it really subvert and radically interrogate those rules and structures?" (p. 60).

This question, White argues, can only be answered historically, and it is one which is particularly pertinent to the representation of transgression in adolescent fiction. Transgression is a function of the social construction of subjectivity. The forms of resistance or transgression initiated by a person can only be defined as such through their being situated in a conflictual relation to given social or cultural codes, these codes being subject to social and historical change. Furthermore, opposition to one set of cultural codes can often entail compliance with another—even anarchy, insofar as it is manifest as resistance to all social codes, operates within the context of a codified system. Transgression, then, might be thought of as a rather tenuous interplay between positions of resistance and complicity. Adolescent fiction, on the whole, functions within a dominant humanist and liberal paradigm of personal maturation which valorizes intersubjective responsibility. Thus, the representation of transgressive behavior frequently has a conservative social function. While transgression may destabilize, subvert or interrogate the boundaries of represented social codes and structures, it is frequently co-opted by an ideologically inscribed model of maturation which values socially cooperative forms of intersubjectivity, as in *A Game of Dark* (Mayne, 1971). Adolescent novels, such as those of Robert Cormier and some recent Australian novels—for example, Sonya Hartnett's *Sleeping Dogs* (1995) or Marsden's *Dear Miffy* (1997)—in which characters remain radically alienated and solipsistic, represent transgressions of received cultural codes which define the boundaries of "adolescent fiction." In breaching those boundaries, however, they also modify them. In embracing ideological positions which are critical and hostile to humanism, they implicitly dismantle the ideological premises of children's literature. On the other hand,

they are also very instrumental in sustaining and strengthening those humanist paradigms and the conventional boundaries of the fiction insofar as re-
actions of outrage from the media, educators, and parents usually restate
(and in doing so reaffirm) precisely those ideological paradigms that have
been breached.

REPRESENTING TRANSGRESSION

In *Speaking to Miranda* (Macdonald, 1990), the problem of how to define
transgressive or resistant forms of subjectivity is inextricable from questions
of representation and point of view. As I suggested in Chapter 3, Emma/
Magda's transgression of social conventions and her deliberate self-effacement
draws attention to the limitations of these conventions and of textuality itself. By effacing her own identity and concealing her past, she implicitly refuses and denies herself a subject position. She is represented in the text as a
series of "flickering" images derived mostly from *The French Lieutenant's
Woman* (Fowles, 1969/1985) and from culturally constructed representations
of female promiscuity, mystique and passivity—the whore, the mysterious
enigmatic (nameless) female figure, and the passive unambitious wife/mother.
These images combine to denote a central absence; the trace of an
unrepresentable person or consciousness lies behind them, but is not assimilable to or in any way contained by them. In this way, the cultural, narrative
and textual forms used to represent Emma/Magda replicate her own self-effacement, thereby denying her a subject position within either the represented
society or the text itself. Whereas the correlation between transgression, agency
and subjectivity is seen as positive in *A Game of Dark* (Mayne, 1971), it is
represented negatively in *Speaking to Miranda*. For Emma/Magda, transgression and resistance to social and cultural codes leads to a denial of agency and
a loss of self. Ideologically, these textual processes function as strategies of
exclusion, whereby the transgressive other is denied an active subject position
by the textual structures through which s/he is made present.

In *Eva* (1988), Dickinson also draws attention to the implications of
representation and point of view for narrative depictions of transgression
and resistance. *Eva* is an overtly oppositional text. As both chimp and
woman, Eva is situated on the margins of both human and chimpanzee society, from where she is able to observe similarities between chimp and human codes of behavior. Focalization strategies represent both societies as
culturally alien, and from this position the novel presents a negative critique
of humanity and of the homocentric assumptions which underlie conventional humanist ideas. Underlying the text is a dialogue between humanist
and antihumanist viewpoints which is constructed through the represented

speech of other characters, such as Eva's father (p. 80), Grog (p. 111) and Joan Pradesh (p. 136), who each represent a different social and ideological viewpoint.

Eva's story is to some extent a reversal of conventional evolutionary and originary myths in that it depicts a movement backward from a "civilized" human self to a more "primitive" animal self. The oppositions implied by these terms are, however, progressively deconstructed. This reversal culminates in a crucial scene where Eva rips the human clothing from her chimp body. This scene is narrated twice, first from Eva's point of view as it is happening (pp. 137–138), and then later as a taped image on the zone (three-dimensional television) as it is seen, again from Eva's point of view (pp. 145–146). The main difference between the two descriptions of the scene lies in the construction of point of view. The first time it is narrated, Eva is a participant and her chimpness is foregrounded, as in "making her pelt prickle and bush out" (p. 137) and "knuckled away" (p. 138). The second time the episode is narrated, she is in the position of a human observer watching an image of herself and her "humanness" in the observer role is given emphasis in the phrase "Eva could feel it too, with her human mind" (p. 146). Both times the episode is described, there is a shifting interplay between cultural values associated with humanness and animalness. These are initially represented through a series of oppositions which both assert and undermine notions of essentiality:

> human versus animal
> social versus natural
> clothed versus naked
> outer versus inner
> "words" versus "bark"

Eva's literal stripping is a metaphoric stripping away of her human, external and socially constructed (clothed) self and display of her animal, natural and inner self. These oppositions ostensibly imply an assertion of essentialist notions of selfhood associated with this inner self, despite Eva's ambiguous status as human/chimp. However, repeated references to the (baying) "human pack" (pp. 137–138) undercut the opposition between words and "bark," and hence between human and animal ("baying" and "pack" having connotations of the latter). The second time the episode is narrated, Eva perceives her own image on the video as that of an other, as in the reference to "the chimp" (p. 145). The effect is similar to the earlier use of the mirror in the novel, and articulates a moment of split subjectivity, which undermines the simplistic oppositions between human and animal.

Eva's action is transgressive in two ways. It violates specific human social codes of behavior about dress and undress, and it questions the imposition of these codes onto another species. The wearing of clothes, by Eva and by other chimps, has a humanizing function in that it disguises their otherness from humans. (In the novel, chimps are dressed mainly so as to conceal their sexuality and their lack of toilet training.) For Eva's mother, the prospect of Eva mating with a chimpanzee is horrific, and the butterfly overalls in which she dresses Eva represent an attempt to assert Eva's state of being as human and as a young girl over her status as an adult chimpanzee. Eva's transgressive action then represents a refusal of the subject position constructed for her by humans as either human or as chimp. The significance of the action lies in her ambivalent state of being human/chimp; it would mean something quite different if Eva were either all chimpanzee or all human.

An important part of the effect of Eva's action lies in its status as a visual image and a textual sign which is appropriated, interpreted and ascribed with meaning by her human audience. This occurs through a range of discursive and narrative strategies. The first time the episode is narrated, the distance between Eva and her human audience is emphasized. Furthermore, she is clearly conscious of her own actions as performance, as in "she had to do or say something more. They were waiting. Not words, nothing human" (p. 138). The status of her action as performance, and thus as a visual image or sign to be ascribed with meaning, is foregrounded the second time the episode is narrated by the shift in point of view, because Eva is now an observer, and by the fact that it is a visual representation. Furthermore, the discursive register of this second description is rhetorical and metaphoric, as in, "They [Eva's actions] spoke for Kelly, and the other chimps, and all the children of earth, the orangs and giraffes and whales and moths and eagles, which over the past few centuries had turned their backs on humankind and crawled or glided or sunk away into the dark" (p. 146). These strategies combine to objectify Eva's actions, and to inscribe the image with abstract and generalized meanings. The shift from the viewpoint of a chimpanzee to that of a human being highlights the process whereby Eva's transgressive action is reappropriated by the human discursive structures to which it is opposed through the construction of meanings which would transcend the differences between Eva, other chimpanzees and animals, and other human beings.

Grog and his fellow campaigners for chimpanzee rights subvert the antisocial and antihuman significance of Eva's action and put it into the service of their ideological program. The idea of rights for animals can only be asserted from a humanist position, that is, as being analogous with the idea of human rights. It thereby implies the imposition of human cultural values onto another species. However, this move involves an assertion of those humanist values which are so clearly lacking in the human society represented in the text. In the process of becoming more homocentric, selfish and exploitative of other species, this society has discarded humanist values associated with altruism, humanitarianism and hope for a future. And it is these kinds of values that Grog and his friends transpose onto Eva and the other chimps. Metaphorically, Eva stands in for all chimpanzees, all animals, and ultimately, she also stands in for those human beings, such as Grog, who have given up on the human race. In this way, the moment at which Eva rips the human clothing from her chimp body is both a metaphoric stripping away of her human self and a disclosure of the endemic lack of positive humanist values in the represented human society.

Within the social and historical context represented in the novel, antihuman gestures and discourses function as positive assertions of the value of humanism and as a critique of the negative implications of humanism, namely cultural solipsism. These kinds of ideas are also explored through an interplay between intertextual references. There are two main intertexts for the novel which imply teleological and moral narrative structures against which the text is situated. The Genesis story is a fairly obvious intertext to which the title and an early reference to an "Adam and Eve" cartoon (p. 15) which Eva watches refer. Eva's story is a reversion of the Genesis story—this is implicit in references to beginnings in the first chapter (p. 10). The genre of postdisaster (apocalyptic) fiction, of which *Eva* is a variant, is a second intertext for the novel. The cartoon retells the Genesis story in a way that replicates some crucial aspects of her society (p. 15). The plot, or "story" structure of this cartoon is "always the same," but it is significantly different from its biblical pretext. There is no tree of knowledge, (or life), no concept of God, transgression or retribution. The conventional roles of Adam and Eve are reversed (it is Adam who "gets into trouble," and his sin is "arrogance and impulsiveness" rather than breach of interdiction). The Great Snake is always present as a threat, though Christian concepts of salvation and the defeat of evil are absent. In other words, what is missing from the story is its conventional moral significance. There is no suggestion that this morality has been either dismantled or replaced: it has been merely discarded in favor of a simplistic discourse which treats the text as "story." The lack of a moral outcome or conventional ending in this version of the biblical story is analogous with the absence of human or moral significances or teleological fictions in the society of the primary text. Biblical narratives and postdisaster fictions have in common teleological narrative structures oriented toward apocalyptic endings and new beginnings. Human civilization in *Eva* is represented as simply winding down, rather than as having a conventional apocalyptic ending, and the absence of a sense of an ending displaces the mythic and teleological functions of biblical and postdisaster fictions, as well as subverting their moralistic assumptions.[6]

Although *Eva* presents a critique of the homocentric assumptions of humanist ideologies implied by its intertexts, it is not opposed to humanism as such. Dickinson's recognition of the implications of privileging the human species at the expense of other humanist values collapses any simplistic opposition between humanism and antihumanism. Furthermore, the ending of the novel forecloses a monologic reading of this dialogue. While Eva's death implies story closure, it in fact signals a number of narrative openings, possible futures for this group of chimpanzees. The ending does signal "the defeat of humankind and all that cleverness" (p. 204), but the displacement of these human significances, "the threads of human knowledge" (p. 206), onto the chimp society implicitly subverts, but positively reaffirms, human values. Within a society which has no concept of hope, and no capacity to see beyond the here and now, Joan Pradesh's justifications for her experiments, such as the sanctity of human life, or humanity's "unconscious moral standards" (p. 136), signify only a human potential for a monological cultural and ethical solipsism. Individuals in this society are isolated, unable to communicate with each other, able to interact with the world only through the images of the "shaper" (futuristic 3–D television), and are thus unable to construct either positive fictions or interactive self-other relations. The human need for purposes, for teleological and evolutionary myths, is postulated by characters such as Grog (p. 111), whose descent into madness perhaps signifies his exclusion from the dominant culture. Eva's purpose, however, is discursive and intersubjective; and Dickinson's use of humanist assumptions to subvert humanism implicitly reaffirms human needs for meaningful fictions and for nonsolipsistic interrelations amongst self, other and world.

CONCLUSION

Bakhtin, Vološinov, Lacan and Althusser all address the social, cultural and linguistic influences on the formation of subjectivity and place a varying emphasis on the power of individuals to resist social ideological determination. This chapter has examined the use of such narrative strategies as displacement, alienation and transgression in the exploration of relationships between individuals, language and social structures. I have touched on many ideas which are pertinent to later chapters. The interrelations between language, society and subjectivity as they have been formulated by theorists like Bakhtin, Vološinov, Lacan and Althusser are central, though my focus in later chapters will be oriented toward Bakhtinian theories of the novel and the representation of forms of subjectivity. Vološinov's work, in particular, foregrounds the social and ideological basis of language and of thought, and thus of concepts, theories and narrative representations of selfhood. The represented relations between characters and social settings in novels are indicative of underlying ideological assumptions about the relations between individual subjects and social and discursive practices. The idea that language determines and constructs for its speakers enunciative positions within a heteroglossia is particularly pertinent to my concerns in Chapter 7, where I will be examining the textual construction of the subject within polyphonic and heteroglottic texts.

In adolescent fiction, the representation of transgressive or alienated states of being has up until quite recently usually had a conservative social function. However, notions of alienation and transgression are a function of the social construction of the subject. That is, actions or experiences are not in themselves inherently transgressive, alienating or conformist. Rather, they are defined as such in relation to existing social codes and structures, these codes being subject to social and historical change. Thus, novels such as *A Game of Dark* (Mayne, 1971), *Eva* (Dickinson, 1988) and *Speaking to Miranda* (Macdonald, 1990) highlight the fact that the ideological value and significance of concepts such as alienation and transgression can only be ascertained contextually. While the narrative strategies I have been discussing may destabilize, subvert or interrogate the dominant paradigms for personal development and socialization, they are frequently assimilated into an ideologically inscribed model of maturation which values socially cooperative forms of intersubjectivity. This model is represented in relatively positive terms in most of William Mayne's fiction, but its more negative implications are explored in novels like *Speaking to Miranda* and *Eva,* wherein notions of an alienated and transgressive subjectivity are resituated within gendered and humanist dialogues. The discussion of negative implications of humanism, in *Eva* especially, anticipates the central concern of Chapter 5, which will look at two polyphonic multitemporal novels which represent positive and negative variants of modernist humanism.

ENDNOTES

1. Seeman (1959) first identified these six social psychological aspects of alienation. *See also* Kalekin-Fishman (1989) and Oldenquist and Rosner (1991).

2. The implication in Bakhtin's argument of an empowered subjectivity allows

for active subject positions to be inferred for represented characters and for readers, as I have argued in Chapter 2.

3. Antar's narrative, especially the journey into the underground, conforms in many ways with Joseph Campbell's (1968) pattern for a heroic life (*see* the discussion of Campbell in Chapter 4 of *Retelling Stories*, Stephens and McCallum, 1998). It is also noteworthy that Mayne has doubled the motif of exile and return.

4. The term *mise en abyme* refers to a representation or narrative segment, embedded within a larger narrative, which reflects, reproduces or mirrors an aspect of the larger primary narrative (McCallum, 1996b, p. 404; *see also* Hutcheon, 1980, pp. 54–56; Prince, 1988, p. 53; McHale 1989, pp. 124–125).

5. *See* Briggs (1991), Part A, Vol. 1, pp. 373–375.

6. Dickinson's reshaping of the Genesis story of the Fall in *Eva* has also been discussed in Chapter 2 of *Retelling Stories* (Stephens and McCallum, 1998).

5 SUBJECTIVITY, COGNITION AND CERTAINTY

The gods have departed, more or less, and so has the marvelous clockwork machinery, and what is left is ourselves. We stand where God once stood, at the center of explanations. If someone has blundered, we have only ourselves to blame; but on the other hand, we can stop accepting responsibility beyond our powers, which is really a metaphysical form of taxation without representation! We are not fully free and fully capable, and the human condition, let alone the circumstances and characters of each of us, was not chosen by us.

Jill Paton Walsh, "Disturbing the Universe"

This chapter explores two variants of modernist humanism and their implications for representations of subjectivity. These are: a positive and optimistic strand, which is affirmed by writers such as Jill Paton Walsh, Penelope Lively and Virginia Hamilton; and a more negative and pessimistic strand, exemplified by Alan Garner and Robert Cormier. The discussion will focus on *Unleaving* (Walsh, 1976) and *Red Shift* (Garner, 1973/1989), two very complex and sophisticated novels for young people. Both novels are premised on a critique of Cartesian subjectivity and religious truths, but whereas Walsh affirms the possibility and value of traditional humanist concepts in the absence of philosophical or religious truths, Garner stresses the alienating consequences of this absence for individuals, and the problems it poses for the construction of meanings.

As Bullock (1985) has demonstrated, twentieth century humanism is characterized by a doubleness. The early twentieth century saw the emergence of a negative strand of humanism which expressed an alienation, discontinuity, fragmentation and despair (p. 137), which is evident in Garner's work. However, as Bullock has noted, modernism "found as many ways of affirming life as of rejecting it" (p. 154), and novels by writers such as Walsh,

Lively and Hamilton exemplify this in their emphasis on central humanist concepts, in particular the possibility of interpersonal relationships necessary for personal maturation. Bullock's own positive humanism stresses "the desire to develop human relationships, the need for affection and for cooperation and the need to belong to human groups" as "an essential part of human life without which the identity of the individual remains stunted" (p. 181). A crucial difference between the writing of Walsh, Lively and Hamilton and that of Garner and Cormier lies in the representation of this connection between interpersonal relationships and personal maturation. The optimism which pervades Walsh's *Unleaving* (1976), despite the seriousness of its themes and story, is contingent upon the central characters' progress toward intersubjectivity. Intersubjectivity is present in Garner's *Red Shift* (1973/ 1989) only as an absence, an essentialized impossibility against which the alienation and fragmentation of the subject is measured. Garner's pessimism is comparable with that of Cormier and other American fiction for young people in the 1970s and 1980s and with a negativity which has emerged more recently in Australian writing in the late 1980s and 1990s (for example, novels by Gillian Rubenstein, Sonya Hartnett and John Marsden).

Stephens (1992b) has noted that the incursion of modernist narrative forms and themes into children's literature has been limited and partial; they are most frequently used by writers such as Mayne, Walsh, Hamilton and Garner in novels which are often deemed "too difficult" or "too dark" for children. Criticism of Garner's work in particular typically attempts to ameliorate its implicit negativity about human relationships, this negativity being incompatible with the mainstream concerns of children's literature. The avoidance of modernist themes and strategies in children's literature is indicative of premodern ideological assumptions, which typically underlie writing for and about children. As I suggested in Chapter 1, these assumptions entail a privileging of essentialist concepts of subjectivity and childhood associated with liberal humanism and romanticism, and a prevalence of traditional realist narrative techniques. Eighteenth and nineteenth-century romanticism certainly had its "darker side," but the dominant ideologies of childhood are heavily indebted to Wordsworthian and Blakean images of childhood innocence. Narrative strategies which are typically modernist include unreliable first person narrators; extensive character focalization; indirect modes of discourse representation; and multiple narrative frames, strands and voices. Modernist forms and themes are oriented toward a critique of positivist notions of meaning and subjectivity, and tend to imply a view of the world and meaning as being subjectively constructed (Lodge, 1990, p. 26; Stephens, 1992b, pp. 53–54).

Chapter 2 concentrated on multivoiced novels in which the narrative voices or strands are situated in the same spatial and temporal context, but which are narrated from different narratorial or character points of view (who speaks and/or sees). In this chapter, as well as in Chapter 6, I will be looking at what can be loosely termed "polyphonic multitemporal narratives." These are multistranded novels in which the narrative strands are differentiated by shifts in the temporal and spatial relationships (or what Bakhtin referred to as "chronotopic" relationships) as well as narrative voice or point of view.[1] Concepts of temporality and history are an important aspect of both positive and negative forms of modern humanism. In his discussions of novelistic time, LaCapra (1987, p. 204) has distinguished between diachronic and synchronic dimensions of time. Diachrony designates movement over time involving change; synchrony "stops" time at a given moment and displays its "sameness" or "nowness" (p. 204). Novelistic time is the interaction of these two dimensions, and modernist narratives emphasize the synchronic dimension of time through the concept of "repetitive temporality", that is, processes of recurrence with change (p. 205). The use of narrative and discursive repetitions in novels such as *Unleaving* (Walsh, 1976) and *Red Shift* (Garner, 1973/1989) disrupts linear and teleological concepts of time associated with diachronic dimensions of time, and implies instead cyclical concepts of time. These are linked in *Unleaving* with personal memory and in *Red Shift* with mythic or collective memories. Chapter 6 will go on to deal at greater length with the interrelationships between diachronic dimensions of narrative time, history and representations of subjectivity in *The Court of the Stone Children* (Cameron, 1973), *Voices after Midnight* (Peck, 1989/1991), *The Callender Papers* (Voight, 1983/1991), *The Driftway* (Lively, 1972/1985), *A Bone From a Dry Sea* (Dickinson, 1992), as well as in *Red Shift* (Garner, 1973/1989).

In multistranded narratives, each strand constructs a context in which other strands are read and interpreted. The location of narrative strands in different times means that each narrative is read in the context of other past and future narratives; a primary effect, then, is to represent a dialogue between the textual past and present. The processes through which readers attribute meanings to narratives (and feel compelled to construct meanings) are foregrounded in novels such as *The Driftway* (Lively, 1972/1985), *Red Shift* (Garner, 1973/1989), *Unleaving* (Walsh, 1976) and *A Bone from a Dry Sea* (Dickinson, 1992) where the links between narrative strands are for the most part implicit. Readers are required to actively exercise inferential and analytic skills in their attempts to make meaningful connections between narrative strands. In *Unleaving* and *Red Shift,* repetition is a primary strategy for implying "story" and thematic interconnections between narrative strands in these novels. Repeated story elements (such as place, characters and events) and discursive elements have implications for the representation of the subject in time, and for concepts of subjectivity. Multistranded and multivoiced narrative strategies are instrumental in the construction of characters in both past and present narrative strands who occupy active subject positions within the discourse of a text. By implication, these strategies carry with them cultural assumptions about subjectivity and the positions human subjects occupy within time and history.

The discussion in this chapter will focus closely on the narrative techniques and philosophical concerns expressed in *Unleaving* (Walsh, 1976) and *Red Shift* (Garner, 1973/1989). Both novels are structured as interlaced multistranded narratives. Both incorporate a range of literary and extra-literary intertexts and discourses which imply contexts in which to formulate questions about subjectivity raised by their narrative techniques. *Unleaving,* a sequel to *Goldengrove* (Walsh, 1972/1985), comprises two parallel narrative strands, both of which are focalized by the same character, Madge, but from two points in time about forty or fifty years apart, and from two quite different subject positions. These are strategies which problematize the possibility of positing a single coherent and essential subjectivity for Madge. *Red Shift* comprises three parallel narrative strands, all of which are situated at different historical times: the second century A.D.; December 1643; and a time roughly contemporary. Repetitions and parallels between the three strands imply interconnections which raise questions about essentialist concepts of subjectivity and the possibility of transcendent meanings. Both novels are highly complex and sophisticated in both narrative technique and thematic concerns, and they both require considerably more reader participation than many adolescent novels. I suggested in Chapter 2 that polyphonic narrative strategies are instrumental in the construction of active implied reader positions. The next section will outline the narrative techniques and positioning of implied readers in *Unleaving* and *Red Shift,* before examining the implications these have for the representation of subjectivity.

POLYPHONIC MULTITEMPORAL NARRATIVES AND IMPLIED READER POSITIONS

The narrative technique of *Unleaving* (Walsh, 1976) is unusual in that there are two interlaced narrative strands, both of which are narrated from the viewpoint of the same character at different points in time. This is important for the representation of subjectivity and for the positioning of implied readers. Both narrative strands are narrated in the third person. One is almost entirely focalized by Madge, age seventeen, and the other is mostly focalized by an older Madge (or Gran) some forty or fifty years later. The connection between these two focalizers, however, is not immediately obvious, and the shifts from one narrative to the other are confusing, particularly as Madge's grandmother is also referred to as "Gran." The chronologically earlier narrative begins with Madge returning to Goldengrove to attend her grandmother's funeral. Madge inherits the house and the main part of the story concerns a summer which she spends at Goldengrove with an Oxford reading party, consisting of two philosophy professors, their families, and students, to whom she has rented the house. The second narrative strand takes place many years later; Madge is now Gran, and the narrative spans a summer during which her daughter, grandchildren and her niece, Emily, come to stay with her at Goldengrove.

The double narrative structure of *Unleaving* has two main effects: it represents both the younger and older Madge(s) as occupying different subject positions within the text, and hence destabilizes notions of an essential singular subjectivity; and it encourages quite complex reading strategies. In "On Wearing Masks," Walsh (1989) claimed that the narrative technique of the novel was a deliberate attempt "to induce young readers to identify with a character (Madge) so strongly when she was young that they would be tricked into finding themselves inside the skin of an old woman later in the book" (p. 172). Implied reader point of view is mostly aligned with that of the younger Madge: the sections of narrative focalized by Gran tend to be shorter, and on an initial reading (i.e., a reading primarily for "story") seem peripheral to the main narrative, and the chronologically earlier narrative strand constitutes the primary story interest. These sections are almost entirely focalized by the younger Madge, and thematically she is the most central character. Focalization constructs an implicit position from which to "see" and interpret the textual world which is perceptually and attitudinally aligned with that of Madge. An implication of Walsh's comment is that once readers realize that Gran and Madge are the same character, they will be "tricked" into identifying with Gran. However, an odd effect of Walsh's strategy is that while by the end of the novel we know that Madge and Gran are the same character—and attentive readers will have formed a hypothesis about their sameness by at least page 24—it is still difficult not to think of them as two different characters, because they occupy different subject positions which, for readers, exist simultaneously. One implication of this is that the subjectivity of the character(s) Madge/Gran is being represented as contingent upon, and constructed through, the subject positions which she/they occupy within various contexts, rather than as essential or given. Furthermore, Walsh's strategies actually deny readers a position from which to identify fully with either Madge or Gran, and thereby encourage a retrospective and analytic reading.

If we compare the narrative strategy of *Unleaving* to that of retrospective narration from a single temporal point of view, we can see more clearly what Walsh is doing. In retrospective narrative, for example, Robert Louis Stevenson's *Treasure Island* (1883) or Charles Dickens's *Great Expectations*, events are narrated from the perceptual viewpoint of a character's younger self, but from the conceptual and linguistic position of this character's older self (Chapman, 1980, p. 158). Thus, there is a temporal and ideational disjunction between the time of the "story" and the time of narration, but the disparity between the narrator's older and younger selves is diminished by the contextualizing narrative voice. However, double-stranded narration and dual focalization in *Unleaving* foreground this disparity. Because the older and younger Madge(s) both focalize, they both occupy discrete and equally valid subject positions. They might represent aspects of the same character, but they are not identical. They occupy independent subject positions, which for readers are coexistent and not entirely assimilable to each other.

I suggested in Chapter 2 that the spatial and temporal interconnections between story strands in multistranded narratives like *Salt River Times* (Mayne, 1980) and *Finders, Losers* (Mark, 1990) enable readers to infer a central "story" linking the various narrative strands. The restriction of narrative time in *Unleaving* to Madge's life and interconnections between narrative strands enables readers to deduce that Gran and Madge are the same character, and to infer a linear narrative connecting them. Though there are two narrative discourses, there is really only one "story," and a retrospective reading of the novel reveals how the two narrative strands are interconnected so as to clearly link Madge and Gran very early in the novel. Implied readers of Garner's *Red Shift* (1973/1989) are, however, denied a position from which to construct a single linear "story" linking the various narrative strands. The novel comprises one narrative strand situated in a time roughly contemporary, and two other strands situated in a historical past. These constitute distinct parallel "story" strands, the interconnections between which are more overtly oriented toward the development of interconnecting themes than toward the construction of a linear "story" structure. Like *Unleaving*, though, the interconnections between narrative strands remain implicit, and the narrative strategies assume a predominant use of inferential and inductive reading strategies whereby readers infer thematic significances for interconnections between narrative strands, as well as much of the "story" material conveyed in individual narrative strands.

There are three narrative strands in *Red Shift,* each of which is situated in the same place at different historical times. Each is narrated in the third person, and they may be summarized as follows:

1. *The contemporary strand.* This consists of thirteen episodes or sections, and it spans nine months. The story concerns the relationship between Tom and Jan, two adolescents who, when Jan moves to London at the beginning of the novel, meet once a month at Crewe. Tom lives with his possessive parents in a caravan at Rudheath, in what is a physically and emotionally claustrophobic atmosphere. Toward the end of the novel, Tom realizes that Jan has had a lover (though this has actually occurred prior to the opening of the novel) and the relationship breaks up at the end of the novel. The novel ends with a letter written in code by Tom, which he has put in Jan's bag, in which he says that if she is not at Crewe next time he will go to Barthomley, the implication of this being that he will jump from the tower of the church (Nikolajeva, 1989, p. 131).[2]

2. *The civil war strand.* This is narrated in nine episodes or sections, and narrative time spans twelve hours. The story centers on an actual historical incident, the Barthomley massacre of December 1643. The broad outlines of Garner's story and some of the names of characters, for example John Fowler, are derived from a number of historical sources.[3] Briefly, the people of Barthomley had taken refuge from royalist soldiers in Barthomley church and, after the soldiers were apparently fired upon, the church was set on fire and most of its occupants slaughtered. Garner's story focuses on the relationship between three (fictional) characters who had taken refuge in the church; Thomas, Margery and John Fowler, the rector's son. John taunts Thomas about Margery's prior relationship with Thomas Venables. After seeing Venables amongst the royalist soldiers while he is standing watch, Thomas has what appears to be an epileptic fit and accidentally fires his gun, thereby provoking retaliation from the royalist soldiers. Margery and Thomas survive the massacre, though Thomas is injured and Margery is raped by Thomas Venables, who kills John Fowler and helps Thomas and Margery to escape.

3. *The Roman strand.* This is set in the second century A.D., spans nine months, and is narrated in nine episodes or sections. The story concerns five (fictional) fugitives of the Ninth Roman legion, last heard of in 117 A.D., who have apparently deserted the Ninth and gone "tribal" in order to survive. They are Logan (the leader), Magoo,

Face, Buzzard and Macey (Logan kills Buzzard and Face). It would seem that these last four are Celts who have joined the Imperial army—only Logan is Roman—and Garner represents them using language and behavior associated with that of American soldiers in Vietnam (Philip, 1981; Benton, 1974). They attack a settlement of native Celts at Barthomley, where they take a native woman, who it seems is responsible for their later deaths. She is raped by all except Macey, who befriends her and stays with her at the end of the novel.

There has been some dispute as to whether the two chronologically earlier story strands are subordinate to the contemporary story (Chambers, 1973; Townsend, 1979; Nikolejeva, 1996) or whether, "the weight of the narrative rests fairly equally on all three strands" (Philip, 1981, p. 87). Philip sees the assumption that the contemporary strand is dominant as indicative of the reader's expectation of a novel which "fulfils a set, expected narrative pattern" in which the primary object of reading is the extraction of one dominant "story," which other strands would merely reflect (1981, p. 87). Most commentators on the novel have noted the "elliptical, condensed and allusive" style of the narrative discourse (Philip, 1981, p. 86). The novel requires a good deal more reader participation than many children's novels, making "heavy demands of the reader's intelligence, concentration and background knowledge" (Townsend, 1979, p. 82), and for these reasons the question as to whether it is really a children's novel at all is frequently raised. Again Philip has suggested, however, that much of the controversy surrounding the novel is indicative of the assumptions made by its critics, namely "that reading is a passive activity, and that narrative connections should be explicit, rather than implicit" (1981, p. 87).

The narrative techniques used in the novel construct active implied reader positions which assume a complex of inferential and analytic reading strategies. The absence of explicit cohesive links between and within narrative strands situates readers at some distance from narrative events and existents. A primary reading of the novel involves two simultaneous processes: a "bottom-up" decoding of the narrative discourse of individual narrative strands; and a "top-down" interpretation of the three strands and the novel as a whole according to acquired social, cultural and intertextual knowledge[4] The first process is problematized by Garner's elliptical narrative style. Each strand is narrated in the third person, but there is very little actual narrated description or character focalization, a strategy which denies overt reader identification with characters and events. The narrative discourse consists almost entirely of dialogue, and many "story" details must be either inferred or posited by readers (i.e., details such as place and time, who is speaking, the relationships between characters, what has happened prior to discourse time and character's actions occurring during conversations). Some of these narrative gaps can be filled retrospectively, but many are left open, for example, the nature of Margery's relationship with John Fowler and Thomas Venables prior to the opening of the novel. The second reading process depends upon a reader's knowledge of cultural codes, and involves a recognition of complex interconnections, repetitions and patterns of similarity and difference within the three narrative strands. Such recognitions are rendered problematic by the fact that these interconnections are only ever implied. (Links between the narrative strands are established primarily through place, character names and roles, objects and repeated story and discursive features. These will be elaborated more fully later in this chapter.)

The interaction between the two assumed reading processes can be seen by a comparison of the interpretative positions implied by narrative strategies used to represent sexual activities in the three narratives. As many commentators have pointed out, virtually all of Tom and Jan's sexual relationship in the contemporary strand occurs in the pauses between their speech utterances (*see* Philip, 1981, p.106; Hunt, 1991, p.113), as the following passage shows:

> 'Bikini!'
> 'It's hurting you too much,' said Jan, 'I'll get rid of it.'
> 'Have you caught up?' said Jan.
> 'Don't.'
> 'I only want to know.'
> 'I can't cry.'
> 'Should you?'
> 'I was by myself.'
> 'Yes.'
> 'I'm sorry.'
> 'You couldn't help it.'
> 'Next time—'
> It was Jan who cried. Tom held her, kissed her hair.
> 'Next time,' she said. 'Is that all? Next time—'
> 'What can I do?' said Tom. 'Make it better—.' (1989, p. 130)

As Philip (1981) and Hunt (1991) have suggested, the predominance of dialogue, restricted speech tags and absence of narrative description in this passage denies readers access to a passive voyeuristic position from which to view and interpret textual events. The inferences which readers make about characters' actions and thoughts depend on a bottom-up decoding of the narrative discourse and a top-down reading according to acquired social knowledge. A bottom-up reading infers a narrative gap between lines 2 and 3 which is implied by the apparent lack of cohesion in the dialogue and by repeated *inquit*-tags "Jan said" which "bracket the implied sexual act" (Hunt, 1991, p. 113), or incompletion of the act, as the case may be. Top-down reading strategies enable readers to attribute the represented conversation with cohesion and reference and to ascribe (sexual) meanings to Jan's question "Have you caught up?".

Philip stresses the effects of Garner's narrative technique in this passage for the development of thematic concerns, namely, "the incompatibility of the inner and outer worlds". The omission of intrusive narrated detail represents sexual activity as a private experience, whereas narrative description would objectify and distance it, and imply an observer (1981, p. 107). However, the absence of focalized detail and the gaps between utterances in the dialogue also suggest the inability of either character to apprehend the other and the absence of an interpersonal relationship between them. Philip's shift from narrative technique to thematic significance is problematic, as becomes clear when we compare Garner's use of similar strategies of omission to represent sexual activity elsewhere in the novel, where the location of sex within the narrative gaps, on the margins of the text so to speak, represents it more ambivalently. For example, the use of euphemisms by Tom's parents to talk about sex—"We wondered if you'd had any occasion to do anything to make us ashamed of you" (p. 17), "been intimate," and "had relations" (p. 37)—works in a similar way, but here its effect is parodic. Conversely, narrative strategies similar to those used in the passage quoted above are also used to represent some of the more violent sexual scenes in the novel, such as Tom's treatment of Jan at Mow Cop,[5] or Thomas Venables' rape of Margery (pp. 139–140), and that of the native woman by the Roman soldiers (pp. 33–34), both of which also occur "between the lines" of conversation and, in the case of the latter, on the margins of the represented scene. Furthermore, these textual strategies also represent sex as simply an act of doing something to someone else whose subjectivity is either effaced or not recognized; this is emphasized in the Roman strand by the native woman's lack of a name. Thus, the omission of narrated detail works here to situate the sexual violence on the margins of the discourse. The impact of this violence for readers is heightened, since it is being represented as implicit, rather than explicit, it is not simply described and objectified for readers; rather, it must be inferred and constructed by them.

Garner's narrative techniques and structures draw attention to ideological assumptions implicit in the interpretative strategies assumed of readers. Clearly, readers will make sense of each narrative strand through its contextual relationships with the other two narratives, but the meanings ascribed to the novel will depend to some extent on whether readers stress the similarities or the differences between them and on the significances attributed to these similarities and differences. An emphasis on repeated narrative elements implies that the three narratives are versions of the same story; hence, the characters in each narrative represent aspects of the same person. However, the differences between interpersonal relationships and social and historical contexts problematize any simple transition from narrative interconnections to thematic significance. The question of sameness and difference foregrounds ambiguities in the text, and it hinges on a distinction between concepts of the self as *ipse* and as *idem* (Ricoeur, 1993). *Ipse*-identity posits self-sameness on the basis of character or self-identity, and thereby implies "a selfhood without sameness" (Ricoeur, 1993, p. 106). *Idem*-identity posits self-sameness on the basis of *"uninterrupted continuity"* and *"an invariable structure"* (p. 105) corresponding to an individual, and thereby implies "a sameness without selfhood" (p. 106). The idea of *ipse*-identity underlies the notion of an essential selfhood (common to Tom, Thomas and Macey) anterior to social and historical contexts. The idea of *idem*-identity implies essentiality on the basis that the three characters occupy the same position within the same place and the same narrative structure. In this way, Garner's narrative strategies represent a complex interrogation of both essentialist and provisionalist constructions of meaning and concepts of subjectivity.

The narrative techniques used by Walsh in *Unleaving* (1976) and Garner in *Red Shift* (1973/1989) raise similar concerns. The implication in both novels that the central characters are aspects of the same person destabilizes notions of essential selfhood and meaning by foregrounding the distinction between concepts of self as *ipse* and as *idem,* and by thereby generating a disparity between these concepts. Both novels are grounded on a critique of Cartesian subjectivity. However, the narrative processes and philosophical and literary traditions which Garner and Walsh are drawing upon are very different. Walsh is working from a secular humanist position, from where she critiques essentialist assumptions underlying premodernist philosophical and literary intertexts and acclaims the modernist rejection of religious and philosophical "truths." This rejection is taken as given in *Red Shift,* but Garner sees it as implying a displacement and alienation of the subject. *Unleaving* presents a positive view of a subjectivity that is contingent, provisional, and which depends upon positive intersubjective relations with others. *Red Shift* presents a more negative view of the modernist enterprise, wherein subjectivity is the site of loss and alienation and positive interpersonal relationships are a diminishing possibility. Ultimately, Garner's narrative strategies assert an unattainable desire for essentiality of meaning and selfhood and, hence, for transcendence of historical and cultural difference, a desire which, in the context of Garner's modernist vision, is fundamentally unachievable. The next section will examine Walsh's use of philosophical and literary intertexts. These construct a dialogue between different conceptions of subjectivity, and thereby provide a context in which to consider the implications of representations of subjectivity.

INTERTEXTUALITY AND SUBJECTIVITY IN *UNLEAVING*

In *Unleaving* (1976), Walsh makes extensive use of literary and philosophical intertexts. Much of this material is implicitly concerned with notions of subjectivity, and it implies a context in which to formulate questions about subjectivity raised by the narrative techniques of the novel. While readers are able to infer that Madge and Gran are the same character, textual strategies imply that the subjectivity of this character resides within intersections in a dialogue between older and younger selves. Are we to think of Madge and Gran, then, as the same character, aspects of the same character or two different characters? In other words, is the subjectivity of a person conceivable as a unique essential being, that is, the self as *ipse*, or as the conglomeration of positions which that person occupies and has occupied, that is, the self as *idem*? Intertextual material alludes to and articulates complex philosophical issues about subjectivity underlying these questions, and also indicates the kinds of cultural and intellectual contexts in which such questions are raised.

Philosophical discussions in the novel center on conventional topics, such as human knowledge, actions and consequences, immortality and so on. Underlying much of this material is a dialogue about human knowledge of which Descartes and Locke are representative.[6] Descartes asserted the existence of an innate cognitive predisposition, unique and essential to human beings, which enables us to grasp general truths about reality independent of experience (*see*, for example, Wilson, 1969). Locke (1690/1981), however, maintained that there are no such general, allegedly innate, principles which compel universal assent (pp. 67–68), and that the human mind is like "white paper, void of all characters, without any ideas," which is "furnished" with "the materials of reason and knowledge" from experience (p. 89). Both of these positions clearly have implications for how we think about subjectivity, and they imply a context in which to reformulate questions about subjectivity raised by narrative techniques used to represent character. The Cartesian notion of innate ideas implies an essential basis for a human being's experience of subjectivity; and Locke's emphasis upon the relationship between knowledge, experience and education implies that an individual's experience of subjectivity is socially and culturally determined. These two positions are not, however, diametrically opposed in Walsh's novel, nor is either presented unequivocally. Instead, the narrative discourse articulates and explores both positions. Toward the close of the novel, for example, Gran makes a series of observations dialogically intertwined with snatches of quotation from Yeats's "Sailing to Byzantium":

> And one's mind takes it hard, she thinks; one's soul is as lithe as ever, and as volatile, and is amused, patronizing and irritated by the body's decrepitude.
> *An aged man is but a paltry thing . . .*
> yet inside I feel no different; I feel the same as ever, rather, which is more important, as many different things as ever . . .
> *A tattered coat upon a stick, unless*
> *Soul clap its hands and sing, and louder sing*
> *For every tatter in its mortal dress . . .*
> though it isn't monuments of magnificence for me (yet Santa Sophia is more like a vision than a building, I do remember), it's more the brightness falls from the air, the eternally changing sea, and the view of Godrevy light. Yet what could this be inside me, that feels unchanged, through so many and so great revolutions of matter? (Walsh, 1976, pp. 142–143)

The contradiction in Gran's experience of subjectivity, as in "I feel the same as ever, or rather . . . as many different things as ever," articulates a central ambiguity in the novel. Gran's experience of subjectivity is one which is grounded in sameness and difference, which parallels readers' apprehensions of Madge/Gran. Although Madge and Gran represent the same character, they occupy subject positions which are, for readers, simultaneous and discrete. From a Cartesian viewpoint, they are essentially the same character. What we think of as self is, then, an homogeneous accumulation of past facets of the same person, the same essential self—an implication too of Yeats' poem. Such notions of selfhood, that is, that which is "inside me, that feels unchanged," are defined by Madge in opposition to "the body's decrepitude" (p. 143), but, at the same time, this unchanging quality is also defined as changeability or difference. The difference which also grounds Gran's sense of selfhood, combined with the narrative techniques used in the novel to represent Madge/Gran, implies a Lockian conception of selfhood. What we think of as self, then, is a heterogeneous conglomeration of past and present conceptions of selfhood, each of which is formed and situated within and through different temporal, personal and cultural contexts, in other words, that which is "as many different things as ever." Furthermore, as Gran's qualification of Yeats's poem implies (in "though it isn't monuments of magnificence for me") essentiality and spirituality are to be located not in human achievements (such as knowledge and art which, for Yeats, are symbolized by Byzantium), but in the landscape, the natural tangible world.

An overriding concern in the novel is with the relationship between the discourses of philosophy and literature and the immediate world of experience. Ultimately, Walsh privileges an empirical secular humanist approach to ideas and the world as opposed to an abstract universalizing approach. Implicit here is a traditional humanist view of the importance of ideas, but this is combined with a modernist assertion of the validity of empirical observations and subjective constructions of the world which distrusts the elaboration of abstract ideas in isolation from social and historical contexts (Bullock, 1985, p. 156). Philosophical material is incorporated in the novel in ways which foreground its discursive otherness, that is, its status as a specific discursive form, or language system, through which we represent and attribute meanings to the world and to relationships between our selves, others and this world. Such material mostly occurs in the chronologically earlier narrative strand, where it is represented as direct quotation—for example, the excerpt from Locke (quoted in *Unleaving*, 1976, pp. 52–53)—or as direct or indirect character dialogue which is usually reported from, and thereby framed by, Madge's point of view. For Madge, the discourse of philosophy is an unfamiliar one and she usually takes no part in the formal discussions between the professors and the students, but is mainly situated on the outskirts of these discussions, listening. Character focalized descriptions of these discussions indicate the limitations of Madge's point of view. The effect of this can be both parodic and subversive. For example, the narration of the discussion about innate knowledge culminates with Madge's exclamation, "how marvelous such knowledge would be—*I want it!* How does one get it?" (p. 55), wherein she completely misses the point, but at the same time undermines and dismantles the premise of the argument.

By representing philosophical discussions from Madge's limited viewpoint, the narrative frequently constructs a dialogue between the reported discourse (the philosophical discussions), the reporting discourse (character-focalized narration) and the represented social context. This can be seen in the discussion about innate knowledge on Zennor Hill (pp. 55–56). The following passage, an excerpt from this discussion, is narrated from Madge's viewpoint:

> They are saying, now, that if God exists, then the innate could be his mark upon the soul, the potter's fingerprint. Is there perhaps innate knowledge of God?
>
> "But could innate knowledge then be lost?" asks Matthew Brown, in his flat northern accent. For no knowledge of God has ever appeared to *him*. There is something wrong with this remark, for it does not impress the others as clever, as it does Madge. They find it both expected, she sees, coming from him, and unsubtle.
>
> "Were we to *accept* that there is innate knowledge," says Mr. Jones, "we should have to tackle Locke's refutation."
>
> "Which is," says Professor Tregeagle, "that no idea alleged to be innate, even the simplest, does in fact command universal assent." Behind him the bobbing golden heads of the children dip and bounce between the sunlit stones. "For it is evident that children and idiots have not the least apprehension or thought of them."
>
> Madge stares at Molly, whose coarse features and sluggish understanding are thus enough to strip the soul of God's fingerprints, extinguish the undeniable truth, and send us into the world naked with all to learn. Molly has gathered a handful of stones, and is putting them at random on top of the nearest boulder. (p. 56)

The passage draws attention to rules and conventions of philosophical discourse. Although the discussion is represented as a dialogue, it proceeds according to a particular pattern, and the argument which it presents is structured monologically from an unquestioned *a priori* assumption—namely, that there is a fundamental connection between the intellect (cognition and knowledge) and human subjectivity. This is indicated partly through the lack of response to Matthew's apparently inappropriate question, "But could innate knowledge then be lost?" and through the manner in which Locke's argument is incorporated by Mr. Jones. However, the philosophical material in this passage is contextualized in such a way as to undercut the philosophers' assumptions, and to construct a dialogic opposition between the discursive practice of philosophy and the immediate social context within which it is situated and of which the speakers remain largely unaware. This occurs through ironic parallels between character dialogue and the narrative discourse. Professor Tregeagle's reference to Locke (and to "children and idiots") is paralleled by the descriptions of the children playing and that of Molly in particular, Professor Tregeagle's Downs syndrome child (who is focalized here by Madge). The childrens' lack of awareness of the discussion that is going on around them reflects and reinforces Locke's position that human knowledge is not innate but, rather, learned and acquired through experience, and undercuts the Cartesian position, but there is also a contrast in terms used to describe the children in general and Molly in particular which implies two conceptions of childhood and of subjectivity.

Lockeian and Cartesian ideas are further undermined later in the novel by Molly's learning of the phrase, *cogito ergo sum,* and her repetitions of it as "Coggletoe. Petrolpump . . . Butterknife" and "Cogito ergo butterknife" (pp. 110–111). The phrase, *cogito ergo sum,* which has become representative of Cartesian subjectivity, asserts a correlation between a posited innate cognitive predisposition and the essential humanness of a subject. Molly's transposition of sounds and words foregrounds the disparity between the signifying sign-shape and the signified meaning, and between linguistic performance and competence. In doing so, the correlation between cognition, consciousness and essential selfhood upon which Cartesian subjectivity is grounded is dismantled, as is Locke's correlation between language, consciousness and selfhood. Molly also repeats the phrase "correctly" and Patrick's ironic comment, "Well, is that proof good, or isn't it? Because she can say it as well as anyone else!" (p. 111), poignantly highlights the extent to which their father's philosophy marginalizes Molly.

Although there is, throughout the novel, a refusal to represent philosophical concepts unequivocally, assertions about the correlation between intellectual capacity and essentiality, of either the self or the humanness of the subject, implicit in the represented philosophical discourses are constantly questioned and undermined. These ideas are both parodied and censured through Walsh's representation of the character of Professor Tregeagle, whose valuing of the intellect painfully informs his perceptions of Molly, his inability to comprehend and relate to her as another person and his ignorance of how his use of philosophical discourses impinges upon her subjectivity—and effectively denies her a subject position. Underlying this is a failure to recognize that philosophical ideas do have implications for how relationships between selves, others and the world are perceived and attributed with meaning.

The philosophers and their students all use philosophy as an abstract discourse which they perceive as having little bearing upon the immediate and actual world. Madge's more pragmatic and empirical approach to philosophical ideas is clearly affirmed and privileged. She continually contextualizes philosophical questions, relating them to her own experience, her relationships with others and her perceptions of the world and of other people. There are two main implications of this. First, Walsh is using Madge to assert that apparently abstract philosophical ideas do have implications for the ways in which we interpret and make sense of the world, and that empirical observations about the world also have validity. That this is also Walsh's position would seem clear from her article, "Disturbing the Universe" (1987), from which the epigraph for this chapter is taken. In this article she rejects various religious and philosophical explanations for human action and responsibility in a similar way to Madge in *Unleaving*, insisting upon a secular humanist position with regard to human responsibility for actions and for the consequences of these actions. In answer to the question, "in a world in which God has become only one possible explanation among many others, may we do exactly what we like?" she concludes, "I am among those modern consciousnesses who believe that we may act without fear of hell or hope of heaven, but not without regard to the consequences. And considering the consequences of human actions—their physical, moral, social, and psychological consequences—considering what, if God asks nothing, we may yet ask of one another, is complicated and hard" (p. 163).

Second, Madge is represented as selectively appropriating and assimilating the discourses of others, as ways of understanding and representing the world to herself.[7] Subjectivity is thus represented as a conglomeration of appropriated discourses and subject positions. Incorporated philosophical and literary intertexts imply an intellectual and literary context within which the character of Madge/Gran is situated, and which clearly informs the manner in which she perceives and represents the textual world. Madge is actively appropriating these texts and discourses as an interpretative schema through which she articulates her sense of herself in relation to this world. Philosophical and literary intertexts are also a primary means through which the narrative positions and voices of Gran and Madge are represented as merged or intertwined. Both of these effects can be seen in the following passage, for example, wherein intertextual literary material is combined with three narrative voices—those of a narrator, Gran and Madge:

1.   But Gran looks and smiles, holding the window-catch and never dreaming of shutting the window. And in her mind the rain is an element of eternity, showing in its brilliant light-catching instant of fall the eternal aspect of the momentary now. Just let it catch the light in such a way, and the whole world shows this double aspect, an immor-

tal brevity, an infinite particularity. It was Traherne—(will I never outlive quoting, and telling myself where the quotation comes from?)—who saw the orient and immortal wheat, which knew no seed and yet no harvest time. And boys and girls playing like moving jewels. "I know not that they were born, or shall die," she murmurs. (p. 74).

The discourse shifts between third person character focalized narration, indirect and free direct character thought. Intertextual quotations and allusions are used to represent character thought and speech in such a way as to dialogize the discourse and represent the various narrative voices parodically. Though the passage is focalized by Gran—as is signaled by "Gran looks" and "in her mind"—what is seen is represented through a mixture of quotations and appropriated discourses. These include overt quotations of Traherne and Madge (from *Goldengrove*, Walsh, 1972/1985), and a parodic imitation of the elevated poetic discourse of romanticism, as in "the eternal aspect of the momentary now," and "this double aspect, an immortal brevity, an infinite particularity." The point at which the narrative slips into direct thought—"will I never outlive quoting, and telling myself where the quotation comes from?"—is almost a straight quotation of Madge in *Goldengrove*—"will I always be quoting in my head, and telling myself where the line comes from?" (1985, p. 8). This implicitly signals to readers (presuming they have read *Goldengrove*) the identity of Gran, and also suggests a merging of the identities and voices of Gran and Madge; it implies that the two voices denote one unique subject. However, the quotation from *Goldengrove* is itself embedded within another quotation, that of Traherne. And its status as quotation draws attention to the processes of representation whereby this moment of convergence, wherein the identities and voices of Gran and Madge are intertwined, is represented as utterly intertextual. The implication that the two narrative voices might denote one unique subject is disclosed as only a deconstructive possibility—this subject can be posited only as the object of a specific mode of representation.

The overall effect of the mixing of voices in this passage is to represent Madge, Gran and Traherne parodically, and thereby reinscribe an implicit authorial position. But it also foregrounds the extent to which the processes through which Madge/Gran perceives and represents the world to herself, and attributes this world with meanings, are inherently bound up with the interpretative strategies she has developed and the texts and discourses to which she has access—namely, philosophy and literature. If we compare this passage to that of Traherne, from which Gran quotes, we can see more clearly how Walsh is doing this.

2.   The corn was orient and immortal wheat, which never should be reaped, nor was ever sown. I thought it had stood from everlasting to everlasting. The dust and stones of the street were as precious as gold: the gates were at first the end of the world. The green trees when I saw them first through one of the gates transported and ravished me, their sweetness and unusual beauty made my heart to leap, and almost mad with ecstasy, they were such strange and wonderful things. The Men! O what venerable and reverend creatures did the aged seem! Immortal Cherubims! And the young men glittering and sparkling Angels, and maids strange seraphic pieces of life and beauty! Boys and girls tumbling in the street, and playing, were moving jewels. I knew not that they were born or should die; But all things abided eternally as they were in their proper places. Eternity was manifest in the Light of the Day, and something infinite behind everything appeared: which talked with my expectation and moved my desire. (Traherne, 1927, pp.152–153)

The two passages are linked through the image of the children playing, and the repetition of terms—for example, "eternity, eternal, infinite" in (1) and "everlasting, eternally, eternity, infinite" in (2). However, a crucial difference between them lies in the relations between the signifying discourse and the signified concepts and referents to which the discourse refers. The passage by Traherne is religious prose, and the scene being described is a vision of the Celestial city; there is no actual referent, rather, it refers to a vision of transcendence which impacts upon the observer, as in "the green trees . . . ravished and transported me." The scene in passage (1) refers to an actual textual event which is being seen by Gran and inscribed with transcendent meaning through the representational codes brought to bear upon what is seen. Thus, whereas the children "were moving jewels" in (2), they are "like moving jewels" in (1). "Eternity was manifest in the Light of the Day" in (2) has religious connotations, as in the idea of Christ as the "light of the world" and way to eternal life (see John 8:12, 9:5 or 12:46, for example). However, these are secularized in (1) through the literal function of the term "light" in "its [the rain] brilliant light-catching instant." Traherne is using discursive conventions characteristic of religious prose, such as paradox—"never should be reaped, nor was ever sown" and "knew not that they were born or should die." The generic context in which the paradox occurs and the chiastic patterning through which it is represented—as in reaped/sown and born/die—implies meanings which would transcend the binary opposition between life and death. Although Gran almost directly quotes Traherne, Walsh has undone the chiastic structure used by Traherne—as in seed/harvest and born/die—thereby stressing the linear direction from birth to death, rather than the conventional Christian notion of the soul's transcendence of death implicit in the passage from Traherne. In this way, although the description from Gran's point of view uses many of the same terms, such as "eternity, eternal, infinite," the semantic scope of these terms is shifted through the contextual features of the discourse in which they occur. Both passages emphasize synchronic dimensions of time, but whereas Traherne represents a vision of religious transcendence, of eternity outside of and encompassing the present moment, Walsh locates Gran's experience of transcendence precisely within the present moment, within the "thisness" of the here and now. In other words, the mixing of discourses and voices in Walsh's text secularizes the religious import of the (mis)appropriated intertext in a way which, by treating the voices of Gran, Madge and Traherne parodically, implicitly affirms the validity of empirical and humanist interpretative strategies.

The dialogue between humanist empiricism and abstract idealism culminates in the representation of Molly's death, when she falls from a cliff while walking with her brother, Patrick, a key moment in the chronologically earlier narrative. While Madge sees Patrick push her, Paul sees him try to save her, and the disparity between their viewpoints is left unresolved. The episode is narrated three times in the following passages: as third person narration focalized by Paul and Madge (1); by Paul in direct speech (2); and by Madge as indirect thought (3).

1.   Up the path on the brink scramble Molly and Patrick. She is picking the thrift at the edge, brightly visible in her emerald green dress. Patrick points; she leans out, stooping over the outermost clump of flowers; and behind them both Paul and Madge see Patrick's arm suddenly lifted, see him stretch out towards her as she falls . . .

It cannot have happened! says Madge's mind. Desperately it replays the sequence; Patrick points, Molly leans . . . (my ellipsis, p. 114)

2.   "Patrick was walking with Molly along the cliff-edge path," says Paul. "We could see them ahead of us. Molly went very near the edge after some flowers growing there, and Patrick tried to grab her, but he just didn't catch her in time, and she fell off the edge." Madge's head swims. She can hardly believe . . . Paul *is* lying! He is lying, unasked, out of sheer good will.

"Patrick Tregeagle tried to catch hold of Molly, and just missed her . . . are you certain of that, young Fielding?" asks the policeman.

"Oh, *quite* certain. I saw his arm go up and stretch towards her. Madge will tell you; she must have seen it too." And it is borne in

on Madge that Paul is not lying; Paul is telling the truth according
to Paul. He tells what he saw; it is what she saw that is untellable.
(pp. 122–123)

3.   Paul did not lie, she tells herself; he saw—since he says so—
Patrick try to save Molly and fail. But I saw Patrick push her over;
there's no denying that's what I saw. (pp. 122–3)

The episode is initially narrated from a detached and objective viewpoint,
and events are described as a series of actions: Patrick points, Molly leans,
Patrick stretches toward her and she falls. However, the relationships between these actions are omitted and it is here that the interpretations of Paul
and Madge crucially differ. Both Madge and Paul see Patrick's arm stretch
toward Molly, but they encode this action with different intentions: Paul sees
Patrick try to save Molly; and Madge sees him push her. This difference between their interpretations lies in the philosophical positions they occupy.
In an earlier episode, where Paul, Madge, Matthew and Patrick discussed
means and ends, actions and consequences (pp. 100–104), Matthew had
suggested that Paul believed in "absolute moral values," that is, that ends
do not justify their means. This position also informs his ascribing of Patrick's
action with intentionality. Madge's description of Paul's interpretation as "the
truth according to Paul" implies that "the truth" is relative to a person's point
of view, but is also an implicit allusion to New Testament Pauline doctrine,
suggesting an analogy between Paul's absolutist moral stance and that of his
namesake. Paul's viewpoint is essentially idealistic; he interprets Patrick's
actions according to what he is capable of believing about himself and hence
about another person. Madge is however more capable of perceiving and
comprehending the viewpoint of an other. In the same discussion, she had
taken a "common sense" utilitarian viewpoint: how one justifies means and
ends depends on the circumstances (pp. 100–103). She recognizes that it
would be possible, from Patrick's point of view, to justify pushing Molly off
the cliff. Her perception and interpretation of events is based upon her
knowledge of Patrick's thoughts and feelings. However, her encoding of this
recognition is based upon her understanding that the relationship between
actions and consequences, means and ends are not always clear-cut. What
she saw is "untellable," because of the harm it might cause others. The question of whether Patrick tried to save Molly, or did in fact push her remains
ostensibly open, and in this context, the relationship between language and
ideas and the world of experience is implicitly reformulated. To the extent
that Patrick had contemplated pushing Molly, and that both Madge and
Patrick believe it is possible that he may have pushed her, this possibility

that Patrick had contemplated pushing Molly, and that both Madge and Patrick believe it is possible that he may have pushed her, this possibility informs the way in which they think about the world and themselves. Though neither Paul's nor Madge's interpretations are presented as the truth, Paul's approach to events is represented as less exemplary than Madge's. Paul's essentially idealist approach merely imposes an abstract belief system on the world—this is also Professor Tregeagle's approach. Instead, Madge's ability to comprehend a point of view other than her own and her combination of a pragmatic empiricism with appropriated philosophical discourses and ideas is valorized in the novel.

The narrative of *Unleaving* represents a systematic rejection of religious and philosophical abstractions, and it insists on the value of humanist concepts and the possibilities of positive human relationships in the absence of philosophical or religious truths. Walsh's positive version of modern humanism is constructed via a direct critique of premodernist philosophical doctrines, and she uses intertexts to explore complex concerns underlying narrative techniques and themes. The conception of subjectivity that closes the novel is radically optimistic and represents a shift in Walsh's writing away from the sense of loss that *Goldengrove* (1972/1985) closed with. Garner's use of intertexts in *Red Shift* (1973/1989) is more implicit, and relies more on modernist discourses and strategies, in particular the wasteland myth, the concern with temporality and the use of repetition to imply mythic significances, as well as scientific concepts, namely "red shift." These issues are the focus of the next section.

REPETITION, TEMPORALITY AND TRANSCENDENCE IN *RED SHIFT*

As I suggested earlier, *Red Shift* (Garner, 1973/1989) implicitly constructs two main reading positions, which presuppose different kinds of interpretative strategies. The concept of "red shift" suggested by the title constructs a top-down reading position. It implies a metanarrative, anterior to the discourse and to the process of reading, which teleologically structures and orders the three narratives according to linear and diachronic notions of time. A bottom-up reading is aligned with the discourse time: the interlacing of narrative strands means that for readers the three narrative strands exist simultaneously and that the interconnections between them are lateral, rather than linear. Narrative interconnections thereby emphasize synchronic dimensions of narrative time and imply mythic and cyclical concepts of time. Although these two interpretative positions intersect, they do not produce coherent readings. The first implies that the three narratives represent different versions of the same story, and emphasizes teleological and linear notions of historical continuity; the second implies that the three narrative strands represent three similar stories situated in different social and historical contexts, and implies an interplay between notions of alterity and circularity. The two positions are not diametrically opposed, and through them Garner constructs a dialogue between relativist notions of cultural and historical difference and modern humanist notions of temporal and cultural transcendence.

The title of the novel seems to offer readers a top-down interpretative position from which to produce a coherent reading of the novel. "Red shift" is an astronomical term of which Stephen Hawking's *A Brief History of Time* (1988) provides an accessible account. The term refers to the phenomenon, first observed by Edwin Hubble in 1924, whereby "stars moving away from us will have their spectre shifted to the red end of the spectrum (red-shifted)" (Hawking, p. 41). Hubble also observed that "most galaxies appeared red-shifted", that is, "nearly all were moving away from us" (pp. 41–42), and that "the size of a galaxy's red shift . . . is directly proportional to [its] distance from us. Or in other words, the farther a galaxy is, the faster it is travelling away" (p. 42). One of the most important implications of Hubble's findings is that "the universe itself must be expanding and that there must therefore have been a time in the past known as the big bang when the distance between neighbouring galaxies must have been zero" (p. 50); that is the time which scientists refer to as "the big bang" (p. 50). As Hawking has explained, "all our theories of science are formulated on the assumption that space-time is smooth and nearly flat, so they break down at the big bang singularity, where the curvature of space-time is infinite" (p. 50). Thus, the laws of science cannot predict what happened before the big bang; so as far as scientists are concerned the big bang constitutes the beginning of time (p. 50; *see also* pp. 9–10). The title of Garner's novel is usually interpreted metaphorically: the image of an expanding universe and of galaxies moving further and further away from each other is an analogy for an increasing distance between and loneliness of human beings, who are less and less able to communicate with and understand each other and to maintain loving relationships (Philip, 1981, p. 88; Chambers, 1973, p. 494; Nikolajeva, 1989, p. 128). As Philip has suggested, "the book's basic premise is that the most important, and the most difficult, task in life is the establishment of loving contact between two people, the breaking down of barriers, and it is against this private, internal struggle that the seemingly random violence of the outside world is measured" (1981, p. 88). The notion of an infinitely large and expanding universe also obviously puts a damper upon homocentric illusions about humanity's place and relevance in the universe, and the title is seen then as a symbol of a resulting modern existential angst about the alienation, emptiness, futility and the unknowability of the world (Philip, 1981, p. 91), and the "instability of man's place in the scheme of things" (Benton 1974. p. 7).

The title, "red shift," and the notion of an expanding universe which it suggests, implies a developmental metanarrative which structures the novel and informs the kinds of meanings which might be attributed to it. However, there are a number of problems with this kind of top-down interpretation of the novel. First, if the expanding universe is an analogy for human relationships, then the distances between people will be represented as greater, and the possibilities of communication more difficult, in the present than in the past. Hence, the relationship between Tom and Jan is to be seen as a failure, attributable to a lack of communication. However, the difficulties of effective communication are not peculiar to the contemporary relationship. It is a problem which recurs throughout the three narratives, and is foregrounded in the civil war strand in particular, wherein the same episode is narrated differently three times from three different character viewpoints (Garner, 1989, pp. 73–77, 91–94 and 100–101). Second, the notion of an expanding universe presupposes a beginning, and hence a notion of time as linear, which implies that the three narratives should be read as teleologically structured, beginning with Macey and ending with Tom. However, for readers, the interlaced structure of the narrative, and the ending in particular, implies nonlinear concepts of narrative time; a linear teleological (top-down) reading can only be produced retrospectively.

A central problem with the novel is how to interpret all of the repetitions and interconnections interwoven through the three narrative strands. Clearly, readers will make sense of each narrative in terms of its contextual relationships with the other two narratives, but the kinds of meanings that are ascribed to these interrelations will depend upon whether readers stress the similarities between narrative strands or the differences. Is the novel three different versions of what is essentially the same story, or is it three similar stories situated in different social and historical contexts? The question hinges on how we conceive of the role and status of a repetition: does a repeated event, situation or experience have the same meaning, or does the specific context in which it occurs change its meaning? The three narrative strands in the novel are primarily linked through place and through repeated story and discoursal features. The central characters of each narrative are to varying degrees displaced and alienated, culturally, socially and psychologically. Interconnections and repetitions imply parallels between characters and events in each narrative strand, and imbue places and objects with mythic and transcendent qualities.

The three narratives all center on three places: Barthomley, Rudheath and Mow Cop. Each place is represented as being sacred and as associated with violence and desecration at some point in time. Recurring wasteland images and references have a cumulative effect, and though they are strongest in the contemporary strand, they imply a cyclical pattern whereby the representations of place oscillate between being places of personal or cultural sanctity and wastelands symbolic of the alienated subjectivity of characters. Browning's "Childe Roland to the Dark Tower Came" is a crucial intertext for the wasteland and dark tower images throughout the novel, and for the negativity and despair that pervades the contemporary strand in particular. The phrase "the dark of the tower" is used repeatedly to describe the church at Barthomley (*see,* for example, 1989, pp. 77, 93, 100, 126 and 133). The church is the site of the tribal settlement which the Roman fugitives attack in the opening of the novel where they find and rape the young woman (pp. 26–35); it is also where the massacre occurs in 1642 and Margery is raped, and where Jan and Tom eat sandwiches and attempt to make love (p. 130). The implication in Tom's coded letter, that he will jump from Barthomley tower (Nikolajeva, 1989), echoes the link in Browning's poem between the dark tower, death and the object of the Romantic quest. Rudheath is a birch wood which was a medieval sanctuary (Philip, 1981, p. 96). In the Roman strand it is a sanctuary of the Cats, whose shrine has been reconsecrated by the Mothers (the Cats and the Mothers are the two Celtic tribes in the Roman strand) and which is desecrated by Logan (pp. 23–24). In the civil war strand, it is a temporary place of refuge for Thomas and Margery after the massacre at Barthomley, and in the contemporary strand it is the caravan site where Tom lives. The birch wood connects the three strands (pp. 12, 20 and 145–146), but, as Philip has argued, the shrine has lost its sacredness in the contemporary narrative and become a "dead place," a modern wasteland (Philip, 1981, p. 97). Mow Cop is a hill in Cheshire which in the Roman strand is a sacred place for the tribes: it is "the netherstone of the world. The skymill turns on it to grind the stars" (p. 64). Here the fugitive soldiers make their headquarters and die; Margery and Thomas are on their way to Mow Cop at the end of the novel; and for Tom and Jan, it is a special and private place, where they also find the stone axe and read the graffiti on the walls of the ruined cottage which closes the novel, "not really now not any more" (pp. 88 and 155).

The three strands are also linked through repeated objects, story motifs and discursive features. The central male characters each possess a stone axe or thunderstone, which the female characters each recognize as special, or sacred, and which the male characters all misuse in some way. Macey carries it with him (it is linked to his fits) and uses it as a weapon at Barthomley (p. 20), where he later buries it (p. 150). It is found at Barthomley by Thomas, who wants to break it (p. 42), and at the end of the novel Margery speaks of putting it in the chimney of the house she and Thomas will build at Mow Cop (p. 154), at which point we already know that Tom and Jan have found the axe in a ruined cottage at Mow Cop (p. 82) and that Tom has sold it to a museum (p. 131). Each story centers on a love relationship, and the women in each story are sexually and/or physically violated. Each story contains triangular relationships between different combinations of characters: Tom, Jan and the German wine grower or Tom's mother; Thomas, Margery and Venables or John Fowler; Macey, the young woman and Logan or Magoo or Face. Repeated references and phrases occur in each strand (for example, the star constellation of Orion (pp. 29 and 39), or "it was the waiting" (pp. 42 and 49) and quotations, such as "Let there be no strife, for we be brethren" (pp. 30, 46 and 70)—which both Thomas and Tom read on the chapel screen and to which Margery and Jan both reply "How do I know?".) Garner has claimed that the novel is a reworking of the "Tam Lin" ballad (1976, p. 125). There are no obvious references to the ballad in the novel, and as Philip has argued, the connections between them are tenuous (1981, p. 105). Parallels between the novel and the ballad include: the names of the three male characters, Tom/Thomas/Macey; their "need to be held and mothered" and to be "saved by instinctive, unreserved female love" as Thomas and Macey are, though Tom is not (Philip, 1981, p. 104). Further, the connection between *Red Shift* and "Tam Lin" implies that we are to assume that Jan and Margery are, like the native girl, pregnant at the end of the novel (Philip, 1981, p. 104). Although Watson (1983) does not mention "Tam Lin," it seems to underlie his interpretation of the rape and seduction of the three women as "willing submission" through which they "save" (or attempt to save) the three male characters (pp. 81–82). The two historical narratives differ from the ballad in that the women are raped by an other (or others), and that Macey and Thomas would only be the "putative or substitute" fathers (Philip, 1981, p. 104); in the contemporary strand, Jan is willingly seduced by another, though it seems likely that, if she is pregnant, Tom is the father. An implication of these substitutions is that the other male characters, Macey's "mates," Thomas Venables, and the German Wine grower, are the doubles or counterparts of Macey, Thomas and Tom.

The three male characters are linked through their names (Tom, Thomas and Macey, short for Thomas), their susceptibility to fits and by their momentary apprehensions of each other. Each character is prone to having fits: Macey's behavior has the features of a "berserker" (R. Walsh, 1977, p. 38n; Philip, 1981, p. 98); and Thomas's "fits" seem to be a form of epilepsy.[8] Both characters' fits are interpreted by other characters according to cultural conventions as a form of divine possession or apprehension—for example, the Celtic woman asks Macey, "When did the god come to you?" (Garner, 1989, p. 59), and John Fowler says of Thomas, "that man sees God" (p. 45). Tom's emotional outbursts of physical and verbal rage are more difficult to interpret (many commentators posit mental illness). They are clearly linked with those of Macey and Thomas through the use of time-slip strategies, whereby characters are momentarily aware of each other, during their fits. For example, Macey's description of "two hands—pressing at me—a long way off against my eyes" (p. 23) repeats and conflates two descriptions of Tom: "he rammed the backs of his fists into his face, dragging his eyes open" (p. 19) and "he pressed his open palms against the window gently, relentlessly" (p. 20). During his fits, Macey also sees the tower on Mow Cop (which exists only in Tom's time), and the church tower at Barthomley (p. 60). The colors which Macey also sees—"blue silver and red" (pp. 20, 22, 59 and 60)—are repeated in the contemporary strand in the description of the train on the last page—"The red doors closed. The blue and silver train" (p. 155). This awareness of characters is only one-way. While Macey apprehends Thomas and Tom, and Thomas apprehends Tom, Tom is aware of neither of the past characters. Past characters thus have an apprehension of the future, but no apprehension of the past, a pattern which reverses historical concepts of time, and which underscores Tom's alienation and displacement in time and place. Tom's comment "I could do with a red shift. Galaxies and Rectors have them. Why not me?" (p. 126) makes a connection between science, the physical world and religion, and implicitly questions the possibility of truth or certainty. His need of a "red shift" suggests the need for a meaningful belief system or tradition with which to position himself in relation to the world, and with which to order his experiences and construct them as meaningful.[9]

It is possible to read *Red Shift* within the context of negative or positive modernist traditions and produce two divergent readings. A negative approach privileges diachrony, history and chronology, and stresses cultural and historical difference. Fragmentation and alienation is seen as endemic, neither specific to the modern experience, nor transcendable. A positive modernist approach, such as that of Philip (1981), privileges synchrony, myth and circularity over diachrony, history and chronology, and posits the possibility of transcending the fragmentation and alienation which characterizes the modern experience (*see* LaCapra, 1987, pp. 130–131). Thus, in a positive reading, Garner's negativity about personal maturation and interpersonal relationships can be recuperated through the evocation of modernist concepts of repetitive temporality and transcendence wherein repeated narrative patterns are seen as constructing circular mythic concepts of time grounded in an originary and transcendent moment and an essentialized subjectivity. In this way, the pessimistic ending of the contemporary strand can be ameliorated via the more positive endings of the chronologically earlier narratives. Such an interpretative approach stresses the interconnections between Tom, Macey and Thomas, and the implication that they are essentially the same person. They have been described as "one person living simultaneously in three times, or rather in one boundless, nonlinear time" (Nikolajeva, 1989, p. 129), "all aspects of the same person [who] possess each other's minds" (Gillies, 1975, p. 115), and the "alter egos" of each other (Gillies, 1975, p. 115; Townsend, 1979, p. 89).[10]

However, an interpretation which sees Tom/Macey/Thomas as a unifying figure must either ignore or transcend temporal and cultural differences between narrative strands. It presupposes the possibility of transhistorical notions of human experience and subjectivity and the essentiality of the subject. I am not suggesting that the novel does not imply this interpretative position, but rather that it is an ambivalent position which is inscribed in the text at the level of desire, rather than as a point of closure. As Watson (1983) has commented: "Garner's imagination craves a kind of pure virgin-self, untrammelled by the past and uninjured by parents . . . but, paradoxically, his great artistic gift is his ability to make dramatic the complexities of the confused and entangled psyche, suffering and raging and volubly articulate. What is the tormented modern consciousness to do, knowing it has lost—perhaps never had—the virgin self?" (p. 86). Watson's discourse is evocative of a Lacanian conception of the subject as the site of irremediable loss and alienation and of a darker and more negative version of modernist humanism, which focuses on the (deferred) quest of the subject for integration amid fragmentation (Hutcheon, 1989, p. 108; Gloege, 1992, p. 59). Garner's use of Browning's poem, itself a critique of the romantic quest for the self, inscribes this quest as an unrealizable desire for completion and presence.

The ambivalence generated by Garner's modernism is highlighted in Philip's (1981) interpretations of the fits of the three characters and the time-slip strategies used to represent their apprehension of each other. Garner has expressed admiration for societies in which epilepsy and mental illness are seen as a form of divine possession (Garner, 1976, p. 132)—as indeed are Macey's and Thomas's fits represented by other characters. Philip (1981) argues that this admiration implies that the fits experienced by Tom, Macey and Thomas are a form of religious ecstasy and "seem to posit 'the intersection of the timeless moment' as the source of conventional ideas of divinity" (p. 100). However, as Philip points out, what these characters actually apprehend is not God but a confused sense of each other (p. 100). Philip interprets this as the effect or manifestation of an "engram" or "memory-trace," a phenomenon described by Garner in "Inner Time" (1976). An engram is "a memory-trace, a permanent impression made by a stimulus or experience" which is located within "inner time" (pp. 127–128). As Garner points out, "intensely-remembered experiences . . . will be emotionally contemporaneous, even though we know that the calender separates them by years." Inner time is "one-dimensional—or infinite" and not bound by the linear temporality of "outer time" (p. 128). In fiction, a "disorientation leading towards madness can be induced when the engram is made present simultaneously in inner and outer time" (p. 129). Garner also extends this concept, linking it with the notion of a "collective unconscious" or "inherited inner time" (p. 129). Clearly, then, the fits experienced by Tom, Thomas and Macey can be understood as the manifestation of a memory trace which is inscribed within the collective memory or unconscious common to the three characters, as well as being present within certain situations and places. Thus, for Philip (1981), Tom's inarticulate outbursts "proceed from the confluence of an individual psychological upheaval with the energy inherited from analogous historical situations" which exist in inner time and thus transcend temporality (p. 101). The fits each character experiences are to be understood as the manifestation of a transcendent essential aspect of human experience, and the fact that they apprehend each other (rather than divinity) is explicable as an assertion of a form of secular humanism which replaces notions of God with a conception of human experience as essential and therefore transcendent. Furthermore, the notion that individual experiences construct a memory-trace locates the source or cause of such moments of transcendence firmly in the past. They are, in fact, a projection of the past onto the future, and Tom's inability to apprehend past characters as they apprehend him corresponds to his temporal and cultural displacement from this originary moment.

The main problem with Philip's interpretation is that it ignores the differences between the three narrative strands and the historical and cultural situatedness of characters and events, through which Garner asserts the cultural construction of meaning and notions of historical continuity. In other words, the text also implies a position from which to interrogate the positive version of modern humanism which Philip's reading seems to assume. By representing the fits which Thomas and Macey experience as a form of divine possession (from the viewpoints of other culturally situated characters), Garner is also then drawing attention to the cultural situatedness of interpretations of human behavior and of the meanings that cultures ascribe to behavior. The fact that during these moments of heightened awareness characters are only able to apprehend visions which are reflections or projections of themselves, rather than God, also suggests that Garner is perhaps parodying the notion of divine apprehension by representing it as an extreme form of solipsism. The desire for transcendence is ultimately a desire for essential selfhood, but it is also the site of fragmentation and loss of self. The question remains though, as to whether this parody asserts a secular humanist notion of transhistorical transcendence (as Philip and other commentators seem to think it does). Or does it also extend to humanist notions of transcendence, in which case Garner would seem to be critiquing the extreme cultural solipsism of humanist practices wherein the other is perceived through the logic of identity? Certainly, the severe alienation and inability to perceive the subjectivity of an other, or to form interpersonal relations, that links the three male characters suggests this analogy between individual and cultural solipsism.

Garner's narrative techniques thus foreground ideological problems with modernist concepts of repetition and transcendence, and, in my reading, present a negative version of modern humanism. Walsh's *Unleaving* (1976) raises similar kinds of questions to those raised in *Red Shift*, about the relations between repetition, meaning and context. These center on the relations between repetition, recollection and point of view. Repetitions in the discourse of *Unleaving* draw attention to shifts in meaning corresponding to shifts in narrative point of view and the temporal positioning of the subject in relation to an experience or event. These issues provide the focus for the next section.

Repetition and Recollection in *Unleaving*

Repeated episodes and discourse elements in both narrative strands of *Unleaving* (Walsh, 1976) have a cumulative effect, which focuses attention on thematic concerns, disrupts temporal linearity and implies a circular narrative structure, as in *Red Shift* (Garner, 1973/1989). However, whereas in *Red Shift* narrative circularity has a mythic function, which posits an originary moment of transcendence anterior to the temporal context of the text, Walsh uses repetition and circularity to assert the phenomenality of the here and now, and to foreground differences between present and recollected experience and, hence, to assert the provisional construction of the subject. Both novels use strategies which disrupt diachronic dimensions of narrative, but the notions of synchronic time that they assert are very different.

Repetitions in *Unleaving* are of two types: repeated story motifs and elements; and repeated discursive features. Both types foreground narrative discontinuities between story order and discourse order, and implicitly highlight thematic concerns, in particular, concerns with age and death. The two narrative strands are interconnected so as to clearly link Madge and Gran and establish that they are the same person quite early in the novel. In the opening sections, there are some indications that the chronologically earlier narrative is Gran's memory. This is implied by strategies indicating point of view in narration focalized by Gran, and by shifts in tense in that focalized by Madge. For example, the account of Madge's grandmother's funeral, which is clearly narrated from the point of view of Madge, is preceded and followed by descriptions of Gran, which suggest that she is in fact remembering the funeral: "Gran sits, eyes closed, looking out to sea" (Walsh, 1976, p. 15) and "Gran starts a little as she hears him, for she was far away . . . There have been other deaths, other rescues" (pp. 21–22). Also, the syntactic form of the first three sections focalized by Madge imply retrospective narration: they begin in the past tense, as in, "There had been a journey" (p. 7; *see also* pp. 10 and 15), and shift into the present tense.

Repeated episodes include the younger Madge and Emily both taking the same route from the train station to the house (pp. 9 and 39) and both retrieving a bottle from the sea (pp. 35 and 39); and references to lost children (pp. 58–59 and 59–61), deaths (p. 22), Oxford (p. 24) and falling (pp. 29 and 48). These repetitions establish story links between the two narratives. They mainly have a proleptic function; they allude to later story events or to events which have happened in between the two narratives. There is also a considerable amount of repetition in the discourse of the novel: in descriptions of actions and the landscape; in opening phrases, (e.g., pp. 7, 15 and 22); and in quotations (in particular, quotations from Locke on pages 52 and 134 and Job on pages 64 and 136). Repeated references to the action of entering the living room on pages 7 and 10 are the most overt early clue that Madge and Gran are the same character and when this same action is repeated again toward the close of the novel (p. 147), it has a cumulative effect which focuses story and significance on Madge's entry into the living room where her grandmother's dead body has been laid out.

Discursive repetitions also disrupt the linear direction of the narrative, so that the significances of earlier references become clearer retrospectively. For example, on pages 49–50, the lighthouse is described from Gran's point of view in terms which, at this point in the novel, seem ominous and ambiguous: "Though she knows how it lies, dark against the sun on its sloping island in a sea that glitters with floating but unextinguished stars of light; how it looms, peering over the top of the cliff with its one Cyclops eye." It is described again, on page 114, from Madge's point of view, just after Molly has fallen from the cliff: "over the humped back of the cliff's edge rises Godrevy light—just the top of it, looking over the crest of the land at them with its one dark Cyclops eye." The repeated phrase, "with its one (dark) Cyclops eye" clearly links the two passages and, retrospectively, we know that Gran is seeing the lighthouse from Godrevy Point, from where Molly fell. The first reference is a retrospective prolepsis, and it makes sense only once readers know of Molly's fall; Gran is in effect remembering events which for readers are yet to happen. The temporal disjunction between story order and discourse order disrupts the linear temporal progression of the narrative (story and discourse are at this point moving in opposite directions) and implies a circular narrative structure.

This circularity also occurs through discontinuities between story order and discourse order, whereby the two narratives are represented as literally interlocked. This has important thematic implications for how the subjectivity of Gran/Madge is represented, and for the novel's central concern with age and death. Whereas story order and narrative order in Gran's narrative are fairly close, in Madge's narrative there is a crucial gap at the beginning of the novel between her entry into the living room, where her grandmother's body is laid out, and the funeral, which is not filled until the end of the novel where it is narrated from the point of view of Madge as Gran (pp. 146–7).[11] The delayed narration suggests a necessary emotional distance, but it also disrupts readers' sense of the narrative as strictly chronological, and imposes a circular narrative structure. Gran's account occurs quite near the close of the novel, so the novel begins and ends at the same point in time, with Madge's journey to Goldengrove after her grandmother's death (pp. 7–10, pp. 146–147). This foregrounds Walsh's thematic concerns with age and death; the novel begins and ends with Madge's grandmother's death and anticipates Madge/Gran's death. The title of the novel, "Unleaving," an allusion to Hopkins's poem "Spring and Fall," has two main associations: the association with autumn implies a metaphoric allusion to aging and to death; and it also suggests the idea of remaining (or not leaving). The first anticipates Madge/Gran's death. The second figures the circularity of the novel, that is, the sense in which it begins and ends at the same place and time and that Madge/Gran and Madge's Gran each, in a sense, remain at Goldengrove; subjectivity and place are inextricable. This circularity also emphasizes the connection between Madge and her own grandmother. One reason that the identities of characters in *Unleaving* is initially confusing is that Madge as Gran is so reminiscent of Madge's Gran in *Goldengrove* (Walsh, 1972/1985). The Gran of *Unleaving* is an intertextual construct—both Madge and Madge's grandmother. An implication of this is that subjectivity is not a stable or singular phenomena. By playing at being Gran, Madge is always actively constructing her own subjectivity. The narrative techniques work, then, to represent the subjectivity of Madge/Gran as an accumulation of, and dialogue between, older and younger selves, and between Madge and Gran's sense of their own identity in relation to place and to others.

The narrative structures of *Red Shift* (Garner, 1973/1989) and *Unleaving* are similar in that the narrative strands merge together at the end of the novel, a strategy which can potentially achieve narrative closure and thereby construct a stable position for readers to interpret the interrelations between narrative strands. In the close of *Unleaving*, the overt identification of Gran as Madge, and the retrospective narration of past events narrated previously or omitted from Madge's narrative, implies a circular narrative structure, linking the ending of Gran's narrative to the opening of Madge's. In this way, the ending suggests the merging, or overlapping of the voices and subject positions of Madge and Gran, and constructs a position from which readers are able to infer a linear "story" structure connecting the two narratives. In *Red Shift*, the three strands are represented as merged through the omission of textual breaks marking shifts between narrative strands, and of the names of the speakers (1989, pp. 154–155). However, while the narratives are thereby typographically interlocked, it is still possible to disentangle them, and to identify the various speakers through the content and the discursive style of character speech. The novel, then, comprises three discrete narrative strands, each of which attains a sense of "story" closure. The interconnections between the three stories are lateral, rather than linear, and readers are denied a stable position from which to infer a linear "story" structure. For readers, the three narratives coexist simultaneously, and for this reason the ending of the novel is most frequently taken to imply an assertion of the "insignificance of time" as it is experienced by an individual relative to larger concepts of time (Benton, 1974, p. 6). Notions of time, then, are merely culture-specific ways of ordering what is a comparatively limited experience (Benton, 1974, p. 7) and the physical merging of the three narratives is analogous to the merging of the temporal contexts in which they are situated. However, in stressing the similarities between stories, this move seems to assume that the three narratives represent three versions of the same story with alternative endings, and closes off the possibility that they might also be three different stories situated in three different temporal and cultural contexts.

CONCLUSION

I began this chapter with a quotation from Jill Paton Walsh's "Disturbing the Universe": "the gods have departed, more or less . . . and what is left is ourselves." Walsh's hypothesis constitutes an ideological basis for both of the novels that I have been discussing. However, while they offer much the same answer to the question as to what is left "in a world in which God has become only one possible explanation among others" (Walsh, 1987, p. 163), that is, ourselves, the concepts of selfhood that the two novels offer are very different. In a sense, the question that I have extracted from Walsh's statement is fundamental to contemporary writing for young people, though Walsh's and Garner's responses perhaps articulate this question with more complexity than most novels for teenagers. They also express two extreme, and to some extent opposed, voices with which an answer might be offered. For Walsh, the absence of philosophical or religious truths allows for the affirmation of a positive humanist stance, which insists upon the possibility and value of human relationships and the validity of empirical and subjective observations about the world, and at the same time asserts the value of literary and philosophical cultural traditions within which complex ideas can be explored. For Garner, such philosophical relativism poses problems for the construction of meanings and results in a personal and cultural alienation, fragmentation and loss of self. In *Red Shift*, the central image of the expanding universe articulates a vision of humanity in which individuals are distanced from one another, unable to communicate effectively and unable to form intersubjective relationships. For both writers, the absence of "truth" offers freedoms, but it also constitutes restraints on those freedoms. A crucial difference in their work lies, then, in how such freedoms and restraints are to be viewed.

While the questions that novels such as these pose are central to fiction for young people, *Unleaving* and *Red Shift* are very unusual adolescent novels. They utilize very sophisticated narrative techniques and so highlight the complexity of the philosophical issues that they deal with. Both novels utilize modernist narrative strategies, including multiple character focalizers, indirect modes of discourse representation, and multiple narrative strands, that is strategies which are relatively uncommon in texts for children and teenagers. The narrative techniques of both novels also foreground problems of reading and interpretation, namely, how to interpret recurrent narrative patterns. Both novels are structured through multistranded narration and

In *Unleaving*, this circularity is linked with personal time and memory; in *Red Shift*, it is linked with mythic or collective memory. Chapter 6 continues my analysis of temporally structured multistranded novels which construct a dialogue between the past and the present, but my focus will be on the diachronic dimensions of narrative time and the representation of history and of subjectivity within history.

ENDNOTES

1. Bakhtin's concept of the chronotope is discussed and elaborated on in Chapter 6, with regard to historical fictions.

2. Nikolajeva (1989) has also included a transcription of the coded letter.

3. *See* Philip (1981, pp. 94–96) for a full account of Garner's historical sources.

4. *See* Stephens (1992a, pp. 29–41) on top-down and bottom-up reading.

5. "She carried the pain of his strength without a sound, and raised her head when she felt his tears. As he looked at her, he retched, and threw her from him, slamming her body against the wall, and caught her as she fell, held her as if he were a woman, such gentleness" (Garner, 1989, p. 114).

6. This dialogue is made explicit in the philosophical discussion that takes place on Zennor Hill (pp. 55–56).

7. These two strategies can be seen in her quotations of Locke, Job and Wittgenstein, where she is deliberately repeating previously quoted material so as to imply other meanings, and also when she asks of Matthew, "Have you ever seen a dead body, Matthew?" (p. 107), wherein she relates Matthew's argument to her own experience and thereby situates an abstract idea in a literal context.

8. This is implied by Margery's comment about Thomas, "Where's God when you're stiff as a plank and your tongue's down your throat?" (p. 45).

9. Chambers (1973) offers another interpretation of this passage: "Everyone needs a little distance from the deepest pains of living before the pain is understood and can be coped with, before experience can be given perspective, and be made bearable" (p. 496).

10. Watson (1983) applies this to the female characters in each of the narrative strands; they are also to be seen as essentially the same character.

11. The fact Madge's Gran has died is implicit in the mention of the telegram (p. 8), but this information is only ascertained retrospectively.

6 SUBJECTIVITY AND HISTORY

In any case, why should the development of a child's perception about the past matter? To have a sense of history is, above all, to have a sense of one's own humanity, and without that we are nothing. For the child, it is a step toward an awareness of other people, which is the most vital step toward being not just an adult, but a mature adult.

Penelope Lively, "Children and Memory"

We must drop our habit of taking the different social structures of past periods, then stripping them of everything that makes them different; so that they all look more or less like our own, which then acquires from this process a certain air of having been there all along, in other words, of permanence pure and simple. Instead we must leave them their distinguishing marks and keep their impermanence always before our eyes, so that our own period can be seen to be impermanent too.

Bertolt Brecht, *Brecht on Theatre: The Development of an Aesthetic*

This chapter focuses on the historical dimensions of the concepts of subjectivity and individual and cultural forms of solipsism. As Lively's assertion of the relationship between child development and a sense of history in the first epigraph suggests, concepts of personal identity are formed, in part, through an awareness and understanding of the past and of a sense of a relation in the present to personal and social histories. However, the apprehension, understanding and representation of the subjectivity of historical persons present a particularly problematic area for both fictive and non-fictive forms of historical writing. As Brecht's comments in the second epigraph imply, the problem lies in how to perceive and comprehend the otherness of a past culture, race or person without anachronistically projecting present concerns and ideological assumptions onto that past and, conversely, without representing it as an earlier (either less "civilized" or more ideal) stage of the present. These kinds of concerns are foregrounded in historical novels concerned with the relations between a narrative past and present, particularly in novels which incorporate multiple temporal contexts. The narrative techniques used to represent the past and the present ascribe meaning to concepts of subjectivity, time and history. This chapter will examine the implications that narrative structures have for the construction of the subject in history and for the dialogic representation of the past. In the last chapter, I concentrated on personal concepts of time, memory and narrative repetitions in polyphonic multitemporal novels. This chapter will focus on historical novels which structure the relationship between the past and the present dialogically.

Historical fiction for children is primarily oriented toward the development of an understanding of the present and of the relations between one's self, time, place and others through attaining a sense of history. To this end, historical fiction for children—such as that by Sutcliff, Treece or Lively—and the teaching of history, have traditionally been dominated by humanist approaches to history, wherein events in the past are conceived of as "changing particulars" within an unchanging system of representation "that would itself transcend the historical process" (LaCapra, 1980, p. 273). History is conceived of as a system of universals which validate and authenticate experience in the present. Stephens has also noted that "notions of the 'universality of human experience' . . . may amount to no more than a matter of re-presenting the past in our own image" (1992a, p. 207); in other words, the evocation of universals can be indicative of culturally solipsistic textual practices. Traditional humanist approaches are also apt to represent historical processes as developmental and teleological and to generate "closed" versions of history—that is, what LaCapra has termed "documentary" views of history, which reconstruct the past for readers in a "digestible and assimilable" form (1980, p. 263). The developmental model used to schematize historical processes is frequently that of child development. This analogy between the formation of a culture, or nation, and that of an individual subject is pervasive within traditional humanist approaches to history and the teaching of history in particular. It is implicit, for example, in Egan's (1989) claim that historical understanding in Western culture has followed a sequential and chronological development, and in his assumption that there exists a correspondence between stages of linguistic and cognitive development and historical development (pp. 280–282). Representations of primitive species or cultures as being childlike and solipsistic also construct cultural development according to a model of child development, which thereby correlates modern western culture and moral and intellectual concepts associated with adulthood.

In Chapter 5, I outlined LaCapra's distinction between diachronic and synchronic dimensions of narrative time (1987, p. 204). I suggested that modernist narratives, such as *Red Shift* (Garner, 1973/1989) and *Unleaving* (Walsh, 1976), emphasize the synchronic dimensions of narrative time and use repetitive temporal patterns to disrupt linear and teleological concepts associated with diachrony. Diachrony designates movement over time involving change (LaCapra, 1987, p. 204). In this chapter, I will be looking at narrative forms used to construct (and subvert) diachronic dimensions of time and their interrelations with concepts of history and subjectivity. LaCapra (1980) has extended the Bakhtinian concept of dialogism in his work on history writing and interpretative approaches to the past. The discussion will also link Bakhtin's concepts of dialogism, polyphony and the chronotope with the insights of LaCapra (1980; 1987) and Hayden White (1980; 1987) about the relations between history writing, narrative and interpretation. The codes and practices of history writing are culture-specific, and any historical record or interpretation is selective and partial, reflecting the concerns and interests of the historian or commentator and the cultural, ideological and intellectual context in which it is produced (H. White, 1980). As Hutcheon (1989) has argued, a primary way in which modern historians organize, interpret and represent the past is through the use of narrative forms, comprising beginning, middle and end, and logical cause-and-effect structures. These are forms which imply "a structuring process that imparts [culturally inscribed] meaning[s], as well as order," coherence and closure (p. 62). White's discussions of narrativity have suggested that the privileging of narrative forms within modern historiography is indicative of a desire to ascribe the past (and hence the present) with coherence, integrity, fullness and finality (1980, p. 24). There is a strong humanist interest in the construction of progressive and developmental versions of history and the privilege accorded to narrative lies in its capacity to represent linear, chronological, causal and teleological relationships between events and persons (LaCapra, 1980; Miller, 1974).

The novels discussed in this chapter all represent a dialogue between the past and the present. They do this either by incorporating multiple narrators and/or character focalizers, by timeshift strategies and the construction of multiple temporal settings or by using narrative motifs such as characters who are involved in historical research. These narrative strategies can potentially, structure the relationship between past and present dialogically, and they can draw attention to the textuality of a text, and hence to the textuality of history. The combination of polyphonic narration with multitemporal narrative represents characters situated in both narrative past and present as narrators and as focalizers, in other words, as agents who occupy active subject positions within the narrative discourse. These strategies can have the effect of representing history as open, subject to other representations and interpretations, and they can inscribe a range of historically and socially situated interpretative positions within texts. At the same time, narrative strategies also carry with them implicit cultural and philosophical assumptions about subjectivity and the relations between human subjects, time and history. Appropriated discourses and intertexts are used to represent characters, events and discourses of the past, thereby implying that the past of a place or culture and the subjectivity of persons is radically intertextual and heteroglottic, and that history is a complex process of textualization and, hence, ideological inscription.

There are three main interrelated aspects of narrative which effect the representation of subjectivity within history: the narrative techniques used to represent the subjectivity of characters located in the past, and to mediate and dialogize representations of the past; the Bakhtinian concept of the chronotope and the use of evolutionary and developmental chronotopes in narrative; and the intertextual construction of histories, and of alternative histories in particular. These aspects will be examined in *The Driftway* (Lively, 1972/1985), *The Court of the Stone Children* (Cameron, 1973), *Red Shift* (Garner, 1973/1989), *The Callender Papers* (Voigt, 1983/1991), *Voices After Midnight* (Peck, 1989/1992), *Donald Duk* (Chin, 1991) and *A Bone from a Dry Sea* (Dickinson, 1992). The next section will examine the textual inscription of documentary and dialogical approaches to history, and narrative strategies used to represent historical persons as focalizers and as subjects and to position characters and implied readers in interpretative relations to the past.

HISTORY AND AGENCY

LaCapra (1980) has distinguished between two main approaches to the past in modern historiography: a documentary approach and a dialogical approach. These are not mutually exclusive, but rather represent different emphases within history writing, which are indicative of different modes of representation, reading practices and subject positions. A documentary approach functions primarily as a "processing of primary source material" (p. 263) which reconstructs the past and represents it for readers in a digestible and assimilable form (pp. 272 and 263). A dialogical approach constructs "a dialogue or conversation with the past" (p. 272) and aims to stimulate readers to respond critically to the interpretations offered. By masking the selectivity and partiality of interpretative processes involved in the writing of history, documentary approaches present "closed" versions of history and assume fairly passive reader subject positions, wherein a reader's subjectivity is relatively effaced. Dialogical approaches "present interpretation as the 'voice' of the historical reader in 'dialogue' with the past" (p. 274), and in doing so assume more active reader subject positions.

In Voigt's *The Callender Papers* (1983/1991), Peck's *Voices After Midnight* (1989/1992) and Chin's *Donald Duk* (1991) dialogic and documentary approaches to the past are represented as interdependent. In *The Callender Papers* the narrator, Jean, is employed by Mr. Thiel to sort and collate historical documents relating to the Callender family. At the outset, her approach to this historical material is methodical and scholarly. She sorts and catalogs the various papers into groups according to chronology and theme—personal and family papers, public papers, business-of-life papers and so on. As her response to the past changes from a scholarly interest to an emotive and empathetic evaluation, her objectives and hence her approach also change from a documentary processing of primary source material to an interactive and dialogic relation with what she discovers is her own past. Furthermore, Jean's discoveries (namely that Mr. Thiel is in fact her father and Irene Callender was her mother) have implications for her own present and for her identity.

Jean's access to the past is via two kinds of sources: textual material (the Callender papers) and the stories told by other characters—namely, Mac, Mrs. Bywall and Enoch. The title of the novel and Jean's initial function stress the textuality of history and hence her access to the past. However, her evaluation of the past and ability to interpret and thus enter into dialogue with it depend also on how she interprets the stories that other characters tell. Thus, a dialogic relation to the past depends on her initial ability to adopt a documentary approach, to survey and process the textual past and also to evaluate the different textual and actual selves that others, such as Enoch and Mr. Thiel, construct and project of themselves. These factors combine in the construction of an active subject position for Jean in relation to the past, though it is only through the intervention of others, such as Mac, that she is able to ascertain the truth about the past and about other characters.

Documentary and dialogic approaches are also represented as being interdependent in Peck's time-shift novel *Voices After Midnight* (1989/1992). In this novel both approaches are linked with the concept of agency. The narrator Chad and his younger brother, Luke, are able to cross over into the past. However, they are not perceived by other characters outside of their own time and are able only to passively observe characters and events occurring in the past. Thus, although they recognize that there is something that they must accomplish, they initially find themselves unable to act. Heidi, their sister, occupies a much more active subject position: she is perceived by characters in the nineteenth century and attends the 1887 New Year's party where she dances with Tyler (a character in the past who will become her own great-great grandfather) and plays out a comic Cinderella role.

Heidi's capacity to act within the past is achieved in two main ways: through her ability to construct a subjectivity for herself and through her reading of historical romance. Although it is clear that she is perceived in the past because she wears a white lace dress of the period that she has found in the attic, her ability to shape and "makeover" her own image is also stressed throughout the novel; for example, Heidi's appropriation of Jocelyn's image is an attempt to construct another self. As Chad observes, when Heidi first finds the dress and holds it up against herself, "she was being the kind of girl for a dress like this" (1992, p. 50). Thus, Heidi "fits in" to the past because she is able to adopt an appropriate subject position within it. In contrast, Chad and Luke are able to intervene and act in the past only after they conduct research in the present on what has already happened, that is, only after they have adopted a documentary historical approach. In this way, the past can only be altered once all three characters have attained agency within the present and past. An implication of the novel is that engagement with the past and the types of agency that characters can achieve in the past and the present are gendered. Heidi's capacity to act in the past is clearly gendered as feminine through the evocation of conventional feminine attributes, especially the idea of the makeover. For Chad and Luke, agency is enabled through research (conventionally typed as masculine); for Heidi, it is enabled by imaginative and conscious self-construction. Agency (of all characters) is necessary for a dialogic relation between the narrative past and present. As in *The Callender Papers* (Voight, 1983/1991), this dialogue is implicit in the idea that the past shapes and makes the present possible. Like Jean, Chad and Luke research their own past, and, furthermore, they also in fact make their own present possible through their actions in both the past and the present.

Both *The Callender Papers* and *Voices After Midnight* depict dialogic relationships between the past and the present by stressing the textual nature of the past—as in *The Callender Papers*—and through an exploration of the role of agency and empathy in positioning characters in an active relationship with the past. The notion that characters are researching their own pasts and thereby shaping their own presents and futures entails that an awareness and understanding of the past are crucial to the formation of subjectivity in the present.

In a third novel, *Donald Duk* (Chin, 1991), dialogic and documentary approaches to the past are seen as interdependent, but at the same time, as not producing consistent versions of history. The history books that Donald and Arnold read about the building of the railroads in nineteenth century America are written from the viewpoint of Anglo-Irish Americans; in playing down the role of Chinese American's, they are complicit in the perpetuation of biased and limiting images of the Chinese in America. Donald learns a different version of events partly through his dreams, which give him access to the past and allow him to engage dialogically with that past, and partly through "filling the gaps" in the history books. An alternative history is constructed via the textual gaps in the received history. Thus, dialogic and documentary approaches to the past work together to imply a history which is open and contestable, and which enables Donald to reassess his sense of identity as American and Chinese.

Sensitivity to history and the cultural past is also seen as crucial for personal development in Cameron's *The Court of the Stone Children* (1973), and the past and present are also mediated via a combination of dialogic and documentary historical methods. This is a time-shift fantasy in which a character from the past is displaced into the present and from France to San Francisco. Domi is a young French woman from seventeenth century France who exists as a kind of ghost in contemporary San Francisco, though she is only seen by Nina, a young girl who has recently moved to San Francisco from Silver Springs. Domi's home, a French chateau, has been demolished, but the rooms, furnishings, doors, paneling and chandeliers were all brought to a San Francisco museum, which Nina visits. Domi, along with her home, has been both physically and temporally displaced. Nina feels lonely, homesick and at a loss in San Francisco, and her personal maturation is dependent upon her making a separation between self and place. Subjectivity is seen as formed through an understanding of the cultural past, and is not dependent on a specific place. Domi's existence in the present also implies essentialist notions of subjectivity, that is, that the self exists independent of the body, time and space. In this way, the text assumes a universality of human experience and subjectivity which transcends physical, historical and social contexts and which grounds the possibility of historical dialogue.

Documentary and dialogical approaches to the past are both represented in the novel. Gil and Mrs. Staynes both demonstrate a scholarly treatment of time and history, as does Nina's job in the museum and her reading of Odile's journal. Nina also has a special feeling for the past and for objects belonging to and made by people in the past that she refers to as her "Museum Feeling" (p. 79). Thus, she enters into a dialogue with the past through her capacity for emotive, imaginative and empathetic responses. Nina's apprehension of seventeenth-century France is mediated by Domi's narration (pp. 114–123) and by dreams, where it is described using evocative and emotive language, as in the following passage:

> As she stood there, she felt someone behind her—and there it was: her Feeling, the sense of timelessness, an acute awareness of being freed of the moment. She held her breath, looked down at her own hand resting on the windowsill, and it seemed scarcely to belong to her. She looked at the shadows on the wall and they seemed not shadows any longer but living shapes of an indescribable beauty against color so deep as to invite her to enter it, as if it were no longer solid but some depthless medium in which she might become lost. The flowers and fruits were no longer painted, but hung there, giving out color like light, yet rounded and fluted and planed as if you might touch them and hold them. They had a fragrance, and Nina heard the stillness of this Moment piercing her brain in a tone beyond the pitch of sound. (pp. 16–17)

Nina's "museum feeling," her sense of the past, is located within a "timeless" moment; it is, in other words, an idea of history that actually transcends time and history. The passage is focalized by Nina, and markers indicating point of view, such as "seemed" and "as if," imply that this moment of transcendence is an aspect of her own emotive response. However, the language used in the passage, in particular the omission of verbs—as in "they seemed not shadows"—and the attribution of agency to the objective world—as in "color so deep as to invite"—suggests Nina's loss of agency. The novel closes with Nina's realization that Domi has gone and that the timeless "Moment had passed" (p. 191). In this way, Nina's understanding of the historicity of the past is associated with her personal maturation, and notions of transcendence are correlated with childhood. Thus, the relation between the past and agency is treated in a more ambivalent way than in Voigt's or Peck's novels.

The Court of the Stone Children (Cameron, 1973), The Callender Papers (Voight, 1983/1991), Voices After Midnight (Peck, 1989/1992) and Donald Duk (Chin, 1991) are not overtly polyphonic in their narrative techniques. The first two are narrated in the first person and neither includes substantial material narrated by or from the point of view of characters other than the narrator. Donald Duk is narrated in the third person and focalized by one main character. Cameron's novel is narrated in the third person and does include extracts from Odile's journal and narration from Domi's point of view. However, like *The Callender Papers* and *Voices After Midnight*, *The Court of the Stone Children* is mostly narrated from the viewpoint of one character in the present. The next section looks at historical novels which incorporate multiple narrators and focalizers in the past and the present, and which are therefore more overtly dialogical in their narrative techniques.

NARRATIVE TECHNIQUE AND THE REPRESENTATION OF PAST AND PRESENT SUBJECTS

The two approaches described by LaCapra (1980) also distinguish the narrative techniques and assumed reading strategies typical of conventional (single-voiced) time-shift narratives and other more overtly dialogical (polyphonic) historical narratives. Conventional time-shift narratives, such as *Charlotte Sometimes* (Farmer, 1969/1992), *Playing Beatie Bow* (Park, 1980), *Voices After Midnight* (Peck, 1989/1992), *The Devil's Own* (Lisson, 1990) and *Donald Duk* (Chin, 1991) most frequently represent the past from the point of view of a character or narrator from the present who has been displaced into that past. Multistranded historical narratives, such as *A Bone from a Dry Sea* (Dickinson, 1992), and polyphonic time-shift fantasies, such as *The Driftway* (Lively, 1972/1985) or *Red Shift* (Garner, 1973/1989) represent the past from the viewpoints of characters or narrators located in both the past and the present. They do this by incorporating multiple narrators or character focalizers and/or constructing multiple narrative strands situated in different temporal contexts.

As I suggested in Chapter 2, the representation of a character as a subject depends on that character being positioned in the narrative as a focalizing agent. In conventional time-shift narratives, it is usually only characters from the present who focalize; characters situated only in the past are not usually represented as focalizers. *Voices After Midnight* (Peck, 1989/1992), for example, is narrated in the first person by Chad. "Scenes" from the past are represented as reported discourse, conversations and situations which are overheard and watched by Chad and Luke. They do not enter into dialogue with the "voices" that they hear after midnight and the viewpoints of Tyler and Emily in the past are not represented in the narrative, apart from snatches of reported speech. Narrative voice and point of view are thereby restricted to one temporal and cultural position, that of the present. Insofar as Tyler and Emily are only ever represented as they are perceived by Chad, they are denied agency. Furthermore, their fates are directly determined by Chad's, Luke's and Heidi's actions. One effect of this strategy is that characters located in the past are denied active subject positions. This can have crucial ideological implications in that the nature of selfhood and identity is seen as essentially the same for subjects existing in the past or the present, irrespective of social, cultural and ideological differences. Also, to the extent that the significance of a past event is interpreted from a position in the present, the past is represented as objectified and closed—as in LaCapra's (1980) description of a documentary concept of history. I am not suggesting that all single-stranded time-shift narratives are monological; novels such as *Voices After Midnight* (Peck, 1989/1992) and *Charlotte Sometimes* (1969/ 1992) are dialogical in other ways, but the idea of history which they represent is essentially closed.[1] By representing the relation between past and present as an intersection which centers on the position of one character whose viewpoint is grounded in the present, the dialogic potential of the past/ present narrative form is thereby limited. LaCapra's (1980) description of a dialogic interpretative position which recognizes "that the past has its own 'voices' that must be respected, especially when they resist or qualify the interpretations we would like to place on them" (p. 274) aptly describes Lively's narrative technique in *The Driftway* (1972/1985). The novel literally represents a dialogue between past and present by constructing historical characters as focalizers and narrators who tell their stories to a character in the present whose own viewpoint is modified as a consequence of this exchange.

In multistranded historical novels, such as *Red Shift* (Garner, 1973/ 1989), *The Driftway* (Lively, 1972/1985) and *A Bone from a Dry Sea* (Dickinson, 1992), characters situated in both past and present narrative times are represented as narrators and/or focalizers. Characters thereby function as agents who occupy active subject positions within the narrative discourse. These strategies can potentially structure the relationship between the textual past and present dialogically. *A Bone from a Dry Sea* is a double-stranded novel in which narrative strands are interlaced. One narrative is set in a time roughly contemporary, and the other four million years in the past. The contemporary narrative concerns a young woman, Vinny, who has come to stay with her taphonomist father on an archaeological dig where they uncover the fossil remains of (presumably) two key characters in the past narrative strand. This narrative also concerns a young woman, Li, a member of an aquatic hominid tribe who have rudimentary linguistic, cognitive and tool-using abilities. Dickinson's account of Li and her tribe is based on the "aquatic ape" theory, a controversial theory which postulates an aquatic phase in the evolution of human beings between about four and eight million years ago (Morgan, 1972; Roede, 1991). *The Driftway* (Lively, 1972/

1985) comprises a primary narrative and multiple secondary narratives situated in a range of historical contexts: ancient Britain, the ninth, seventeenth, late eighteenth, nineteenth and early twentieth centuries. The primary narrative concerns the journey of a young boy, Paul, along the driftway, an old droving road. The secondary narratives comprise the stories of other past characters who have also traveled along the driftway, and whom Paul apprehends at various points during his journey—these apprehensions are referred to as "messages" in the novel. These narratives are incorporated partly as an element of fantasy—it is the effect of the road playing "its tricks" (p. 31)—and partly as being induced by Paul's heightened perceptual state.

Both novels are narrated in the third person and are focalized by characters situated in the past and the present. Narrative strands in *A Bone from a Dry Sea* (Dickinson, 1992) are focalized by Vinny and by Li, neither of whom is aware of the other. The narrative structuring of *The Driftway* (Lively, 1972/1985) is more complex and uses a range of techniques for incorporating the voices and discourses of past and present characters. The primary narrative is focalized by Paul. There are eleven secondary narrative episodes, six of which are at least partially focalized by Paul, and they are interconnected so as to form seven separate narrative strands. Most of the past characters either focalize or narrate their "stories", and they are thereby constructed as "subjects of their own directly signifying discourse" (Bakhtin, 1984a, p. 7). For example, the story of a prehistoric boy's meeting with a stranger is narrated in the third person and focalized by the boy (pp. 83–88), and the story of Jennet Haynes is set in the nineteenth century, and begins as third person narration focalized by Paul which shifts into first person account by Jennet (pp. 143–145). Both characters occupy discrete (active) subject positions, and are not merely the objects of another character's perception.

These narrative strategies also structure the relationships between the past and present narratives and between the text and its implied readers dialogically. In *The Driftway*, narrative techniques used to represent the shifts between primary and secondary narration textually represent a dialogue between the past and the present, and construct interpretative positions in relation to the past. Thus, the interpretative positions of implied readers and of Paul the main character focalizer, are analogous, and the narrative strategies which position Paul in relation to the secondary narratives also construct implied reader positions in relation to the textual past and present. In *A Bone from a Dry Sea* (Dickinson, 1992), the positions of implied readers and those of Vinny and Li are disparate. Unlike Li and Vinny, readers have access to both narratives. The connections between the two strands are implicit, and there is not a textualized reading position mediating the narratives, as there is in *The Driftway*. Implied readers in *A Bone from a Dry Sea* must infer interconnections, and are thus positioned in more active reading positions than in Lively's novel. In both novels, however, the narrative structures imply ideological and cultural parallels between the past and the present. These parallels ascribe meaning to human experiences, characters and events in the past and the present, and are thereby indicative of underlying concepts of historical continuity and change.

The construction of past characters as focalizers and narrators can present problems of representation in that a subjectivity is retrospectively inferred for a person situated in a remote and alien past or culture. As I suggested in Chapter 4, the formation of subjectivity is inextricably tied up with language and with social and cultural practices. Thus, representations of the viewpoints of past persons—either fictive or non-fictive—are always implicated in problems of language. The capacity to comprehend and represent the viewpoint and culture of an other is determined by a person's access to the discursive codes and conventions which constitute that culture, and it is limited by the socioideological position from which it is viewed. Dickinson's interest in these kinds of issues is foregrounded by the narrative techniques he uses in *A Bone from a Dry Sea* (1992) to represent Li's point of view and by bracketed narratorial comments in the past narrative strand. For Dickinson, the problem of representing events from the viewpoint of a character situated in a remote and alien past culture whose cognitive and cultural viewpoint can only be imagined centers on two issues: the use of culture-specific narrative codes and structures; and the relationship between thought and language. In order for Li's "story" to be told, it must be encoded using familiar narratorial conventions and structures. For example, Li and the members of her tribe have no names, but in order to "tell their story" the narrator must use names (p. 20). Dickinson uses an image of an "invisible lens" through which the past is seen and distorted to describe the process whereby this past is perceived and imagined:

> Light bends as if it were passing through invisible lenses. The people seem to dwindle, stretch, vanish, stand clear for a moment and distort again. We are looking through lenses of time, right at the edge of imagination's eyesight. To give the tribe names distorts them, but its the best I can do from where we're standing. (p. 20)

In this sense, the difference between fiction and history is minimal—they use similar representational codes and conventions, and both are limited by the socio-ideological position from which they are written. The image implies the inaccessibility of the past itself; it can be neither perceived nor imagined without being distorted by the present because it is only from a position in the present that it can be imagined or represented. The present narrative also stresses the processes through which historians and archaeologists imaginatively reconstruct an idea of the past which is essentially grounded in their idea of the present.

As I suggested in Chapter 2, focalization strategies have important ideological implications for the representation of subjectivity. Characters are often denied subjectivity when they are focalized, rather than focalizing, and in time-shift narratives these strategies can effect the subordination of past characters to a single socio-ideological position in the present. The past narrative in *A Bone from a Dry Sea* (Dickinson, 1992) is mainly narrated in the third person and focalized by Li, but bracketed comments in the opening chapters are narrated in the voice of a first person narrator. These shifts in narrative point of view represent Li as focalized, rather than focalizing, and thereby foreground her otherness. This is emphasized in the following description:

> (Suppose for a moment that the time-lens lets us see her undistorted, what does she look like, this single, night-black figure crossing the glaring flat? She walks erect, but is still not quite a metre tall. Her body is hairless but her head has a glossy black mane falling over her shoulders. She is plump, roly-poly, from the layer of insulating fat beneath her skin. Her feet are like ours, but webbed between the toes, and her long fingers have webs to the first knuckle. Her head is the shock, tiny to our eyes, with a face more monkey than human. What room can there be in that cramped skull for thoughts, imaginations, questions, wonders, for all that makes us human? Can this be where we came from?) (p. 22)

By suggesting the possibility of seeing Li "undistorted," the narrator draws attention to the discourses and cultural assumptions through which she is represented and to the narratorial position, viewpoint and voice through which she is objectified and denied subjectivity. The commentary thereby ironically underscores the impossibility of representing Li from an unmediated and undistorted point of view. Though the discourse aims at some level of objectivity—as in terms like "figure" and "walks erect"—the description is focused on her similarity to and difference from humans in the present, and thus stresses the narrator's humanness and position in the present. The discourse mixes colloquial and scientific registers—as in "plump, roly-poly . . . layer of insulating fat"—and terms associated with animals—as in "mane"—and with humans—"plump, roly-poly." This mixing of registers echoes Morgan's style in *The Descent of Woman* (1972), a fictionalized account of the aquatic ape theory. The "invisible lens" through which the past is perceived thus comprises the discourses of both history and fiction, and is teleologically determined by the positioning of the (human) narrator in the present. The lens through which Li is seen is most visible when the narrator comments on, and hence draws attention to it, but, ironically, it is least visible when Li focalizes—that is, when narrative techniques associated with fiction are used to posit a subjectivity for her.

The past narrative also foregrounds the relationship between language and thought. The tribe has only a rudimentary language system, which presents a problem for the narrator in the present. If the formation of cognition, consciousness and language are interdependent, as theorists such as Vološinov (1986) and Vygotsky (1962) have suggested, then how can the thought and consciousness of a person who lacks a complex linguistic signifying system be conceived of and represented? A pre-text for *A Bone from a Dry Sea* is Golding's *The Inheritors* (1955)—a novel about a Neanderthal tribe which is focalized by Neanderthal characters. As Halliday (1971) has shown, narrative point of view is constructed in Golding's novel through the prominence of certain syntactic features and repeated references to the activities of cognition and verbalization, and thought is represented as a picturing process. Like Golding, Dickinson is concerned with how a person whose linguistic capacity is limited perceives and understands the world and others, and how this can be represented in narrative. However, the narrative discourse of Dickinson's novel is considerably less disjointed and unfamiliar than that of Golding. Repeated references in Dickinson's novel to "seeing" and "understanding" imply a link between perception and cognition, and foreground the relationship between language and thought. Dickinson represents Li's thought processes as being in the process of becoming more complex, and hence recognizable. The double narrative structure draws parallels between the cognitive and social development of Vinny, a contemporary child, and that of Li, a primitive hominid child. Insofar as Li's development is metonymic, that is, it represents the direction of the development of the tribe as a whole, the text implies an analogy between child development and the development of a species.

Dickinson represents the function of primitive language as social and pragmatic. This position conforms with that of Malinowski, for whom language is a "mode of action and not an instrument of reflection" (Malinowski, 1956, p. 312). The tribe is "only half-way toward words" (p. 20). They have a repertoire of "calls," such as "Come-help, Shark!, Big wave!, Follow me," but they do not have words or sentences (p. 21). All of these calls are significant within a social context and have concrete pragmatic functions. The fact that these "calls" do not constitute "words" implies that the language of the tribe is structured as a denotative sign system in which there is little slippage between the sign-shape and its meaning. Syntactic structures articulate logical, causal, spatial and temporal relations between signs and referents, and construct relationships between speakers and addressees. The absence of sentences in the tribe's language suggests a limited ability to conceive of complex or abstract concepts, and a limited range of interpersonal relations between characters. Thus, Li's inventions and problem-solving activities occur within a practical context, for example, making a net by watching a spider spin a web. Furthermore, the fact that she is moving toward more abstract forms of problem-solving is represented as simultaneous with her interest in forms of otherness (p. 35), which signals a move out of solipsism. This is paralleled by Vinny's maturation in the contemporary strand, wherein she is depicted as gradually coming to know and understand her father as another self. The significances to be discerned from the interrelations between the two narrative strands are clearly oriented toward a universalizing of human social and personal experiences and developmental processes.

The interrelations between narrative strands in *The Driftway* (Lively, 1972/1985) also express a concern with personal and cultural forms of solipsism and the possibility of developing out of solipsism into intersubjectivity. The relationships between subjectivity and narrative point of view, however, are treated in less direct ways than in *A Bone from a Dry Sea*. Although characters located in the past either narrate or focalize their own narratives, the secondary (past) narratives are framed and mediated by the primary (present) narrative, which constructs a range of interpretative positions in relation to the past. These positions, however, delineate a limited number of socio-ideological viewpoints on the past and on history. There are two main approaches to the past represented in the novel. The first is given expression in Bill's interpretations of Paul's visions of the past; and the second is expressed through focalization strategies used to represent Paul's relations to the past. Underlying Bill's interpretations is an essentially monologic approach to history. He describes Paul's visions of the past as "messages":

> Messages about being happy, or frightened or downright miserable. Messages that cut through time like it wasn't there, because they're about things that are the same for everybody, and always have been,

and always will be. That's what the Driftway is: a place where people have left messages for one another. (Lively, 1985, p. 32)

For Bill, the "messages," or stories from the past which Paul apprehends, represent what we think of as history—"history's just another word for messages" (p. 34). These messages communicate similarities between people living in the past and the present, and thus imply a sense of historical continuity which is grounded in a logic of identity. This approach implies analogies between Paul's social development and personal experiences living in the present and those of characters in the past and, as in *A Bone from a Dry Sea* (Dickinson, 1992), it universalizes processes of maturation. Furthermore, this approach subordinates the past to the present: the primary function of historical awareness and understanding lies in the interpretation of experience in the present. Bill's interpretation of the significance and function of these messages, and of history, is based on a liberal humanist view of history which, through assuming the universality of human experience—that "things that are the same for everybody" (p.32)—implies a correlation between historical and cultural continuity. However, while Lively to some extent naturalizes and authorizes Bill's views of history—especially the need for an awareness of the past in order for maturation to occur—his interpretative position in the novel is ambivalent because it is undermined by strategies mediating secondary narratives and by the past narratives themselves. By focusing on similarities between past and present, his approach limits and contains the possible significances of the secondary narratives and imposes a monologic interpretation upon the past. Furthermore, the idea that the past exists as tangible traces within the present, and that it is possible to apprehend these traces in an unmediated way, assumes that the past is "always recoverable because it is what the present is made out of" (Phelan, 1989, p. xvi). Bill's position thus also assumes the transparency of the discourses and narrative codes and conventions through which the textual "messages" are mediated and through which histories are written.

A second dialogical approach to the past is constructed through the narrative strategies used to represent Paul's apprehension of the past and by the range of narrative techniques used to construct secondary narratives. Shifts from primary to secondary narrative are usually mediated by third person character focalized narration. Characters are represented as visions which appear to Paul (or, as in the case of the capture of Driftway Jim, overheard by Paul) and they are represented from his point of view. Focalization techniques used at these points of transition textually represent interpretative positions and strategies in relation to the secondary narratives.

These imply subject positions in relation both to the text and to the past and the characters that it represents, thereby suggesting an analogy between the ways in which fiction and history are read and interpreted, and between these interpretative practices and a subject's cognizance of others. Thus, narrative strategies also imply assumptions about the status of the past, the possibility of apprehending the past and the capacity for intersubjectivity.

Paul's apprehensions of the past generate a range of reader subject positions. These vary according to the degree of reader passivity and activity, and they demonstrate a development from limited socio-ideological (culturally solipsistic) interpretative positions toward more dialogical modes of interpretation which recognize and attempt to negotiate the otherness of an other's viewpoint and subject position. Thus, Paul's development of historical understanding and interpretative skills parallels his personal and social development. For example, his apprehension of the narrative of the prehistoric boy in the following passage articulates dialogical relationships between text and reader, present and past, the self and an other.

> A dog barked somewhere to the right, a long way away. They must
> be following the rim of a valley, for the sound defined a distance, com-
> ing from below and quite far, clear and undistorted. The rhythm of
> Bessie's trot changed imperceptibly in response, and then levelled out
> again, as though it had told her something. Paul found himself stiff-
> ening a little in sympathy, trying to read the sound, invest it with sig-
> nificance, as though he was stirred by a memory of a time when the
> signals people lived by were different, simpler and yet more intense,
> the senses more acute, the store of knowledge small and immediately
> related to the business of survival, when every message must be sifted,
> considered, for it might be crucial . . . (pp. 81–82)

This description foregrounds the particularity of the past, and it expresses this in terms of the otherness of another person's viewpoint, language and conceptual systems. Paul's attempts to focalize, and hence imagine himself in the position of a prehistoric boy, imply the limited accessibility of both the past and the viewpoint of the other. The idea of a collective memory that Paul accesses is suggested only as a metaphoric possibility—"as though he was stirred by a memory." That he tries "to read the sound" overtly places him in the position of a reader of an alien text—which is the physical world. That he tries to "invest" sounds in the world with "significance" implies that they are not inherently meaningful; rather, they are attributed with meaning according to the social and discursive practices of a given culture. Paul's socio-ideological position in relation to the past is thus similar to that of the narrator of the past narrative in *A Bone from a Dry Sea* (Dickinson, 1992). The narrative which follows on from the passage is the only secondary strand narrated in the third person and focalized by a character other than Paul. These strategies represent the viewpoint of the boy as a particular way of looking at the world and of representing this world to himself. However, like Dickinson, Lively uses third person narration to solve the problem of how to represent the thought and language of another whose thought, language and culture are radically different from our own. Like Dickinson, Lively foregrounds the different relationships between the physical referential world and the signs through which this world is ordered, represented and ascribed with meaning in the past. It is not just that the representational signs used by another culture are different, but also that the these sign systems conceive of the referential world differently and thereby ascribe varying ideological significances to this world. In other words, the sign systems of any one culture not only selectively invest the physical world with culturally specific meanings, but are also a means with which to conceive of that world.

The narrative techniques used in polyphonic multitemporal narratives to represent the subjectivity of characters located in the past incorporate a range of interpretative positions in relation to this past, and construct dialogic representations of history. The combination of multiple temporal contexts means that the interactions between the synchronic and diachronic dimensions of narrative time can be quite complex and that time-shifts frequently incorporate a range of different concepts of time. The next section will examine Bakhtin's concept of the chronotope as a means of analyzing the interactions between diachrony and synchrony and the interrelations between narrative time and space in time-shift fantasies and historical narratives.

THE CHRONOTOPE IN HISTORICAL FICTION

The chronotope is possibly the most elusive of Bakhtin's concepts. As Holquist has remarked, "at the conclusion of the 200–page monograph on the chronotope . . . many readers will find themselves hard pressed to answer the question, 'What exactly is a chronotope?'" (1990, p. 109). The term literally means "time-space" and refers, in its most general sense, to the "intrinsic interconnectedness of temporal and spatial relationships that are artistically expressed in literature" (Bakhtin, 1981, p. 84). According to Bakhtin, particular narrative genres are characterized by specific formal combinations of time and place (or "chronotopes") which structure a novel. The concept of the chronotope has two main aspects: narratological and ideological. Holquist (1990, pp. 109–110) has suggested that the chronotope is a unit of narrative analysis similar in function to recurring plot types or devices central to structuralist analyses of narrative. He has demonstrated the relevance of the chronotope to narratological analyses of the relations between the story and discourse components of narrative (pp. 113–115). These theoretical interconnections are pertinent but, as Holquist has argued, Bakhtin also stresses the cultural and ideological specificity of the chronotope, and hence its capacity to be "in dialogue with specific, extraliterary historical contexts" (p. 112). Thus, the chronotope is not merely interchangeable with structuralist archetypal plot types, but is rather an attempt to describe their cultural specificity within particular literary genres. For example, the quest narrative as it is used in adolescent fictions takes on particular culturally and ideologically inscribed chronotopic forms. For Bakhtin, narrative genres are characterized by specific chronotopic configurations which structure a narrative and through which characters are constructed and represented. Insofar as narrative genres are historically and culturally situated, narrative conceptions of spatial/temporal relationships entail particular culturally constructed images of human life.

Nikolajeva (1988, 1989, 1996) is perhaps the only children's literature critic to apply Bakhtin's chronotope in the discussion of children's texts. In *Children's Literature Comes of Age* (1996), she primarily uses it to make distinctions between various genres of writing—fairy tale from fantasy, "quality" texts from popular literature (or what Nikolajeva terms "paraliterature") and historical from retrospective novels (p. 151). Of particular interest is her suggestion that novelistic chronotopes are gendered: "male" texts structure time as linear and space as open while "female" texts structure time as circular and space as "closed and confined" (p. 125). Nikolajeva combines this generic approach with a historicist perspective and hence, as with her use of the concept of polyphony,[2] charts a development within children's literature which proceeds from the "classical (epic) narrative"—that is, narratives which use "relatively simple structures with a concrete place and a logically arranged, chronological action"—to the contemporary "sophisticated [or polyphonic] children's book"—that is, texts which express "an intricate network of temporal and spatial relationships, which better reflect our own chaotic existence" (p. 151).

Most of the texts discussed throughout this book fall into Nikolajeva's "sophisticated" category, but my interest in this chapter is primarily in multistranded time-shift novels, where the chronotope is a useful concept for analyzing the intricacies of spatial and temporal relations and the ideological assumptions implicit in how these relations are conceived. I am using the concept of the chronotope in reference to time-shift narratives in two interrelated ways: as a narratological concept, to refer to spatio-temporal relations within and between narrative strands; and as an ideological concept, to refer to spatio-temporal images or concepts which structure and organize narratives. These two functions can also be linked with LaCapra's (1987) distinctions between diachrony and synchrony; the chronotope is an aspect of the interaction between these two dimensions. The temporal and spatial interrelations in time-shift narratives are often quite complex, because of the multiplicity of temporal contexts, especially when there are also multiple narrative strands. This means that the interactions between discourse time—the time of narration and of reading—and story time—the duration of the purported events of the narrative—can generate a range of configurations. The positioning of narrators and character focalizers in different temporal contexts also produces multiple discourse and story times. Time-shifts in multistranded narratives frequently incorporate a range of different concepts of time, which vary according to the emphasis on diachronic or synchronic dimensions. Thus, narrative time will vary in perspective—in its production of personal, historical, mythic or collective temporal concepts—and in structuration—in its construction of linear, developmental, circular or transcendent time schemas. As I suggested in Chapter 5, diachronic time is disrupted in *Unleaving* (Walsh, 1976) and *Red Shift* (Garner, 1973/1989) through the use of repetitive and circular narrative structures, and by an emphasis on personal concepts of time in Walsh's novel and on collective time in Garner's novel.

Clearly, different chronotopes will have ideological implications for how human subjects are represented in relation to time, place and history, and for the representations of historical change and continuity. The narrative strands of novels such as *Unleaving, The House that was Eureka* (Wheatley, 1985) and *The Hillingdon Fox* (Mark, 1991) are all set in the same historical period and have the same physical or spatial setting; and the time spans of each novel are confined to the personal time and space of (at least one or more) characters' lives: *The House that was Eureka* and *Unleaving* both span about fifty years, and the houses in these two novels have a central plot function which metonymically defines space as domestic (female) space. Though there are crucial gaps in "story" information, readers are able to infer a biographical (linear) chronotopic structure which interconnects the characters and events within various narrative strands. These novels thus incorporate different chronotopic conceptions so as to construct a dialogue between synchrony (associated here with personal and recollected time/space) and diachrony (associated with linear biographical time). The dialogization of chronotopes is more diverse in novels, such as *The Driftway* (Lively, 1972/1985), *The Court of the Stone Children* (Cameron, 1973), *Red Shift* (Garner, 1973/1989), *Strange Objects* (Crew, 1990/1991) and *A Bone from a Dry Sea* (Dickinson, 1992), wherein narrative strands are located in different historical and prehistoric times and places. In these novels, it is more difficult for readers to infer a linear "story" structure connecting the narrative strands, and the texts represent a dialogue between characters' conceptions of personal time and space and more abstract spatio-temporal concepts.

The second way that I am using the concept of the chronotope is to refer to spatio-temporal images or concepts which structure and organize narratives, and which ascribe texts with larger cultural and ideological significances, particularly in this last group of novels. As Nikolajeva (1996) has suggested, the chronotopic structuring of many contemporary novels does, in part, "reflect our own chaotic experience" (p. 151). However, narrative chronotopes also structure experience, and thereby impart it with order and meaning—even when such experience is constructed as "chaotic," as the case may be, in *Red Shift* (Garner, 1973/1989), perhaps. For example, the idea of the expanding universe in *Red Shift,* the "driftway" in *The Driftway* (Lively, 1972/1985), historical objects in *The Court of the Stone Children* (Cameron, 1973) and the fossil record in *A Bone from a Dry Sea* (Dickinson, 1992) are all chronotopic images which structure and organize the spatial and temporal aspects of narrative strands. Furthermore, these chronotopes also express broad underlying assumptions about history, time, human experience and subjectivity. As I suggested in Chapter 5, the idea of the expanding universe in *Red Shift* interconnects the three narratives in a way that implies the transcendence of linear concepts of time and of cultural and historical difference. Similarly, the fossils in *A Bone from a Dry Sea* and the "driftway" in *The Driftway* imply the literal inscription of time, history and human action on place. This is contrasted in *The Court of the Stone Children,* where time and history are seen as inscribed within personal possessions, furnishings and objects which have belonged to particular people. For Nina, "it was the paradox and somehow, the sadness of Time that drew her to the possessions of those long gone: objects, unthinking, unfeeling objects that yet have their own voices, and that outlast the loving flesh that created them" (pp. 91–92). Thus, the past inheres in objects and in the emotive responses they evoke, rather than in place, and it is manifest in intensely personal terms independent of geographical place.

Although place in *The Driftway* (Lively, 1972/1985), *Red Shift* (Garner, 1973/1989) and *A Bone from a Dry Sea* (Dickinson, 1992) remains relatively constant—narrative strands are situated in the same place at different times—the representations of space and time are interdependent, and different narrative conceptions of time entail variations in how human subjects are positioned and represented in relation to place and history. Thus, the chronotopic images used in these novels are oriented toward the construction and inscription of ideological metanarratives. The image of the expanding universe in *Red Shift* evokes transhistorical notions of subjectivity and place, similar to notions of transcendence evoked by personal possessions in *The Court of the Stone Children*. Chronotopic images in *The Driftway* and *A Bone from a Dry Sea* inscribe developmental and evolutionary narrative schemas which both structure and are undermined by the narrative discourses of the texts.

The image of the "driftway" in Lively's novel is a pervasive feature of the narrative structure, and it illustrates aspects of Bakhtin's discussion of the chronotope of the road (1981, pp. 243–245). It also explicitly demonstrates functions of the chronotope which are more implicit in other novels. According to Bakhtin, the chronotope of the road depicts the intersection of "the spatial and temporal paths of the most varied people . . . people who are normally kept separate by social and spatial distances" (1981, p. 243). In doing so, it represents the sociohistorical heterogeneity of the countryside through which characters travel (p. 243). By combining this chronotope with multitemporal narration, Lively thus incorporates a range of characters who would normally be kept separate by historical distances, as well as by spatial and social distances, and represents the social and cultural diversity of history and place.

Lively has said of *The Driftway* that she wanted to use the landscape and the road in particular as a "channel for historical memory" (Lively, 1973, p. 405). In *The Presence of the Past* (1976), a nonfiction introduction to landscape history, she describes the landscape as lying "like a ghostly jigsaw puzzle under the modern map—a message in code to be deciphered by the ingenuity of today's historians" (1976, p. 104). It is a silent and often barely visible record of the past. The ancient drove roads, green lanes and bridlepaths form an important part of landscape history because they provide a particular kind of evidence about how people in the past lived and traveled, which is inscribed onto the landscape. By traveling along these old roads in the present, "the landscape suddenly becomes a thousand years older: we see it through someone else's eyes" (1976, p. 64). The "driftway" along which Paul travels, in Lively's novel, is an old droving road, now sometimes called Banbury Lane, "which follows the B4525 from Banbury to

Northampton" (Lively, 1973, p. 405), and which has been used since pre-history as a droveroad to herd animals.[3]

The "driftway" has four main functions in the novel: (1) it themati-cally interconnects the narrative strands; (2) it is a metaphor for historical and narrative processes; (3) it implies a dialogical relation between the past and the present; and (4) it is a metaphor for a child's development out of solipsism. The driftway physically links characters and provides thematic interconnections between narrative strands. The term "driftway" refers to "a lane or road along which cattle are driven, a droveway" (Shorter Ox-ford English Dictionary, 1992), but this usage is fairly specific and rare, and the term itself is subject to semantic drift. It implies both a road along which one is carried by external forces—as in "to drift" with the sea or wind cur-rents—or upon which one might wander aimlessly—as the image of Bill, a drifter, would imply. Thus, the image of the driftway suggests a state of dis-placement, of being adrift. Many of the narratives are concerned with forms of physical, cultural and personal displacement. For example, Jennet Haynes, a young widow living during the nineteenth century, has been dispossessed of a home by the practices and institutions of the society in which she is situ-ated, and is in a continual state of displacement. This has implications for how she constructs a sense of identity. She does not know her father's name and her husband was "of Nowhere," hence she has no place to live and re-fers to herself as "I, Jennet Haynes, Widow of Nowhere" (Lively, 1985, p. 144). Like Jennet, many of the characters, such as Driftway Jim and Sam and Nelly Slatter, occupy positions which are either physically, socially or culturally marginal. Other characters, such as the prehistoric boy and Mat-thew Cobham, cross physical, personal and cultural boundaries and acquire experiences which do not fit their accepted knowledge and predictable re-sponses, as indeed does Paul in the primary narrative.

A second way that the driftway works is as a metaphor for histori-cal and narrative processes: it represents the intersection of diachronic and synchronic dimensions of time. Paul's journey along the driftway constructs a linear and progressive narrative, and thus represents diachronic time. Synchronic time is represented by the "messages" or momentary apprehen-sions of the past that he encounters along the way, which "stop" time and imply the intersection of multiple times within the same place. History and narrative are conventionally thought of as linear and progressive (Miller, 1974, pp. 459–460), and are thus associated with diachrony rather than synchrony. However, by representing the past as an aspect of the synchronic dimension of time, the text generates a tension between conventional no-tions of temporal continuity and linearity and a historical heterogeneity. The secondary narrative strands are not arranged in any tidy linear or chronological sequence; rather, they often intersect and cross over each other, and each narrative is more or less incomplete, often representing only a portion of a larger story. The lack of chronology and incompletion thus disrupts teleological and linear notions of history and narrative.

A third way that the driftway works is to dialogically structure relations between past and present. By combining the chronotope of the road with multivoiced narration, the landscape of the past is represented as it is seen "through someone else's eyes" (Lively, 1976, p. 64). It conveys an image of the past as tangibly present within places in the present, and represents that presence as discursive, human and subjective. The following passage articulates Lively's ideas about the relationship between landscape and human history (it is spoken by Bill):

> You see the way the shape of a country's made the people in it, and you see the way they've written themselves all over it, too, people who're dead and gone now. In the way the fields go, and the roads . . .
>
> Most people look at a bit of country and they just see it as an arrangement of hedges, and trees, and lanes, and they don't think of how it's all come about, like. They think it's natural. There's hardly such a thing as a natural landscape. It's something always on the move, changing every few years. And if you get to know a bit about it you can see all the layers of changes, going right back to in olden times . . .' (p. 79)

The image of the landscape as a text, which both writes and is written upon by the people who occupy it, implies a sense of the past of places and cultures as radically textualized and intertextual. The absence of any "natural landscape" is in part due to the necessary processes of time and change—a "virgin" countryside could only exist as an originary moment independent of time—but it is also partly tied up with the processes of textualization and representation through which we apprehend and conceptualize what we see. Implicit in this is the recognition that particular perceptions and representations of a place are always subject to prior cultural representations in and through which they have been attributed with meanings. These ideas have analogies with historiographic practices. The idea that places are significant to the extent that human actions have constructed them as significant also applies to history. Thus, the significance of an event lies partly in the meanings that are attributed to it, but also in the fact that it is recorded at all. There is a subtle interplay in Lively's fiction between places which are "historical" because of certain "great" events which have occurred there (such as the Battle of Edgehill), and the idea of places being inscribed with the history of "ordinary" people and events. The notion that an event can leave "a shadow on a place" (p. 32) suggests that the experiences of humanity are inscribed on the landscape, a process which is also analogous with historical textual practices. Thus, the writing of history is a way of ordering time and representing the passage of time as meaningful.

A fourth way that the driftway works is as a metaphor for the child's development out of solipsism. Paul's journey along the driftway is also a psychological journey of personal maturation, wherein he progresses from a solipsistic state toward intersubjectivity. Paul's father has been recently remarried to Christine, and though Paul is ostensibly running away from the police, having been accused of shoplifting, it becomes clear that his actions are informed by his inability to accept his father's remarriage and to perceive Christine as another self, a person rather than "her" (p. 6). The fact that he is beginning to move out of solipsism is indicated in observations toward the close of the novel, such as "Her. No, Christine. She's got a name, hasn't she? She's a person isn't she?" (p. 112). The problem of solipsism, and the processes through which a child negotiates categories of otherness and thus moves toward intersubjectivity, are a central concern in Lively's fiction. In her nonfiction she has stressed the importance of "that step toward maturity a child takes when it ceases to see people as static, frozen at a moment in time, but sees them instead as changing and developing creatures" (Lively, 1973, p. 400). For Lively, an important stage in the move toward intersubjectivity is "the development of a child's perception of the past" and of their own place in relation to history as she suggests in the passage quoted as an epigraph for this chapter, "for the child, it is a step toward an awareness of other people and toward being . . . a mature adult" (1973, p. 401). This concern with the relationship between a child's recognition of historical continuity and of the selfhood of others is expressed overtly in *The Driftway* by Bill:

'To my way of thinking other people's not just the few blokes you happen to come across. It's them you never knew as well, because they're in other times, or other places. Because they're the same as you and me, aren't they, in the end? You've got to want to know about them, unless you're going to spend your time shut up inside your own head, and there's quite a few like that, more's the pity. But this road'll talk to you if you're the kind of person wants to be told things. There's some don't care one way or the other: they're not bothered. They'll live out their lives shut up inside themselves, just looking straight in front of them like old Bessie here, between two blinkers.' (pp. 33–4)

There is an ambivalence in Bill's conception of a historical awareness, in that the recognition of the selfhood of others entails a conception of the other as inherently like one's self—"they're the same as you and me." In other words, Bill's (and Lively's) idea of historical continuity is based on the assumption that there is an essential human nature that links subjects in the past and the present. Lively's concerns with the relationship between a perception of history and the move out of solipsism are thus inextricable from her humanist assumptions about history, namely, that "to have a sense of history is, above all, to have a sense of one's own humanity, and without that we are nothing" (Lively, 1973, p. 401). However, there is an implication in Lively's argument that though the recognition of historical continuity represents a move out of individual solipsism, it is actually a move toward a form of cultural solipsism which represents the past as an image of the present and ignores cultural alterity. Thus Lively's conception of the relationship between place, time and human subjects is grounded in a teleology which encodes chronology as causality, and temporal progression as cultural and historical continuity.

A Bone from a Dry Sea (Dickinson, 1992) is not dominated by any single chronotopic image, but the two narratives are interconnected so as to imply culturally specific narrative conceptions of time and space. The narrative both constructs and disrupts conventional humanist notions of history and evolution. The historical process that it represents combines concepts of evolution and of universal aspects of human experience. Evolutionary and linear conceptions of time are represented through story links between the two narratives, and the cultural and intellectual contexts that these links evoke. I mentioned earlier that the fossil record conveys the idea of time and human history as being inscribed upon a place. The double narrative, the implication that the fossils Vinny finds belong to Li, and the parallels between the two characters, especially between their cognitive, social and personal maturation, reinforce the suggestion that Li is Vinny's ancestor and that they are part of the same evolutionary chain. As I have already suggested, Li's development is metonymic of the development of the tribe as a whole. Thus, the text implicitly asserts the conventional analogy between child development and the historical evolution of a species and a culture. Parallels between the personal development of the two characters also imply essential or universal aspects of human experience, which are grounded in their common experiences of otherness. The relation between being and otherness is most fully explicated in Li's narrative in her recognition of the otherness of her mother and of other members of the tribe (pp. 35–36), but it also impinges on Vinny's negotiations with her father. Lively is also most explicit about relations between the self and others in the prehistoric strand in *The Driftway* (Lively, 1972/1985) which centers on a young boy's apprehension of the selfhood of an other whom he perceives as "the same as I, we are of one kind" (p. 87). In Lacanian terms, the apprehension of the other is an aspect of the mirror phase, and is the site of the split subject. Thus, in representing the experience of otherness as essentially human and as originary, the view of human evolution implicit in both novels accords with a model of child development. Dickinson, in particular, makes the explicit link between the ability to distinguish between self and other, consciousness and the capacity for abstract thought in his characterization of Li.

Dickinson's novel also disrupts and subverts conventional evolutionary paradigms and humanist histories. It does this through the two central characters and through the representation of the past society. Both Li and Vinny are female children, and as such are socially and culturally marginal. Both are also intelligent and are appropriated by key male adults within their social groups who use them to exercise power and dominance over other members of the group. This is emphasized in the parallel episodes where Li is carried first on the shoulders of Presh (p. 52) and then Greb (p. 73), and Vinny is picked up by Dr. Hamiska (p. 119). Both Li and Vinny reflect on the social function of this action and its meaning within specific social codes of behavior.

Conventional (male-centered) models of evolution are also disrupted through the use of Elaine Morgan's controversial aquatic ape theory (1972) and the central roles attributed to women. Morgan's theory is outlined by Vinny in the contemporary narrative, and the past narrative supports and validates Vinny's position. Furthermore, the past narrative displaces traditional "man the hunter" versions of early evolution through its characterization of Li, whose innovations and inventions are oriented toward traditionally feminine activities, such as food gathering, reproduction, ornamentation and medicine. She invents a net for catching shrimps and a splint to mend Presh's broken leg, and develops primitive tools for making birth ornaments. Thus, another intertext for the past narrative is perhaps Miles's *The Women's History of the World* (1989). Miles has argued that the "man the hunter" theory of human evolution is a "phallacy" (1989, p. 3) and has demonstrated the role of women, of female inventions—such as food-carrying bags—and social skills necessary for cooperative behavior—

such as food gathering and the raising of dependent young—in the early evolution of the species. The social organization of the tribe in the past narrative of Dickinson's novel is of particular interest. With Presh's injury and the tribe's rejection of Greb, the nature of leadership changes, depending "less upon dominance and more upon consent" (p. 124), and Li occupies a crucial position through her intellect and skills. This move toward a form of social organization based on cooperation and consent constructs an alternative to conventional (masculinist) models of social evolution which see early societies as being based on male aggression and dominance (Miles, 1989, p. 13). This model is represented by Greb and his tribe. The social group with which the novel closes—the survivors of a tidal wave—is overtly female-centered, thereby again subverting conventional male-centered theories. However, the male-centered model is only displaced; although Greb is killed in the tidal wave, the threat that he constitutes is reproduced in the parallels between masculine codes of behavior in the past and present narratives, so while the past narrative has a fairly positive close, the close of the novel is ambivalent. In this way, Dickinson has constructed an ideologically powerful chronotope which is critical of social institutions based on aggression, dominance and selfishness. As I suggested in my discussion of *Eva* in Chapter 3, Dickinson's critique of the negative implications of humanist ideologies, namely homocentrism and cultural solipsism, also functions as an assertion of the need for positive human values within society, namely, values associated with altruism, compassion and cooperation. As with Lively, the ideological significances of Dickinson's chronotopes are essentially humanistic.

The chronotopic relations in time-shift fantasies and multistranded narratives, such as *The Driftway* (Lively, 1972/1985), *The Court of the Stone Children* (Cameron, 1973) and *A Bone from a Dry Sea* (Dickinson, 1992), are narratologically complex, and they are an important way of inscribing ideologies within narrative. Like historical fictions in general, they are grounded by ideological assumptions about the social and cultural positioning of human subjects within time and history. However, insofar as they depict historical processes, they are also a powerful means of representing shifting power relationships within societies and hence possibilities for change. Novels, such as *A Bone from a Dry Sea*, *The Driftway* and *Red Shift* (Garner, 1973/1989), are also constructed out of and are read within the context of other cultural and literary historical texts and intertexts. I have touched on this in my discussion of intertexts for Dickinson's novel, and in the final section will focus on the intertextual construction of historical fiction.

In *The Driftway* (Lively, 1972/1985) and *Red Shift* (Garner, 1973/1989), Lively and Garner construct fictions which combine discursive strategies characteristic of conventional historical fiction with intertextual and poly-phonic narrative strategies, so as to foreground questions about how we apprehend, understand and interpret the past. In doing so, they signal concerns with the status of history as a particular kind of discursive practice, and with the ideological implications of writing histories and historical fictions. The image in *The Driftway* of the landscape as a text which writes and is written upon by the people who occupy it has an analogy with the intertextual structure of the novel as a whole and of other novels such as *Red Shift.* This image represents the past of a place as a complex multilay-ered heteroglottic structure, within which events and persons are inscribed as a residual conglomeration of voices, discourses and narratives. Both of these novels are structured through a range of incorporated literary, historical and contemporary intertexts and discourses. Combined with the use of mul-tiple narrators and character focalizers, these intertextual strategies have the effect of representing the past as a heteroglottic layering of other voices, dis-courses and texts, and history as a complex process of textualization in which narrative conceptions of the past are culturally and ideologically inscribed. Both novels utilize specific literary pretexts, such as the Tam Lin ballad in *Red Shift* and Robin Hood stories in *The Driftway,* and generic discourse styles and narrative forms derived from a range of historical and literary writings to represent characters and events. *The Driftway,* in particular, is constructed out of a range of intertexts and discourses appropriated from other types of historical fiction—it is as much a history of historical fiction written for children as it is a historical novel.

In *Red Shift* (1973/1989), Garner combines disparate cultural, liter-ary and historical discourses and intertexts. These include literary and bib-lical quotations (particularly from *King Lear*); contemporary and archaic dialect terms; literary and historical pre-texts (such as the Tam Lin ballad and Browning's "Childe Roland to the Dark Tower Came"); and actual his-torical sources. In the two historical strands he combines diverse cultural, literary and historical discourses, intertexts and sources. The English civil war narrative is closely based upon a well-documented actual historical in-cident (Philip, 1981, pp. 94–95) and the Roman episode is a fictionalized account of fugitives from the lost Ninth Roman legion. Dialogue in both narrative strands is represented using archaic and dialect terms—for example, "skirking" (p. 101), "borsant" and "skriking" (p. 92) in the civil war strand, and "beck," "garth" and "clemmed" (pp. 48–49) in the Roman strand. The use of dialect and archaisms is a conventional strategy of historical fiction, which renders strange both the discourse of the text and the historical world which it seeks to evoke (Stephens, 1992a, p. 220). Archaic registers in the Roman strand denote the native Celtic dialects of the Cats and the Mothers (the native Celtic-British tribes), which the Roman soldiers learn and appropriate. They also speak a mixture of contemporary jargon and slang, which Garner has appropriated from that spoken by American soldiers in Vietnam—for example "alternative analysis," "hit the infrastructure," "go tribal" (p. 24) and "gook" (p. 102). In this way, Garner produces a register clash between the overtly anachronistic discourse spoken by the Roman soldiers, and the archaic and dialect discourses which they have appropriated and which are also spoken by characters in the civil war strand. This clash works in two main ways. First, it foregrounds the conventionality of archaic forms of novelistic discourse used to represent the past. The use of dialect terms in the civil war strand may be more "scholarly" than the anachronistic dialects used to represent the dialogue in the Roman strand in the sense that the linguistic style is more accurate for this period (Philip, 1981, p. 91), but its appropriateness is also a measure of its conventionality. Both archaic and anachronistic discourse defamiliarize the text and the events being represented in the conventional manner of historical fiction, but by combining them they each call the other into question as an appropriate mode of discourse representation. Second, in the Roman strand in particular, the clash of different linguistic registers and styles represents a complex process of cultural and linguistic struggle. The Roman soldiers, four of whom are probably Celts, and possibly once members of the tribes whom they seek to imitate, are represented as actively appropriating the native dialects, in order to assimilate to and infiltrate the alien culture, and to perpetuate what Logan perceives to be the dominant (Roman) culture.

Garner's sources for the historical narrative strands in *Red Shift* comprise a diverse range of cultural and historical material. His research files for the novel "contain numerous cuttings on My Lai" (a Vietnamese village where American soldiers massacred villagers during the Vietnam War) and "a picture of three manic American soldiers dragging a dead comrade behind them . . . labelled Logan, Magoo and Macey" (Philip, 1981, p. 94). There are parallels between accounts of this more recent event at My Lai and Garner's account of fictive events at the settlement Barthomley in the second century A.D. (Benton, 1974, pp. 10–11). Philip has also suggested parallels with "the numerous similar massacres of Red Indians chronicled in Dee Brown's *Bury My Heart at Wounded Knee*" (Philip, 1981, p. 94) and between the circumstances leading to the Wounded Knee outrage in 1890 and those leading to the massacre at Barthomley in 1643.[4] Furthermore, in the film version of *Red Shift,* "Tom's copy of Dee Brown's book is deliberately visible" (Philip, 1981, p. 94). As Philip has suggested, Garner is drawing from a range of historical accounts, so as to imply an analogy between the fictionalized accounts of massacres in the two narrative strands on the one hand, and an analogy between fictive events in the novel and actual contemporary events.[5] Though the connections with Vietnam are not overt in the text, the discourse used by the Roman soldiers constructs a position for readers to make connections between Garner's historical fiction and the contemporary world. Thus, the intratextual connections imply a pattern of repetition within the novel which suggests the possibility that patterns of human actions and significances transcend historical and social differences.

Conventional historical novels, such as those by Rosemary Sutcliff or Henry Treece, form a cultural and literary context in which novels like *The Driftway* (Lively, 1972/1985) and *Red Shift* (Garner, 1973/1989) and are received—though not necessarily produced—and within and against which they are read. Though Garner's sources for his account of the Ninth legion in *Red Shift* are more likely to be historical, Sutcliff's *The Eagle of the Ninth* (1954) is a likely pre-text for readers of Garner's novel, and certainly Sutcliff's elevated register and implicit cultural values form a context for Garner's work. Sutcliff is writing within a humanist tradition, a primary assumption of which is the possibility that there are human significances and values which span cultural and historical differences and, as I have been arguing here and in Chapter 5, Garner's narrative and discursive strategies also posit notions of historical transcendence. Like Garner, Sutcliff also uses archaic and appropriated discourses to represent character speech—a convention of the genre. A key strategy of Sutcliff's historical fiction is to represent the past in a way which reflects and validates the cultural values of the sociohistorical context in which it is written (namely, postwar 1950s Britain) so as to imply a pattern of human action and significance that transcends historical and cultural difference. Like many writers of historical fiction, Sutcliff uses an elevated (literary) register which functions ideologically in the valorization of hegemonic social and political institutions (*see* Inglis, 1981, pp. 217–219 and Stephens, 1992a, pp. 220–226). In contrast, however, Garner uses overtly anachronistic and archaic forms of dialect for subversive purposes; the clash of registers articulates a process of linguistic and cultural struggle for hegemony. The novel is thus implicitly critical of those hegemonic institutions (like Roman culture) which Sutcliff valorizes. Furthermore, the analogies between the various narrative strands, and hence between the past and the present, center upon forms of social, sexual, physical and psychological violence between individuals and between social and cultural groups. The pattern of human action and significance that readers infer from the novel is one which is grounded upon an implicit violence, loneliness and personal alienation and inadequacy that underlies human relationships.

Conventional historical novels, such as those of Sutcliff, also form an intertextual and cultural context for Lively's *The Driftway* (Lively, 1972/ 1985). The use of archaic and dialect discourse, and the construction of setting in the narrative strands set in prehistoric and Saxon England in particular, are reminiscent of Sutcliff's or Treece's novels set during the same periods. There are also echoes of a range of texts and literary genres throughout the secondary narrative strands in Lively's novel. For example, Lively's story of the Welsh drovers, Jack Trip and Driftway Jim, probably has its sources in the nineteenth-century novels and "penny dreadfuls" wherein the highwayman figure was romanticized and elevated to the folk hero status of Robin Hood by writers like Ainsworth and Viles (Turner, 1975, pp. 46–48; Avery, 1975, pp. 237–139). Lively's appropriation of these pretexts is parodic and self-conscious. Driftway Jim is the son of a gentleman who, in the style of Ainsworth's *Jack Sheppard,* becomes a highwayman in order to make available to himself "that style of life" to which he feels he is "naturally entitled" (Lively, 1985, p. 119). The tone of Driftway Jim's narrative is ironic. He deliberately and self-consciously appropriates the image of Robin Hood, robbing only the rich, though he does this to gain the sympathy and silence of the ordinary people, rather than for any reasons of social conscience (p. 120). He thereby constructs a social purpose for his work: he lightens the material burden of the people he steals from and brings them closer to spiritual salvation, and provides the "humble people" with pleasure, interest and the idea of a "challenge to that ordering of society which condemns them always to have the least and suffer the most" (pp. 119–120). Thus, Driftway Jim appropriates and subverts literary images and intertexts in a manner that reflects Lively's own intertextual strategies.

There are two main views as to the cultural and ideological implications of Lively's historical fiction. Inglis (1981) sees Lively as "breaking the ranks" of what he calls "the Tolkien formation": the tradition of historical romance writing, of which Rosemary Sutcliff is representative, which takes up the "great themes of a nation, its history and its heroes," and which is involved in the legitimation of conservative interpretations of history (p. 214). He suggests that, in *The Driftway,* Lively "is consciously if clumsily seeking a way out of historical romancing" (p. 227). An implication of Inglis's view is that Lively is writing against the liberal humanist assumptions which inform the conventional historical romance as a cultural practice. However, Abbs (1975) sees Lively as writing precisely within this tradition, and as thereby seeking to retain and to reinstate humanist values of cultural continuity (p. 118).

These two positions on Lively's fiction are interesting for various reasons. Inglis and Abbs are opposed not so much on Lively's politics, but rather in how they define their own (essentially humanist) position (and that of Lively) in opposition to two different cultural and textual practices. Abbs sees Lively's fiction—and children's literature in general—as an alternative to postmodern (adult) literature and the social and psychological fragmentation that it reflects, in that it embodies traditional cultural values and a visionary and transcendent aesthetics which he sees as lacking in postmodern literature and culture (p. 118). Inglis seems to see Lively as an alternative to the "regressive" nationalist and imperialist traditions inscribed in more conservative historical fiction. Their different ways of situating themselves and Lively are indicative of an ambivalence in Lively's fiction and in historical writings and rewritings in general.

Like many writers of conventional historical fiction for children, Lively does take as her subject matter some of "the great historical peaks": the civil war, the Danish invasion of Saxon England, and so on. However, unlike other novelists of this genre, she uses characters who are "ordinary" common people, rather than "great heroic individuals," and who are often on the "wrong side," so to speak. For example, the civil war strand is narrated from the viewpoint of a parliamentary soldier—rather than from a royalist's point of view, as is more usual (Leeson, 1976)—and, furthermore, it presents a bitter indictment of the war, its violence, and its false valorization of social virtues such as loyalty, valor and honor. Similarly, as I have already suggested, her highwayman figure is a cynical parody of both Robin Hood and highwayman literary (and cultural) traditions. Thus, like Garner, Lively appropriates subjects and narrative techniques characteristic of other historical genres in order to parody and thereby subvert and interrogate their ideological basis. Whereas conservative forms of historical writing present British history as progressive, that is as teleologically structured toward the "settlement of a morally excellent and commonly assented-to political order" (Inglis, 1981, p. 216), Lively's emphasis on repetitive patterns of personal, social and cultural displacement, and the marginalization of the weak and the powerless, is situated against this programmatic legitimation of dominant political and social orders. At the same time, then, the ideological concerns that inform Lively's revision of history are dependent on a positive evaluation of the possibility and necessity of universal human values.

The educational concerns that inform much historical fiction for children, in particular the view that sees the formation of subjectivity and personal maturity as being attained via the development of an understanding of the present and of the past, entail the inscription within narratives of ideological assumptions about the relations between human subjects, time and history. Interpretations and representations of the past are always to some extent grounded in the concerns of the present. This is stressed in the present narrative of *A Bone from a Dry Sea*, for example, where images of the past imaginatively reconstructed by historians and archaeologists are informed by their ideas of the present. Historical narratives are a primary means with which to assert and interrogate universalist notions of historical process, human experience and subjectivity. The combination of multistranded and multivoiced narration in historical fiction can potentially structure the relationship between past and present as a dialogue. These strategies can have the effect of representing history as open, subject to other representations and interpretations. At the same time, these strategies also carry with them implicit cultural and philosophical assumptions about subjectivity and the relations between human subjects, time and history.

The construction of multiple temporal contexts in narrative means that the interactions between the synchronic and diachronic dimensions of narrative time can be very complex. These interactions create a tension between different conceptions of historical change and continuity. Bakhtin's concept of the chronotope provides us with a way of analyzing the cultural and ideological specificity of interrelations between narrative time and space and their implications for how human subjects are represented in relation to time, place and history. The ideological force of a chronotope can, hence, be programmatic for contemporary patterns of behavior.

In my discussions of *Red Shift*, *The Driftway* and *A Bone from a Dry Sea*, I have focused on the intertextual construction of narrative histories—and of alternative versions of history, in particular. The following two chapters also deal with intertextuality, though the focus is shifted to the use of nonliterary texts and discourses in fiction. Chapter 7 looks at the implications of these strategies for the textual representation of subjectivity, and Chapter 8 focuses again on the representation of history and subjectivity, this time in historiographic narrative genres.

ENDNOTES

1. Likewise, conventional historical narratives which use historical focalizers may use strategies—other than time-shift—to dialogize the past, but such narratives

are outside the scope of the present study.

  2. *See* my discussion of Nikolajeva's use of Bakhtin's concept of polyphony in Chapter 2.

  3. It is of interest that in *Red Shift*, the lane which Jan and Tom follow from Crewe, through the railway sidings, to Barthomley and later to Mow Cop is also a "green lane," or driftway (pp. 67–69). This is the same route as that taken by the Roman fugitives and by Margery and Thomas. The following exchange echoes Lively's comments about green lanes:

> "Have you any idea where we are?' said Jan.
> "I'm more uneasy about the "when".' [Tom] (p. 67)

Mayne also uses a "green way" in *Over the Hills and Far Away* (1968) to interconnect past and present.

  4. According to historical accounts of the events at Barthomley in 1643, John Fowler, "the son of the Rector fired from the steeple upon the troops marching past and killed one of them"; the slaughter which followed was motivated by revenge for his death (Philip, 1981, p. 96). As Philip has noted, Garner's changes to the story, whereby Thomas "sets off his gun" by accident (p. 96), echo events at Wounded Knee, where Black Coyote also "fired his gun into the air," so provoking retaliation from the troops (p. 94).

  5. Benton identifies fictional and historical events more closely than Philip, and sees Garner as "in reality" writing about "Americans in Vietnam" (Benton, 1974, p. 11). This identification would seem to narrow the range of significances that the text has to offer.

7 THE TEXTUAL AND DISCURSIVE CONSTRUCTION OF SUBJECTIVITY I

EXTRALITERARY GENRES

... the whole of the enunciation is an empty process, functioning perfectly without there being any need for it to be filled with the person of the interlocutors. Linguistically, the author is never more than the instance of writing, just as I is nothing other than the instance saying I: language knows a 'subject', not a 'person', and this subject, empty outside of the very enunciation which defines it, suffices to make language 'hold together', suffices, that is to say, to exhaust it.

Roland Barthes, "The Death of the Author"

This chapter and Chapter 8 both focus on the textual construction of subjectivity in novels which use extraliterary genres and discourses to represent heteroglossia and polyphony. The incorporation of extraliterary genres is the fourth of the four forms for representing heteroglossia outlined in Chapter 2, and the one I have so far not directly addressed. For Bakhtin, the representation of extraliterary discursive genres within the novel is one of the most basic and fundamental forms for incorporating and organising heteroglossia (1981, p. 320). Extraliterary genres, such as the diary, personal letter, confession, travel notes and biography, have played an especially significant role in structuring novels and in the historical development of the novel. This chapter examines the use of extraliterary genres and discourses and the implications that these textual strategies have for the ideological construction and representation of subjectivity in narrative. Chapter 8 will go on to deal at greater length with modes of extraliterary discourse representation in historiographic genres, with special reference to historiographic metafiction.

As I explained in Chapter 4, the term "heteroglottic" is used by Bakhtin to refer to the structuring of language out of diverse socially typifying discourses and idiolects representative of different socio-ideological groups and interests. There are two main implications of Bakhtin's position that concern me in this chapter and in Chapter 8. First, the novel, for Bakhtin, is an inherently heteroglottic genre in that it appropriates, represents and is structured by these diverse discourses. Second, Bakhtin's ideas entail that the formation of subjectivity is contingent upon the construction of a subject position from which to speak and the appropriation of social and ideological discourses from within a heteroglossia with which to speak. Many of the novels discussed in these two chapters self-reflexively foreground the texts and discourses through which they are constructed, and thus draw attention to the textual and discursive construction of the subject and of the socio-ideological contexts in which subjects are positioned. Subjectivity is represented as an intersection of a range of appropriated cultural discourses, genres and intertexts.

This chapter will examine two main narrative forms: (1) narratives which mix literary discourse and extraliterary discourses derived from the mass media, popular culture and other nonliterary forms of writing; and (2) diary and epistolary genres of the novel. In novels such as *I am the Cheese* (Cormier, 1977/1991), *Backtrack* (Hunt, 1986), *The Blooding* (Wheatley, 1987/1989), *Strange Objects* (Crew, 1990/1991) and *The Hillingdon Fox* (Mark, 1991), overt mixing of diverse nonliterary genres functions as a way of representing and examining the sociocultural influences on the formation of subjectivity and the function of language in the construction and textual representation of subjectivity. Diary and epistolary narratives foreground the construction of subjectivity within language by problematizing the voice and subject position of the diary/letter writer. In these novels, the diary and epistolary form is used to express a concern with the formation of subjectivity within time and in relation to represented social and cultural contexts. The next section will examine Bakhtin's discussion of extraliterary genres, modes of representation and implications of strategies for the construction of narrative point of view and textual subject positions.

INCORPORATED EXTRALITERARY GENRES

Bakhtin outlines two ways in which extraliterary genres are incorporated in novels. First, they can be incorporated as structural components within a text (1981, p. 323). The following are some examples of adolescent novels which use extraliterary genres as structural components:

Newspaper items: *The House that was Eureka* (Wheatley, 1985); *The Blooding* (Wheatley, 1987/1989)

Letters: *Dear Nobody* (Doherty, 1991), *Dodger* (Gleeson, 1990), *The Toll Bridge* (Chambers, 1992), *Came Back to Show You I could Fly* (Klein, 1989)

Diary entries: *Mandragora* (McRobbie, 1991), *Eleanor, Elizabeth* (Gleeson, 1984)

Interview: *I am the Cheese* (Cormier, 1977/1991)

Mixed genres—newspaper items, letters, diary entries, historical or legal documents and other extraliterary discourses: *Backtrack* (Hunt, 1986), *Breaktime* (Chambers, 1978), *Dance on my Grave* (Chambers, 1982), *Strange Objects* (Crew, 1990/1991)

In these novels, extraliterary genres are incorporated as discrete embedded textual elements. The last group is indicative of what has become a trend in recent adolescent fiction, where a range of nonliterary genres and discourses are combined—for example, the use of reports, documents, "nonfiction" informational texts, newspaper items and editorials, as well as paratextual strategies, such as footnotes, epigraphs, editorial comments, citations and so on, and typographical experimentation. This mixing of discursive genres functions primarily as a way of incorporating polyphony in novels.

Second, extraliterary genres can be incorporated as organizing principles which directly determine and organize the structure of a novel (Bakhtin, 1981, p. 323). The following are some examples of adolescent novels which use these extraliterary genres as an organizing principle:

Diary: *The Hillingdon Fox* (Mark, 1991), *So Much to Tell You* (Marsden, 1987), *Breaking Up* (Wilmot, 1983), *Z for Zachariah* (O'Brien, 1975), *Emma Tupper's Diary* (Dickinson, 1971)

Letter, diary, confession: *The Blooding* (Wheatley, 1987/1989), *Dance on my Grave* (Chambers, 1982)

Personal letters: *Letters from the Inside* (Marsden, 1991)

In these novels, extraliterary genres determine the form of a novel as a whole and, as will be clear from repeated texts in these two lists, both strategies for incorporating discourse can be combined in one novel.

All forms for appropriating and representing heteroglossia in the novel permit language to be used in ways that are indirect, conditional and distanced (Bakhtin, 1981, p. 323); that is, they can enable appropriated discursive genres to be the object as well as the mode of representation. For example, in *I am the Cheese* (1977/1991), a multistranded novel, one narrative strand is represented entirely as an interview conducted within an institution of the central protagonist Adam by Brint (a mysterious character whose role and purpose in interviewing Adam is not clear). The interview is being used in part to communicate events concerning Adam's family lead-

ing up to his institutionalization, but it is not simply a way of framing retrospective narration. Instead, the interview mode itself is also the object of
representation, in the sense that it becomes metonymic of Adam's
disempowered subject position. The purpose of the interviews remains ambiguous, partly because the interviewer's role is never made clear—is Brint
a psychiatrist trying to help Adam, or is he an interrogator trying to ascertain how much Adam knows, and if the latter, then whose side is he on?
Thus, the interviewer-interviewee relationship is a power relation which reflects (or is a microcosm for) relations between institutionalized systems and
political processes, and individuals enmeshed within these processes. As the
interviewee, Adam is subjected by the interview process in the same way that
he and his family have been subjected by political processes.

Incorporated discourses are usually linguistically marked by stylistic
conventions discernible in aspects of register, lexis and syntax associated with
specific generic discourses. The textual conventions for incorporating
extraliterary genres in many contemporary adolescent novels can heighten
these stylistic conventions. Hence, incorporated discourse becomes the object of representation. For example, the variation of print and layout conventions, and the use of marginalia, footnotes, epigraphs and other textual
conventions associated with specific genres are strategies which draw attention to the physicality of texts.

Bakhtin distinguishes between two modes of representation whereby
extraliterary genres are incorporated in the novel. They may be represented
as directly intentional, that is, they "refract authorial intentions"; or they
may be treated objectively, "not as a word that has been spoken, but as a
word to be displayed, like a thing," and, thereby, deprived of authorial intentions (1981, p. 321). Bakhtin's essay on novelistic discourse was written
in the 1930s and, in the context of more recent critical discussions of authorial intentionality, terms like "intentional" and "objective" are misleading. Some commentators have substituted other more critically "neutral"
terms: Todorov (1984), for example, uses the terms "passive" and "active"
(p. 70). The distinction Bakhtin is making is not so much about authorial
intentionality as the diegetic level at which incorporated discourses are represented and the degree to which the discursive otherness of these discourses
is foregrounded. The incorporation of extraliterary discursive genres can thus
be understood as a form of discourse representation, and for this reason I
use the terms "indirect" (intentional) and "direct" (objective).[1] In the case
of "intentional" discourse, incorporated genres are represented as indirect
discourse which is diegetically subordinate to a narratorial voice or authorial position, and their discursive otherness is thereby often masked or re-

pressed. In the case of "objective" discourse, incorporated genres are represented as the quoted or direct discourse of another which has other contexts and meanings, and their linguistic or stylistic peculiarities are thereby generally foregrounded.

Both modes of representation can potentially effect a doubleness. That is, both modes can be used to represent incorporated discourse as another text situated in a dialogic relation to the focused text in which it is incorporated, and which refers to other texts and contexts outside of the focused text. However, direct modes of representation are potentially more overtly dialogic, while the dialogicality of indirect modes tends to be more covert. Indirect modes incorporate extraliterary discourses within the discourse of characters or narrators as direct or indirect quotation, paraphrase or appropriated discourse. In *The Hillingdon Fox* (Mark, 1991), for example, although the diaries of the two brothers are represented directly, media discourses are represented indirectly as either quoted or appropriated discourse within the writing of the two diarists. Direct modes foreground the distinctive textual and discursive features of extraliterary discourses by physically representing these discourses as diegetically and textually distinct from the narrative discourse. This is indicated usually by typographical, linguistic and paratextual features specific to the discursive modes being imitated. For example, newspaper pages in *The House that was Eureka* (Wheatley, 1985, pp. 77–78 and pp. 113–115) are physically represented using the typography associated with the newspaper genre—headlines, subheadings and double columns—as well as linguistic features peculiar to that genre. Paratextual strategies include footnotes, epigraphs, prefaces, illustrations, editorial comments, documents, reports and so on; that is, textual conventions associated with discursive genres such as historical, legal or other nonfiction texts (*see* Hutcheon, 1989, pp. 82–92).

Direct representation of extraliterary genres can enable the incorporation of a range of social and ideological viewpoints in texts. Readers will potentially be situated in positions not directly aligned with character or narratorial point of view. In *Backtrack* (Hunt, 1986), *The Blooding* (Wheatley, 1987/1989) and *Strange Objects* (Crew, 1990/1991), incorporated texts, such as newspaper items or documents, represent aspects of a story in ways which distance readers and involve them in active processes of inferring and constructing both story and meanings. For example, in *The Blooding*, paratexts in the form of endnotes to newspaper items refer to other articles, and thereby construct another level of story (for example, 1989, pp. 30, 34, 75 and 149). This format thus stresses the complexity of events, the multiplicity of causes and implications that events can have, and thereby implies that the fictive world comprises multiple layers and interconnections. The function of extraliterary discourses in incorporating a range of political and social viewpoints is particularly important in *The Blooding,* the discourse of which is otherwise virtually straight first person narration. In contrast, *I am the Cheese* (Cormier, 1977/1991) mixes literary and extraliterary genres in combination with multistranded narration. There are three narrative strands: a first person account Adam's bike ride from Monument to Rutterburg narrated in the present tense; an interview by Brint (a psychiatrist, perhaps?); and an account of Adam's childhood and events leading up to the death of his parents narrated in the third person in the past tense. Up until almost the close of the novel the temporal relations between these three strands are unclear, and readers cannot be sure whether the bike ride takes place before or after the interviews. It is finally revealed, however, that Adam is in fact riding his bike within the confines of the institution where he is being held, and that this narrative strand thus occurs on a different diegetic level, rather than at a different point in time. The meaning of this narrative strand remains ambiguous: does it represent Adam's imaginings or desires, his plans for the future, or is it symbolic of Adam's life insofar as he, like his bike-riding counterpart, is left utterly alone, alienated and unable to trust anyone by the end of the novel. The novel ends "I keep pedalling, I keep pedalling . . ." (1991, p. 191), but the fact that the journey from Monument to Rutterburg to see his father has merely taken him around the grounds of the institution suggests that his "pedalling" will get him nowhere; he will eventually be "obliterated" or "terminated" (p. 190). This narrative structure combined with the interview genre positions readers in active subject positions which, once the "story" has been disclosed, are oriented toward making thematic and metaphoric links between the three narratives and making interpretative decisions about the interviews themselves—postulating answers to questions such as—What is the purpose of the interviews and who is Brint working for?

Incorporated extraliterary discourses can be used to articulate concerns with the interrelations between the self, the world and others. These discourses often refer not so much to any specific text as such, as to a particular set of textual conventions and cultural and ideological assumptions associated with specific discursive genres. The generic codes and discourses associated with the mass media, in particular newspaper and television, constitute a special group of extraliterary cultural discourses through which the public, political and social spheres are mediated, represented and disseminated. These kinds of discourses are usually quite overtly inscribed with socially constructed cultural assumptions and values. Their incorporation within novelistic discourse performs an important function in the representation of social and cultural influences on the formation of subjectivity and of cultural values and ideologies in relation to which characters and narrators position themselves and are positioned as subjects. For example, news items in *The Blooding* (Wheatley, 1987/1989) and *The Hillingdon Fox* (Mark, 1991) construct a recognizable social and cultural context for represented events in relation to which characters are positioned. Characters in both novels are in the process of becoming more aware of social roles and codes of behaviour, and extraliterary material in these novels is crucial for the representation of subjectivity as being formed within a social context. Whereas extraliterary texts in *The Hillingdon Fox* and *The Blooding* gesture outside of the text so as to imply analogies with extratextual social and historical contexts, extraliterary material in *Strange Objects* (Crew, 1990/1991) and *Backtrack* (Hunt, 1986) is, by comparison, more intratextual and, in the case of *Backtrack,* radically self-reflexive.

Extraliterary genres also have an important function in the ideological construction of subjectivity in language and the representation of intersubjectivity in novelistic discourse. Discursive genres are "specific points of view on the world" and each possesses its own verbal and semantic forms for assimilating various aspects of reality (Bakhtin, 1981, p. 290). In other words, they are ideologically inscribed. Represented in the novel, these genres usually preserve their own structural integrity and independence, and their own linguistic and stylistic peculiarities (Bakhtin, 1981, p. 321). The effects of incorporating extraliterary genres can potentially be similar to those of using multiple focalizers or narrators. They can enable the representation of a variety of linguistic styles and registers and ideological viewpoints, and the construction of characters and narrators as "ideologues," that is, as "subjects of their own directly signifying discourses" (Bakhtin, 1984a, p. 7) who occupy subject positions not dominated by a narratorial voice or authorial position. However, as I argued in Chapter 2 about the use of multiple narrators, focalizers and narrative strands, the presence of extraliterary genres in a novel does not automatically ensure its dialogicality. This resides not merely in the presence of different styles and dialects, but also the "dialogic angle at which these styles are juxtaposed and counterposed in the work" (Bakhtin, 1984a, p. 184).

Typographical experimentation and overt genre mixing have become increasingly common in adolescent fictions but, as Stephens (1992b) has suggested, these strategies "seem to be settling into [their] own formulaic conventions: two or three clearly delineated genres or modes . . . are juxtaposed in order to suggest restricted perspective and to complicate otherwise flat, everyday surfaces" (p. 53). The narrative context in which extraliterary discourses are incorporated is a major determining factor in the dialogic function of incorporated discourse. The heteroglottic potential of incorporated extraliterary genres can be contained and repressed through the presence of a dominant authorial or narratorial point of view. This can also occur through a lack of register differentiation, whereby the stylistic and linguistic peculiarities that characterize particular forms of social and professional discourse are either disguised or ignored, and through the treatment of narrative discourses in general as transparent media which simply conveys information rather than as specific linguistic codes which construct and inscribe this information with meanings. For example, in novels such as *Came Back to Show You I Could Fly* (Klein, 1989), *Dodger* (Gleeson, 1990), *Letters from the Inside* (Marsden, 1991) and *The Toll Bridge* (Chambers, 1992), the dialogic potential of extraliterary discourses and double-stranded narration is repressed by the presence of dominant authorial viewpoints, naive realist assumptions about the representational function of language, and a common failure to represent register variation in represented character discourse. These three characteristics combine to deny characters and implied readers subject positions independent of the dominant authorial position. In comparison, novels such as Chambers's *Breaktime* (1978), Hunt's *Backtrack* (1986), Crew's *Strange Objects* (1990/ 1991), and Mark's *The Hillingdon Fox* (1990) consistently foreground their own textuality and discursivity and use extraliterary genres to construct characters and readers as active subjects.

HETEROGLOSSIA AND POLYFOCALIZATION IN <u>BACKTRACK</u>

Peter Hunt's use of extraliterary discourses in *Backtrack* (1986) is particularly complex and self-reflexive. He combines a range of extraliterary discourses, narratorial modes and focalization strategies so as to explore and play with notions of historical accuracy and authenticity. The plot centres on a "mysterious" train crash. This event is narrated at least five times from different characters' points of view and using different narrative and discursive modes, as the following passages show. Passages (2) and (4) are third person narration focalized by characters present; the other three are all represented as retrospective accounts using extraliterary discourses, namely, newspaper, report and letter. Passages (1) and (5) are represented directly using typographical features peculiar to newspaper and letter genres and (3) is represented indirectly. In all of these five passages, narrative point of view and discursive mode are used to construct subject positions for speakers and focalizers in relation to the represented events—subject positions are determined by time and place, social position and occupation, attitude and emotional viewpoint and, in the case of the textual accounts, implied audience and the context of writing. The different meanings attributed to the event are indicative of the varying contexts, viewpoints and discourses used to describe it.

1.   Newspaper report (direct representation)Our correspondent in Hereford last night informed us of another shocking railway catastrophe. A train which was carrying the Rt-Hon Sir Edward Marks, His Majesty's Minister for Military Supply, was derailed near the village of Elmcote with terrible results. Eight persons are reported to have perished in the holocaust occasioned by fire. Sir Edward, who was fortunately uninjured, gave such assistance as he could together with other rescuers.

    Further details will be given in later editions, but it is already conjectured that the accident may represent an attempt on the life of the Minister by agents of a hostile nation.

The Times
Friday, 3rd September, 1915 (p. 3)

2.   Third person narration focalized by Harry, George and Will
And through the trees down to the footpath just as the light changes and the gush of heat sears up the eyes and up the carriages; one hanging half off the viaduct, another on its end, resting on the tender of the engine, and leaning against the pillar of the second arch. The engine still shuddering and the upper cranks turning in the plough of trees and path, the black nose among burning bushes. Lit faces over the parapet. (p. 11)

3.   Inquest Report: third person retrospective narration, quoted by Jack (indirect representation)
"The engine crossed the up line, broke through the parapet of the viaduct, and fell directly into the lane below, dragging the first coach with it. The couplings between the second and third coaches fractured, and the second coach remained suspended on the parapet at an angle of about 40 degrees from the vertical. The third coach was slewed across the running lines, and the fourth had over-ridden it and was at a steep angle; the front half of the first-class set had over-ridden this, and was at a similarly steep angle; the second half was on its side. Due to the superior construction of these vehicles, there was comparatively little structural damage to them. The remainder of the train remained upright on the rails." (p. 61)

4.   Third person narration, focalized by Edward
The door that was on the right seems to be underwater: dark green

light: no, just bushes and unmistakably a rail down in the ground. The carriage creaking and smelling worse, momently. But at least there's an open window, or a hole, and Edward leans across and up, elbowing his body out of the open space to air and trees; the carriage almost on end, and on its side. Climbing out and looking down the streaked roof, and an horrific sight: splintered and shattered wood, and crushed shapes, and the coach hanging off over the parapet of a bridge. People running to the broken brickwork and looking down, where there is smoke and fire and noise. The sides of the carriage pitted and seared with gravel, like a heavy bombardment of shells. (p. 62)

5.   Letter: first person retrospective narration by Ashley Cartwright (direct representation)

When I came to myself, the air was filled with smoke and steam, and I found that the carriage had reared upwards. Getting to the window, I perceived that I was nearly 20 feet from the ground, and as I looked out (risking injury from the shards of shattered glass) I felt the carriage lurch violently, and the carriage that was caught aslant the turn on the parapet of the viaduct fell away in a terrible gush and inferno of flame. At the very last second, I saw a man leap from it to the parapet, where he was barely held from plunging to his death by two other men. The scene was lighted by an unearthly glow, as of stygian fires. (p. 68)

There is a lot of repetition of descriptive and nominal terms in the five passages, and the physical positioning of the carriages and engine is roughly the same in each account. However, speakers and focalizers are constructed in subject positions which vary according to their physical, emotional and attitudinal relation to the event, their occupation and social position, and hence their access to technical, social and cultural discursive codes. Passage (1) is represented as reported indirect discourse of an unspecified other—as in "Our correspondent in Hereford informed us of . . ."—and is the most physically distanced from the event. Passage (3) is narrated by an unspecified person from an unspecified position, but the detail of the account suggests a position of physical and temporal proximity. Passages (2), (4) and (5) are all narrated from the viewpoints of characters present, though their physical positions are different—Harry, George and Will (2) were all outside the train, while Edward (4) and Cartwright (5) were inside it. The time of narration also varies. Cartwright's account is retrospective and the repetition of the first person pronoun—as in "I came," "I found," "I perceived"—

draws attention to the status of his account as narrated text, and hence mediated and re-presented. In contrast, the use of present tense indirect narration and the omission of pronouns denoting the perceiving subject in passage (4) implies an illusion of unmediated narration of events. By describing the same event from a number of different viewpoints using different kinds of discourse at different points in the novel, the text raises questions about the status and significance of the event(s) described and their ontological dependence on the position, voice and discourse of the narrating/focalizing subject. Insofar as each passage represents a different version of events, the meanings ascribed to these events vary according to point of view, context and, in the case of passages (1), (3) and (5), the purpose for writing. Does each passage represent the same event, and can it mean in the same way each time it is described?

Of the five passages, the language used to describe the accident in (1) is the most sensationalized—as in "shocking," "terrible," "perished," "catastrophe" and "holocaust." However, terms like "catastrophe" and "holocaust" actually generalize the event and subordinate it to the war at large. The semantic impact of terms such as "shocking," "terrible" and "perished" is diminished, and the discourse thus conveys the speaker's physical and emotional distance from both the accident and the war. As "another shocking railway accident," it is a plot element in the metanarrative of war. This contrasts with the reference to war in passage (4)—as in "like a heavy bombardment of shells"—the specificity of which implies the immediacy of the perceiving subject (Edward) to both the train accident and to war itself. Ashley Cartwright's letter also features a mixture of sensationalist and generalizing discourse similar to that of the first passage, though the register is elevated and overtly literary. Cartwright's vocabulary—particularly the lexical set "inferno," "unearthly" and "stygian"—makes an intertextual link with mythic and religious metanarratives. The effect, however, of Cartwright's over-the-top language and literary allusions, combined with the long preamble which precedes his account, is parodic.

The five passages each reflect how register is used to invest the scene with significances which are largely determined by the attitudinal position of the focalizing or narrating subject and that subject's access to specific social and cultural codes and conventions. The generalizing discourse used in (1) and (5) is contrasted by the specificity of terms used in passages (2), (3) and (4). The semantic range of descriptive and referential terms in these three passages corresponds to the emotional stance and social and cultural knowledge of perceiving subjects. The emotive register of terms in (2) and (4) is roughly similar—as in "sears," "shuddering" and "burning" in (2), and "splintered," "shattered," "crushed," "pitted" and "seared" in (4)—and this contrasts with the more neutral and objective technical register of terms in (3). However, passages (2) and (3) both use a technical register—as in "viaduct," "tender," "upper cranks" and "couplings," which contrasts with the vague descriptive terms used in (4), such as "the parapet of a bridge." These contrasts in register are indicative of characters' physical and attitudinal points of view as well as their access to technical codes and knowledge. Will, George and Harry, who focalize passage (2), and the unspecified writer of passage (3) are familiar with the technical language used to talk about trains and viaducts, whereas Edward (4) is not. The textualized subject positions of speakers and focalizers also constructs different significances. The three textual accounts [(1), (3) and (5)] are overtly oriented toward an addressee, the construction of a narrating voice and the production of significances within a larger social and cultural context. The newspaper is primarily concerned with representing an accident of war and the audience constructed by the discourse is characterised by an interest in sensation, disaster and narrative complication and resolution—hence the postulation of causes and the subordination of events to the metanarrative of war. The account in the inquest report is an implicit attempt to affirm that liability for the accident did not lie with either the train or the railway. And Cartwright's letter is an overt attempt by Cartwright to construct and present himself as a writer, within a literary tradition of (Dickensian) writers about train crashes and of grand mythical narratives.

Extraliterary discourses and genres which are incorporated in texts as textual components have an important function in the dialogizing of the narrative discourse. They incorporate a range of social and ideological viewpoints within texts and foreground the role of language in the construction of meanings for represented events, and thereby construct more active implied reader subject positions. The remainder of this chapter will examine the use of diary and epistolary genres as organizing principles which determine the structure of the novel as a whole and the implications these narrative strategies have for the representation of subjectivity.

DIARY AND EPISTOLARY NOVELS AND THE CONSTRUCTION OF SUBJECTIVITY

Diaries, journals and letters are extraliterary discursive genres which have had a significant role in the historical development of the novel (Porter, 1984; Martens, 1985). For Bakhtin, they also have an important function for the incorporation and representation of heteroglossia in the novel (Bakhtin, 1981, p. 323). The remainder of this chapter examines the use of diary and epistolary genres in *The Blooding* (Wheatley, 1987/1989), *Strange Objects*

(Crew, 1990/1991) and *The Hillingdon Fox* (Mark, 1991), where they function mainly as organizing principles to structure the novels. Diary forms in each of these novels represent characters as occupying narrative subject positions not dominated by an authorial or narratorial position or voice. A common concern is with the textual construction of the writing or narrating subject: the act of writing a diary entails the simultaneous construction of a narrated or represented self and a narrating voice. The latter involves the construction of a subject position from which to write or narrate and the appropriation of socio-ideological discourses and narrative forms with which to write or narrate.

Diary genres are used in these three novels to construct double narrative structures. *The Hillingdon Fox* (Mark, 1991) and *Strange Objects* (Crew, 1990/1991) both comprise two parallel journals which frame and contextualize each other. *The Hillingdon Fox* is a double-stranded diary novel which consists of the two diaries of two brothers written eight years apart, Hugh (age seventeen in 1990) and Gerald (age eighteen in 1982). The diaries are represented in the novel as alternating daily extracts. Both diarists are involved in documenting a war: Gerald records the Falklands War; and Hugh records the opening of the Gulf conflict. Both also record events concerning their family and friends. The viewpoints of both narrators are limited and this, combined with the time gap between their narratives, produces narrative gaps and discrepancies. Implied readers are thereby positioned in active reading roles and are required to infer both story details and significances. *Strange Objects* is a double-stranded multitemporal novel in which diary genres are represented at two diegetic levels of narration. The primary narrative is set in 1986 and concerns a young man, Stephen Messenger, who finds a series of "strange objects," among them the (fictive) diary of Wouter Loos (a Dutch murderer who was cast away on the coast of Western Australia in 1623 with another murderer Jan Pelgrom). The primary narrative is represented as a project book, entitled "The Messenger Documents," which Messenger has apparently compiled and assembled before disappearing, and this manuscript is presented as evidence in an inquiry into his disappearance. The project book functions as a structuring principle which organizes the novel as whole, and it includes within it a newspaper copy of a translation of Loos's journal.

The Blooding (Wheatley, 1987/1989) centers on a conflict in a small Australian logging town between the local timber cutters and a group of conservationists. It is narrated by Colum, who in lives in the town, and who has an affinity with the forest and spends much of his time in a secret place in the forest that his grandfather showed him as a child. His father is a logger, however, and when the conservationists arrive in town Col comes into conflict with his father through his involvement with them. The novel opens with Col in the hospital with two broken legs, having fallen from a tree which was in the path of a bulldozer driven by his father, and his lawyer asks him to write a statement, giving an account of events leading up to this. Thus, the narrative takes the form of a retrospective account written by Col. However, the status of the document that he writes is ambiguous. It is a letter, a diary and a confession, and thus combines the narrative strategies of the epistolary novel, the diary novel and a legal statement or confession. Throughout the narrative Col remains unsure about whom the document is addressed to—the lawyer, himself or an unknown future reader—and why he is writing it. This ambiguity destabilizes Col's subject position (as diarist, letter writer, confessor) and his own notions of story and significance, thus generating multiple story/discourse times and textualized subject positions both for addressees and for Col himself.

Epistolary and diary novel genres have received critical attention from narrative and genre theorists who have focused primarily upon the temporal disparities between the narrative discourse and the story and relations between narrators and narratees (Prince, 1975; Porter, 1984; Martens, 1985; Genette, 1986). Diary and epistolary novels are an example of what Genette terms "interpolated narration": narration which occurs "between the moments of the action" and in several narrative instances (1986, p. 217). The journal or letter are to some extent both "a medium of the narrative and an element in the plot" (p. 217); in other words, the acts of writing and narration are both the object of the story and elements of the discourse. A crucial aspect of narrative which diary and epistolary genres foreground is the construction within language of a speaking subject (the narrator or diarist), a narrated subject, and an addressee or narratee. However, a peculiarity of diary fiction is the apparent absence of a narratee: the diary is most frequently seen as a private mode of writing in which the diarist writes "essentially for himself" (Martens, 1985, p. 4). If, as Bakhtin argues, all utterances are oriented toward an other, toward a speaker's idea of that other, then to whom is the diary addressed, and what is the relation between the narrator, the narratee (or apparently absent narratee) and implied readers? A tacit assumption in conventional diary and autobiographical fiction is that the narrating subject denotes a centered and unified self which coincides with the narrated subject. However, Barthes's (1977b) parody of autobiographical genres has foregrounded the implicit doubleness of the subject in the act of self-narration, generated by disparities between the narrating and the narrated subjects (Hutcheon, 1989, p. 40). The convention that the diarist writes for her/himself creates a further split between the subject as narrator, narrated and narratee. These fragmentations and doublings are comparable to the use of the *doppelgänger* that I discussed in Chapter 3, and can also be understood in Bakhtinian and Lacanian terms as configurations of the relations between self and other and of the fragmented subject. The idea that the diarist writes for, about and in the voice of different selves represents a variation on the idea of the subject as being constructed via the appropriation of the position and viewpoint of the other. The narrated subject and the narratee are both aspects of the subject's internalization of the other. The disparity between the subject as narrator, narrated and narratee is analogous to that disparity described by Lacan and Bakhtin between the subject as perceiver and perceived in relation to the mirror. The text of a letter or diary, like the mirror, constitutes the field of the other in which the subject is constructed or narrated.

TIME AND ORDER IN DIARY FICTION

Interpolated narration in novels such as *The Blooding* (Wheatley, 1987/ 1989), *Strange Objects* (Crew, 1990/1991) and *The Hillingdon Fox* (Mark, 1990) problematizes narrative order, beginnings and endings, and it foregrounds disparities between the story and its representation in the narrative discourse. Characteristically, the diary is a fragmented, discontinuous and incomplete form. Its apparently random and contingent narrative structure implies the illusion of an unstructured spontaneous "artless," and therefore "natural" account, lacking a beginning and an ending, but potentially focused on significant events or incidents. However, any fictional account always begins and ends somewhere, thereby implying a narrative structure "that imparts meaning as well as order" (Hutcheon, 1989, p. 62). The problem of beginnings is flaunted in *The Hillingdon Fox,* for example, in Hugh's comments about starting a diary:

> I'm already beginning to wish I'd started to write all this when I first thought of it, last month. Then I'd have had a complete record of the conflict. . . It's *annoying*, that's all, starting in the middle of something. Still, that's life isn't it? You always come in in the middle. I was born in 1973. I must find out what I arrived in the middle of. (my ellipsis, Mark, 1991, p. 9)

The narrative structure of the diary apparently reflects the structure of a human life; it opens and closes *in medias res.* Hugh's comment contrasts ironically with the first entry of Gerald's diary in which he overtly attempts to construct a subject position from which to begin:

> Greetings to the Twenty-First Century! Let me introduce myself. My
> name is Gerald Marshall and I am eighteen years old, having been
> born on January 17th 1964. I live at 8, Grosvenor Avenue, Calderley,
> Oxon, with my parents Anthony and Elizabeth Marshall, and my
> brothers, Geoffrey and Hugh. (p. 10)

Gerald's listing of his name, age, address, family members, their names, ages
and so on is an overt attempt to situate himself and to construct an illusion
of a narrative beginning, as opposed to an opening. Implicit here is also an
attempt by Gerald to construct an image of himself as an objective reporter
of events. The novel ends abruptly when the two brothers cease writing, at
the point at which Gerald decides to put the diary in the time capsule (and
is about to find out the truth about whether or not his father is having an
affair) and Hugh is about to open the time capsule where Gerald's diary is
hidden (along with other unknown items). Thus the point at which the novel
closes is also the point at which it opened; it begins and ends in the middle
of things.

The temporal situatedness of the act of narration is also foregrounded
in *The Hillingdon Fox* by disparities between the story and the narrative
discourse. This relation is treated playfully in Gerald's unintentional and
indirect reporting of a relationship between two of Gerald's friends, Jo Ann
Rugg and Mark Lovell, through which the disparity between discourse order (Gerald's narration) and story order (as it is reconstructed retrospectively
by Gerald and by readers) is ironically foregrounded. The main events of
the story are narrated inadvertently by Gerald—for example, his note of Jo
Ann and Mark's absence from the meeting (p. 24) and account of Jo Ann
crying in the library (pp. 59–60). The story is also recorded, again inadvertently, on a video which contains footage of Jo Ann visiting an ante-natal
clinic, Mark and Mr. Rugg having a fight outside a Laura Ashley store, and
Mark and Jo Ann meeting outside the town hall. These story components,
which take place on the third and fifth of April, are only gradually revealed
in Gerald's narrative over the period from the fourth to the eighteenth of
April as he inadvertently narrates them and, especially, as he describes the
video film (pp. 76–77, 89–91 and 94–95). It is only after he sees the video
for the second and third times (pp. 89–91 and 94–95) that he begins to no-
tice the relationship between what had appeared to be unrelated contingent
occurrences and to construct these story elements as a connected narrative
sequence, which is that Jo Ann, thinking she was pregnant, had told Mark
(the father to be) and her parents, and after a fight with Jo Ann's father, Mark
had run away (pp. 111 and 116–117).

In *Strange Objects* (Crew, 1990/1991), Crew incorporates the conventions of interpolated narration in a way which opposes story and discourse aspects of the narrative. The documentary material comprising Stephen Messenger's scrapbook is in chronological order, a fact that ostensibly implies that it has been compiled over the four-month period which it covers. In this way, it constructs an implied reader position which would assume a reading of the text as a diary narrative. However, the only entry narrated by Messenger which is dated is the final letter to Hope Michaels (p. 175). It would seem, then, that "The Messenger Documents" (as Messenger's scrapbook is referred to in the novel) have been selectively collected and arranged by Messenger from a retrospective point of view, as if this viewpoint were situated in the present of the story. This retrospective structuring of the discourse, by a clearly unreliable narrator, has the effect of undermining and subverting the story represented in the narrative discourse. "The Messenger Documents" are framed and structured by an introduction and afterword by. Dr Hope Michaels, to whom the manuscript has been addressed and sent, and who occupies a diegetically higher editorial position. Michaels also disrupts the apparent chronology of the story when she withholds crucial "story" information until the final pages of the novel, namely, that Stephen Messenger's father had died three months prior to the point at which the novel begins—a detail which possibly explains Messenger's dreams of blood and clearly unhinged state of mind. Thus, Michaels replicates the strategies of deception deployed by Messenger, and ultimately by Crew. Whereas disparities between story and discourse components in *The Hillingdon Fox* (Mark, 1991) place characters and readers in similar interpretative positions (that is readers infer the "story" along with Gerald and Hugh) the treatment of story/discourse relations in *Strange Objects* isolates, and ultimately disempowers, its readers who are deceived not just by the "author," but also by characters and narrators at all levels of narration.

Beginnings, narrative order and the very act of narration are all also problematized in the opening of *The Blooding* (Wheatley, 1987/1989), where the narrator, Colum, is instructed to write an account of the events leading up to his confinement in hospital:

> The Lawyer said to write down what happened.
> *'Everything?'* I said.
> *'Everything,'* he said, 'The whole sequence of events.' (1989, p. 1)

> 'Just begin at the beginning,' he said very patiently, 'and work through to the middle, and end at the end. Pretend you're just telling a story.' (1989, p. 2).

Colum's attempts to follow the lawyer's instructions are frustrated from the outset, as the point at which the sequence of events could be said to have "begun" becomes more difficult to situate. The temporal disparity between the story and the discourse is foregrounded by the combination of interpolated and retrospective narrational modes and a range of addressees. Colum writes a journal (wherein he records daily events in the hospital), a letter (which is addressed to a fictive reader and is personal in tone) and a (retrospective) legal statement or confession (which is addressed to a lawyer and which strives for objectivity and linearity). The temporal relation between story and discourse is further complicated through the construction of four kinds of time: story, discourse, historical and mythic. The interrelations between these concepts of time can be seen in the following passage.

> The story I'm simply trying to tell about what happened in Cornwall in that little bit of time from Thursday afternoon when I met Jade when I was hunting, till Monday morning when the old man ran me down with the bulldozer, all seems to get gobbled up by talking about the hospital or how I got into the gang with Scott or how I used to get on best with Mum till I won the old man to me with fighting and sport or how the happiest times of my life have been in my land. Plus there's the stuff about Grandad too. (p. 37)

Story time corresponds to "that little bit of time from Thursday afternoon . . . till Monday morning." However, the present moment of narration in the hospital (discourse time), events which happened in Colum's past and in the past of his forebears (historical time) and the stories told to Colum by his grandfather (mythic time) constantly impinge upon his attempts to "just tell the story." These strategies draw attention not only to the effects of retrospective narration and appropriated discourses upon the perception and representation of past events, but also to the need to historically situate these events within the confines of a metanarrative through which events are inscribed with cultural meanings. Each of these notions of time presupposes a beginning and a narrative structure, and thematically the novel centers on the (deferred) desire for an originary moment and a stable subject position from which to narrate.

The secret "palace" that Col's grandfather had shown him as a child, and which is Col's own secret or private place, is in fact the site of an earlier settlement. The fairy tales which his grandfather tells represent this historical settlement as myth or folklore, thereby obscuring its historical significance, as the "first settlement" of the town of Cornwall, in Australia [2]. The representation of the settlement as a "palace," that is, as a mythic place, constructs the past and the original moment of settlement as mysterious and other (it is unfamiliar for Colum and for readers). The moment of (white) settlement is located in mythic or fairy tale time rather than in historical time and is thus represented as immanent, that is, outside of conventional linear concepts of time. In this way, the "palace"—that is the archaeological remains of the earlier settlement—is represented within the generic conventions of the pastoral, that is as a part of the forest and its metaphoric "greenness"; it is a "natural" place outside the closedness of Cornwall society. However, growing at the center of this "palace," this archetypal "wilderness," are magnolias and herbs— plants which are not native to Australia. These exotic plants disclose the pastoral myth underlying Grandad's (and the text's) construction of history; a myth which is not only homocentric, but also anglocentric (*see* Scutter, 1991). Finally, the forest is "saved," not because of any intrinsic value it might have in itself as wilderness, as conservationist discourse might imply, but because it is centered around, enclosing and preserving, a remnant of the colonial past, that is, a remnant of (white) human society. The pastoral myth merely legitimates the colonialization of the wilderness and postulates an originary moment which is coterminous with (white) human civilization. While the ending of the novel demystifies Col's reading and thus reveals the cultural constructedness of place and the past, the ideological apparatus through which the moment of colonization is constructed as originary is neither interrogated nor dismantled.

Authority and Authenticity in Diary Fiction

Historically, epistolary and diary genres have been associated with the conventions of literary realism (Porter, 1984, p. 18). Typically, these genres have been used as a means of authenticating the fictive text and the world it depicts, though in self-reflexive modes of fiction they are often also a means of interrogating that world. The diary novel has a double status as fiction and as written document, which depends upon the implicit agreement that the fictive act of writing coincides with that of narration. For example, in *The Hillingdon Fox* (Mark, 1991) Hugh declares that his diary will record his "innermost thoughts" and that he will not "cross anything out" because "you can't cross out what you think" (p. 7). The assertion implies that writing, narrating and thought are all coincident, that is, they occur simultaneously. Thus, two dominant thematic concerns in diary fiction are with the physical processes of writing and the materiality of the written document, and with the relations between representation, authenticity and authority (Prince, 1975, p. 479). The use of the diary form is associated with a desire to confer authority through a pretence of authenticity. The documentary status of the diary enables it to function as a literary found object, as the diaries of Wouter Loos in *Strange Objects* (Crew, 1990/1991) and Gerald in *The Hillingdon Fox* are represented, though its fictive status potentially undermines and subverts this authority, particularly in metafictive novels. This ambiguity as to the status of the fictive document also underlies Gerald's journal and the time capsule itself in which it is to be placed. A "time capsule" is a sealed container in which objects and documents are placed in the hope that they will display the current state of a civilization to whomever might eventually find it at a later time. In other words, a time capsule is an attempt in the present to construct the present as a historical (pretextualized) artifact, and to dictate future representations of that present as past. The stated purpose of the contributors to the time capsule in *The Hillingdon Fox* is to put together "as true a picture as we can contrive of the state of the nation" (p. 10). However, the term "contrive," with its connotations of stratagem, plot and trickery, draws attention to the extent to which this picture is one which is inscribed with cultural (and possibly fictive) assumptions about the present and future and about history.

This concern with authenticity and authority extends to the positions and functions of represented diary writers. The idea of the "time capsule" as an attempt to inscribe and circumscribe narrated events in the present with meaning underlies the motivation of journal writers such as Gerald in *The Hillingdon Fox* (Mark, 1991), and Wouter Loos in *Strange Objects* (Crew, 1990/1991), both of whom are overtly motivated by a concern to produce and project a specific image of themselves. The activity of writing a diary or letter entails the representation of a narrated subjectivity and the construction of a narrating subject. Both are contingent upon the writer's adoption of a subject position in relation to the represented world and to an actual, imagined or absent narratee. These relations hinge on the diarist's conception of the context of her/his writing and of whom s/he is writing for. In *The Hillingdon Fox* and *The Blooding* (Wheatley, 1987/1989), the context of journal writing is inherently double: it is both a public and a private activity. As a transcription of daily events, a diary can be an impersonal daily record of public social and historical events, as terms like "journal" or "chronicle" would imply. This is suggested in Hugh's description of the practice of "Mass Observation" in *The Hillingdon Fox*—this is "a kind of national diary of what it was like to be alive at the time" (Mark, 1991, p. 7). A diary is also a private, secret and personal record of one's "innermost thoughts," and Hugh's description of himself as "sitting alone in an empty room . . . writing down innermost thoughts" (Mark, 1991, p. 7) is a conventionalized image of the fictive diary writer (Porter, 1984, pp. 15–16). However, even where it is essentially a private activity, it is one situated within a specific time and place.

The complexity (and inseparability) of this double context is a central thematic concern in *The Hillingdon Fox,* where Gerald and Hugh write for quite different reasons and with different addressees in mind. Both have a sense that they are living in politically significant times and thus see themselves as involved in the activity of recording political and social "history" as it occurs. For Gerald, this means constructing an accurate and objective social history (p. 10). Although he writes with a hypothetical reader in mind, he finds himself writing increasingly for himself in his obsession to understand and ascribe meanings to the events and incidents he records. Hugh is more conscious than Gerald of his own personal reasons for writing: he writes about the political events around him in an attempt to make sense of his own position in relation to them. Both brothers attempt to exclude themselves, their families and relationships from their accounts in order to focus on larger social and political issues. However, both find that their own positions and viewpoints impinge upon the objectivity of such a document in ways which foreground the relations between representation, the context of writing and the socio-ideological position of the writer.

Gerald and Hugh each record a war: Hugh records the start of the Gulf conflict in 1990; and Gerald records the Falklands War in 1982. These external events imply a cultural context within and against which they are writing and, to some extent, structure their writing. Their diary entries either begin or end with references to the current state of the "international situation," and they both appropriate media terminology to describe public and political events. These appropriated media discourses mediate historical and social contexts and ideologically situate the two narratives. A dominant concern for both diarists is the relation between the self and the world, and Gerald and Hugh appropriate media discourses as a means of constructing for themselves subject positions in relation to the public political worlds they describe, and in relation to their imagined addressees. Gerald's use of appropriated discourse tends to be unreflective. He simply reiterates the discourses of economic rationalism, Thatcherism, late capitalism, war and patriotism—as in "Perhaps all this will revive the sense of what it means to be British, slow to anger but terrible when roused!", for example (p. 23).

One effect of the double narrative structure is that Hugh's narrative constructs a position from which to interrogate the ideological assumptions inscribed in the discourses which comprise Gerald's narrative, and hence draws attention to the semantic instability of these discourses. Hugh's writing about war and the public world is more introspective than that of Gerald. His incorporation of the discourse of war tends toward the parodic, such as "'A search for a way back from the brink'— is what they said on the News last night after dinner. It *was* calamaris, by the way . . ." (p. 13), where the serious and the mundane are ironically juxtaposed. His appropriations of literary and popular humanist discourses—as in references to *1984* (p. 118), Donne (p. 123) and Bob Geldof (p. 125)—further undermine Gerald's position. The double narrative structure and the temporality of the diary mode also draw attention to the restrictions placed on interpretation by interpolated narration, and by the already textualized form of the history which Gerald and Hugh record. The time of narration is transient and momentary, and both diarists lack the necessary distance from events from which to interpret retrospectively their historical and political significances. Their access to events occurring in the Falklands and Gulf wars is only via the television and newspapers, that is, already textualized accounts of events. The instability of knowledge about the present, or the past, for that matter, is highlighted in the last entry in Gerald's diary, which refers to the sinking of the *General Belgrano* (apparently) inside the exclusion zone (p. 159). Hugh has already described the process whereby this event was selectively recorded, and how the account was changed as the war progressed (p. 119). Although the actual circumstances of the sinking of the Belgrano did eventually emerge—that it was sunk outside the exclusion zone, though the reasons for this are still open to question—Hugh's narrative draws attention to the processes through which events are constructed and obsfucated within language. This destabilizing of the capacity of language to represent and ascribe meaning to events is replicated within the text, particularly in Gerald's narrative. In early diary entries, he attempts to list events which occur and so represent the world objectively. However, as his diary progresses, he becomes increasingly obsessed with the relations between different events and people and the meanings of events.

Narrators, Narratees and Implied Readers in Diary Fiction

The construction of a subjectivity and representations of the relations between the self and the world are tied up with the diary or letter writer's conception of the other for whom they perceive themselves as writing. Prince and Porter have both argued that while a fictive diarist typically claims that s/he is writing for him/herself, they often have an addressee or reader in mind (Prince, 1975, p. 479), and that even the commonplace notion that a diarist "writes for him/herself" implicitly assumes the trace of an "addressee in that self sufficiently objectified to be written for" (Porter, 1984, p. 10).

In other words, the text of the diary writer who writes for him/herself functions like a Lacanian or Bakhtinian mirror as the field of the other within and through which the subject is constructed.

The main difference between a diary novel and an epistolary novel is that the latter constructs a more active textual role for its narratee (Porter, 1984, p. 10). The narratee of epistolic narration can take a number of forms: a possible future reader (who may be the diarist's future self), an addressee who is implicitly constructed within the discourse, or a narrated self as distinct from the self who narrates. The writings of Colum in *The Blooding* (Wheatley, 1987/1989), of Wouter Loos and Messenger in *Strange Objects* (Crew, 1990/1991) and Gerald in *The Hillingdon Fox* (Mark, 1991) all constitute examples of epistolic-diary narration. Each of these diary writers is to some extent aware of an addressee, either implicit or explicit. Hugh is the only diary writer in these novels who writes essentially for himself, but he is always self-consciously aware that someone might read what he writes, even if that someone is only his future self. A significant portion of Colum's narrative in *The Blooding* is taken up with his attempts to work out who he is writing for and why. He attempts to write a legal statement or confession, but his narrative style and register constantly shift between public and private modes of address to both an other and to himself. Gerald, Stephen Messenger and Wouter Loos attempt to construct their narratees more overtly than either Hugh or Colum. This is contingent with their attempts to "narrate" themselves, that is, to use their narration to construct and inscribe themselves as unified subjects. Ambiguities in Colum's and Hugh's narration (and which also develop in Gerald's narration) articulate a view of a subjectivity which is provisional and subject to change.

In *Strange Objects* (Crew, 1990/1991), there are overt (though clumsy) analogies between the narratorial positions of Loos and Messenger and the Barthesian notion of the split narratorial subject (Hutcheon, 1989, p. 40). These are represented in a disagreement between Professor Hans Freudenberg, the translator of Wouter Loos's journal (pp. 59–60), and the writer of a letter to the editor signed "sceptic" (p. 72) about Wouter Loos's journal. This disagreement concerns the relation between the intention and personality of Loos (the author) and the "voice" and subject position of the writer, as it is inscribed in and constructed by the discourse of the journal. Loos's journal is addressed to his peers and is clearly an attempt to clear his name (regarding the charges of murder for which he was cast away). Freudenberg's interpretation assumes a direct correspondence between the "voice" of the writer and the personality of the author—that is, between the narrated and narrating subject. The sceptic interprets this relation as disparate: the author has adopted a voice which does not correspond with his personality in order to achieve certain intentions and to disempower his readers—the intended reader of Loos's journal, according to the "sceptic," is one who will be seduced by the "honeyed tones of its author" (p. 72). Presumably, the reader who can read between the lines of these "honeyed tones" and deconstruct the text can also gain access to the "real" (murderer/rapist) author. Both commentators are concerned with what of Loos's character, anterior to the journal, can be extracted from the text, and with how to reconcile what they know of Loos the person with Loos the writer. And while the sceptical letter writer distinguishes between implied readers and actual readers, both reading positions are, in Barthesian terms, "author-centered": "The explanation of a work is always sought in the man or woman who produced it" (Barthes, 1977a, p. 143). Both Freudenberg and the sceptic, in assuming that narrative discourse can simply reflect or disguise its author, rather than construct an image of that author as a narrated (and therefore represented) self, thereby confuse the personality of the author, anterior to writing (a construct of what is known of his past actions), with the subject of the enunciation, the speaker inscribed in the text of the journal. The notion of the essential subject underlies this confusion and the disagreement between Freudenberg and the sceptic hinges on how to define this essentiality. The sceptic sees Loos as inherently evil—essentiality is thus correlated with the idea of original sin. Freudenberg sees Loos's writing as an act of atonement whereby Loos redeems his inherent humanity—essentiality is thus correlated with the humanity of the subject. The biblical discourse of Loos's journal implies that the writing is a form of baptism or redemption—"I will not become new through blood but through words. I will use the words of this book to begin" (p. 173).

These ideas have implications for the representations of Stephen Messenger, constructed in "the Messenger Documents" by Messenger himself and by Hope Michaels, the "editor" of those documents. Messenger experiences subjectivity as fragmented and doubled through the presence of a *doppelgänger*, the "other Stephen Messenger." In a letter to Messenger, Hope Michaels compares him to James Dean and Messenger subsequently describes his *doppelgänger* as a James Dean figure. Crew thus represents the relation between self and other as locked in the narcissistic stage of the mirror phase wherein the narrating subject identifies with the image of the self which is constructed by the other. Underlying the novel, then, is a desire for an authentic and stable subjectivity which would transcend the alienation and fragmentation that Messenger and Loos experience and which would thus transcend the gap between the narrating and narrated subject(s) and the narratee.

The diary novel functions on two interrelated levels: the narrator's purposes for writing, which are informed by assumptions about whom s/he writes for; and the functions the diary form has within the fiction itself for the production of meanings and the construction of implied reader subject positions. The narratee of a diary novel is a function of the narrator's discourse and intentions—whether implicitly or explicitly stated by the narrator. The fictive act of writing a diary or letter is a framed communicative act outside of which implied readers are situated (Martens, 1985, p. 33). It thereby constitutes an element of the story as well as the discourse, and the position of an implied reader depends not on the actuality of a narratee, but on the relations between the narrator, the narrative discourse and story. In *The Hillingdon Fox* (Mark, 1991) the double narrative structure and Gerald's overt construction of a narratee foreground the distinction between narratees and implied readers and the status of the narratee as a function of the narrating subject. The narratee position is constructed overtly through direct address, and covertly in Gerald's implicit assumptions about his readers and as an adjunct of the subject position that he constructs for himself. Direct address and explanations are overt attempts to construct a narratee position and to predict, dictate and circumscribe expected attitudes and responses. His use of the discourse of patriotism, references to "feminist" friends (p. 29) and to "the liberal egalitarianism that has for decades undermined our schools" (p. 39) covertly situate the narratee in a position which is attitudinally and ideologically aligned with his own. The narratee position is thus a replication of the narrated subject position. It is an ideal other through and for whom Gerald constructs an image of himself, as narrated subject. The overt construction of the narratee in Gerald's narrative effectively denies implied readers a passive reading position. His use of pretentious registers—such as, "We stand on the threshold of maturity and prepare to disperse into adulthood" (p. 17)—and his narration of ironical exchanges between his parents (e.g., pp. 16–17), undercuts his viewpoint and makes his discourse the object of irony and parody. Hugh's construction of a narratee is much less overt than that of Gerald, but the double narrative structure constructs two narratee positions. This, combined with strategies which undercut Gerald's and Hugh's narratives, effects a clear distinction between narratee and implied reader positions.

CONCLUSION

Incorporated extraliterary genres and discourses shape the textual construction and representation of subjectivity by enabling the inclusion of a wide range of ideological and social discourses and viewpoints and the construction of active implied reader subject positions. The effects of using a range of discursive genres in narrative can potentially be similar to those of the polyphonic strategies discussed in Chapter 2, in that characters and narrators can be represented as occupying discrete subject positions within a text and the role of language and subject position in the construction of meaning(s) can be foregrounded. As my discussion of *Backtrack* has shown, the combination of multiple extraliterary textual elements and multiple character focalizers complicates the representation and meaning(s) of events because of the range and number of social, ideological and discursive points of view that are represented.

Diary and epistolary genres have an important function in the textual and discursive construction of subjectivity. I have focused on some of the peculiar narrative features of these genres, such as interpolated narration, the ambiguous position of the narratee and the distinct positions that these genres imply for narratees and implied readers, and their function in foregrounding concerns with representation and authenticity in the novels discussed. A common concern is with the simultaneous construction of a writing or narrating subject and a written or narrated self via the act of writing. This interest can in turn effect a fragmentation and/or doubling of the narratorial subject. Diary and letter genres in *The Hillingdon Fox*, *The Blooding* and *Strange Objects* all represent subjectivity as provisional and as formed in relation to others and to the world, despite character narrators' more or less articulated desires to project a stable and centered subjectivity for themselves.

The novels discussed in this chapter self-reflexively foreground the texts and discourses through which they are constructed, and the textual and discursive construction of the subject. The discussion has thus touched on some issues which are taken up more fully in the next chapter, where the focus is on the representation of extraliterary discourses in historiographic genres, with special reference to historiographic metafiction.

ENDNOTES

1. On discourse representation *see*, for example, Leech and Short (1981), McHale (1978) or Pateman (1989).

2. For Wheatley's Australian readers, the allusion to the "first settlement" of Australia—that is the arrival in Sydney of the first white settlers in 1788—is obvious. The term, "first settlement" mythicises the colonizing process, implying that the land was "unsettled" and therefore unoccupied, and that this moment marks a beginning for a history of Australia. Grandad's fairy tales in *The Blooding* take this mythicising process a step further, locating this moment of settlement in a mythic and therefore immanent past.

8 THE TEXTUAL AND DISCURSIVE CONSTRUCTION OF SUBJECTIVITY II

HISTORIOGRAPHIC GENRES

What is "imaginary" about any narrative representation is the illusion of a centered consciousness capable of looking out on the world, apprehending its structure and processes, and representing them to itself as having all of the formal coherency of narrativity itself. But this is to mistake a "meaning" (which is always constituted rather than found) for "reality" (which is always found rather than constituted).

Hayden White, *The Content of the Form*

This chapter will expand on ideas introduced in Chapter 6 regarding the relations between the past and its textual representation in fiction. Now the focus will be on the function of extraliterary discourse in historiographic genres for the representation of subjectivity, with special reference to historiographic metafictions. The novel has traditionally used historical data as a means of authenticating the fictive world, and conventional historical novels usually incorporate this historical material using realist representational strategies. The term "historiographic metafiction" has been used by Hutcheon (1987; 1989) to refer to historical fictions which self-reflexively mix fictive and historical discourses so as to undermine realist assumptions and pose questions about the relationships between fiction, history and reality (*see* Hutcheon, 1989, pp. 14–15 and 35–36). In Chapter 7, I outlined Bakhtin's distinction between intentional and objective modes of representation and suggested that these can be understood as forms of discourse representation, that is, as direct and indirect discourse. This chapter examines the implications of different discourse modes for representing history and subjectivity in conventional historical novels such as *The Devil's Own* (Lisson, 1990) and *Mandragora* (McRobbie, 1991), and in metafictive novels, such as *Backtrack* (Hunt, 1986) and *Strange Objects* (Crew, 1990/1991).

A primary consideration in examining historical fiction is the ontological nature of history and historiography. In writing about historiography, Hayden White (1987) and LaCapra (1980) have suggested that our capacity to know and understand the past is determined by the textual forms through which it is represented and apprehended. To the extent that the past is only accessible via its documents, archives and artifacts, our knowledge of that past is always mediated and determined by prior textualizations, representations and interpretations. The past is thus potentially only knowable as text, and is thereby always already implicated in problems of language, discourse and representation (LaCapra, 1980, p. 297), and, as the epigraph to this chapter suggests, to mistake the texts which constitute "history" for the past is to confuse "meaning" (and by implication, ideology) with "reality." The textual mediation of the past poses problems for the inscription of subjectivity in history because the subjectivity of a historical other can only be inferred from the texts and discourses within which s/he is constructed and made present as a subject. As I suggested in my discussions of *Speaking to Miranda* (Macdonald, 1990) in Chapters 3 and 4 and of diary and epistolary novels in Chapter 7, the texts and discourses which enable the construction and representation of a subjectivity can also constitute a constraint and a limitation upon the apprehension of a textualized other and upon characters' attempts to "narrate" themselves. The difficulty for history writing lies in inferring agency for a historical other as s/he is represented and potentially circumscribed within discourse.

Conventional historical novels usually either represent historical material indirectly (as reported discourse within character or narratorial discourse) or, if it is represented directly, ensure its subordination to a dominant narratorial or authorial position. It is primarily used to authenticate the fictive world and hence to mask the ontological differences between history, fiction and reality. Historical discourse is thereby treated as a transparent means for representing story, character and setting, rather than as an object of representation. Metafictive historiographic novels foreground the discursive and textual conventions of history writing, usually by physically incorporating and representing historical texts and discourses in ways that destabilize the relation between fiction, history and reality. *Backtrack* (Hunt, 1986) and *Strange Objects* (Crew, 1990/1991) both incorporate historiographic conventions such as footnotes, documents and records, reports, and so on; and in drawing attention to the discursivity of these conventions, historical material is treated as the object of representation, as well as a means of representing historical data. Represented historical material in historiographic metafictions may refer to either actual or fictive events: the texts and documents represented in *Backtrack* are almost entirely fictional, whereas those in *Strange Objects* are a mixture of actual and fictive.[1] It is the self-reflexive incorporation of the discursive and textual styles of history writing, rather than their actual historicity, that is characteristic.

History writing constitutes, in Bakhtin's terms, a discursive genre: it is characterized by particular structural and linguistic forms for assimilating and representing aspects of reality; and it is inscribed with particular cultural and ideological assumptions about knowledge and understanding. In conventional historical fiction, historical discourse is treated as if it were transparent, that is, as if the object of representation (past events, persons and settings) could be unproblematically made present independent of the discourses and narrative structures used to represent it. Metafictive novels retain the documentary status and generic conventions of incorporated historical documents, thus drawing attention to the discursive conventions of both historical and fictive writing, to their role in representing and ascribing meanings to events, characters and objects, and hence to their lack of transparency. In metafictive novels such as *Backtrack* (Hunt, 1986) and *Strange Objects* (Crew 1990/1991), historiographic material is incorporated in ways which destabilize the relations between history and fiction and represent the narratorial subject as decentered and fragmented. The representation of subjectivity in historiographic metafictions is a special case and, as I will argue, the outcome can be very different in different texts. In general, the textual strategies of historiographic metafictions can construct positions from which to interrogate the conventional authenticating functions of historical material in fiction and the processes by which we understand and interpret historical discourses. In the next section, these ideas will be illustrated through a comparison of the ways in which historical material and discourse are incorporated in two conventional historical novels *The Devil's Own* (Lisson, 1990) and *Mandragora* (McRobbie, 1991), with their incorporation in two metafictive novels, *Strange Objects* and *Backtrack*.

DISCOURSE REPRESENTATION IN HISTORICAL FICTION AND HISTORIOGRAPHIC METAFICTIONS

In Chapter 6, I argued that if the past is represented only from the viewpoint of characters in or from the present, as in conventional (single-voiced) time-shift narratives such as *Playing Beatie Bow* (Park, 1980), then history can, potentially, be constructed as objectified and closed. Similarly, in conventional historical novels like *The Devil's Own* (Lisson, 1990) and *Mandragora* (McRobbie, 1991), historical material is incorporated using narrative strategies that subordinate this material to a central perceiving or narrating subject in the present, thus representing history as closed and the discourses which mediate it as transparent. Furthermore, these strategies also deny historical characters subject positions and, hence, subjectivities. *Backtrack* (Hunt, 1986) and *Strange Objects* (Crew, 1990/1991) self-reflexively foreground incorporated discourses so as to highlight problems associated with the apprehension and understanding of the past and its textual representation.

The Devil's Own and *Strange Objects* retell fictionalized versions of the same actual historical event: the wreck of the Dutch ship *Batavia* on the Abrolhos Islands off the coast of Western Australia in 1629 and its aftermath, a mutiny which resulted in the murder of 125 of the shipwrecked survivors and trial of the mutineers, after which two, Wouter Loos and Jan Pelgrom, were cast away off the coast of Western Australia. The opening chapters of *The Devil's Own* have two narrative strands: italicized portions of text represent events of 1629, narrated in the third person; the other strand is set in the present (probably the late 1980s) and is focalized by a young woman Julie who, through a timeslip strategy, is transported into this past (subsequent events are represented from her point of view). This kind of narrative structure is potentially dialogic, but any disparity between historical past and fictional present is minimized by a reconstructive narrative mode which treats the incorporated historical material as "story" and through focalization strategies which represent the past from the point of view of a character from the present. Thus, the novel constructs the illusion that the past can be simply reflected and that access to it can be unmediated. The problem of language posed by the fact that the *Batavia* survivors were Dutch is solved rather neatly when it emerges that Julie speaks Dutch. The epigraph of the novel is a quotation from documents made by the *Batavia* mutineers, but otherwise historical material is represented indirectly. It is incorporated as "story" material, which is either narrated, focalized or reported by characters, and which is unproblematically apprehensible. Two obvious sources for *The Devil's Own* are already largely fiction: Hugh Edwards's *Islands of Angry Ghosts* (1966/1985), a history-adventure novel which combines a fictionalized account of the shipwreck with a documentary account of the discovery of the wreck in 1963; and Henrietta Drake-Brockman's *The Wicked and the Fair* (1957), a historical romance about the *Batavia*.

The events surrounding the wreck of the *Batavia* function more as a catalyst for Crew's novel, *Strange Objects* (1990/1991), than as "story" material. However, the historical and fictive discourses, texts and genres through which the *Batavia* episode has been recorded and reconstructed implicitly and explicitly inform the discursive and textual structuring of *Strange Objects*. A primary historical source for the circumstances of the shipwreck and subsequent events is the journal of Francisco Pelsaert, commander of the *Batavia,* who after the shipwreck sailed to Java in an open boat, apparently to obtain help (Drake-Brockman, 1963). There are parallels between the structure and form of Pelsaert's journal and the narrative structure of *Strange Objects.* The journal itself is a heteroglottic text comprising: (1) an account of the wreck and the journey to Java and back to the islands; (2) copies of the mutineers' documents; (3) evidence given at the trials of the mutineers; (4) confessions; (5) decisions and sentences passed by the disciplinary council; (6) a copy of the letter of instructions given to Loos and Pelgrom; and (7) descriptions of the native wildlife in the Southland. Crew's novel imitates this heteroglottic structure. It comprises an epigraph, introduction, afterword, newspaper clippings, photocopied historical, archaeological and pseudoscientific articles, letters, illustrations, the (fictive) journal of castaway Wouter Loos, and first person narration by Stephen Messenger who, like Pelsaert, has (apparently) compiled and assembled these "documents" into a scrapbook entitled, "The Messenger Documents." These documents are in an itemized form which imitates discursive conventions associated with legal procedures—they are, in fact, presented as evidence at the inquiry into Messenger's disappearance. This itemized form was also used by Pelsaert to record the trials, confessions and crimes of the mutineers (Drake-Brockman, 1963).

A common feature of Pelsaert's journal, "the Messenger Documents" and Wouter Loos's fictive journal (included in those documents) is that the discourses used simultaneously construct a persona for each of the writers/ compilers, but also conceal the personality of those writers. Editors and commentators on Pelsaert's journal, such as Henrietta Drake-Brockman (1963), have tended to use the journal to infer answers to questions about Pelsaert and his actions which remain unanswered by history—questions such as What sort of person was he, and why did he, the commander of the ship, leave the shipwreck? Answers to these questions can really only be extrapolated and inferred from the image Pelsaert presents of himself via his activities of recording and documenting. (As I suggested in Chapter 7, Professor Freudenberg and the "sceptical" letter writer also evince this same desire to infer subjectivity and agency for Loos from his journal.) Readers of Crew's novel are involved in a similar process of inferring a subjectivity for Stephen Messenger. *Strange Objects* thus foregrounds two problems faced by historians interpreting historical documents and artifacts: a chronicler or compiler such as Pelsaert, Messenger or Loos may present a deliberately false image of themselves and the events they describe; and the discourses used by historians to describe, interpret and make sense of those documents and artifacts may implicitly ascribe them with cultural and ideological meanings. Thus, Hope Michaels's descriptions of the peritextual aspects of "the Messenger Documents" (passage 2 below) imitate objective discourses used to describe archaeological and historical artifacts, in particular, a description of Pelsaert's journal by Burkitt, quoted by Drake-Brockman (1963):

1.   Pelsaert's journal or day book consisted of about 84 pages of hand-made paper in sheets of about 15 in. long, 10 wide, without any covering; being simply bound together with other records of a similar nature in a huge folio . . . The writing was clear-cut old fashioned script [Gothic] in old Dutch, with a clear left hand margin of about 2 in. There were occasional flourishes and excursions into it . . . The writing was still perfectly clear, distinct, and copy-book, and impressed me as being written by someone of strong character. . . . (my ellipsis, p. 94)

2.   The project book was of the conventional pulp-paper type, with ninety-six pages, measuring 24 by 30 centimeters. When the news paper cover [The Hamelin Herald, Friday 29 August 1986. (ed.)] had been removed, the cardboard beneath showed a still from the 1979 George Lucas film, *Star Wars*. The caption printed at the bottom right-hand corner read: 'A lifepod lands on the barren surface of Tatooine.'

      Inside were pages covered in handwriting (black ball-point pen, generally uniform and labelled 'Messenger, Midway Roadhouse') or pasted-in press clippings and photocopied articles from books and magazines. Each item—whether hand written or in print—was individually numbered and its source (newspaper, book, etc.) had been carefully recorded. Many of the larger newspaper articles were neatly folded in order to prevent their protruding beyond the edges of the project book cover. (p. 3. *See also* the "Interim Report" on Loos's journal, pp. 29–38.)

The language in both descriptions is objective and detached, but the excess of detail in Michaels's description parodies Burkitt's historicist/archivist discourse. The descriptions of the newspaper cover and the picture beneath it parody archaeological processes, but the significance of these cultural artifacts, as signs, lies not so much in any "meaning" they might have as in the endless processes of quotation they enact. An unstated implication in Michaels's description is that a "character" for Messenger can be extrapolated from his project book in the same way that Burkitt infers a "strong character" for Pelsaert from his handwriting (and that Freudenberg infers a character for Loos from his journal). However, this possibility is simultaneously affirmed and undermined by analogies between "the Messenger Documents" and the characterization of Messenger. Both are constructed from a bricolage of appropriated texts and discourses which imply the fragmentation of the subject and denote the absence of a unified subject or text.

Strange Objects incorporates discursive genres peculiar to historical writing, and the textuality of the past and of subjectivity is foregrounded through parodic representation of these genres. Direct representation of incorporated discourse places it in quotation marks, so to speak, and thereby foregrounds the discursive nature of our knowledge of the past. However, the degree of authorial intervention whereby these discourses are framed and mediated also effects their status and that of the past to which they refer. This is clear in another more conventional historical novel, David McRobbie's *Mandragora* (1991), where documentary historical material is represented directly as quoted text in the form of letters, a family Bible and a diary. The novel centers on the relationship between two characters in the present, Catriona and Adam, who are involved in transcribing these nineteenth-century documents and investigating a mysterious shipwreck which occurred 100 years earlier. Although the text does imitate some historiographic conventions, the documentary material is framed and mediated by narratorial and character focalized commentary, which for the most part assumes that the discourse of incorporated material is transparent and unproblematic, as the following passage shows:

> *The Diary of Ewart MacColl, Esq. Farmer,*
> *lately of Maybole, Ayrshire.*
> *On board the barque* Dunarling, *Saturday*
> *6th March, 1886.*

It was going to be a massive job transcribing the diary of Ewart MacColl, Esq. and Farmer; many of the pages were damaged and torn and some were badly water stained making the words faded and almost unreadable. As for the handwriting, it was old fashioned but neat in its way, with little curly decorations on the capital letters. (italics in original indicating text is a quoted document; p. 30)

The passage uses discursive elements associated with historiography, such as typographical representation of the incorporated (fictive) text and a description of observable aspects of the artifact (the pages, words and handwriting). However, the linguistic modifiers—such as "neat," "little" and "curly"—signal character focalization, thereby indicating that the diary is mediated and represented via the consciousness of its transcriber, Adam. It is thus ironic and significant that Adam merely "transcribes" the diary, a process which implies a transparency of language and voice and an immediacy of the past and of the diarist. Adam's vision of Ewart MacColl, "the man who'd written these words so long ago . . . writing with a scratchy steel nib" (p. 31), assumes an unproblematic correspondence between the voice and person of the diarist and between the text of the diary and the world which it describes. Diary entries are represented in the form of paragraph or page-long italicized entries interspersed within the primary narrative which frames and explicates the diary, its writer, and the context of its writing, and hence constitutes an authoritative narratorial position to which the secondary historical material is subordinate. Parallels between characters in the primary and secondary narratives are overtly spelled out so that the diary of Ewart MacColl merely reflects the thoughts and feelings of its transcriber, Adam. For example:

> *I wonder what could have driven them apart?*
> Adam sighed deeply as he read over those last words he had typed. Driven apart summed up his own situation very neatly. As the days passed he worried more and more about the state of his mind . . . (italics indicate diary entry; p. 60. *See also* p. 120.)

Furthermore, the relationships between Catriona and Adam and between Margaret Colquhoun and James Ramsey (recounted in the diary) are represented in the form of parallel narratives (*see* pp. 82–89, for example), and the disparities between past and present are minimized through strategies of replication whereby characters occupy interchangeable positions within represented relationships—for example, Adam occupies the position of James (as lover) and Ewart (as voyeur). Although incorporated material is represented directly, thereby implying its discursive otherness, it is subordinate to the primary narrative and its particularity and otherness is effaced by the narrational strategies used to frame it. The significance of this material is thereby limited to the level of "story." There is no real interest in the discourse of the diary (apart from the definitions of a few archaic words) or its writer; in fact, the question of the narratorial role and reliability of Ewart MacColl is never raised. While the past in *Mandragora* is textually mediated, this text is constructed as quite transparent, and the past which it represents is simply revealed through the process of transcription.

A fourth novel which I want to look at here is *Backtrack* (Hunt, 1986), a novel in which direct and indirect modes for representing discourse are combined so as to virtually efface any sense of a narratorial center or presence. The novel poses questions about the possibility of knowing and interpreting events and persons located in the past from a position in the present. There are two main narrative strands. The primary narrative centers on two characters, Jack and Rill, who attempt to solve a mysterious train crash which occurred seventy years earlier, and is mainly focalized by Jack. Secondary narratives are situated in the past and comprise versions of past events narrated from the viewpoints of at least seven different characters.[2] Shifts between these two narrative strands are clearly marked by textual breaks and narrative strategies indicating focalization. However, it would seem that the secondary narratives are Jack and Rill's "fictional" reconstructions based on their investigations and hypotheses about the cause of the accident, the individuals involved and the course of events leading up to it. The narrative discourse of both strands shifts typically from third person narration (direct discourse) to free direct discourse (*see* the primary narrative on pages 4–5, for example). These shifts tend to problematize narrative point of view and imply the absence of a centered narratorial position, and thus destabilize implied reader point of view by denying implied readers a stable subject position from which to interpret events.

Incorporated extraliterary material is comprised of a newspaper article; diary entries; a letter; the inquest report of the accident and excerpts transcribed from a cassette recording of James Fraser, the signalman's, retrospective account of the accident; and excerpts from nonfiction books, mostly about trains, railway accidents, the setting *(Walks Around Hereford),* early twentieth-century espionage; and so on. Most extraliterary discourse in *Backtrack* is represented as typographically marked direct discourse, as it is in *Strange Objects* (Crew, 1990/1991) and *Mandragora* (McRobbie, 1991). However, for the representation of James Fraser's account (in Chapter 3) and the inquest report (in Chapter 4) the narrative shifts constantly between primary and secondary narration and between direct and indirect discourse modes.

Hunt's use of representational modes, extraliterary discourse and primary and secondary narration is quite complex, and particularly pertinent to my concerns with the representation of subjectivity and the past in narrative. This complexity can be demonstrated using a typology of discourse modes derived from Leech and Short (1981, pp. 318–351). Leech and Short identify four modes of discourse representation used to represent the speech or thought of characters: direct discourse (DD), indirect discourse (ID), free direct discourse (FDD), and free indirect discourse (FID).[3] In Chapters 3 and

4 of *Backtrack,* these four modes of discourse representation are used to mediate extraliterary discourse in varying ways, resulting in six distinct modes of discourse representation:

1.   indirect discourse represented within the free indirect speech or thought of characters [ID/FID]
2.   indirect discourse represented within the indirect speech or thought of characters [ID/ID]
3.   indirect discourse represented within the direct speech of characters [ID/DD]
4.   direct discourse represented within the indirect speech of characters [DD/ID]
5.   direct discourse represented within the direct speech of characters [DD/DD]
6.   documents: typographically marked direct discourse [document]

Now watch me pull a rabbit out of my hat. These strategies for representing the extraliterary discourse problematize its authoritative status and communicative function. Constant shifts in diegetic level and discourse mode construct a range of subject positions for characters and readers, which are focused less on the content of the documents and more on the discourses which represent and interpret it and the subject positions which these discourses construct for characters. For readers, the relationship between Jack and Rill which frames and mediates the documentary material also provides another point of focus. The following discussion of the six discourse modes uses examples from pages 60–65 of Chapter 4 where Jack and Rill read the transcripts of the inquest report. The order in which discourse modes are listed and discussed here proceeds from the least direct (free indirect discourse) to the most direct (direct representation of documents), and it highlights the ways in which, in *Backtrack,* the closer the narrative account approaches a direct report of what was actually said at the inquest, the more ambiguous and obfuscatory the discourse becomes.

The first three discourse modes (ID/ID, ID/FID and ID/DD) represent material from the inquest report indirectly; that is, "what is said" is expressed in the words of the reporting character of narrator as free direct, indirect, or direct speech or thought (Leech and Short, 1981, p. 318). For example:

1.   *Indirect discourse represented as the free indirect speech or thought of these characters (ID/FID).* Pages of technical evidence. Weight of engine (97 tons); number of carriages (10: six wooden-bodied second-

class 6–wheelers, one articulated first-class set, two four-wheel ex-Midland Railway third-class, and brake van. Total tare weight. ("The weight and the tares?" "Do be quiet, dear." "Is this interesting?") Estimated speed at time derailment, 47 mph. Recommended speed on approach curve to viaduct, 10 mph. Well, that accounts for that, then. Dum de dum. (p. 60)

2. *Indirect discourse represented as the indirect speech or thought of these characters [ID/ID].* "Charming." This page has a helpful note from the supine barrister. 'What strikes you as particularly piscine about this?' ("Why can't he use English?" "He's a barrister; it's against union rules"). Jack looking down the page, trying not to appear too thick. Something fishy? (p. 63)

3. *Indirect discourse represented in the direct speech of these characters [ID/DD].* Rill coming round and looking down the page. "Except that he also says that none of that would explain why the train just belted through Elmcote without stopping." (p. 63)

In these three passages, the distinction between direct and indirect (character) discourse is clear, though the distinction between reported material and indirect (character) discourse, that is, the reporting context, is frequently blurred. In 1, where the report is represented indirectly as the free indirect speech or thought of characters, the two discourse modes interact so as to construct the illusion of the reading process. The discourse shifts between these two modes freely, conveying the illusion of the characters simultaneously reading and processing what they read. In 2, where material from the inquest report is represented indirectly as the indirect thought or speech of characters, it becomes difficult to ascertain what exactly is written in the report because there is minimal distinction between these two categories of discourse. In contrast, in 3, where the report is represented indirectly as the direct speech of a character (Rill), the distinction between character discourse and reported discourse is much clearer. A feature which emerges in this example is that in focusing on facts and legal issues, the report generates more questions than it answers. This situation is exacerbated in the following three examples, where direct discourse modes are used to represent the report, that is, it is quoted verbatim (Leech and Short, 1981, p. 318), but either as indirect (narrator or character focalized) discourse, as direct discourse (that is quoted by a character), or as a textual document. For example:

4. *Direct discourse represented as indirect discourse [DD/ID].* Rill holding out a slip of paper, rather as if she had discovered a cigarette end

in the smoked oysters. Jack raising his eyebrows. "Sexist rubbish," Rill said. The paper fluttering and weaving into Jack's hand. Where it reads, `Cherchez la femme.' (p. 63)

5.   *Direct discourse represented in the direct speech of characters in the primary narrative [DD/DD].* Rill running her hand lightly down the page. "Evidence from the inquest states that both the driver and fireman were previously in good health, although their bodies were terribly injured." (p. 63)

6.   *Documents: typographically marked direct discourse.*

   a.   TRANSCRIPT OF EVIDENCE GIVEN AT THE CORONER'S COURT, LADBURY SUB-DISTRICT
   Wednesday, 8th September, 1915
   Presiding Coroner: Sir James Paradis, Bart.
   Clerk to the Court: Mr Arnold Morris
   "Which femme, then?"
   "There's only une."
   82. Evidence of Rachel Gertrude HAND, spinster, of Hereford Road Cottages, Elmcote, Herefordshire (p. 63–64)

   b.   Q: You are Rachel Gertrude Hand, of Hereford Road Cottages, Elmcote?
   A: Yes, sir.
   Q: Were you acquainted with the late David Lee?
   A: I knew him, yes, sir.
   Q: What was your opinion of his character?
   A: He was always a very kind and upright man.
   Q: Were you aware of any defects in his character?
   A: I don't understand, sir.

(No fool, our Rachel. Jack and Rill mouthing the dialogue together). (p. 65) The first passage, 6a, follows directly from 4; a segment of secondary narrative in which Sir James and the constable discuss Rachel's "character" before having her called before the bench, occurs between 6a and 6b.

There is a conventional historicist assumption that the closer an account of an event is to that event in time and place, the more accuracy and credibility it can be accredited with. Thus, there is an expectation (on the part of characters and readers) that the inquest report will in some way disclose the key to the mystery. However, the reported and actual transcripts of the inquest report are characterized by their refusal to disclose information, and attention is thus drawn to the discursive strategies which structure the report and to the narrational strategies through which it is reported. The report features marked shifts in register and discursive genre which foreground the function of language in constructing (and concealing) its object. Note, for example, the contrasting registers used in 2—which uses an objective descriptive register—and 4 and 5—which use literary and emotive registers respectively. The order of these six examples follows a trajectory from less direct to more direct and, hence, we might expect the last three passages to have more credibility than, and provide us with more information than, the indirect accounts in examples 1–3. However, there is a further play with the idea that the more direct a representation is of its object, the more accurate or truthful it is. The discourse becomes more ambiguous the closer the account approaches a direct report of what was actually said at the inquest. This process culminates in the documentary representation of Rachel's evidence, wherein the opacity of the discourse compels Jack and Rill (and readers) to read hidden significances into the flat question-answer exchange.

Hunt's strategies for representing material here imply an analogy between legal and historical discourses and practices. Both law and history are characterized by specific rules governing the investigation and representation of evidence, and both represent events in the past as the product of specific protocols of investigation (Bennet, 1990, p. 55). Hunt's combination of the discursive practices of law and history highlights the possibility that an event and a person can be both constructed and concealed by the discourses through which they are represented. In the primary narratives Rachel is a crucial, though ambiguous, figure in the mystery. The opacity of her discourse in the inquest report implies the limitations of the discourses of law and history, and of textuality itself to represent Rachel as a subject. Her position in the text is analogous to that of Emma/Magda in *Speaking to Miranda* (Macdonald, 1990)—discussed in Chapters 3 and 4—in that she is circumscribed, and denied subjectivity, by the discourses through which she is made present. Furthermore, the discourses about Rachel which precede and frame her evidence (particularly the phrase "Cherchez la femme" in example 4, above) construct her according to culturally constructed paradigms of sexual behavior which are reinforced by other characters' characterizations of her in the secondary narrative (e.g., *see* the exchange between Sir James and Constable Ellis on page 64) and by the sexual teasing implicit in the primary narrative. Rachel's answers in the inquest report (example 6b, above) are thus both opaque and semantically loaded (as in, "I knew him," for example, where it is possible to read "knew him" in a variety of ways). The use of the borrowed literary phrase "cherchez la femme" also blurs distinctions between the discourses of fiction and law.

Historiographic metafictions such as *Backtrack* (Hunt, 1986) and *Strange Objects* (Crew, 1990/1991) foreground the texts and discourses through which they are structured so as to raise questions about the relations between history writing and our apprehension and understanding of the past. Typically, incorporated genres are represented directly, but as my discussions of the uses of direct discourse in *Mandragora* and the mixing of direct and indirect modes in *Backtrack* have demonstrated, the narrative strategies used to frame and mediate incorporated discourse effect their metafictive status and function. In conventional historical fictions, historical discourses are generally treated as transparent. By foregrounding the function of language in representing and inscribing meaning to events and persons, metafictions draw attention to the ontological status of represented events and persons and the role of the narratorial voice in constructing and representing events and persons. The remainder of this chapter examines the implications of narrative strategies in *Backtrack* and *Strange Objects* for the representation of subjectivity, the construction of implied reader subject positions and the ideological inscription of interpretative positions constructed in both novels.

DIALOGISM AND MONOLOGISM IN HISTORIOGRAPHIC METAFICTION

As I argued in Chapter 2, the strategies for inscribing polyphony in different novels can be similar, though the effects of these strategies can vary depending on the ideological function of discourses and voices. Likewise, in historiographic metafictions, genre-mixing can produce diverse ideological effects. A primary effect of the genre-mixing that occurs in metafictive novels such as *Backtrack* (Hunt, 1986) and *Strange Objects* (Crew, 1990/1991) is that it constructs the illusion of a decentered and fragmented narratorial subject. At the same time, however, frame-breaking strategies also dismantle this illusion and imply a narratorial or editorial presence which shapes and constructs the narrative and which positions implied readers. The two above-mentioned novels differ crucially in the conceptions of subjectivity inscribed in them, and in the subject positions constructed for implied readers. Hunt's narrative techniques represent subjectivity as provisional and as simultaneously constructed and concealed by the texts and discourses through which the subject is made present. The idea of a fragmented subject underlying *Backtrack* conforms with a Bakhtinian view of subjectivity as being formed in dialogue with social and linguistic practices. Crew's novel reflects a Lacanian view of subjectivity in that the characters of Loos and Messenger are represented as inherently split on the one hand, but as structured by a desire for a unified and essential selfhood on the other hand. Both novels center on an unsolved mystery, the resolution of which hinges on the possibility of inferring a subjectivity for a textually constructed other. Ultimately, both are hoaxes. However, whereas Hunt constructs informed, complicit, and thus empowered implied reader positions, Crew's narrative strategies tend to ideologically disempower implied readers and thus reinscribe essentialist versions of history, subjectivity and language which the text ostensibly sets out to dismantle. Thus, Hunt's strategies are apt to produce dialogic effects, whereas Crew's strategies produce a monologic orientation.

DIALOGISM IN *BACKTRACK*

Frame-breaking devices in *Backtrack* comprise characters who occupy interpretative positions in relation to a historical past and thus function as analogies for implied readers; the overt representation of the textual and interpretative strategies common to history and fiction writing; and the use of paratextual conventions, namely, a footnote and an epigraph. The central mystery in the novel remains unsolved, and this lack of narrative resolution draws attention to the discursive genres which Jack and Rill use in their attempts to solve it: namely, historical research, conjecture and narrative reconstruction using conventionalized genres, narrative codes and cultural assumptions. Thus, they combine and mix various fictive and historical discursive codes, subsequently blurring fiction and history, and at the same time drawing attention to the conventionality of these discourses. History writing and fiction share common narrative strategies and forms for representing events and historical persons or characters; hence, they are not always easily distinguishable from each other, especially in novels which self-consciously mix both genres. Furthermore, such strategies inscribe both fictive and historical events with meaning (*see* LaCapra, 1980, pp. 269–270). The possibility remains that the act of narration, in either genre of writing, might construct and thereby construe its object.

Jack and Rill hypothesize two main solutions to the mystery, both of which are structured as narratives: the espionage plot and the crime of passion plot. Both are modeled on cultural metanarratives common to historiography and literature. In the first plot, the train accident is part of a foiled plan to kill Edward (Rill's great-great uncle), and Rachel (Jack's great grandmother) harbors the anarchist, Richard Rathbone, and a hired killer, McGillis, in the cellar of her house. This explanation is largely discounted by Jack and Rill. The second plot comprises a range of narrative variations: Rachel is imagined to be romantically involved with David Lee (the train driver), Harry, George and/or Will in various configurations. The "crime of passion" theory is also implicit in documents from and secondary narration of the inquest (*see* Hunt, 1986 pp. 63–65), but rather than proving the theory, this coincidence suggests that such narrative schema are common to legal conjecture as well as to historical and fictive processes. It becomes clear by the end of the novel that the key to the mystery of the accident (if there is in fact any mystery) lies with Rachel, David, Harry, George and Will. The lack of narrative resolution finally hinges on the fact that indisputable facts about the personalities of past characters, their relationships with each other, and the "truth" about what happened, are inaccessible and unknowable. It is thus significant that Rachel, George and David Lee, central characters in the "crime of passion" plot, are not represented as focalizers; readers have no access to their points of view. Thus, the mystery plot is also a displaced version of a quest for the subjectivity of an other.

Jack and Rill's hypotheses and imaginative reconstructions of events center on issues such as representation and narration, point of view and subjectivity, order and causality, all of which pose problems for both fictive and historical genres of writing. Concerns with these issues are clearly foregrounded in the epigraph to the novel, the preface (p. 1) and the final "Lead out" chapter (pp. 126–136), each of which have a frame-breaking function. The epigraph reads: "Reader, beware, for you are now entering the country of fiction, where everything should be believed, but everything must be suspected" (not paginated). This is a conventional metafictive device for drawing attention to the fictive status of a novel, and does not really disrupt reader positions. The preface, however, enacts metaleptic disruptions which overtly destabilize the positions of the narrator, the narratee and characters, and the relations between fiction and history within the text. This occurs partly through the ambiguous position of the narratee addressed in "Look over your shoulder" (p. 1) and also in a footnote alluding to an exchange between Jack and Rill:

> Rill, who just at this minute is in Livorno or Rome or somewhere, being an *au pair* girl among the rich, says that's the most disgusting page she's ever read. Relishing nastiness. If you're going to write about charred bodies, you'd better think about it. I mean, if it really happened, it would be better to forget about it, and if it's fiction, then you ought to be ashamed of yourself. There's enough horrible without making up more.
>
> I suppose it's a good moral point. But whether it happened or not, *I* didn't murder them. But someone did. I think. (p. 1)

The implication that the preface is narrated (and written) by Jack constructs another narrational level diegetically higher than, but in a dialogical relation with, the primary narrative. In the "Lead out," Jack is attempting to compose a reply to Rill, which suggests that the preface, and possibly the whole text, is that letter. The preface and the final "Lead out" chapter are situated in the same time and place, five years after the primary narrative, though the reference to Rill's whereabouts in the footnote to the preface implies an ambiguous gap between the time and place of narration, and Rill's reading and reply. Furthermore, the exchange between Rill and Jack alluded to in the footnote blurs textual distinctions between fiction and history, and narration and authorship. The implication is that Jack, in narrating (and writing) the narrative account(s), also (re)constructs and fictionalizes events. To the extent that the past is not objectively knowable and is subject to prior textualizations, any (re)telling of a past event is also a (re)textualization and a (re)construction. The narrative forms used to structure such a retelling not only inscribe the event with meanings, but also potentially constitute its textual (and hence possible ontological) existence. The speaker's disclaimer of responsibility for the actuality of events represented in the narrative "whether it happened or not" problematizes the status of "historical" events, but in doing so also asserts the actuality of fictional events outside of the act of narration: "Whether it happened or not, I didn't murder them. But someone did. I think." While the distinction between history and fiction is blurred, the speaker's disclaimer implies a more subtle distinction between the activities of narration and authoring, between telling and authenticating. In a final metafictive twist, it is ultimately the author, Peter Hunt, who murdered the characters.

MONOLOGISM IN *STRANGE OBJECTS*

Hunt's use of extraliterary discourse and framing devices, and his narrational strategies, are complex and playful. They dismantle the fictional frame of the text and imply positions from which readers can interrogate the various narrative versions of events and the socio-ideological assumptions which inform them. Crew uses similar narrative strategies in *Strange Objects* (Crew, 1990/1991), but they function more to disguise textual processes and to disempower implied readers.

There is an ideological tension in *Strange Objects* generated by the co-presence of contradictory approaches to meaning, culture and subjectivity. Genre-mixing foregrounds the textual construction of "history," implying a cultural relativist viewpoint, that is, a view of history, meaning and subjectivity as being contingent and provisional. However, this position is underwritten by an implicit assumption that a "true" version of history and of selfhood lies beneath these textual constructions. This process is enacted within the two narrative strands that comprise the novel, both of which are structured as mysteries: the first centers on the unknown fate of Wouter Loos and Jan Pelgrom, and the second on the disappearance of Stephen Messenger.

There has to date been no historical evidence of Loos or Pelgrom after they were cast away. Since the historical episode lacks closure, the unknowability of their fate generates a range of possible narrative openings and closures—part of the reason, perhaps, for the appeal the episode has in the popular imagination. However, in postulating a solution to the mystery in the form of Loos's fictive journal, *Strange Objects* closes off the range of narrative possibilities in deference to a desire for historical continuity and teleological closure. In other words, it poses a fictive resolution which supports a traditional view of Australian history to an otherwise open-ended narrative. Insofar as history is generally written by and from the point of view of the dominant social and cultural groups within a society, accepted versions of history tend to reflect and validate the ideologies and values of the dominant culture. Notions of historical "truth" can be destabilized by either drawing attention to the radical textualization of the past, or by constructing an alternative version of history—as Dickinson does, for example, in *A Bone from a Dry Sea* (1992). Crew combines these strategies in *Strange Objects*. However, while the discourse reveals the radical textualization of the past, the alternative version of Australian history which is disclosed does not differ radically from traditional versions of Australian history.

In history writing, paratextual conventions, such as footnotes, quotations and citations, refer to and construct parallel texts (or paratexts), which authenticate and verify textual material. In *Strange Objects,* these conventions are parodied by a mixing of different genres and registers, and fictive and actual discourses. For example, the "interim report" on Loos's journal (pp. 32–34) combines an objective register, characteristic of historical and scientific writing (it has numbered sections and subheadings, and uses conjectural terms, editorial footnotes and so on), with an ironic approach to the actual texts cited and quoted. These mostly comprise popular and fictional texts, such as Edwards's *Islands of Angry Ghosts* (1966/1985), rather than academic or authoritative texts. Thus the use of epithets, such as "the definitive authority" (p. 33) for Drake-Brockman, a writer of historical romance and popular history, parodies historiographic citational conventions. Ironically, fictive texts are used to verify the historical probability of fictional events.

Although these strategies blur distinctions between fiction and history and thereby draw attention to the textual construction of the past, the cultural and ideological assumptions implicit in these textual constructions are not questioned—in fact, Crew's treatment of extraliterary discourses reinforces their ideological implications. Quotations from these popular and literary texts are recontextualized and edited so as to represent them as secondary historical sources and, hence, as having an authoritative function. For example, the following passage quoted by Crew from Edwards's (1966/1985) *Islands of Angry Ghosts* (a historical-adventure novel) has been selectively edited so as to obscure its fictive status and foreground certain meanings which have gained a mythic status within (European) Australian history:

> **Their story may [well] be among the most interesting sagas of early Australian history; but we will not know it, for they were never seen or heard of again** . . . [—though later ships were instructed to keep an eye out for them.] **They were swallowed up by that huge, mysterious, unknown continent called the Southland** . . . [They may have been drowned in a few days or weeks, trying to sail north. It is more probable that they were taken into the tribe by the gentle Murchison natives, and they may have lived for years—two centuries before the first white settlers came to Western Australia—taking aboriginal wives and fathering a clutch of coffee-colored children who wondered why their fathers were always looking hungrily at the sea.] . . . **So far from the windmills and green fields of Holland** . . . (Edwards, 1966/1985, pp. 78–79; Crew, 1990/1991, p. 34; boldface indicates Crew's text and brackets indicate his omissions.)

Crew omits from the passage Edwards's more overt fictionalizing about the fate of Loos and Pelgrom, and thus represents Edwards as an authoritative source. Insofar as most of Crew's readers will be unaware of the ways in which Edwards's text has been edited, this strategy is a disempowering one, particularly as ideological assumptions about Australia and its history implicit in the quoted discourse remain unquestioned, and are in fact reinforced and authorized by the framing narrative context. The discourse used by Edwards in "they were swallowed up by that huge, mysterious, unknown continent called the Southland," which is retained by Crew, is of particular interest. It is representative of an ideological discourse about Australia that mythologizes place and history by representing Australia as a vast, mysterious and unknown continent, which is, by implication, empty of human beings, culture and history prior to white settlement. (Until recently, Australian histories conventionally began with Cook's "discovery" of Australia in 1770 or the "first settlement" in 1788; Australia was represented as culturally isolated prior to European contact and the past of the Aborigines was represented as "myth" or "legend" rather than as "history.")

This discourse constitutes a metanarrative complicit with the discourses of colonialism which, through a mystification of the land, marginalize its native inhabitants and their culture in order to confer legitimacy upon colonization (Hodge, 1990). Ostensibly, Crew's use of the story of Loos and Pelgrom constructs an alternative version of the history of white settlement in which European migrants introduce disease, decline and death for the native occupants, rather than culture, progress and civilization, as in traditional accounts of the colonization process. The novel is thus critical of the history of white settlement in Australia and of some of the ideological assumptions underpinning the extraliterary texts which it quotes and cites. At the same time, however, the setting in *Strange Objects* conforms to mythic conceptions of the land as vast, empty and hostile (*see* pages 25–26, for example). Furthermore, while Crew's version of colonization differs from traditional Australian histories in terms of its point of view, the structure of this alternative history is not so different. As with such traditional histories, European migration to Australia constitutes an originary moment in history from which the rest of recent Australian history proceeds causally and teleologically; conjectures about Pelgrom's and Loos's fate made by Crew, Edwards, Bates and other writers about the episode simply displace that originary moment and reinscribe it at an earlier point in time. Such conjectures thus evince a desire for presence and historical continuity, that is, a desire for the event of Loos and Pelgrom being stranded to constitute a beginning and a subsequent causal structure, and finally, a faith in the idea of history as grand narrative.

The second mystery in *Strange Objects,* Stephen Messenger's disappearance, is represented through a series of itemized documents presented as "evidence" in an inquiry into Messenger's disappearance. Implied readers are constructed in positions similar to those of Jack and Rill in *Backtrack* (Hunt, 1986), that is, as historians or archivists whose role it is to decipher and interpret the documentary evidence. As in *Backtrack,* this central mystery remains unsolved. Further, resolution of the mystery pivots on the possibility of inferring a subjectivity for a textually constructed subject, Messenger, thereby implying an analogy between Messenger's fragmented subjectivity and that of the text itself. However, just as Crew's version of the Loos/Pelgrom episode is teleologically closed, the Messenger mystery, though unsolved, ultimately leads to thematic and ideological closure.

This closure is effected by strategies which deny implied readers interpretative agency, through the bricolage construction of the text, which simultaneously opens and forecloses meaning, and through the use of narrative motifs of displacement and doubling. In the first instance, strategies such as the withholding of story details (e.g., the fact that Messenger's father has been killed in a road accident three months before the events of the novel, Crew, 1991, p. 183) and the use of red herrings (such as references to blood, severed hands and so on) retrospectively imply a dominant authorial presence structuring and ordering the narrative. In the second instance, repeated intertextual images, motifs and discourses generate an excess of signs, which simultaneously evoke and defer a center of significance. The novel is a pastiche of appropriated literary and cultural intertexts and pretexts: it contains references to specific pretexts, such as *Robinson Crusoe;* intertextual allusions, such as Messenger's name (which has associations with death) and the town of Hamelin; literary motifs, such as the magic ring and the castaway motif; and cultural discourses and genres, such as the "hitchhiker" story, and quotations from science fiction films, books, popular culture, and so on. All these appropriated images and discourses function in a similar way to the use of repetition in Garner's *Red Shift* (1973)—discussed in Chapters 5 and 6; that is, they imply isomorphic patterns and links between events and characters in different narrative strands which suggest the possibility that these narrative strands are assimilable to a single metanarrative that transcends historical and cultural difference, despite the narrative components being culturally and historically situated. For example, the "strange objects" referred to in the title—the "cannibal pot," mummified hand, ring and journal—have multiple narratival functions. They are archaeological artifacts and fantastical signs, and as such are not inherently meaningful. Instead, they are ascribed with historical, social, cultural and metaphysical meanings through the discourses used to describe and represent them. Magic rings, for example, are a common motif in fantasy texts, and Messenger and Loos each represent the ring accordingly; Loos links it with the story of *El Dorado,* and Messenger's description of it floating above him like a "spacecraft" (p. 38) evokes popular science fiction texts. The ring itself is literally a floating signifier, the meaning of which is deferred by the processes of intertextual quotation whereby it is made present. This deferral of meaning structures the text around a recursive play of absence, and the discourse consequently keeps hedging toward the evocation of metaphysical and transcendent meanings. However, the dissolution of determinate meaning outside of cultural and ideological paradigms inscribes this transcendence as deferred desire.

The third way that closure is effected through the novel is through the use of displacement and doubles. In Chapters 3 and 4, I argued that by representing a character's solipsism as a form of social or cultural displacement and alienation, texts construct an analogy between individual and cultural solipsism. In *Strange Objects,* a cultural relativist position is articulated via the solipsistic viewpoints of the two central narrating characters, Loos and Messenger. Both Loos and Messenger occupy culturally alienated and transgressive subject positions and they perceive and interpret the world from an utterly solipsistic point of view. For example, Loos, a murderer and rapist, has been cast out from his own society and is physically displaced and alienated within a foreign country and culture. Although he presents his relationship with the Aborigines as intersubjective, his narrative assumes their subjection and lack of subjectivity. Like Beni in *The Blue Chameleon* (Scholes, 1989, discussed in Chapter 3), he attempts to interpret Aboriginal culture using representational codes of his own culture. In Crew's novel, however, this reveals the limitations of Loos's viewpoint and of the interpretative paradigms of his own culture. For example, in one journal entry Loos writes that he has managed to "communicate" with the aborigines. However, the iconic signs which he uses to communicate include the Christian cross and the coronet; thus, the episode discloses the cultural specificity of language and narrative (p. 106).

Parallels between the two narrative strands imply analogies between Messenger's and Loos's ways of perceiving and representing the world and other characters. Both use cultural stereotypes to represent other characters, and both clearly perceive the other—Pelgrom, Kratzman and Aborigines—as barbaric and threatening. Thus, their solipsism implicitly discloses the culturally solipsistic implications of Crew's relativism. Characterization in *Strange Objects* features a complex arrangement of doubles. As in some of the novels discussed in Chapter 3, the double is perceived as a mirror inversion of the subject, as a character's opposite, other self or alter ego, as in Loos's representation of Pelgrom, and Messenger's representation of Kratzman. Messenger's references to his own imagined double, "the other Stephen Messenger," imply an internally fragmented subjectivity. The "other" Stephen Messenger is an inverted self upon whom Messenger's own illness is displaced, in the same way that Loos's disease is displaced upon Pelgrom and upon the Aborigines.[4] The link between the double, death and disease suggests that the double represents a character's other "evil" self, or alter ego—this idea is implicit in the correlation between essentiality and original sin in the novel, which I suggested in my discussion of Loos in Chapter 7.

Insofar as the fragmentation of the subject in *Strange Objects* is conceived of as an aberration, rather than as a condition of subjectivity, the novel implicitly asserts the desire for and possibility of a unified and essential self.

This idea is also expressed metaphorically by Messenger's fascination with skeletons and his invention of the inaptly named "life frame," and through the absence of his father. The life frame is a wire frame in which he places a lizard; he then places the frame over a bull ant's nest, in the hope that the skeleton of the lizard will be revealed. The life frame is thus an attempt to objectify and frame the hidden essential life or self; it implies the desire for an interior self, anterior to cultural and social practice. In a discussion of the myth of the individualized self, Booth (1993) remarks that "the search [by troubled adolescents] for `the real me,' a search performed by peeling away all 'inauthentic' influences, reveals nothing at the core" (p. 80). This comment could easily be about Stephen Messenger's quest for subjectivity in *Strange Objects* and, as Booth's comments imply, the "search" for the individualized self actually constitutes "a kind of refutation of individualism" (p. 80). As Messenger discovers, the "life frame" reveals nothing; it results in the negation and dissolution of life, and of any concept of an inner self or of agency. As I mentioned earlier, the absence of any mention of Messenger's father until the revelation of his death in the afterword is crucial. Ostensibly, the afterword thus offers readers a clue with which to retrospectively piece together Messenger's fragmented narrative, but it also inscribes an authoritative and closed interpretative position which denies implied readers interpretative agency. Conventionally, the father denotes legitimacy, tradition and authority, and the absence of these concepts signals Messenger's dispossession and alienation. The parallels between Loos and Messenger imply an absence of traditions and authoritative fictions with which to mediate the social world and to construct a coherent sense of selfhood within an alien culture. Thus, the privileging of a relativist position in the novel is on Crew's part a logocentric move, whereby he ultimately disempowers the implied reader and reinscribes a closed, monological and authoritative position.

CONCLUSION

This chapter has focused primarily on the strategies and effects of historiographic metafictions in contrast with conventional historical fictions. The function of historiographic discourses and genres may have two very different effects on the representation of subjectivity, depending on whether historiographic material is used in accord with the representational strategies of realism or metafictionally. Historical data is conventionally used in fiction to authenticate the fictive world, as it does in novels such as *The Devil's Own* or *Mandragora,* wherein historical discourse is thus treated as a transparent means for representing story and character. Historiographic metafictions treat historical discourses as the object, as well as the means, of representation, and hence draw attention to their lack of transparency and to the discursive conventions of historical and fictive writing. Metafictions use historiographic discourses to raise questions about the relations between history, fiction and the world, and the ontological status of represented events and persons in either history or fiction, rather than simply to authenticate the fictive world.

Historical material can be represented indirectly or directly, but neither mode is inherently dialogical or metafictive. Though metafictive forms of narrative tend to favor direct modes of representation, the function and status of historical material is primarily determined by the strategies used to frame and mediate discourses, and hence the degree of authorial presence and intervention. Metafictive historical fictions typically foreground questions about representation and the possibility of knowing and interpreting events and persons located in the past from a position in the present. Novels such as *Strange Objects* and *Backtrack* suggest analogies between the textuality of the past and of subjectivity, and between the fragmented, disjointed structure of texts and of narratorial subjects. Both novels are structured as a bricolage of appropriated social and ideological texts and discourses which imply an illusion of decentered and effaced narration; both also pivot on an unsolved mystery, the resolution of which hinges on the possibility of inferring a subjectivity for a textually constructed other. These two novels differ radically, however, in the representation of subjectivity, the construction of implied reader subject positions and the ideological inscription of interpretative positions. In a sense, the two novels encapsulate a dialogue running through this book between Baktinian and Lacanian visions of subjectivity. Bakhtin saw the subject as formed in dialogue with social and linguistic practice (as *Backtrack* would also seem to suggest), and Lacan saw the subject as inherently split but structured by a desire for completion (the same desire would seem to underwrite *Strange Objects*). While, as my analysis almost certainly implies, I see *Backtrack* as an infinitely more sophisticated and dialogical novel than *Strange Objects,* the dialogue between Bakhtin and Lacan ultimately remains open.

ENDNOTES

1. Actual texts in *Strange Objects* include excerpts from Hugh Edwards (p. 34) Daisy Bates (p. 34), Henrietta Drake-Brockman (p. 33–34), Aldo Massola (p. 109), K.G. McIntyre (p. 109)). Fictional texts occur on pages 124–126, 39–41 and 41–45 for example, though some of the events which these fictional texts represent are historical.

2. Focalizers include Harry and Will (Jack's great-great Uncles), Edward (Rill's great-great Uncle), James Paradis, Mr Weeks (the stationmaster), James Fraser (the signal man) and Rathbone (an anarchist).

3. Leech and Short (1981) distinguish between represented speech and thought, and thus classify these categories: direct speech (DS); direct thought (DT), and so on. I am using the term "discourse" to refer to both represented speech and thought as it is frequently difficult to discriminate between these categories in *Backtrack*. The area of discourse representation has received a great deal of critical attention, and was also of interest to Bakhtin (1984a, pp. 181–269) and Vološinov (1986, pp. 109–159). See also, McHale (1978) and Pateman (1989).

4. The idea that it is in fact Loos who carries and spreads disease amongst the Aborigines was suggested by Gary Crew in a lecture given at Macquarie University in 1993. The implication that Loos displaces his own illness, and responsibility, upon the other creates an interesting analogy with Messenger.

9 CONCLUSION

What is essential about [the social] self is not found primarily in its differ-
ences from others but in its freedom to pursue a story line, a life plot, a drama
carved out of all possibilities every society provides: the amount of overlap
with other story lines matters not a whit. The carving is done, both con-
sciously and unconsciously, by a self that is social at birth and increasingly
socialised, colonised in response to penetration by other selves.

Our true authenticity, in this view, is not what we find when we try
to peel away *influences in search of a monolithic, distinctive identity. Rather*
it is the one we find when we celebrate *addition of self to self, in an act of*
self-fashioning that culminates not in an in-dividual at all but in . . . a kind
of society; *a* field *of forces; a* colony; *a* chorus *of not necessarily harmoni-*
ous voices; a manifold *project; a* polyglossia *that is as much in us as in the*
world outside us.

Wayne C. Booth, "Individualism and the Mystery of the Social Self;
or, Does Amnesty Have a Leg to Stand On?"

As I suggested in the introduction to this book, and as many theorists have
argued, the idea of an essential, unique and individualized self has been systematically interrogated and deconstructed virtually since its inception, and
poststructuralist deconstructions of the essential self merely explicate an
implicit predisposition within the humanist tradition. Humanism has always,
at least implicitly, accepted that the "search for 'the real me,' a search per-
formed by peeling away all 'inauthentic' influences, reveals nothing at the
core" (Booth, 1993, p. 80); nothing, that is, except fictions and ideologies
of identity. The gods have departed, and, in the absence of religious and
philosophical "truths," we are ultimately left with fictions, theories and ideologies as to the nature, purpose and meaning of what we conventionally
refer to as "selfhood." Furthermore, poststructuralist visions of socially con-

structed and fragmented selves are as fictional, and as ideologically inscribed, as those fictions they seek to dismantle and replace. However, this recognition of the constructedness of humanist and poststructuralist selves alike does not mean that we should discount the power such fictions and ideologies have in fashioning identities and in shaping the ways in which we relate to the world. Some ideologies of identity are more empowering than others, nevertheless, and Booth's vision of a self that is free to pursue a story line and carve out a drama implies an agential subjectivity, while at the same time asserting the essential sociality of that subject in terms which are recognizably Bakhtinian and, as Booth's use of fictional metaphors implies, admitting its essential fictionality.

Another, similar, ideology of identity on which this book is premised is that concepts of personal identity and selfhood are formed in dialogue with others, with language and with society. The idea that subjectivity is dialogical presumes the coexistence of concepts of a personal identity as both a subject and an agent. Thus, ideas about and images of the self are defined in relation to existing social codes, structures and practices, but at the same time they also facilitate and are the product of conscious and deliberate actions. I maintain that these issues are of major relevance to an understanding of adolescent fiction, because ideas about and representations of subjectivity are always inherent in the central concerns of this fiction: that is, in the concerns with personal growth and maturation, and with relationships between the self and others, and between individuals and the world, society or the past. It therefore seems to me to be a deficiency in discussions of adolescent fiction that they seldom directly address the centrality of subjectivity or, hence, the ways that it is produced in and by fiction.

Bakhtinian theories of subjectivity, language and narrative have a significant contribution to make to the study of children's and adolescent fiction, especially with regard to the many dialogic representations of subjectivity to be found there. Bakhtinian theory is not just a way of talking about texts, but more importantly, a way of examining how texts exist in the world as representations, and hence how they interact with the social and cultural contexts in and through which they are produced and received. Insofar as we use language and narrative to represent, mediate and comprehend the world and our relations with others (as well as to construct fictions), an examination of how texts mean entails assumptions about, and has implications for, how the world is ascribed with meaning and how we structure our relationships with other selves.

Bakhtin's work has in common with adolescent fictions a preoccupation with interpersonal relations and the influence of society, culture and language on cognition, maturation and the formation of concepts of personal identity. He develops these ideas within an essentially humanist context. Although aspects of his theory are hostile toward some elements of humanism, in particular the impulse to essentialize the self, the individual and meaning, there is in his work an ideological resolve which stresses the centrality of human experience, language and culture. His notion of dialogism has ethical implications which are closely aligned with the central concerns of modern humanist writings and of many adolescent and children's fictions.

Children's and adolescent fiction is, on the whole, dominated by humanist conceptions of the individual, the self and the child, and subjectivity is almost always conceived of within a dominant humanist ethic which values socially cooperative forms of intersubjectivity. On the other hand, many of the novels discussed destabilize essentialist concepts of the subject and construct reading positions which implicitly interrogate the universalizing implications of humanism. Very few of the novels that I have been looking at could be said to be wholly antihumanist and negative in their outlook, though many censure or negate aspects of humanist practice, for example, Dickinson's *Eva* (1988) and Garner's *Red Shift* (1973).

Oppositions between humanism and various forms of antihumanism (Marxism, structuralism and poststructuralism) hinge on questions about meaning, about how the self relates to others and to the world, how individuals relate to society and how the world is ascribed with meaning. The postmodern subject is as much a construction as the humanist self, and philosophical arguments about subjectivity and meaning operate within social, ethical and political contexts. If, as I have suggested, subjectivity is formed in dialogue with existing social codes, structures and practices, in particular textual and discursive practices, then the inscription of these kinds of questions within adolescent texts has implications for the representation and textual construction of adolescence as a cultural fiction through and against which individual subjects define and construct their subjectivity.

Children's and adolescent fictions typically valorize the capacity to act independently of social restraint and, in doing so, assume humanistic concepts of individual agency. This is an idea which presents problems for the depiction of characters within social relationships in fictions for adolescents. As I suggested in Chapter 1, the image of empowered individuals capable of acting independently and making choices about their lives presents young readers with a worldview which for many is simply idealistic and unattainable. Alternatively, to overemphasize the construction of subjectivity within society implies a mechanistic view of individuals constructed within and determined by social institutions. Such visions offer young readers relatively negative worldviews and more recent "bleak" fiction for adolescents in Australia, which depicts young people in irresolvable states of alienation, is perhaps characterized by this implication and might be criticized on the grounds that it does not offer its young readers the possibility of making empowered choices. Many of the novels discussed in this book, such as Jill Paton Walsh's *Unleaving* (1976), for example, pivot thematically on the question of how to negotiate these two ideologies of identity. The ending of a recent Australian novel, *the best thing* (Lanagan, 1995) suggests a dialogue between the two positions: "They didn't tell us this at school; they told us we were all individuals carving out places for ourselves. No one ever warned me that someone else could take my heart and bare it to the world for breaking over and over again, the way Bella [the narrator's infant child] does" (pp. 180–181). The dominant ideology, inculcated through schooling, conforms to a liberal humanist ideology which sees individuals as empowered to make choices about their lives; the reality for Mel, the narrator, is that subjectivity is not singular. She is not one individual carving out a place for herself, but instead occupies various subject positions in relation to others— her daughter, her boyfriend, her mother and father—and in relation to the social world around her.

This book has focused on two main aspects of adolescent fiction: the representation of subjectivity as being dialogically constructed through interrelationships with others, through language, and in relation to social and cultural forces and ideologies; and the use of dialogical narrative strategies to structure narratives, to represent subjectivity and intersubjectivity and to position implied readers as subjects in texts. These two aspects are closely interrelated, though, as the discussion of texts has made clear, narrative techniques and structures do not in themselves determine representations of subjectivity. The presence in a text of dialogical narrative techniques does not automatically ensure the representation of dialogical conceptions of the subject, since particular narrative forms or techniques are neither inherently dialogic or monologic. Instead, novels are, like language, structured by an interaction between monologic and dialogic forces which position implied readers and which inform and shape representations of subjectivity.

Although adolescent fiction is underpinned by a central humanist ethic, it is also a particularly eclectic and heteroglottic novelistic genre which borrows pervasively from other cultural genres and discourses, and in doing so appropriates a range of cultural and intellectual ideas and narrative and discursive forms. Bakhtinian theory, with its range of concerns and interests, provides a theoretical frame for examining this eclecticism and heteroglossia. Bakhtin's concept of dialogism provides us with ways of examining the interactions between various ideological positions and tensions expressed in adolescent fiction through the incorporation of humanist, modernist and postmodernist strategies and themes. His theories of narrative—in particular the concepts of polyphony, intertextuality and heteroglossia—provide ways of analyzing narrative strategies and techniques that have gained popularity in contemporary children's and adolescent fiction, such as genre-mixing, varied discourse modes, the use of multiple narrative strands and voices and extraliterary discourses and genres, as well as narrative motifs such as the *doppelganger* and the *quest*. These are all strategies which can potentially position implied readers in active subject positions. The concept of addressivity has important implications for a theory of language and of reading. If discourse is always oriented toward an other and toward that other's response, then language has an important function in the construction of relations between the self and others, and in the textual production of implied readers. In writing about intersubjectivity, Bakhtin uses an analogy between the self and the other, and an author and a character. Despite the problems I have identified in this analogy, it still offers the crucial observation that there is a relationship between the social and interpersonal construction of subjectivity, the textual representation of subjectivity and the orientation of a text toward an implicit audience.

The theory of reading which might be extrapolated from Bakhtin's work contends that readers employ a range of strategies for reading and response, and that the novel—by virtue of its inherent capacity to incorporate a diversity of narrative techniques and voices, and a diversity of social and ideological discourses—can potentially construct a multiplicity of implied reader subject positions. Thus, implied readers are conceived of as actively involved in the production of meaning. However, as I have been arguing, the construction of implied reader subject positions in narrative is determined by the narrative techniques used. Texts which use a limited range of narrative techniques and discursive genres, and are dominated by a single (monologic) voice and ideology, generally construct more passive reading positions. Texts which use dialogic narrative structures and techniques, such as multivoiced and multistranded narration, and/or a range of genres and extraliterary discourses, generally construct more active reading positions. With the case of inexperienced readers, this is of particular importance, since these techniques can implicitly equip readers with a wide range of reading strategies and skills for ascribing meanings to texts and for ascribing experiences in the world with meanings. Furthermore, in many of the novels discussed, these strategies also facilitate a questioning of conventional notions of selfhood, meaning and history.

In the course of this book, I have often found need to canvass difficult and rather complex ideas in order to find ways to define and articulate the radical diversity in adolescent fiction, in the representations of subjectivity and ideologies of identity, the constructions of implied readers, the narrative techniques, structures and intertextual strategies, and the ideological inscriptions of texts. What I think the process defines is the often subtle and deeply inlaid models of selfhood offered to readers in adolescent fiction, models which are not expressed overtly by means of philosophical, moral or sociological discourses, but are expressed implicitly through storytelling and narrative forms. It is a tribute to the potential power of such fictions that they are able to use narrative form to represent and communicate ideas of such complexity and of such significance for any young reader's quest for meaning and self-definition.

GLOSSARY

addressivity: the orientation of discourse toward an other and that other's response. "Every word is directed toward an *answer* and cannot escape the profound influence of the answering word that it anticipates" (Bakhtin, 1981, p. 280). This concept is used to discuss the role of language within relationships between the self and others, and the construction of implied readers in narrative within active subject positions. Ideally, addressivity is dialogical. An other addressee (reader or listener) is allowed a position from which to respond, and his/her response taken into account; in narrative, active subject positions are constructed for implied readers. Monological forms of address either ignore the other's potential response or deny that other a position from which to respond.

chronotope: literally means "time-space." A chronotope is a formal combination of time and space specific to a particular narrative genre. As such, the concept is comparable to structuralist plot types or devices, although Bakhtin also stresses that these plot types are culturally and ideologically specific. The term chronotopic refers to the "intrinsic interconnectedness of temporal and spatial relationships that are artistically expressed in literature" (Bakhtin, 1981, p. 84). Chronotopic configurations have an important function in the construction and representation of particular ideologically inscribed images of human life in relation to time, space and history. I use the term in two main ways: to refer to spatio-temporal relations within narrative, and to refer to spatio-temporal images or concepts which structure and organise a narrative—for example, evolutionary, or developmental, chronotopes used in historical fiction.

dialogism: the semantic range of this term is very broad. At its most abstract it refers to the centrifugal forces in language and culture, that is, those elements associated with linguistic and cultural diversification. A general sense of the meaning of **dialogic** is that of "dialogue": a verbal interchange between individuals where there is an exchange of words, ideas and viewpoints, as opposed to monologue, wherein only one person speaks. Thus, the term **dialogic** describes a relation of exchange between two positions—between the self and others, between subject and language or society, between two ideologies or discourses, two textual voices and so on. This relation is neither oppositional, dialectical nor monological. Hence **dialogism** is also defined in opposition to **monologism**. The **dialogic orientation of discourse** refers to the orientation of an utterance toward other preceding and subsequent discourses—the intertextuality of discourse—and toward an other and that other's anticipated answering word—the addressivity of discourse (Bakhtin, 1981, pp. 275–280).

diegetic: refers to the levels of narration in novels, such as primary narratives, secondary narratives and so on (Genette, 1986, pp. 227–237). The terms diegesis and diegetic are also used in relation to mimesis and mimetic to distinguish between narrated material (diegesis) and represented material (mimesis), such as character dialogue (*See* Genette, 1986, pp. 162–185; Hawthorn, 1992, pp. 41–43).

focalisation: an indirect mode of narration occurring in first and third person narrative whereby events are narrated from the perceptual point of view of a character situated within the text as if seen through the eyes of that character (Stephens, 1992a, p. 27). Focalisation techniques are important for the construction of characters as "ideologues," for the representation of subjectivity and intersubjectivity, and for the positioning of implied readers.

heteroglossia: literally means "many languages." Bakhtin uses the term to refer to the "internal stratification of any single national language" into "socially typifying languages," or speech genres. These genres have a socio-ideological basis. They represent specific ideological points of view on the world which coexist, intersect and often conflict. Any one language comprises multiple coexisting and competing social discourses and ideologies which "encounter and coexist in the consciousness of real people" (Bakhtin, 1981, p. 292). Heteroglossia is represented in the novel within the speech of characters and narrators, and through the incorporation of intertextual and extraliterary discourses. Linguistic terms such as "sociolect," "idiolect" and "register" are also used to refer to this linguistic diversification. (*See,* Bakhtin, 1981, pp. 262–263 and 291–292; A. White, 1984; Fowler, 1981).

humanism: a concept with a broad range of applications, but with shared assumptions and concerns about the nature of human beings and their relationships to societies. Core assumptions involve the nature of subjectivity and human agency: although people may not be constituted as essential selves, they can make choices as to the kinds of selves they become. They do this be engagement both with personal and inward aspects of being and experiencing, and with the political and social dimensions of existence, the organisation of human life in society. Humanist thought seeks to engage human intellect, imagination and emotions in intersubjective comprehension of other people's worlds and ideas; it fosters a concern with social and political freedoms, and with justice. It resists complacent or deterministic arguments that nothing can be done to change things, that ordinary people cannot strive for and achieve some measure of agency. It contends that although men and women may not have complete freedom, they nevertheless have, or should have, the opportunity to make choices, to forge their own agency (*see passim* Bullock, 1985).

ideologue: the speaking person in the novel who in speaking his/her "own unique ideological discourse" represents a specific ideological position or "language world view" (Bakhtin, 1981, pp. 332–333).

ideologeme: the discourse of a speaker in the novel which is inscribed with their particular socially and ideologically situated way of viewing the world (Bakhtin, 1981, pp. 332–333; *see also,* Bakhtin/Medvedev, 1978, pp. 21–25). The concept is comparable with the linguistic term idiolect, "an individual's personal variety of a particular language system" (Macquarie Dictionary, 1981), as Hawthorn's comments about idiolect suggest: "a writer's achievement in giving a particular literary character a distinctive idiolect can be an important aspect of that writer's success in characterisation" (1992, p. 80).

ideology: a shared system of beliefs or "ideas about the world, about how it is or should be organised, and about the place and role of people in it" (Stephens, 1992c, p. 148). The concept of ideology is crucial for a discussion of adolescent fiction insofar as childhood and adolescence are as much ideological constructions as biological stages of growth. Such fictions are premised on ideological assumptions about what it means to be a child, adolescent and adult, what it means to grow up, and hence what it means to be; in other words, such fictions are premised on culturally specific ideologies of identity.

intertextuality: the interrelations between two or more texts, which has an effect upon how a given ("focused") text is read. Bakhtin's theory of intertextuality implies that meaning is the product of the interaction between a focused text and its intertexts; meaning lies within the space between texts, rather than with one or the other. Some theorists have sought to restrict the meaning of intertext as referring only to those texts to which a text refers, as distinct from pretexts, sources and the related texts that a reader may bring to a text. Others, however, exclude literary allusion from intertextuality. I use the term in its widest sense, to refer to the range of cultural and literary discourses, genres, pretexts and generic precursors of a focused text, as well as specific texts referred to or quoted within it. Intertextuality is an implicitly polyphonic narrative strategy because it enables the representation of multiple simultaneous intersecting voices, discourses and subjectivities within a text.

logocentrism: a term coined by Derrida to refer to (idealist) systems of thought which are reliant upon an extra-systemic validating presence or centre which underwrites and fixes linguistic meaning, but is itself beyond scrutiny or challenge (Hawthorn, 1992, p. 94). This posited presence is also referred to as the transcendent signified, that is, an abstract concept (such as the Logos, or God) correlated with "truth," which fixes meaning and halts linguistic play (Derrida, 1978). Derrida's concept of logocentrism intersects with Bakhtin's concept of monologism (*see* Monologism).

metalepsis: refers to the transgression of logical and hierarchical relations between different (diegetic) levels of narration, that is between authors, primary narrators, secondary narrators and characters (Genette, 1980, pp. 234–236). These transgressions are frequently used in metafictions where they disrupt or "break" the frame of a narrative and draw attention to the fictionality of a text.

metanarrative: a term introduced by Lyotard (1984) to refer to overarching and totalising philosophies of history, which legitimate and privilege cultural practices and ideologies (Fraser and Nicholson, 1989, p. 86). Metanarratives are also referred to as "grand narratives" and "master narratives," and Hayden White's work on history writing is particularly relevant to the notion of history as "grand narrative" (White, 1973, 1987). It should be noted that metanarrative has also been used in quite a different sense by Genette (1980) to refer to a narrative which either "talks about other, embedded narratives," or "which refers to itself and to its own narrative procedures"

(Hawthorn, 1992, p. 104). *See also Retelling Stories* (Stephens and Mc-Callum, 1998).

monologism: this term has a wide semantic range, and can be used to describe language, specific discursive forms, the relation between a speaker and an interlocutor and between the self and others. It refers to the centripetal forces in language (as opposed to the centrifugal, or dialogic forces of language). These forces are associated with "historical processes of linguistic unification" and sociopolitical and cultural centralisation which ensure a "maximum of mutual understanding" between speakers (Bakhtin, 1981, p. 270).

Monologism can refer to specific ideas about language and particular kinds of discourse. A **monologic** approach to language posits a unitary system of linguistic norms, and is essentially logocentric because it is posited on the idea of a central still point at which linguistic meaning can be fixed. Monologic forms of discourse are manifest in the emergence of a dominant official language or ideology (p. 271). These discourses are oriented toward the repression of the inherent heteroglossia of language, and hence the repression of difference. Likewise, monologic narrative forms and strategies repress the inherent dialogic potential of a narrative.

Monologism is also used to refer to the stance of a speaker toward an other and relations between the self and others. "Monologism, at its extreme, denies the existence outside itself of another consciousness with equal rights and equal responsibilities, another *I* with equal rights *(thou)*" (Bakhtin, 1984a, p. 292). Whereas dialogism is associated with the formation of intersubjectivity, monologism refers to a form of solipsism which fails to recognise or effaces the subjectivity of the other.

polyphony: literally means "many-voiced," and is mainly used by Bakhtin to describe the peculiar (**polyphonic**) nature of novelistic discourse. Novels typically appropriate and represent "a multiplicity of social voices" and socio-ideological discourses from within a heteroglossia (1981, p. 263), and they deploy a range of narrational strategies, voices and discursive styles. The term **polyphony** as Bakhtin uses it acquires a fairly specific meaning, wherein it refers to the construction of dialogical interrelationships between speakers and voices represented in narrative. Polyphony is important for the representation of intersubjectivity.

solipsism: the inability to distinguish between one's own self and the otherness of the world and of other people. Solipsism takes two forms: a person may be unable to perceive an other as another self, and hence denies that other a subject position independent of her/his self; or a person may be unable to perceive of her/his self as independent of the world, and to construct a sense of her/his self as agent. Bakthin also uses the phrases "cultural" or "ethical" solipsism, where the term refers to the inability of members of one culture or society to perceive and comprehend the "otherness" of another culture or society.

teleology: when applied to fiction: an interpretation or its structure (or a work's interpretation of its own events and participants) which apparently discloses evidence of design or purpose in nature, society and the universe, so that the meaning of the parts inheres in the outcome toward which they move.

References

Primary Sources

Cameron, Eleanor. *The Court of the Stone Children*. New York: E. P. Dutton, 1973.

Chambers, Aidan. *Breaktime*. London: The Bodley Head, 1978.

——. *Dance on my Grave*. London: The Bodley Head, 1982.

——. *The Toll Bridge*. London: The Bodley Head, 1992.

Chin, Frank. *Donald Duk*. Minneapolis: Coffee House Press, 1991.

Cormier, Robert. *The Chocolate War*. London: Lions Teens Tracks, 1988 (1974).

——. *I am the Cheese*. London: Lions Tracks, 1991 (1977).

——. *Fade*. London: Lions Tracks, 1990 (1988).

Crew, Gary. *The Inner Circle*. Port Melbourne, Victoria: Mammoth, 1986.

——. *Strange Objects*. Port Melbourne, Victoria: Mammoth, 1991 (1990).

Dickinson, Peter. *Emma Tupper's Diary*. London: Victor Gollancz, 1971.

——. *Eva*. London: Victor Gollancz, 1988.

——. *A Bone from a Dry Sea*. London: Victor Gollancz, 1992.

Doherty, Berlie. *Dear Nobody*. London: Hamish Hamilton, 1991.

Drake-Brockman, Henrietta. *The Wicked and the Fair*. Sydney: Angus and Robertson, 1957.

Duncan, Lois. *Stranger with my Face*. London: Puffin, 1995 (1981).

Eliot, T. S. *Selected Poems*. London: Faber and Faber, 1954.

Farmer, Penelope. *Charlotte Sometimes*. London: The Bodley Head, 1992 (1969).

——. *Thicker than Water*. London: Walker Books, 1989.

Fowles, John. *The French Lieutenant's Woman*. London: Triad/Panther, 1985 (1969).

Gardam, Jane. *The Hollow Land*. London: Julia MacRae Books, 1981.

Garner, Alan. *Red Shift*. London: Lion Teen Tracks, 1989 (1973).

——. *The Stone Book Quartet*. London: Collins, 1983.

Gleeson, Libby. *Eleanor, Elizabeth*. Sydney: Angus and Robertson, 1984.

——. *Dodger*. Victoria Park, Western Australia, Woodchester Stroud, England: Turton and Chambers, 1990.

——. *Love Me Love Me Not*. Ringwood, Victoria: Viking, 1993.

Golding, William. *The Inheritors*. London: Faber and Faber, 1955.

Hamilton, Virginia. *Arilla Sun Down*. London: Hamish Hamilton, 1977 (1976).

Hartnett, Sonya. *Sleeping Dogs*. Ringwood, Victoria: Penguin, 1995.

Holman, Felice. *Slake's Limbo*. London: Fontana Lions, 1986 (1974).

Hopkins, Gerald Manley. *Poems and Prose of Gerald Manley Hopkins*, selected by W. H. Gardner. Harmondsworth, England: Penguin, 1953.

Hunt, Peter. *A Step off the Path*. London: Julia MacRae Books, 1985.

——. *Backtrack*. London: Julia MacRae Books, 1986.

——. *Going Up*. London: Julia MacRae Books, 1989.

Klein, Robin. *Came Back to Show You I Could Fly*. Ringwood, Victoria: Penguin, 1991 (1989).

Lanagan, Margo. *the best thing*. Sydney: Allen and Unwin, 1995.

Lawrence, Louise. *Children of the Dust*. London: Bodley Head, 1985.

Lisson, Deborah. *The Devil's Own*. Glebe, New South Wales: Walter McVitty, 1990.

Lively, Penelope. *The Driftway*. Harmondsworth, England: Penguin Books, 1985 (1972).

Macdonald, Caroline. *The Lake at the End of the World*. Ringwood, Victoria: Penguin, 1990 (1988).

———. *Speaking to Miranda*. Ringwood, Victoria: Viking Penguin, 1990.

MacRobbie, David. *Mandragora*. Port Melbourne Victoria: Mammoth Australia, 1991.

Mark, Jan. *Finders, Losers*. London: Orchard Books, 1990.

———. *The Hillingdon Fox*. Woodchester Stroud, England, Victoria Park, Western Australia: Turton and Chambers, 1991.

Marsden, John. *So Much to Tell You. . . .* Glebe, New South Wales: Walter McVitty, 1987.

———. *Letters from the Inside*. Chippendale NSW: Pan Macmillan, 1991.

———. *Checkers*. Sydney: Macmillan, 1996.

———. *Dear Miffy*. Sydney: Macmillan, 1997.

Mayne, William. *Over the Hills and Far Away*. London: Hamish Hamilton, 1968. Reprinted as *The Hill Road*, New York: Dutton, 1969.

———. *A Game of Dark*. London: Hamish Hamilton, 1971.

———. *Salt River Times*. Melbourne: Thomas Nelson, 1980.

———. *Winter Quarters*. Harmondsworth, England: Penguin Books, 1984 (1982).

———. *Drift*. Harmondsworth, England: Penguin Books, 1987 (1985).

———. *Antar and the Eagles*. London: Walker Books, 1989.

O'Brien, Robert C. *Z for Zachariah*. London: Victor Gollancz, 1975.

Oneal, Zibby. *The Language of Goldfish*. London: Victor Gollancz, 1987 (1980).

Park, Ruth. *Playing Beatie Bow*. Ringwood Victoria: Penguin, 1980.

Paterson, Katherine. *Jacob Have I Loved*. London: Victor Gollancz, 1983 (1981).

Pausacker, Jenny. *What Are Ya?* North Ryde, New South Wales: Angus and Robertson, 1987.

Peck, Richard. *Voices after Midnight*. London: Macmillan, 1992 (1989).

Rubinstein, Gillian. *Galax Arena*. South Yarra, Victoria: Hyland House, 1992.

Scholes, Catherine. *The Blue Chameleon*. Melbourne: Hill of Content, 1989.

Stevenson, Robert Louis. *Treasure Island*. London: Lamboll House, 1986 (1883).

Sutcliff, Rosemary. *The Eagle of the Ninth*. Harmondsworth, England: Puffin Books, 1954.

Traherne, Thomas. *Centuries of Meditations*. Edited by Bertram Dobell. London: P. J. and A. E. Dobell, 1927.

Ure, Jean. *Come Lucky April*. London: Mandarin, 1993 (1992).

Voight, Cynthia. *The Callender Papers*. London: Lions, 1991 (1983).

Walsh, Jill Paton. *Goldengrove*. London, Sydney, Toronto: The Bodley Head, 1985 (1972).

———. *Unleaving*. London: Macmillan, 1976.

Wheatley, Nadia. *The House that Was Eureka*. Ringwood, Victoria: Penguin, 1985.

———. *The Blooding*. Ringwood, Victoria: Penguin, 1989 (1987)

Wilmot, Frank. *Breaking Up*. London: Willliam Collins, 1983.

Zindel, Paul. *The Pigman*. London: The Bodley Head, 1969.

SECONDARY SOURCES

Abbs, Peter. "Penelope Lively, Children's Fiction and the Failure of Adult Culture." *Children's Literature in Education* 18 (fall 1975): 118–124.

Althusser, Louis. *Lenin and Philosophy and other Essays*. Translated by Ben Brewster. London: NBL, 1971.

Allen, Lynn. "Polyphonic Discourse and Feminist Vision in Christina Stead." In *Literature and Popular Culture*. Edited by Horst Ruthrof and John Fiske, Nedlands, Western Australia: Australian and South Pacific Association for Comparative Literary Studies Conference, 1987, pp. 162–174.

Aries, Philippe. *Centuries of Childhood*. Translated by Robert Baldick. London: Jonathon Cape, 1962.

Avery, Gillian. *Childhood's Pattern: A Study of the Heroes and Heroines of Children's Fiction 1770–1950*. London, Leicester, Sydney, Auckland: Hodder and Stoughton, 1975.

Babbitt, Natalie. "Review of *A Game of Dark*." *The New York Times Book Review* (October 10, 1971): 8.

Bagnell, Norma. "An American Hero in Welsh Fantasy: The Mabinogion, Alan Garner and Lloyd Alexander." *The New Welsh Review* 2, nos. 4, 8 (1990): 26–29.

Bakhtin, M. M. *The Dialogic Imagination—Four essays by M.M. Bakhtin*. Translated by Caryl Emerson and Michael Holquist. Edited by Michael Holquist. Austin: The University of Texas, 1981. (Original Russian edition, 1975.)

———. *Problems of Dostoevsky's Poetics*. Translated by and Edited by Caryl Emerson. Manchester: Manchester University Press, 1984a. (Original Russian edition 1929; revised and expanded in Russian 1963.)

———. *Rabelais and his World*. Translated by Helene Iswolsky. Bloomington: Indiana University Press, 1984b. (Original Russian edition, 1965.)

———. *Speech Genres and other Late Essays*. Translated by Vern W. McGee. Edited by Caryl Emerson and Michael Holquist. Austin: University of Texas Press, 1986. (Original Russian edition, 1979.)

———. *Art and Answerability—Early Philosophical Essays by M.M. Bakhtin*. Translated by Vadim Liapunov and Kenneth Brostrom. Edited by Michael Holquist and Vadim Liapunov. Austin: University of Texas Press, 1990. (Original Russian edition, 1979.)

Bakhtin, M. M. and P. N. Medvedev. *The Formal Method in Literary Scholarship: A Critical Introduction to Sociological Poetics*. Translated by Albert J. Wehrle. London and Cambridge Massachusetts: Harvard University Press, 1978. (Original Russian edition, 1928.)

Barthes, Roland. "The Death of the Author." In *Image-Music-Text*. Translated and Edited by Stephen Heath. London: Fontana, 1982 (1977a). (Reprinted in *Modern Criticism and Theory: A Reader*. Edited by David Lodge. London and New York: Longman, 1988)

———. *Roland Barthes by Roland Barthes*. Translated and Edited by Richard Howard. New York: Hill and Wang, 1977b (Original French edition, 1975.)

Bates, Daisy. *The Passing of the Aborigines*. Melbourne: The Speciality Press, 1944.

Bator, Robert. *Signposts to Criticism of Children's Literature*. Chicago: American Library Association, 1983.

Belsey, Catherine. *Critical Practise*. London and New York: Methuen, 1980.

Bennet, Tony. *Formalism and Marxism*. London and New York: Methuen, 1979.

———. *Outside Literature*. London and New York: Routledge, 1990.

Benton, Michael. "Detective Imagination." *Children's Literature in Education* 13 (1974): 5–13.

Bernard, John and Arthur Delbridge, *Introduction to Linguistics: An Australian Perspective*. Sydney: Prentice Hall of Australia, 1980.

Bernstein, Michael. "When the Carnival Turns Bitter: Preliminary Reflections upon the Abject Hero." *Critical Inquiry* 10 (December 1983): 283–305.

Bialostosky, Don H. "Booth's Rhetoric, Bakhtin's Dialogics and the Future of Novel Criticism." *Novel* 18, no. 3 (1985): 209–216.

Booth, Wayne C. "Critical Response IV: Reply to Richard Berrong." *Critical Inquiry* 11 (1985): 697–701.

——. "Individualism and the Mystery of the Social Self; or, Does Amnesty have a Leg to Stand On?" In *Freedom and Interpretation* Edited by Barbara Johnson, New York: Basic Books, 1993: 69–102.

Bove, Paul A. *Intellectuals in Power: A Genealogy of Critical Humanism.* New York: Columbia University Press, 1986.

Brecht, Bertolt. *Brecht on Theatre: The Development of an Aesthetic.* Edited and Translated by John Willet. New York: Hill and Wang; London: Methuen, 1964.

Briggs, Katherine M. *A Dictionary of British Folk Tales in the English Language.* London and New York: Routledge, 1991 (1970).

Bullock, Alan. *The Humanist Tradition in the West.* New York and London: W. W. Norton, 1985.

Cameron, Eleanor. "Art and Morality." *Proceedings of the Children's Literature Association* 7 (1980): 30–44.

Campbell, Joseph. *The Hero with a Thousand Faces.* 2nd ed. Princeton: Princeton University Press, 1968.

Carroll, David. "The Alterity of Discourse: Form and History and the Question of the Political in M. M. Bakhtin." *Diacritics* 13, no. 2 (1983): 65–83.

Chambers, Aidan. "Letter from England: Literary Crossword Puzzle . . . or Masterpiece." *Hornbook* 49 (October 1973): 494–97.

——. *Booktalk: Occasional Writing on Literature and Children.* London: Bodley Head, 1985.

Chapman, Seymour. *Story and Discourse: Narrative Structure in Fiction and Film.* Ithaca and London: Cornell University Press, 1980 (1978).

Clark, Katerina and Michael Holquist. *Mikhail Bakhtin.* Cambridge, Mass. and London: Harvard University Press, 1984.

Crago, Hugh. "Penelope Farmer's Novels." *Signal* 17 (May 1975): 81–90.

——. "Cultural Categories and the Criticism of Children's Literature." *Signal* 30 (September 1975): 140–150.

Crook, Eugene J., ed. *Fearful Symmetry: Doubles and Doubling in Literature and Film.* Tallahassee: University Presses of Florida, 1981.

Crowley, Tony. "Bakhtin and the History of Language," in *Bahktin and Cultural Theory.* Edited by Ken Hirschkop and David Shepherd, Manchester and New York: Manchester University Press, 1989.

De Man, Paul. "Dialogue and Dialogism." *Poetics Today* 4 (1983): 99–107.

Derrida, Jacques. *Of Grammatology.* Translated by Gayatri Chakravorty Spivak. Baltimore and London: The Johns Hopkins University Press, 1976.

——. "Structure, Sign and Play in the Discourse of the Human Science." *Writing and Difference.* Translated by Alan Bass. London: Routledge and Kegan Paul, 1978. (Reprinted in *Modern Criticism and Theory: A Reader.* Edited by David Lodge. London and New York: Longman, 1988, pp. 108–123.)

Dolar, Mladen. "'I Shall Be with You on Your Wedding-Night': Lacan and the Uncanny." *October* 58 (Fall 1991): 5–23.

Drake-Brockman, Henrietta. *Voyage to Disaster: The Life of Franscisco Pelsaert.* Australia: Angus and Robertson Publishers, 1963.

Dusinberre, Juliet. *Alice to the Lighthouse: Children's Books and Radical Experiments in Art.* New York: St. Martin's Press, 1987.

Eagleton, Terry. "Wittgenstein's Friends." *New Left Review* 135 (1982): 64–90.

——. "Bakhtin, Schopenhauer, Kundera." In *Bakhtin and Cultural Theory,* edited by Ken Hirschkop and David Shepherd, Manchester and New York: Manchester University Press, 1989.

Edwards, Hugh. *Islands of Angry Ghosts.* Great Britain: Hodder and Stoughton, 1985 (1966).

Egan, Kieran. "Layers of Historical Understanding." *Theory and Research in Social Education* 17, 4 (1989): 280–294.

Emerson, Caryl. "The Outer Word and Inner Speech: Bakhtin, Vygotsky and the Internalisation of Language." *Critical Inquiry* 10 (December 1983): 245–264.

Fisher, Margery. "Review of *Charlotte Sometimes*." *Growing Point* 8, no. 5 (1969): 1408.

Foss, Peter J. "The Undefined Boundary: Converging Worlds in the Early Novels of Alan Garner." *The New Welsh Review* 2, nos. 4, 8 (1990): 30–35.

Fowler, Roger. *Literature as Social Discourse: The Practise of Linguistic Criticism.* London: Batsford Academic and Educational Ltd., 1981.

Fraser, Nancy, and Linda Nicholson. "Social Criticism without Philosophy: An Encounter between Feminism and Post-modernism." In *Universal Abandon: The Politics of Postmodernism.* Edited by Andrew Ross. Edinburgh University Press, 1989: 83–104.

Freud, Sigmund. "The Uncanny." *Collected Papers.* Vol. 4. Translated by Joan Riviere. New York: Basic Books, 1959 (1919).

Gannon, Susan. "Robert Louis Stevenson's *Treasure Island:* The Ideal Fable." In *Touchstones.* Vol. 1. Edited by Perry Nodelman, West Lafayette, IN: Children's Literature Association, 1985.

Garner, Alan. "Inner Time." In *Science Fiction at Large: A Collection of Essays by Various Hands about the Interface between Science Fiction and Reality.* Ed. Peter Nicholls. London: Victor Gollancz, 1976.

———. "Achilles in Altjira." *Innocence and Experience: Essays and Conversations on Children's Literature.* Edited by Barbara Harrison and Gregory Macguire. New York: Lothrop, Lee and Shepard, 1987.

Genette, Gerard. *Narrative Discourse.* Translated by Jane E. Lewin. Oxford: Basil Blackwell, 1980.

Giddens, Anthony. *Central Problems in Social Theory, Action, Structure and Contradiction in Social Analysis.* London: Macmillan, 1979.

Gillies, Carolyn. "Possession and Structure in the Novels of Alan Garner." *Children's Literature in Education* 18 (fall 1975): 107–17.

Gloege, Martin E. "The American Origins of the Postmodern Self." In *Constructions of the Self.* Edited by George Levine, New Brunswick, NJ: Rutgers University Press, 1992.

Gombrich, E. H. "They were All Human Beings—So Much is Plain: Reflections on Cultural Relativism in the Humanities." *Critical Inquiry* 13 (Summer 1987): 686–699.

Gough, John. "Alan Garner: The Critic and Self-critic." *Orana* 20, no. 3 (1988): 111–118.

Grosz, Elizabeth. *Jacques Lacan, A Feminist Introduction.* North Sydney: Allen and Unwin, 1990.

Hallam, Clifford. "The Double as Incomplete Self: Toward a Definition of *Doppelgänger*." In *Fearful Symmetry.* Edited by Eugene Crook, Tallahassee: University Presses of Florida, 1981.

Halliday, M. A. K. "Linguistic Function and Literary Style: An Investigation into the Language of William Golding's *The Inheritors*." In *Literary Style: A Symposium.* Edited by Seymour Chatman. London and New York: Oxford University Press, 1971.

Hassam, Andrew. "Literary Exploration: The Fictive Sea, Journals of William Golding, Robert Nye, B. S. Johnson and Malcolm Lowry." *Ariel: A Review of International English Literature* 19, no. 3 (1988): 29–46.

Hawking, Stephen. *A Brief History of Time: From the Big Bang to Black Holes.* London, Toronto, New York, Sydney, Auckland: Bantam Books, 1988.

Hawthorn, Jeremy. *A Concise Glossary of Contemporary Literary Theory.* London, New York, Melbourne, Auckland: Edward Arnold, 1992.

Hellings, Carol. "Alan Garner: His Use of Mythology and Dimensions in Time." *Orana* 15, no. 2 (1979): 66–73.

Hirschkop, Ken. "Critical Response: A Response to the Forum on Mikhail Bakhtin." *Critical Inquiry* 9, (1985a): 672–678.

———. "The Social and the Subject in Bakhtin." *Poetics Today* 6, no. 4 (1985b): 769–775.

———. "Bakhtin and Liberalism." *The Bakhtin Newsletter* 2 (1986a): 139–146.

———. "Bakhtin, Discourse and Democracy." *New Left Review* 160 (1986b): 92–113.

———. "The Domestication of M. M. Bakhtin." *Essays in Poetics* 11, no. 1 (1986c): 76–87.

———. "Introduction: Bakhtin and Cultural Theory." In *Bahktin and Cultural Theory.* Edited by Ken Hirschkop and David Shepherd, Manchester and New York: Manchester University Press, 1989a.

Hirschkop, Ken, and David Shepherd, ed. *Bakhtin and Cultural Theory.* Manchester and New York: Manchester University Press, 1989b.

Hodge, Bob and Vijak Mishra. *Dark Side of the Dream: Australian Literature and the Post-colonial Mind.* Sydney: Allen and Unwin, 1990.

Hollindale, Peter. "Ideology and the Children's Book." *Signal* 55 (January 1988): 3–22.

———. "The Darkening of the Green." *Signal* 61 (January 1990): 3–19.

———. "The Critic and the Child." *Signal* 65 (May 1991): 87–100.

Holquist, Michael. "The Politics of Representation." In *Allegory and Representation.* Edited by Stephen Greenblatt. Baltimore and London: Johns Hopkins University Press, 1981.

———. "Neotextualism: an Antihumanist Threat to Comparative Criticism." *Neohelicon* 10, no. 2 (1983a): 47–61.

———. "Answering as Authoring: Mikhail Bakhtin's Translinguistics." *Critical Inquiry* 10 (December 1983b): 307–319.

———. *Dialogism: Bakhtin and his World.* London and New York: New Accents-Routledge, 1990.

Howe, Irving. "The Self in Literature." In *Constructions of the Self.* Edited by George Levine, New Brunswick, NJ: Rutgers University Press, 1992.

Hughes, Felicity. "Children's Literature: Theory and Practise." *English Literary History* 45 (1978): 542–552. (Reprinted in *Signposts to Criticism of Children's Literature,* Edited by Robert Bator, Chicago: American Library Association, 1983.

Hunt, Peter. "Necessary Mis-readings: Directions in Narrative Theory for Children's Literature." *Studies in the Literary Imagination* 18, no. 2 (1985): 197–121.

———. "Degrees of Control: Stylistics and the Discourse of Children's Literature." In *Styles of Discourse,* Edited by Nikolas Coupland. London: Croom Helm, 1988a: 163–182.

———. "What Do We Lose When We Lose Allusion? Experience and Understanding Stories," *Signal* 57, no. 3 (1988b): 212–222.

———. *Criticism, Theory and Children's Literature.* Oxford: Basil Blackwell, 1991.

———, (ed.). *Literature for Children: Contemporary Criticism.* London and New York: Routledge, 1992.

Hutcheon, Linda. *Narcissistic Narrative: The Metafictional Paradox.* New York: Methuen, 1980.

———. "The Pastime of Past Time: Fiction, History, Historiographic Metafiction." *Genre* 20 (Fall-Winter 1987): 285–305.

———. *The Politics of Postmodernism.* London and New York: Routledge, 1989.

Inglis, Fred. *Ideology and the Imagination.* Cambridge: Cambridge University Press, 1975.

———. *The Promise of Happiness: Value and Meaning in Children's Fiction.* Cambridge: Cambridge University Press, 1981.

Iser, Wolfgang. *The Implied Reader: Patterns of Communication in Prose Fiction from Bunyen to Beckett*. Baltimore: The Johns Hopkins University Press, 1974.

———. *The Act of Reading: A Theory of Aesthetic Response*. Baltimore: The Johns University Press, 1978.

Ivanov, Viacheslav, "The Significance of M. M. Bakhtin's Ideas on Sign, Utterance and Dialogue for Modern Semiotics." *Soviet Studies in Literature* (spring-summer 1975): 186–243.

Jackson, Rosemary. *Fantasy: The Literature of Subversion*. London and New York: Methuen, 1981.

Jameson, Frederic. *The Political Unconscious: Narrative as a Socially Symbolic Act*. Ithaca, NY: Cornell University Press, 1981.

Jefferson, Ann. "Intertextuality and the Poetics of Fiction." *Comparative Criticism* 2 (1980a): 235–250.

Jefferson, Ann. "Realism Reconsidered: Bakhtin's Dialogism and the 'Will to Reference'." *Australian Journal of French Studies* 23, 2 (1980b): 169–184.

———. "Body Matters: Self and Other in Bakhtin, Satre and Barthes." In *Bahktin and Cultural Theory*. Edited by Ken Hirschkop and David Shepherd, Manchester and New York: Manchester University Press, 1989: 152–177.

Johnson, Barbara, ed. *Freedom and Interpretation: The Oxford Amnesty Lectures 1992*. New York: Basic Books, 1993.

Kalekin-Fishman, Devorah. "De-alienation as an Educational Objective." *Humanity and Society* 13, no. 3 (1989): 309–326.

Kessel, Frank S. and Alexander W. Siegel, eds. *The Child and other Cultural Inventions*. New York: Praeger Publishers, 1983.

Kessen, William. "The American Child and other Cultural Inventions." *American Psychologist* 34, no. 10 (1979): 815–820. (Reprinted in *The Child and other Cultural Inventions*, Edited by Kessel and Siegel, New York: Praeger Publishers, 1983a., pp. 261–270).

———. "The Child and other Cultural Inventions." In *The Child and other Cultural Inventions*. Edited by Kessel and Siegel, New York: Praeger Publishers, 1983b.

Kohler, Margaret. "Author study: Alan Garner." *Orana* 16, no. 2 (1980): 39–48.

Kristeva, Julia. "The Ruin of a Poetics." In *Russian Formalism*. Translated by Vivienne Mylne. Edited by Stephen Bann and John E. Bowlt. Edinburgh: Scottish Academic Press, 1973.

———. *Desire in Language—A Semiotic Approach to Literature and Art*. Translated by Gora Jardine Roudizz. Edited by Leon S. Roudizz. Oxford: Basil Blackwell, 1980.

Lacan, Jacques. *The Language of the Self: The Function of Language in Psychoanalysis*. Translated by Anthony Wilden. Baltimore: The John Hopkins Press, 1975.

———. *The Four Fundamental Concepts of Psychoanalysis*. Translated by Alain Sheridan. Edited by Jacques-Alain Miller. London: Hogarth Press, 1977a.

———. *Ecrits*. Translated by Alain Sheridan. London: Tavistock Publications, 1977b.

LaCapra, Dominick. "Rethinking Intellectual History and Reading Texts." *History and Theory* 19, no. 3 (1980): 245–276.

———. *History, Politics and the Novel*. Ithaca and London: Cornell University Press, 1987.

Leech, Geoffrey N. and Michael H. Short. *Style in Fiction: A Linguistic Introduction to English Fictional Prose*. London and New York: Longman, 1981.

Leeson, Robert. "The Spirit of What Age? The Interpretation of History from a Radical Standpoint." *Children's Literature in Education* 23 (1976): 172–182.

Le Mesurier, Nicholas. "A Lesson in History: The Presence of the Past in the Novels of Penelope Lively." *The New Welsh Review* 2, nos. 4, 8 (1990): 36–38.

Lenz, Millicent. "Through Blight to Bliss: Thematic Motifs in Jill Paton Walsh's *Unleaving*." *Children's Literature Association Quarterly* 13, no. 4 (1988): 194–197.

Levine, George, ed. *Constructions of the Self.* New Brunswick, NJ: Rutgers University Press, 1992.

Lively, Penelope. "Children and Memory." *Horn Book* 49, no. 4 (1973): 400–407.

———. *The Presence of the Past: An Introduction to Landscape History.* St. James's Place, London: Collins, 1976.

———. "Children and the Art of Memory." *Horn Book* 54, no. 1 (1978): 17–23; no. 2 (1978): 197–203.

———. "Bones in the Sand" *Horn Book* 57, no. 6 (1981): 641–651.

Locke, John. *An Essay Concerning Human Understanding.* Great Britain: Collins-Fount Paperbacks, 1981 (1690).

Lodge, David. *After Bakhtin: Essays on Fiction and Criticism.* London: Routledge, 1990.

Lurie, Alison. *Not in Front of the Grown-Ups: Subversive Children's Literature.* London: Cardinal, 1990.

Lyotard, Jean-Francois. *The Postmodern Condition: a Report on Knowledge.* Manchester: Manchester University Press, 1984.

MacCannel, Juliet Flower. "The Temporality of Textuality: Bakhtin and Derrida." *Modern Language Notes* 50, no. 5 (1985): 968–988.

MacLeod, Anne Scott. *American Childhoods: Essays on Children's Literature of the Nineteenth and Twentieth Centuries.* Athens and London: The University of Georgia Press, 1994.

Macquarie Dictionary Edited by A. Delbridge, J. R. L. Bernard, D. Blair and W.S. Ramson. McMahons Point, New South Wales: Macquarie Library, 1st edition, 1981.

Malcuzinski, M. Pierrette. "Polyphonic Theory and Contemporary Literary Practises." *Studies in Twentieth Century Literature* 9, no. 1 (1984): 75–87.

Malinowski, Bronislaw. "The Problem of Meaning in Primitive Languages." In *The Meaning of Meaning: A Study of the Influence of Language upon Thought and of the Science of Symbolism.* Edited by C. K. Ogden and I. A. Richards. New York: Harcourt Brace; London: Routledge and Paul, 1956.

Marquis, Claudia. "The Power of Speech: Life in the Secret Garden." *Journal of Australasian Universities Language and Literature Association* 68 (November 1987): 163–167.

Martens, Lorna. *The Diary Novel.* Cambridge: Cambridge University Press, 1985.

McCallum, Robyn. "(In)quest of the Subject: The Dialogic Construction of Subjectivity in Caroline Macdonald's *Speaking to Miranda.*" *Papers: Explorations into Children's Literature* 3, no. 3 (1992): 99–105.

———. "Other Selves: Subjectivity and the *Doppelgänger* in Australian Adolescent Fiction." In *Writing the Australian Child: Texts and Contexts in Fictions for Children.* Edited by Clare Bradford. Nedlands, Western Australia: University of Western Australia Press, 1996a.

———. "Metafictions and Experimental Work" In *International Companion Encyclopedia of Children's Literature.* Edited by Peter Hunt. London and New York: Routledge, 1996b.

McGillis, Roderick. "Calling a Voice out of Silence: Hearing What We Read." *Children's Literature in Education* 15, no. 1 (1984): 22–29.

———. "Secrets and Sequences in Children's Stories." *Studies in the Literary Imagination* 18, no. 2 (1985): 35–46.

———. "The Stream of Fiction: Recent British Children's Fiction." *Touchstones: Reflections on the Best in Children's Literature.* Vol. 3. Edited by Perry Nodelman. West Lafayette: Children's Literature Association Publishers, 1989.

McHale, Brian. "Free Indirect Discourse: A Survey of Recent Accounts." *PTL: A Journal for Descriptive Poetics and Theory of Literature* 3 (1978): 249–287.

———. *Postmodernist Fiction.* London: Routledge, 1989 (1987).

Miles, Rosalind. *The Women's History of the World.* Topsfield Mass: Salem House, 1989.

Miller, J. Hillis. "Narrative and History." *English Literary History* 41 (1974): 455–473.

———. *Fiction and Repetition: Seven English Novels*. Cambridge, Mass: Harvard University Press, 1982.

Mills, Alice. "Written in Blood: *So Much to Tell You* and *Strange Objects*." *Papers: Explorations into Children's Literature* 4, no. 1 (1993): 38–41.

Moon, Kenneth. "Don't Tell it, Show it: The Force of Metaphor in *A Game of Dark*." *School Librarian* 31, no. 4 (1983): 319–329.

Morgan, Elaine. *The Descent of Woman*. New York: Stein and Day Publishers, 1972.

Morson, Gary Saul. "Critical Response II: Dialogue, Monologue, and the Social: A Reply to Ken Hirschkop." *Critical Inquiry* 11, no. 4 (1985): 679–686.

———. ed. *Bakhtin: Essays and Dialogues on His Work*. Chicago and London: University of Chicago Press, 1986.

Neubauer, John. *The Fin-de-Seicle Culture of Adolescence*. New Haven and London: Yale University Press, 1991.

Nikolajeva, Maria. *The Magic Code: The Use of Magical Patterns in Fantasy for Children*. Stockholm: Almqvist and Wiksell International, 1988.

———. "The Insignificance of Time: *Red Shift*." *Children's Literature Association Quarterly* 14, no. 3 (1989): 128–131.

———. *Children's Literature Comes of Age: Toward a New Aesthetic*. New York and London: Garland Publishing, 1996.

Nodelman, Perry. "Searching for *Treasure Island*" in *Children's Novels and the Movies*. Edited by Douglas Stewart. New York: Frederick Ungar Publishing, 1983.

———. ed. *Touchstones: Reflections on the Best of Children's Literature*. Vol. 1. West Lafeyatte: Children's Literature Association Publishers, 1985a.

———. "Interpretation and the Apparent Sameness of Children's Novels." *Studies in the Literary Imagination* 18, no. 2 (1985): 5–20.

Oldenquist, Andrew, and Menachem Rosner. eds. *Alienation, Community and Work*. New York: Greenwood Press, 1991.

Pateman, Trevor. "Pragmatics in Semiotics: Bakhtin/Vološinov." *Journal of Literary Semantics* 18, no. 3 (1989): 203–216.

Pearce, Sharyn. "Identity in Australia: Gary Crew's Adolescent Novels." *Papers: Explorations into Children's Literature* 1, no. 2 (1990): 51–28.

Pechey, Graham. "Bakhtin, Marxism and Post-structuralism." *Literature, Politics and Theory*. Edited by Francis Barker. London and New York: Methuen, 1986.

———. "On the Borders of Bakhtin: Dialogisation, Decolonisation." In *Bakhtin and Cultural Theory*. Edited by Ken Hirschkop and David Shepherd, Manchester and New York: Manchester University Press, 1989: 39–67.

Phelan, James. "Introduction: Diversity and Dialogue in Narrative Theory." In *Reading Narrative: Form, Ethics, Ideology*, Edited by James Phelan. Columbus: Ohio State University Press, 1989.

Philip, Neil. *A Fine Anger: A Critical Introduction to the Work of Alan Garner*. London: Collins, 1981.

Pirog, Gerald. "Bakhtin and Freud on the Ego." In *Russian Literature and Psychoanalysis*. Edited by Danel Rancour-Laferriere. Amsterdam: John Benjamin, 1989.

Plato. *The Republic*. Translated by Desmond Lee. Harmondsworth, England: Penguin Books, 1974.

Polan, Dana. "The Text between Dialogue and Monologue." *Poetics Today* 4, no. 1 (1983): 145–183.

Porter, H. Abbot. *Diary Fiction: Writing as Action*. Ithaca and London: Cornell University Press, 1984.

Prince, Gerald. "The Diary Novel: Notes for the Definition of a Sub-genre." *Neophilogus* 59 (1975): 477–481.

———. *A Dictionary of Narratology*. Aldershot: Scolar, 1988 (1987).

Rank, Otto. *The Double: a Psychoanalytic Study.* Translated and Edited by Harry Tucker. Chapel Hill: University of North Carolina Press, 1971.

Ricoeur, Paul. "Self as *Ipse.*" In *Freedom and Interpretation,* Edited by Barbara Johnson, New York: Basic Books, 1993.

Roede, Machteld, ed. *The Aquatic Ape: Fact or Fiction? The First Scientific Evaluation of a Controversial Theory of Human Evolution.* London: Souvenir Press, 1991.

Rose, Jacqueline. *The Case of Peter Pan or the Impossibility of Children's Fiction.* London: Macmillan Press, 1984.

Ross, Anthony. "The Strangeness of *Strange Objects* and Todorov's Hesitation." *Papers: Explorations into Children's Literature* 3, no. 2 (1992): 82–87.

Russell, David A. "The Common Experience of Adolescence: A Requisite for the Development of Young Adult Literature." *Journal of Youth Services in Libraries* 2, (Fall 1988): 58–63.

Ryan, J.S. "The Tolkien Formation with a Lively Example." *Mallorn: the Journal of the Tolkien Society* 25 (1988): 20–22.

Saussure, Ferdinand de. *Course in General Linguistics.* Edited by Charles Bally, Albert Sechehaye and Albert Riedlinger. Translated by Wade Baskin. New York, Toronto and London: McGraw-Hill, 1966 (1959).

Scutter, Heather. "A Green Thought in a Green Shade: A Study of the Pastoral in Nadia Wheatley's *The Blooding,* Libby Hawthorn's *Thunderwith,* and Katherine Scholes' *The Blue Chameleon.*" In *Children's Literature and Contemporary Theory,* edited by Michael Stone, Wollongong: New Literatures Research Centre, University of Wollongong, 1991.

Seeman, M. "On the Meaning of Alienation." *American Sociological Review* 24 (1959): 783–791.

Shepherd, David. "Bakhtin and the Reader." in *Bakhtin and Cultural Theory.* Edited by Ken Hirschkop and David Shepherd, Manchester and New York: Manchester University Press, 1989.

Shorter Oxford English Dictionary Oxford: Clarendon Press. 3rd ed., 1992.

Shukman, Ann. "Between Marxism and Formalism, the Stylistics of Mikhail Bakhtin." *Comparative Criticism: A Yearbook* 2 (1980): 221–234.

———, (ed.). *Bakhtin School Papers.* Oxford: Russian Poetics in Translation Publications, 1988.

Singer, Alan. "The Voice of History/The Subject of the Novel." *Novel* 21, nos. 2–3 (1988a): 173–179.

———. "The Dis-position of the Subject: Agency and Form in the Ideology of the Novel." *Novel* 22, no. 1 (1988b): 5–23.

Smith, John H. "The Transcendence of the Individual." *Diacritics* 19, no. 2 (1989): 80–98.

Smith, Paul. *Discerning the Subject.* Minneapolis: University of Minnesota Press, 1988.

Soper, Kate. *Humanism and Anti-humanism.* La Salle, Ill.: Open Court, 1986.

Spacks, Patricia Meyer. *The Adolescent Idea: Myths of Youth and the Adult Imagination.* New York: Basic Books, 1981.

Sprinker, Michael. "Boundless Context: Problems in Bakhtin's Linguistics." *Poetics Today* 7, no. 1 (1986): 117–128.

Stallybrass, Peter, and Allon White. *The Politics and Poetics of Transgression.* London and New York: Methuen, 1986.

Stam, Robert. "Mikhail Bakhtin and Left Cultural Critique." *Postmodernism and its Discontents.* Edited by E. Ann Kaplan. New York: Routledge Chapman and Hall, 1988.

———. *Subversive Pleasures: Bakhtin, Cultural Criticism and Film.* Baltimore and London: Johns Hopkins University Press, 1989.

Stephens, John. "Did I Tell You About the Time I Pushed the Brothers Grimm off Humpty Dumpty's Wall? Metafictional Strategies for Constituting the Audience as Agent in the Narratives of Janet and Allen Ahlberg." In *Children's Literature and Contemporary Theory.* Edited by Michael Stone, Wollongong: New Literatures Research Centre, University of Wollongong, 1991.

———. *Language and Ideology in Children's Fiction.* London and New York: Longman, 1992a.

———. "Modernism to Postmodernism, or the Line from Insk to Onsk: William Mayne's *Tiger's Railway.*" *Papers: Explorations into Children's Literature* 3, no. 2 (1992b): 51–59.

———. *Reading the Signs: Sense and Significance in Written Texts.* Kenthurst, New South Wales: Kangaroo Press, 1992c.

———. "Metafiction and Interpretation: William Mayne's *Salt River Times, Winter Quarters* and *Drift.*" *Children's Literature* 21 (1993): 101–107.

Stephens, John, and Robyn McCallum. *Retelling Stories, Framing Culture: Traditional Story and Metanarratives in Children's Literature.* New York and London: Garland Publishing 1998.

Stewart, Susan. "Shouts in the Street: Bakhtin's Anti-Linguistics." *Critical Inquiry* 10 (1983): 265–281.

Stone, Michael, ed. *Children's Literature and Contemporary Theory.* Wollongong: New Literatures Research Centre, University of Wollongong, 1991a.

———. "Postmodernism and Nadia Wheatley's *The Blooding.*" In *Children's Literature and Contemporary Theory,* edited by Michael Stone. Wollongong: New Literatures Research Centre, University of Wollongong, 1991b: 41–49.

———. "The Ambiguity of Hesitation in Gary Crew's *Strange Objects.*" *Papers: Explorations into Children's Literature* 3, no. 1 (1992): 18–27.

Studies in Twentieth Century Literature. Special Issue on Mikhail Bakhtin. 9, no. 1 (1984).

Thibault, Paul. "Narrative Discourse as a Multi-level System of Communication: Some Theoretical Proposals Concerning Bakhtin's Dialogic Principle." *Studies in Twentieth Century Literature* 9, no. 1 (1984): 89–117.

Thomson, Jack. *Understanding Teenagers Reading: Reading Processes and the Teaching of Literature.* North Ryde, New South Wales: Methuen, 1987.

Titunik, I. R. "Bakhtin, and/or Vološinov and/or Medvedev: Dialogue and/or Doubletalk?" *Language and Literary Theory.* Papers in Slavic Philology 5. Edited by Benjamin A. Stolz and I. R. Titunik and Lukumír Dolž. Michigan: Ann Arbor, 1984.

Todorov, Tzvetan. *Mikhail Bakhtin: The Dialogical Principle.* Translated by Wlad Godzich. Theory and History of Literature, Vol. 13. Manchester: Manchester University Press, 1984.

Townsend, John Rowe. *A Sounding of Storytellers: New and Revised Essays on Contemporary Writers for Children.* New York: Lippincott, 1979.

Turner, E. S. *Boys Will Be Boys.* London: Michael Joseph, 1975.

Vološinov, V. N. *Marxism and the Philosophy of Language.* Translated Ladislav Matejika and I. R. Titunik. Cambridge, Mass. and London: Harvard University Press, New York and London: Seminar Press, 1986 (1973). (Original Russian edition, 1929.)

———. *Freudianism: A Critical Sketch.* Translated by I. R. Titunik. Bloomington and Indianapolis: Indiana University Press, Academic Press, 1987 (1976). (Original Russian edition, 1927.)

Vygotsky, L. S. *Thought and Language.* Edited and Translated by Eugenia Hanfmann and Gertrude Vakor. Cambridge, Mass.: The Massachusetts Institute of Technology Press, 1962. (Original Russian edition, 1934.)

Wall, Barbara. *The Narrator's Voice: The Dilemma of Children's Fiction.* London: Macmillan, 1991.

Walsh, Jill Paton. "The Lords of Time." *Quarterly Journal of the Library Congress* 36 (Spring 1979): 96–113.

———. "Disturbing the Universe." *Innocence and Experience: Essays and Conversations on Children's Literature.* Edited by Barbara Harrison and Gregory Macguire. New York: Lothrop, Lee and Shepard Books, 1987.

———. "On Wearing Masks." *The Voice of the Narrator in Children's Literature: Insights from Writers and Critics.* Edited by Charlotte F. Otten and Gary D. Schmidt. New York: Greenwood Press, 1989.

Walsh, Robin. "Alan Garner: A Study." *Orana* 13, no. 2 (1977): 31–39.

Wartofsky, Marx. "The Child's Construction of the World and the World's Construction of the Child: from Historical Epistemology to Historical Psychology." In *The Child and Other Cultural Inventions,* edited by Frank S. Kessel and Alexander W. Siegel. New York: Praeger Publishers, 1983

Watson, Victor. "In Defence of Jan: Love and Betrayal in *The Owl Service* and *Red Shift*." *Signal* 41 (1983): 77–87.

White, Allon. "Pigs and Pierrots: the Politics of Transgression in Modern Fiction." *Rariton* 2 (1982): 51–70.

———. "The Authoritative Lie." *Partisan Review* 50, no. 2 (1983): 307–312.

———. "Bakhtin, Sociolinguistics and Deconstruction." In *The Theory of Reading,* edited by Frank Gloversmith. Sussex: The Harvester press, 1984.

———. "Bakhtin's Masks." *Partisan Review* 53, no. 4 (1986): 634–637.

———. "The Struggle over Bakhtin: Fraternal Reply to Robert Young." *Cultural Critique* 8 (1987–1988): 217–241.

White, Hayden. *Metahistory: The Historical Imagination in Nineteenth Century Europe.* Baltimore and London: The Johns Hopkins University Press, 1973.

———. "The Value of Narrativity in the Representation of Reality." *Critical Inquiry* 7, no. 1 (1980): 5–27.

———. *The Content and the Form: Narrative Discourse and Historical Representation.* Baltimore, London; John Hopkins University Press, 1987.

Wilden, Anthony. "Lacan and the Discourse of the Other." In *The Language of the Self,* Baltimore: The John Hopkins Press, 1975.

Wilson, Margaret, ed. *The Essential Descartes.* New York: Mentor, 1969.

Wilson, Robert R. "Play, Transgression and Carnival: Bakhtin and Derrida on *Scriptor Ludens*." *Mosaic* 19, no. 1 (1986): 73–89.

Young, Robert. "Back to Bakhtin." *Cultural Critique* 2 (1985–1986): 71–92.

Zepp, Evelyn H. "Self and Other: Identity as Dialogical Confrontation in *La Chute*." *Perspectives on Contemporary Literature* 12 (1986): 51–56.

Zima, Peter, ed. *Semiotics and Dialectics: Ideology and the Text.* Amsterdam: John Benjamins B.V., 1981.

Index